The Economics of
a Socialist Enterprise

PRAEGER SPECIAL STUDIES IN
INTERNATIONAL ECONOMICS AND DEVELOPMENT

The Economics of a Socialist Enterprise

A CASE STUDY OF THE POLISH FIRM

George R. Feiwel
Faculty of Commerce
University of Alberta

FREDERICK A. PRAEGER, Publishers
New York · Washington · London

The purpose of the Praeger Special Studies is to make specialized research monographs in U.S. and international economics and politics available to the academic, business, and government communities. For further information, write to the Special Projects Division, Frederick A. Praeger, Publishers, 111 Fourth Avenue, New York, N.Y. 10003.

FREDERICK A. PRAEGER, Publishers
111 Fourth Avenue, New York 3, N.Y., U.S.A.
77-79 Charlotte Street, London W.1, England

Published in the United States of America in 1965
by Frederick A. Praeger, Inc., Publishers
Second printing, 1966
All rights reserved

© 1965 by Frederick A. Praeger, Inc.

Library of Congress Catalog Card Number: 65-21102

Printed in the United States of America

TO MY MOTHER

AND MY WIFE

PREFACE

This study attempts to explore the economics and
modus operandi of a socialist industrial enterprise
within the institutional framework of a centrally planned economy. It is my contention that a fuller and
further understanding of the inner workings of a
Soviet-type economy may be gained by scrutinizing the
constraints imposed on and the performance of the basic
cell of the economy - the enterprise.

At a time when high speed turbulent industrialization
and priority planning reign supreme - as experienced by
the Soviet-type economies during their most intensive
industrialization drives - output maximization becomes
the cardinal target. The central planner then pays
little heed to rational allocation of resources, microeconomic processes, and adjustments. The enterprise's
efficiency and performance are, so to speak, prepon-
derantly subordinated to its ability to augment the
quantity of output. In the following period - and we
are presently witnessing this phenomenon in most Soviet-
type economies - concentration on mere quantity of output is slackened. Preoccupation is then shifted to the
problems of economic efficiency in a growing economy and
the efficacy and limits of central planning in steering
a more adequate and balanced development, fostering
more rational use of resources, and combating inefficiency. The functioning of the economy and working
arrangements for the units of economic activity, the
cohesion, consistency, and interdependence of planning
methods, value parameters, commands, and economic incentives come under searching scrutiny. When the central
planner increasingly focuses his attention on the best,
or better, use of resources, efficiency, flexibility,
output composition and quality, the spotlight falls on
the enterprise's performance, its economics, and modus

operandi.

In view of the necessity to compress the voluminous material into limited space this study concentrates on the Polish state-owned enterprise of key industry and comparison of the firms in several Soviet-type economies and Yugoslavia has been relegated to a study now in progress.

The Polish experience in management of industry is interesting in view of far-reaching ferment and developments in economic thought, remarkable ability of some Polish economists to grasp the dimensions and ramifications of economic problems, and because of the early attempts at decentralization and incorporation of the profit criterion for evaluating the enterprise's performance. But certain modifications miscarried because they were implemented without removing existing constraints which either hampered the expected beneficial effects or resulted in effects quite contrary to those intended. Almost ten years have elapsed since the first attempts at decentralizing the Polish industrial apparatus and rendering the firm's activity more efficient. The time seems ripe to assess the results obtained.

This study is divided into five chapters. Chapter 1 sets the stage by presenting a background of industrial development, ferment in economic thought, and the institutional framework. The following chapters concentrate on the parameters and commands that mold the enterprise's activity and pattern its behavior and adjustment to economic and administrative stimuli. Chapter 2 examines the theoretical issues in the formation of producers' prices and the development of pricing with particular stress on the post-1956 period. But since production costs are the basis for price formation the next logical step seems to be a discussion of the scientific validity of cost concepts employed and to ascertain the validity and reliability of cost data generated by the firm - the subject of Chapter 3. Chapter 4 concentrates on the nature and apportionment of financial accumulation and profit, the incentive role of decentralized funds, and financing the firm's activity. Management's objectives, performance criteria, economic incentives, and adaptation of management to the system are explored in the concluding chapter. My contention is that management's behavior stems from the

inner logic of the present system and unless performance
criteria and the price system are fundamentally over-
hauled no mitigations are likely to produce significant
improvements.

I am at a loss for words to express adequately my
indebtedness to the many people who so liberally and
generously gave of their time, advice, and encourage-
ment. I greatly benefited from the invaluable comments
and incisive criticisms of Professors D.E. Armstrong and
E.F. Beach of McGill University who read earlier drafts
of this work. Dr. Armstrong is chiefly responsible for
making an economist out of me, a fact which by now he
may regret. I was very fortunate to have his good and
friendly advice. Dr. Beach impressed on me the might
of theoretical reasoning and the understanding of the
tools of analysis. Thanks are due to Professor
G. Grossman of the University of California who interested me in the study of Soviet-type economies. Throughout the progress of this work I gained from contact
with Dr. Hu Harries' perceptive and fascinating mind.
His unstinting support was a source of aid and stimula-
tion. Professor Lorne Leitch encouraged me by his kind
interest and support. I had the pleasure of discussing
and exchanging views on some problems of functioning of
a socialist economy with Professors Ivo Moravcik and
Rudy Piñola, all of the University of Alberta. At the
final stages of this work I have incurred a great debt
to Professors Joan Robinson and J.E. Meade and Mr. M.H.
Dobb for clarifying some thorny points of theory. My
thanks are also due to the Faculty Board of Economics
and Politics, University of Cambridge for granting me
the privilege of spending some time as a visitor here
and benefiting immensely from its stimulating intellectual
climate. I have also gained from discussions with
Dr. A. Zauberman of the London School of Economics and
his keen insight into the workings of Soviet-type
economies. It is with gratitude that I acknowledge the
help of many Polish economists and their readiness to
clarify my **queries**. It goes without saying that I
alone bear the full responsibility for errors and
opinions expressed. It was indeed my good fortune to
have had the constant help, advice, and cooperation of
that most understanding and patient of editors -
Mr. Morton Puner, Director of Special Projects,
Frederick A. Praeger, Inc. It was a pleasure to work

with him. At all stages of this work I have benefited
beyond measure from my wife's constructive criticism,
unflinching perserverance, and aptitudes as research
assistant, translator, and typist.

Cambridge   George R. Feiwel
May 1965

CONTENTS

Page

LIST OF TABLES

LIST OF CHARTS

ABBREVIATIONS

CBP   Central Board of Planning (Centralny Urzad Planowania)

CM   Council of Ministers (Rada Ministrow)

CSO   Central Statistical Office (Glowny Urzad Statystyczny)

ECCM   Economic Committee of the Council of Ministers (Komitet Ekonomiczny Rady Ministrow)

FYP   Five-Year Plan

MF   Ministry of Finance

NEP   National Economic Plan

NPB   National Polish Bank (Narodowy Bank Polski)

OES   Office of Economic Studies (Biuro Studiow Ekonomicznych)

PC   Planning Commission of the Council of Ministers (Komisja Planowania przy Radzie Ministrow)

PCNL   Polish Committee of National Liberation (Polski Komitet Wyzwolenia Narodowego)

PUWP   Polish United Workers Party (Polska Zjednoczona Partia Robotnicza)

SCEP   State Commission for Economic Planning (Panstwowa Komisja Planowania Gospodarczego)

SPC   State Price Commission (Panstwowa Komisja Cen)

SYP   Six-Year Plan

TYP   Three-Year Plan

The Economics of
a Socialist Enterprise

CHAPTER 1 CENTRALIZATION AND
DECENTRALIZATION OF
INDUSTRY -
BACKGROUND, FRAMEWORK,
AND ISSUES

THE BACKGROUND

After a prolonged war, German occupation and extensive devastation of the country, fundamental changes
occurred on the Polish political, economic, and social
scene.[1] Politically Poland was gradually being absorbed
into the Soviet orbit of power. Geographically the
balance sheet of the economy was considerably transformed as Poland gained Upper and Lower Silesia, rich
in natural resources, power, and industrial plants,
and lost mainly agricultural land and meager oil and
potassium deposits to the Soviets.[2] The formation of
an administrative and economic apparatus, revitalization
of the economy, repatriation and resettlement of the
population were, inter alia, the pressing problems of
the day.
     Resumption of industrial production had to cope with
serious destruction of capital, decimation of intelligent-
sia, and "ownerless" factories. The bulk of industrial
potential, especially in large scale industry, had been
owned either by the prewar Polish state, the German
occupant, foreign capital, or victims of German exter-
mination. In some cases the spontaneous initiative
of workers could be counted on to reactivate production.
However, extensive resumption of production was fostered by the state.[3] After the first Polish territo-
ries were liberated, the Soviet supported Polish Committee of National Liberation (PCNL) proclaimed that
capital assets formerly owned by the occupant or
absentee owners should pass under the management of the
Provisional State Administration.[4] Banks were na-

tionalized immediately after the seizure of power by the
PCNL.[5] Thus the state gained control over heavy industry,
the greater part of light industry, transportation,
communications, and banks.

At the 1957 Belgrade lectures, Oskar Lange, the inter-
nationally known Polish economist, emphasized the need
for nationalization in activating a socialist planned
economy. The state's control over the "commanding out-
posts" of economic life is, according to Lange, the minimum requirement for establishing a planned economy.
"In the first revolutionary period intervention into
economic processes by political force plays a decisive
role." Consequently the command over economic resources
becomes a condition for implementing the will of the
Party. A large nationalized sector of the economy is a
means towards this end. Lange proclaimed such a policy
a "historical necessity".[6]

The formal act of nationalization passed on January
3, 1946, legalized the state's take-over of key industries
and all enterprises employing more than fifty workers per
shift. The objective of the law was stated in the first
paragraph of the act:

> The state takes over as its property enterprises for
> the purposes of planned reconstruction of the national
> economy, to assure economic sovereignty of the state
> and raise general welfare.[7]

According to article 3 a decree of the Council of Ministers
would be the sole requirement for nationalizing any type
of enterprise. This provided sufficient legal grounds
for further nationalization.[8]

In August,1944, the Office of Economic Studies (OES),
the first Polish economic planning agency, was instituted. The OES was directed to guide current
economic policy, distribute production and consumption
resources, and coordinate the economic activity of
ministries. When the Provisional Government was formed
(December 31, 1944) the Council of Ministers (CM) with
the Economic Committee of the Council of Ministers (ECCM)
became the coordinating organs of the national economy.
Thereafter the OES was subordinated to the ECCM. In
February,1945, the National Polish Bank (NPB) was set up
to finance the state apparatus and industrial production.[9]
In November,1945, the OES was replaced by the Central Board

of Planning (CBP), under the supervision of the ECCM
and accountable to the CM. The decree entrusted the
CBP with "elaboration of state economic plans, coordination of economic activity of the ministries, establishment of plans for the distribution of means of
production and consumption."[10]

Initially economic activity was guided by segmentary
plans of short duration. As industry was reactivated
and the administrative apparatus proliferated, quarterly
plans were drawn up. In 1945 the main efforts were
concentrated on reactivation of industry and communications. Plans were drafted establishing production goals
for industry and tasks for the communications network.
In April, 1945, the CM established the basic production
figures for the coal industry. Simultaneously plans
were drawn up for other branches of state industry.
During the year current monthly distribution lists of
deficit articles were prepared.[11] Reactivation of
industrial production was given decisive priority over
implementation of rational wage and price systems. The
former task was not encumbered by requirements on cost
levels or product mix.[12] The first yearly industrial
plan was drafted for 1946. Whereas the 1945 quarterly
plans covered only production and employment and in the
fourth quarter partly procurement of raw materials and
technical targets, the 1946 plan also incorporated the
first financial indexes.[13] However, the various targets
were badly synchronized.[14]

The basic tenet of the subsequent Three-Year Plan (TYP)
(1947-49) was the reconstruction of industry, communications, and housing. The main efforts were not centered
on construction and development of new enterprises but
rather on restoration of destroyed capacity. A particular
feature of this period was that relatively small investment outlays brought quick returns. Oftentimes repairs
of buildings or overhaul of damaged equipment were the
only conditions necessary for activating large industrial
plants.

The CBP was directed to draw up definite plans and
control the activity of state-owned industries. The
plans drawn up by cooperatives were submitted to the CBP
for coordination. The private sector (farms, shops, handicrafts, and small-scale factories) was guided by state
policies on prices, market regulations, investment,
taxation, etc.[15] The socialists, then still able to

exert their influence through the CBP, were in favor of
a relatively decentralized form of planning for state-
owned industry, a comparatively substantial autonomy for
the cooperative and private sectors, and a moderate rate
of investments. Their immediate goal was raising the
standard of living with tangible benefits for consumers.

By 1948 the TYP showed good signs of fulfilment but
the CBP and its chairman, C. Bobrowski, came under strong
Communist denouncement. The attack was launched on both
theoretical and practical grounds. It was later described
as "a struggle concerning the full use of Soviet experiences in planning".[16] The gist of the attack was that
the CBP was mainly concerned with the immediate raising
of the standard of living and its efforts towards industrialization and development of heavy industry lagged
behind this main goal.[17] A posteriori, B. Minc stated:

> An attempt to plan the national economy on the prior-
> ity of consumption and rejection of the priority of
> production would be the application in our plans of
> false bourgeois economic theory and would mean a
> downward trend in the economy. This type of attempt
> at erroneous planning was the projected national
> economic plan for the year 1948, prepared by the past
> administration of the CBP and rejected by the Polish
> Workers Party.[18]

On theoretical grounds B. Minc denounced the computation
of national income as un-Marxian since it included unproductive services and inflated the importance of the
economy's private sector.[19]

The Communists, headed by Hilary Minc, reaffirmed their
views on centralized economic planning, accelerated industrialization based on the Soviet experience, allowing
only residuals to satisfy the needs of the population.
Minc's argumentation was strongly reminiscent of Stalin's
version of Preobrazhenski's "primitive socialist accumulation".[20]

Referring to the Polish "industrialization debate"
(the CBP discussion), Professor Brus pointed out that:

> Adopting the centralized model as the sole formula
> for centralized planning, the Communists did not
> deliberate on the optimum degree of centralization
> and duration of centralization. Centralization now

had behind it the authority of nearly twenty years
experience in the U.S.S.R., which caused the
principles of Soviet solutions to become the main
criterion of adequacy for the methods of administrating the economy.[21]

In his Belgrade lectures Lange expressed the reasons for
high centralization of planning and management:

The process of rapid industrialization requires...
centralized disposal of resources for two reasons.
First, it is necessary to concentrate all resources
on certain objectives and avoid dissipation of
resources on other objectives which would divert
resources from the purpose of rapid industrialization. This is one of the reasons which leads to
highly centralized planning and management and also
to the allocation of resources by means of administrative establishment of priorities. The second
reason why rapid industrialization demands centralized
planning and management is the lack and weakness of
industrial cadres. With the rapid growth of industry
the cadres are new and inexperienced. Such old
cadres which had some experience in management of
industry and other economic activities are frequently
politically alien to the socialist objectives. In
consequence high centralization of managerial
decisions becomes necessary.[22]

As a result of the attack launched by the Communists
Bobrowski was demoted, replaced by Dietrich, and the
reorganized CBP directed to elaborate more detailed plans
and increase the targets originally stipulated for 1949.[23]
The construction of the 1949 national economic plan
(NEP) involved several steps. The CBP drafted a projected plan on the basis of segmentary plans submitted by
the industrial ministries. After approval of the NEP
draft by the CM, plan instructions were distributed to
ministries, central boards,[24] and enterprises. These
units were to draft their annual plans and transmit them
through the chain of command to the CBP. On this basis
the CBP prepared the NEP for ratification by the ECCM
and the Sejm. Once approved the NEP was in turn redistributed to the lower economic units. By 1949 the
cooperative sector was closely tied into the NEP. The

private sector was indirectly tied in through central distribution of materials.[25]

The last year of the TYP of reconstruction featured further centralization and stress on detailed planning. By 1949 the enterprise's plan consisted of technical and financial parts. The technical plan incorporated indexes of industrial production in physical and value terms, indexes of employment, wage bill and its composition, labor productivity, social contributions, use of electric power, requirements for materials, average costs of the more important products, and total production costs. The financial plan included indexes of wages, social security surcharges, turnover of materials, investments, depreciation, costs, production in value terms, receipts and expenditures, normative (minimum requirement) of working capital, and planned financial results.[26]

At the end of the TYP the CBP was abolished and replaced by the State Commission for Economic Planning (SCEP) headed by Hilary Minc. Poland was to embark on the Six-Year Plan of intensive industrialization.

SIX-YEAR PLAN PERIOD (1950-55)

When the premises of the Six-Year Plan (SYP) were first formulated a concentrated development of ferrous metallurgy and machine building industries was stressed.[27] The principles and targets of the SYP were drafted in 1948, but the targets were subsequently revised and substantially increased by 1950.[28] Moreover, the targets enacted as law in 1950 were augmented during the course of the SYP:

> In 1951 the Six-Year Plan went through a drastic revision aimed at speeding up the tempo of industrialization, at increasing investments allocated for the development of heavy industry. Above all it was important to prevent the productive resources from being used for purposes other than those connected with the rapid expansion of heavy industry.[29]

As a result of Soviet pressures the increased targets of 1951 underwent further upward revisions in 1952 and 1953.[30] Moreover the Soviets found students who were eager to transplant the Soviet pattern to Poland:

> The natural proclivities of Polish Stalinists were
> no different from those of their Soviet mentors.
> They showed similar inclination to combine a roman-
> ticized view of potentialities of modern technology
> with abiding faith in their own ability to manip-
> ulate the rate of saving-investment within wide
> limits and to shorten the gestation period of new
> projects by stern command and fiery exhortation.[31]

The main task of the SYP was an accelerated industrialization of the country with a substantial share of
national income diverted to capital formation.[32] Production of consumer goods was relegated as a subordinate
target.[33] The system of priorities reigned supreme.
The increase of output of "guns" instead of "bread" was
accomplished at the cost of underconsumption. The outstanding feature of this period of forced industrialization was extremely high concentration of investment
expenditures on heavy industry, which absorbed about 88
per cent of total investments.[34]

The investment plan was not fully implemented. The
performance was disappointing in the fulfilment of quantitative targets, composition, timing, sequence, cost,
quality, and the abandonment or postponement of many
projects.[35] The mounting tensions were magnified by a
reshuffle of resources to production of armaments regardless of costs.[36] Simultaneously while over-all gross
investment was increasing the rate of real capital consumption was exceedingly high due to a rapid deterioration of
equipment as repairs were neglected. The planners were
obsessed with construction of gigantic industrial show-
places. The investment program was carried out by building new projects instead of expanding existing potential.
But 90 per cent of the increase in output of the period
is attributed to the old establishments.[37]

Armaments claimed the bulk of investment in machinery
impinging on the requirements of other industries. Total
production of machines for the coal, chemical, construction,
electric power, and agricultural industries did not even
reach 20 per cent of production capacity in the machine
building industry.[38]

Although the highest priorities devolved on the machine
building industry, they were badly drawn and neglected to

assign equally high priorities to the complementary industries. As a result bottlenecks arose.[39] The most flagrant
disproportions occurred between the agricultural,[40] raw
material, fuel, and electric power output and production
capacity of industry as a whole.[41] Discussing the raw
material, fuel, and electric power shortages Lange was
prompted to say that "the basis of those difficulties
are disproportions between the newly created production
capacities and an excessively narrow raw material base,
preventing full exploitation of these capacities."[42]

The disproportions and unsatisfactory "achievements"
of the period were revealed during the heated discussions
of 1956 and 1957. S. Kurowski described the goals of
the period in the following terms:

> The goals put forth to the national economy during
> the Stalinist period could be divided into three main
> groups. They were: reconstruction of the system,
> construction of heavy industry, and construction of
> military power... The decisive meaning for the
> development of the situation was not the ideological
> aspect but the strategic one. As a result a new
> hierarchy of goals came into being, headed by the
> construction of military power. All other goals
> were subjected to this main task... The building of
> military power could not wait, it had to be hastened.
> Since the building of heavy industry and the recon-
> struction of the system were to help in the build-
> ing of military power, these tasks had to be hastened
> as well. Consequently the tempo foisted on the build-
> ing of industry exceeded the production capacity of
> the economy, and the reconstruction of the system was
> conducted at a rate exceeding the development of means
> of production and changes in social consciousness.[43]

An intrinsic feature of the adaptation of Soviet-type
industrialization was overcentralization of the economic
apparatus with all the aspects of a command economy.[44]
Before examining the chief characteristics of a centralized model, let us glance briefly at the methods used
for the preparation of plans during the SYP period.[45]
Prior to 1952 (formally on the basis of a resolution
of the CM) the SCEP prepared control figures (minimum
for output, maximum for inputs) for the ministries which
in turn distributed them to enterprises through the

medium of central boards. On this basis the enterprises
were to draft comprehensive annual plans. When the aggregated enterprises' plans reached the SCEP they were
subject to upward adjustments and recomputation with the
difficult task of balancing and reassigning increased
targets to subordinate units. In this manner the final
plan targets reaching the enterprises bore little
resemblance to their original plans. Quarterly and
monthly plans elaborated by the central boards for the
firms under their jurisdiction consisted of value of
total production in constant and current prices, marketable output in transfer prices, output in physical units,
indexes of labor productivity, employment, average wages,
wage fund, instruction of cadres, procurement, cost reduction, and capital repairs.[46]
        Basing their assumption on Lenin's statement that
"Bolshevism is suited as an example of tactics for all",
the Poles faithfully copied the Soviet planning system,
culminating in the 1952 Polish modifications of the
planning system. As of 1952 the planning procedure
consisted of the following steps: Guided by a resolution
of the CM, the ministries and central boards drafted
plans for the units under their jurisdiction. Those
plans were transmitted to the SCEP which then elaborated
the NEP. On the basis of the NEP the ministries prepared
plans for the central boards. These, in turn, drew up
detailed annual, quarterly, and monthly plans for the
enterprises.[47]
        By 1954 the technical-industrial-economic plan received
by enterprises was a most detailed and intricate structure. The plan incorporated eight main divisions:
production, technical development, employment and wages,
procurement, current and capital repairs, costs, financial,
and investment plans.[48]
        The production plan included value indexes of total
and marketable output. The total production plan was subdivided into the value of producer and consumer goods.
It detailed in physical units production of the more
important goods and specified new production to be undertaken. It also stipulated the subcontracting between
firms. It provided the material and labor input norms.
        The plan for improvement of techniques and organization
of production was composed of a plan of mechanization and
automation of production processes, research undertakings
and study of norms, as well as the introduction and

development of new technological processes and methods
of production planned for new goods.

The plan of employment and wages consisted of the plan
of labor productivity, employment, number of employees
by groups, requirements for additional labor force, and
instructions on the distribution of wages from the
limited wage fund.

The procurement plan was based on the allocation of
materials required to fulfil the production plan according to centrally established norms of input, specifying
the sources of procurement.

The plan of current and capital repairs consisted of
detailed plans for the exploitation and servicing of
machines, execution of repairs, modernization of old
machines, procurement of spare parts and repair materials.
Strict observance of repair discipline, organization and
instruction of repair and maintenance crews, and wages
for repair and maintenance workers was to be enforced.

The plan of costs consisted of cost reduction on
comparable products,[49] a cost plan of total and marketable output, and a plan of costs for the more important
products based on calculated planned unit costs.

The financial plan stipulated profit or loss, division
of profit or financing of losses, changes in normatives
of working capital, the source of investment financing,
financing of capital repairs, and settlement with the budget

The firm's investment plan covered all investments
according to their types. Investments were distinguished
as productive and "unproductive". Separate plans were
drawn up for new investments, improvements, and extensions.
The starting and completion dates were specified.[50]

By 1954 centralization was at its peak in Poland.
Very little, if anything, was left to the discretion of
the enterprises' management.

THE CENTRALIZED MODEL

The centralized model adopted during the SYP period
features more than one organizational level.[51] It is
characterized by 1) concentration of practically all
economic decisions on the central level, except for
individual choice in consumption and employment,[52] 2)
hierarchic structure of plans and vertical ties between
different links in the economic mechanism, 3) transmission

of decisions from top to bottom in the form of direct
orders, 4) predomination of calculation in physical terms,
5) passive function of money in the realm of state ownership,[53] and 6) central establishment of both consumers'
and producers' prices, where the latter are not indicators of economic choice but calculatory magnitudes
facilitating balancing.[54] In this model all decisions
are made at the top and all reported data flow from the
bottom with the intermediary levels serving as channels
for transmitting, aggregating, and disaggregating data
and directives. The directives vary according to the
central planner's preferences with parameters (prices,
taxes, interest rates, etc.) usually petrified and
performing transformed roles (e.g., prices used mostly
for reducing output to a common denominator).[55]

In such a model major economic decisions are made by
the central planner autonomously in that they are not
made in anticipation of microeconomic processes, but
reflect the preferences of the central planner, which in
turn mirror the doctrine and policy of the Party.[56]
Besides the major decisions (distribution of national
income to accumulation and consumption,[57] rate of growth
of investments and distribution among industries, allotment of consumption to collective goods and individual
consumption, consumer goods composition, etc.), the planner also assigns tasks to all economic units in the state
sector. The decisions are transmitted through the administrative hierarchy, thus the planner defines the concrete tasks of enterprises.

In particular the planner decides in this manner the
magnitude and composition of output and production costs,
regulates employment according to skill classifications,
distributes equipment and materials according to state
determined norms, and specifies sources of procurement
and marketing channels. In principle materials are
assigned for specific tasks and must not be used for
other purposes. To coordinate the plan internally the
central authorities divide the tasks of the multi-year
plan into annual, quarterly, and monthly plans. Consequently the major microeconomic decisions as to what,
when, how, and how much to produce are not made by the
firm which is granted only executing functions.

The plan built on the basis of central decisions is
addressed to a given unit at the lower level of the
economic hierarchy (e.g., ministry), which is supposed to

proceed similarly towards its subordinate units (e.g.,
central boards) until the plan reaches the firm. The
intermediaries are administrative extensions of the
central planning apparatus and their latitude in conveying the plan to subordinate units is restricted.
Each unit's plan is an appropriate excerpt of the central
plan, and is in line with the hierarchal structure of the
economy. Transactions between sellers and buyers are
planned and do not play an active role. No change may be
made in those transactions unless information about the
change flows upward and is sanctioned.

    Plan targets are transmitted to the lower echelons as
mandatory orders. Fulfilment of commands is the only
criterion for evaluating performance at all levels. The
commands are often supported by incentives (premiums).
These are not designed to ensure an appropriate choice
at the subordinate level, but only determine that the
orders given will be expediently carried out. Payment of
premiums for fulfilment of the production plan reactivates
prices used to aggregate output. The firms become sensitive
to prices in view of their influence on the size of output
in value terms.[58] As discussed in Chapter V, the linking
of incentives with the production plan often results in
undesirable effects, quite contrary to the ones intended.

    The central planner's production decisions do not result
from an interplay of prices and costs but from dissident
views of Party officials and technicians, without the
possibility of verifying the correctness of the decision
made.[59] Responsible for an "arduous activity that substitutes for the most elementary accomplishment of the
market mechanism",[60] the central planner aims at producing
an internally consistent plan balancing physical magnitudes
of inputs and outputs. The elaboration of the network
of material balances serves as a basis for central distribution and balancing in physical terms of "supply and demand"
for materials.[61] It involves a simplified form of input-
output procedures, carried out rather primitively in view
of the magnitude of the task.[62] Distribution of materials
is based on centrally prepared norms, production requirements are estimated on the basis of constant technological
coefficients.[63] There is unremitting pressure on management
to observe these norms. The technological norms per unit
of output are prepared by the central planner.

    In this model the firm is a legal entity endowed by
the state with financial resources. In principle, its

expenditures should be covered from receipts. But possession of own funds does not entail free disposal of them.
It is of utmost importance that the firms' own funds should
not be sufficient and supplemented with subventions to
permit strict control over adherence to the plan. Such a
control would be seriously hampered should the enterprise
finance all its expenditures from its own funds which
would permit management to deviate from the plan.[64]

The enterprise does not calculate <u>ex ante</u> but <u>ex post</u>.
Within the firm money facilitates recording and reporting
of activity, but not economic choice which, by the very
nature of the system, is non-existent at this level.[65]
Hence economic quantities in monetary terms are only
means of expressing and reporting inputs, outputs, and
results after the targets and methods of production have
been chosen by superiors. Moreover, improved financial
results do not enable enterprises to dispose of the
additional funds. These have to be remitted to the state
budget. Conversely, financial difficulties do not
restrain enterprises from continuing activity since budget
subsidies are almost automatically granted. This model
features an emphasis on quantity of production and
distrust of profit as a measure of performance. It is
easier to control a single target, such as the size of
output, than a residual like profit which is a result
of many factors and more prone to manipulations.[66]
However, in the labor and consumer goods markets money
does play an active role affecting economic choice.

The above description concentrates on the essential
features of the centralized model. But the rigor with
which commands are enforced varies. The planner is
constrained by the impossibility of making decisions on
the minutest tasks of an enterprise. In some cases he
does not have the necessary information or knowledge of
local conditions, and in others he is indifferent, since
the decisions will not perceptively affect his plan.

Owing to command over resources and centralization of
economic and political decisions, the program of compulsory industrialization during the SYP could obtain
highest priority by use of coercion and fiat,[67] disregard of economic cost, and sacrifice of efficiency for
expediency. In Lange's words it was a "sui generis war
economy":

Thus the first period of planning and management of

> a socialist economy, at least according to our present
> experience, has always been characterised by admin-
> istrative management and administrative allocation of
> resources on the basis of priorities centrally estab-
> lished... This is, so to speak, a highly politicalised
> economy, both with regards to the means of planning
> and management and the incentives it utilizes.   I
> think that, essentially, it can be described as a
> sui generis war economy.[68]

CENTRALIZATION DENOUNCED

Although inefficiency of the economy was harshly criticized in the Polish press of 1956 and 1957, a need arose
for more fundamental re-examination of the basic tenets
of the economic system.   It was not sufficient to state
that willfulness guided the economy with no regard for
cost.   The cause of such willfulness had to be exposed.
It is in this spirit that Brus, the one time stanch
Marxist closely associated with the Central Committee
of the Party, spoke at the congress of Polish economists
that took place in Warsaw in June, 1956:

> The State Commission for Economic Planning certainly
> is responsible for many negative items in the balance
> of the Six-Year Plan, but it is a mistake to think,
> as some do, that it will suffice to destroy the
> Commission's premises in order for things to get
> better in Poland.   The State Commission for Economic
> Planning and similar institutions are themselves a
> product of the system, though, it is true, an active
> product that begets other products: nevertheless they
> do not constitute an "original sin".   Definite causes
> in definite conditions lead to definite results; the
> point, then is to discover the causes.[69]

In the course of fermentation of ideas that followed
the congress the excessive centralization, shortcomings
of planning methods, fulfilment of production at all costs,
and flagrant disregard of economic calculation fell under
strong attack.
The economists propounded widely divergent views on the
methods for improving the system, yet they all seemed to
agree that overcentralization was one of the most detrimental factors of the period.   As Lange testifies:

> We actually had a period in the socialist countries...
> when the output of even the least important commodity
> was planned. There was the famous joke in Poland -
> really it was not a joke, but it was true - that the
> production of pickled cucumbers is in the national
> economic plan. Another case which was not a joke
> either but was a fact - was that the State Planning
> Commission made a plan of the number of hares which
> will be shot during the year by hunters. At the
> same time, you could not get, for instance, buttons
> or hairpins for ladies, simply because they had been
> forgotten in the national economic plan.[70]

J. Pajestka, who observed central planning at close range,
remarked that the crisis of central planning in Poland
was provoked by an attempt to equate planning with
command of the economy:

> It is a fact that we planned badly, that almost every-
> thing was done to disgrace planning, that we planned
> without a scientific basis, without calculation,
> hence wilfully, that fixed bureaucratic pattern only
> too often replaced common sense, that we believed
> blindly in administrative decrees, etc.[71]

During the Stalinist era the authorities considered waste
and maladjustments in the functioning of the economy as
manifestations of insufficient centralization. Consequently the remedies offered were increased centralization,
preparation of more detailed plans and indexes, intensified
rationing of materials, and proliferation of commands:

> The system of commands was similar to sucking pumps
> which aimed at reversing the current of a river and
> lead the waters upstream. Sure enough the waters
> came back, taking advantage of any clearance between
> the pumps, any defect in their functioning in order
> to go downstream in accordance with the natural law
> of gravitation. Naturally the system of pumps had
> to grow and improve in order to fulfil its Sisyphean
> labor of reversing the current of the entire economy
> and directing the work of millions of people against
> their most vital needs into a false course.[72]

Inertia at all levels of economic activity could be

observed as all were awaiting instructions from above.
This state of affairs was conducive to a growing necessity
for administrative fiat and strengthening of the central
planner's powers. The ever increasing number of plan
indexes regulated more and more all aspects of economic
life. But as the bureaucratic apparatus grew, less and
less initiative was manifested. "The entire economic
mechanism became a heavy, submissive body, bedeviled by
a jungle of bureaucratic rules and regulations."[73]

Deploring overcentralization and lack of autonomy in
enterprises Brus stated:

> In our economic system we have production or trade
> units which we call enterprises. In fact, however,
> these are not enterprises since they do not have the
> right to make independent decision on the basis of
> their own calculation but must instead accept
> decisions imposed without regard for their economic
> interests. It seems that without appropriate free-
> dom of choice, connected with material interests,
> there cannot be genuine economic accounting. The
> one that exists in our country and to which we
> devote so much space in our economic literature is,
> in fact, a mere shadow of real economic accounting.
> Let the planning organs not take the decisions for
> the enterprises; their role should amount to creating
> such economic conditions so that the decisions of the
> enterprises would go in the direction desired. Then
> the mechanism of economic ties between enterprises
> and the system of accounting, financial sanctions,
> etc., functioning so ineffectively today, will
> operate smoothly.[74]

In a "sui generis war economy" the concern with scarcity
relations, rational allocation of resources, and economic
calculation is not deemed to be of primary importance.[75]
The planner's primary task seems to be assuring compatibility between requirements and availability of production,
hence the importance of material balances. At best the
method of balances will show internal consistency of
requirements and availability, but it will not indicate
the optimal solution as there is a multitude of theoretica
ly possible ones. The lack of economic calculation was
emphasized by Brus:

We have not succeeded in ensuring adequate economic
effectiveness of expenditure of means both in the
sphere of investment as well as in the sphere of
production costs, productivity, full use of production capacity, administrative costs, etc.: there
were many instances of simply criminal waste.[76]

Production targets were assigned without analyzing cost
data in particular firms. Brus continues:

The level of costs is very rarely, or perhaps never,
one of the primary elements for establishing the
production programme of an enterprise, for assigning
production tasks to the various enterprises in such
a way that the average cost of a production unit would
be the lowest possible. The relation between production planning and cost planning is reflected even in
the organizational structure of the State Commission
for Economic Planning and the economic ministries
where the costs departments are separated from the
departments planning production.[77]

Overcentralization caused the familiar occurrences of
squandering and waste of materials, low quality and unsatisfactory assortment of production, high labor inputs,
low labor productivity, slow pace of cost reductions,
weak development of technological progress, incomplete
use of production capacity, wasteful substitution of
materials for labor, and an excessive administrative
apparatus.
   Although the Polish economists were largely concerned
with pointing out past errors, their main objective was
to present proposals for revitalizing the functioning of
the economy and rendering it more efficient.

PROPOSALS FOR CHANGE:
THE MODEL DISCUSSION AND AFTERTHOUGHTS

The discussion on the model was concerned with changes
in the system of planning and administration of the economy within the framework of a socialist system. The
proposals were considered only as technical variants of
the socialist system taken as given. In his recent
appraisal of the development of economic thought in post-

war Poland, Lange referred to the discussion as "a revitalization of Marxist economic thought" and described
it in these terms:

> To the forefront came such problems as centralization
> and decentralization of decision in administrating the
> socialist economy, democratization of administration
> through the workers' councils, the role, on the one
> hand, of economic instruments, and on the other,
> of administrative means in managing the economy, the
> role of economic incentives, the principles of price
> formation, the problem of market equilibrium, etc.
> In Poland these problems were dubbed the economic
> model. The discussion which developed was termed
> the discussion on the model.[78]

Among the debaters, the extremists, so called value-
men, believed that the panacea lay in restoration of
the market mechanism functioning within the socialist
system. Kurowski, "the angry young man" among Polish
economists, postulated that the firm should have absolute
freedom in choosing what and how much to produce and set
prices on its products according to the law of demand and
supply operating in the market.[79] This precept should
apply to manufacturers of both producer and consumer
goods. Furthermore, although the enterprises should
remain socialized their ownership should pass from the
state to the collective of workers. The firms' sole
goal should be maximization of profit. A share of profit
should be divided among the workers employed. The
foreign trade monopoly should be abolished and firms
should decide on the import and export of goods. A
central currency fund should be established where the
exporters would exchange the foreign currency obtained
for their products and the importers would buy this
currency at its market price.[80]
    Kurowski limited the role of the central plan to
forecasting and coordinating the general trend of development in the economy. He envisaged that central authorities would correct market maladjustments. To perform
these functions the planner would use mainly monetary
policy as a mitigating device. Furthermore the power
of the planner with regards to division of national
income between consumption and accumulation would be
strongly curtailed by extending co-decision privileges

to representatives of the working class. Such co-decision would involve struggle between the two forces and
counteract the recurrence of underconsumption.[81] The
central planner's investment program should be limited
to building new enterprises. Prices of investment goods
should be determined by market mechanism and investment
decisions made on the basis of such prices. Investment
funds should bear interest and the rate should result
from the supply and demand for capital and the policy
of the central planner.[82]

Few economists advocated restoration of a free price
mechanism and complete decentralization of decision
making. They rather leaned towards a model in which the
main macro-decisions would be taken by a central authority with prices, at least for the most important products,
set centrally, a few directives sent down from top to
bottom, and mainly economic incentives used in the
process encouraging initiative and improving speed of
adjustment and transmission of information. Within
defined limits, economic choice would be left to management of enterprises. Economic calculation would
become a tool of both management and planning authorities.

The _differentia specifica_ of the so-called decentralized model is that it assumes many levels of decision
making,[83] whereas the strictly centralized model assumes
several organizational levels, all essential decisions
are made at the top. Recently Zielinski suggested that
complete decentralization, with the planner retaining
supreme power in constructing the plan, would mean
governing the _executing_ apparatus exclusively by means
of parameters. Complete centralization would mean
governing the executing apparatus by non-parametric means
(commands). The various degrees of decentralization
would depend on the role performed by parametric versus
non-parametric means. Without detracting from the
planner's essential powers, Lange conceives transformation of a centralized model into a decentralized one
by means of setting up such goals and incentives for the
lower levels that the result of their activity should
conform to the planner's preferences; in other words,
that in a decentralized model the lower echelons should
autonomously execute the tasks previously foisted on
them in a centralized model.[84]

Brus produced a comprehensive literature on the concept
of a decentralized model within the framework of the

present political regime. He appears to have come close
to embodying the prevailing opinion among the majority
of Polish academic economists. At the expense of over-
simplification we have adopted it as a frame of reference.

In this model the central planner is assigned the
task of building the NEP on the basis of "economic and
social rationality". The implication is that the plan
should reflect Party preferences. In this respect there
is no essential difference between the centralized and
decentralized models. The same decision maker is responsible for the major economic decisions in both models.
The central plan would still embrace the major problems:
the rate of growth, production, national income and its
distribution for accumulation and consumption, the division of accumulation for investments and increase of
working capital, determination of the industries' development, localization of investments, distribution of consumption among collective goods and individual consumption
designating changes in the income structure of individual
branches of industry and localities, specification of the
production structure (in branches of industry and on ter-
ritorial basis), designation of major assortments in
physical units, manpower and labor productivity, and
the magnitude and structure of foreign trade.[85]

But, whereas in a centralized model the plan formulated centrally reaches all units of economic activity,
in a decentralized model "the national economic plan
ceases to be a central sun whose rays-directives must
reach all units".[86] According to Brus, in a decentralized model, the central planner decides directly in
the following instances.

1) In the field of national income the planner defines
a) labor's share in national income and the wage structure,
b) the respective shares of the firms' profits designated
for centralized and decentralized funds, and c) distribution of centralized funds among collective goods and
accumulation.

2) It is up to the planner to choose the basic composition of investments, allocating the central investment fund among the various branches of industry, to
determine the size and capacity of plants, and decide
on investment criteria and methods, without necessarily
deciding directly about particulars.[87]

3) Prices should be centrally established as parameters
for enterprises. But when the market is competitive and

firms cannot fix monopolistic prices, and when the state
does not intend to influence the buyer or seller by means
of prices, prices may be formed on the market.[88]
    In this decentralized model all remaining economic
decisions are to be made directly at the enterprise level.
Initially the enterprise is endowed by the state with
fixed and working capital. It autonomously organizes
the production processes, chooses the size and composition
of output, methods and factors of production to be used
to minimize costs. It plays an active role as buyer and
seller of goods. It chooses its sources of supply and
channels of distribution. The firm decides on the division of profit remaining at its disposal and on the
investments from its own funds and/or bank loans. When
investments have been decided centrally and are financed
from centralized funds, the enterprise should be allowed
to decide on methods for their execution. Finally the
enterprise decides on its internal organization, system
of wages and premiums within the framework of centrally
established regulations.[89]
    In a centralized model where economic decisions are
made outside the firm, only production may be maximized
since labor and material inputs are predetermined in both
physical and monetary units. But when the methods and
composition of output are decided by the enterprise, the
use of output criteria as a measure of performance
cannot suffice. Profit, being a synthetic yardstick, is
then the best performance criterion. Hence the firm's
main decisions would be geared to profit maximization.
The profit criterion is usually identified with activating
economic incentives, "a situation stimulating people to
realize a predetermined goal of economic activity."[90]
The supposition is that when profit grows the enterprise
improves its financial situation with respect to further
expansion, improvement of working conditions, and increase
in premiums. Conversely, when profit decreases the firm
may encounter financial difficulties encroaching on
expansion and the size of premiums.[91]
    Attacking profit sharing or premiums based on profit,
Professor Kalecki questioned the practicality of substituting, even to a certain extent, economic incentives
for central planning of production. He pointed out that
if an enterprise is badly managed and profits suffer
there should be no reason for increasing the premiums.
But if technically inferior equipment causes high costs

and low profits, why should the employees be penalized?
Secondly, Kalecki argues, the quantitative effect of the
share in profits is limited by the fact that income from
it cannot constitute a substantial part of remuneration.
But if the share in profit is not substantial, both as
an absolute amount and in relation to basic pay, it would
have only a negligible effect as an incentive. Profit
is not only a function of the volume of production, but
primarily reduction of costs. Kalecki fears that firms
would tend to reduce costs instead of increasing production. He recognizes that in some cases it may be desirable,
but the result might be a complete failure from the over-
all viewpoint. As an example he offers the detriment to
society arising from a substitution of materials and
machinery for labor in case of an oversupply of labor.
He fears that the desire to reduce labor costs may cause
unemployment rather than increase of per capita income.[92]

At the beginning of 1957 the SCEP was abolished and
a new planning body organized under the name of Planning Commission of the Council of Ministers (PC), with
S. Jedrychowski as its chairman. The PC's personnel
was reduced and stress was laid on long range planning
and use of economic analysis in the planning process.
A month after taking office Jedrychowski described the
new economic patterns:

We are now going through a period of transformation
and shaping of our economic model... directed towards
decentralization and democratization, towards organization of workers' councils, towards autonomy for
enterprises and economic autonomy for the People's
Councils. The economic model must take shape in
practice. No ready-made theoretical conception, no
cut and dried patterns or formulas can provide the
details for this economic model which is to take
shape in practice on the basis of our own specific
conditions.[93]

He considered a diminished rate of forced industrialization as a political, economic, and social necessity
stemming from the need for a more rapid and immediate
rise in the standard of living. To fulfil these promises
the economic policy of the state would have to undergo
drastic changes:

In which direction will these amendments go? In the
direction of increasing individual consumption, of
limiting capital investments, of lessening the burden
of defence expenditures on the national income; in
the direction of revising the production plans for
mining... the plans for the metallurgical industry,
and so forth; in the direction of changes in the
principles of foreign trade and the balance of payments.[94]

He explicitly stated that the basic plan indexes--the
wage fund, the investment fund, exports, imports, accumulation of enterprises, and their contributions to
the state budget--will have to be in the nature of
directives. Central allocation of materials should be
curtailed and the quantity of assortments planned centrally for key industries should be reduced to allow firms
some freedom in producing certain assortments according
to buyers' requirements. The discretionary powers should
be wider for consumer than producer goods industries. But:

Central economic administration should not order
enterprises about and deluge them with trifles and
paperwork. It should coordinate the work of firms,
control their activity and help them to attain the
best economic and production results.[95]

During the spring of 1957 a commission of the Economic
Council considered the proposals for change and produced
a set of theses. The document was a compromise of
divergent views and lacks cohesion and clarity. Nevertheless it is important since it was to guide the state
in initiating changes. The salient points raised by the
Theses were:
    1) The crucial industrial investments should be decided
centrally on the basis of analysis of their relative efficiency and guided by the growth rates in the long range
plans. Such investments should be financed by interest
bearing non-repayable credits. The firms should be free
to allocate depreciation and repair funds to investments
or repairs. However, central authorities may limit enterprise investments in part or in full by freezing the
funds.
    2) The central industrial plan should differentiate
between value of marketable output and value added,
identifying quantities of basic raw materials and semi-

fabricates.

3) The establishment of assortment indexes for individual firms should be the exception rather than the
rule. It should be applied to distinctly deficit goods.
Specifically it should be reverted to when sale is subject
entirely to rationing and/or material inputs are rationed.

4) Central establishment of wage funds for enterprises
should be retained. Under no circumstances should the
balancing of income and expenditures of the population
be impaired.

5) Enterprises' activity should be directed by their
own plans, coordinated with the NEP. The principle of
profitability should be the guide and economic incentives
the rule. Whenever directives supplement incentives they
must be observed. The former should never contravene
the latter. Gross value of output should be abandoned
as the main criterion for evaluating performance.

6) Relations between firms and their supervisory units
should be specified, delineating the supervisors' prerogatives beyond which the firm is an autonomous economic
unit. The firm should be allowed to invest from its own
funds from depreciation write-offs, profit, or bank loans.
It may plan its production basing it on an evaluation of
procurement and marketing possibilities, subject to
directives received. It may conduct transactions of procurement and sale directly with other producers **or**
trade centrals. It must divide the wage fund according
to collective agreements. It is authorized to apportion
the part of profit remaining at its disposal as it sees
fit. The workers' council and the director who manages
the firm and is responsible for its activity to the state
are the authorities of the enterprise.

7) The incentive system should be independent of tasks
set in the output plan. Incentives should be tied in with
profit adjusted for results independent of the firm's
activity, e.g., increase in prices, etc. Premium funds
should be stabilized for a period of a few years to
exert a long run influence. The magnitude of the wage
fund prescribed for the firm should not be set as heretofore in relation to gross output but in relation to
value added. Within the frame of legal regulations
governing the wage fund, the firms are authorized to
dispose of it autonomously.

8) In view of the foregoing, an improved price system
must depart radically from the prevailing accidental price

relations. Price formation must consider actual economic
conditions in a given production and exchange sphere.
The different price levels for producer and consumer
goods should be abandoned since they distort calculation
and proportions in the division of national income. The
state should definitely control prices, either directly
by establishing prices or indirectly by influencing
production and the market. The price reform of producer
goods should be based on a calculation of genuine costs
of production, the level and relations of world prices
for goods subject to foreign trade, and ensure profitability to producers. Prices of consumer goods should
ensure equilibrium on the consumer market and assure the
interests of consumers.[96]

Although a relatively wide decentralization is advocated by the Theses, central planning as a conditio
sine qua non for the economy's development is emphatically reasserted. This was not a very "dangerous" document.
But the main changes it proposed were not implemented.[97]
Presumably they did not meet with the blessings of the
Party. The discussion on the model was only an outward
demonstration of a desire for change. The real decisions
were made by the Party.

PROGRESS AND REGRESS

In the spirit of the time greater freedom was granted
to enterprises in making current decisions. Accordingly
the innumerable plan indexes were reduced to eight. In
1956 resolution 704 of the CM stipulated the following
mandatory indexes to be transmitted to enterprises by the
central planning organs: 1) value of marketable production
including value of output for the consumer market, 2)
quantity of production of the most important assortments,
3) total wage fund (including outside labor), 4) profit
or loss, 5) amount of profit to be contributed to the
state budget, 6) budget allotments for investments
determined centrally, including construction work, 7)
financial limits for capital repairs, and 8) total
normative for working capital.[98]

The firms' managers were entrusted with a considerable
number of decisions. They were granted the right to draft
their annual plans on the basis of directives received
and allowed some freedom in breaking down the annual plans

into quarterly and monthly ones. They were permitted to
accept orders not specified in their plans, provided that
such orders would not conflict with plan fulfilment.
They were granted wider freedom in financing their
activity and were permitted to choose their suppliers.
The quantitative effect of the change is revealed by the
reduction of total specified production targets from
1406 in 1956 to 768 in 1957. The number of commodities
subject to central allocation was cut from 1411 in 1956
to 1150 in 1957. The technical coefficients were
reduced from 587 in 1956 to 230 in 1957.[99]

Early in 1956 workers' councils spontaneously sprung
up in several enterprises as a protest of the masses
against the low standard of living, bureaucracy, and
centralization. They were later sanctioned by law and
their formation encouraged in other enterprises. The
law of November 1956 entrusted the workers' councils
and directors with co-management of enterprises.[100] The
importance of the enterprise fund (profit sharing in the
form of premiums distributed from this fund) was enhanced.
The fund was to grow in accordance with profits realized
by the firm. Experimental enterprises were set up.
Decision making by management and workers' councils was
allowed greater freedom there, and was put to the
practical test of workability.[101]

The process of decentralization was one of trial and
error. There occurred a "relaxation of discipline in the
management of enterprises, substantial increases in 'unplanned' wage payments, resulting in inflationary pressures on the consumer market with no offsetting flow of
production reaching the market."[102] Output fell and the
firms were too slow in adjusting to economic stimuli.
The planners found that when management had jurisdiction
over procurement the "self-control" which it was hoped
would guide them was inexistent. Excessive quantities of
materials were ordered and hoarded. Considerable shortages developed and the planners lost control over allocation of materials.

To conciliate the workers, in many cases, no upward
revision of antiquated norms was made. For example, in
most branches of the machine building industry the 1953
norms were still in force. In the metal working firms
work norms were overfulfilled anywhere from 113 to 340
per cent.[103] Moreover:

> Irresponsibility and indiscipline led to overemploy-
> ment, unauthorized investments, overexpenditure of
> the wage fund, excessive overtime and unjustified
> absenteeism. Corruption, embezzlement and theft were
> also common... Many of the weaknesses... could be
> traced back to 1956. Mr. Gomulka on his return to
> power took wide measures to decentralize the economy.[104]

It is generally admitted that the 1956-58 period featured a substantial increase in the real income of the
population at the expense of investment expenditures.
Great stress was laid on the production of consumer goods.
The most important blunders of the SYP were mitigated.
The relative share of investments in national income fell.[105]
   As the process continued and initial results came in
they were judged unsatisfactory. The Party and the central
planner were faced with the danger of losing control over
economic activity at the lower echelons and a process
of reversal and counterreforms was initiated:

> We have all observed the gradual withdrawal of schemes
> intending to increase the autonomy of enterprises.
> This was apparent in the growing number of plan in-
> dexes, weakening of decentralized investments, econo-
> mic incentives, etc.[106]

By 1957 resolution 199 of the CM added a directive plan
index prescribing the wage fund for white collar workers
(managerial, technical, engineering, and office personnel).
In 1958 resolution 392 added two more indexes: the amount
of profit to be contributed to the enterprise's development fund (serving the firm as a source for financing
decentralized investments and working capital) and the
amount of profit to be contributed to the reserve fund
of the association (the unit supervising the firm). Also
in 1958 resolution 450 introduced four more indexes:
number of production workers (engaged in material production only), number of manual workers, the size of the
technical and engineering personnel, and the size of the
administrative and office personnel. In addition resolution 451 of 1958 introduced directive indexes for
export and import tasks, subsidies for housing construction and division of the depreciation fund. By 1959 the
total number of indexes transmitted as binding directives
amounted to anywhere from 18 to 22 depending on the industry.[107]

Concurrently the workers' councils' scope of activity was strongly curtailed by introducing the conference of workers' self-management in November, 1958. The latter institution incorporated representatives of the firm's Party organization, factory council, trade union, and workers' council. Prerogatives which heretofore devolved on the workers' council passed into the hands of the conference and the council became its executing organ. Moreover, the balance of power between the director and the workers' self-management organization in the co-management of the firm decidedly favored the director.[108]

Accompanying the process of recentralization the period after 1958 is distinguished by a relatively slower rate of increase in consumption in comparison to the increase in the flow of production,[109] accompanied by an increase in the share of investments in industry. The growing importance of capital investments may be inferred from the upward revisions of the planned growth index of capital investments in the present Five-Year Plan (FYP) 1961-65. The index (1960=100) was drafted as 146.6 in October, 1958, 149.0 in March, 1959, 150.6 in June, 1960, and enacted by Sejm in February, 1961, as 153.2. The corresponding indexes for investments in industry were 143.2, 140.8, 144.6, and 149.3, agriculture 144.5, 153.0, 183.5, and 183.7, and housing 156.9, 167.5, 159.5, and 147.7. According to the recently revised version of the investment plans for the last two years of the FYP, industrial investments for 1964 were increased by 3.8 per cent and for 1965 by 5.4 per cent. The composition of industrial investment expenditures has been altered at the detriment of agriculture, food, and light industries. The expenditures for the food industry were decreased by 18 per cent and light industry by 32 per cent.[110]

It seems that very little time was given the enterprises to indicate whether or not the decentralized system could work efficiently.[111] Since profit became an important performance criterion, the system could not work efficiently unless prices were reformed so as to become parameters for economic action. As we shall see price reforms did not keep pace with decentralization measures. Consequently the obsolete prices could not be used as guides for efficient allocation of resources. While enterprises were being endowed with greater autonomy little was done in way of amputating the overgrown administrative apparatus and curtailing its powers.[112] In time friction

between the two developed with the balance of power
shifting back to the authorities.

From the process of reforms and counterreforms emerged
the present structure of the Polish economy, which it is
hoped, that unlike Hegel's Prussian state, is not the
apotheosis of the dialectics of history.

PRESENT ECONOMIC ADMINISTRATION

The structure of Polish economic administration has
the shape of a pyramid where the units on the lower echelons are subjected to those on the higher one, forming
thus a hierarchy of power. At the top of the pyramid
is the supreme ruling organ: the Politbureau of the
Central Committee of the Polish United Workers Party
(PUWP). The policy of the Party is implemented by the
highest governing organs of the country: the Sejm, the
CM, the ECCM and the PC.

The Sejm is a legislative body. It supervises the
activity of all executive and administrative state
organs. It enacts into law the annual and multi-year NEP's.

The CM performs the executive role in administrating
the economy. Its Economic Committee's permanent members
are the chairman and vice-chairmen of the CM, the chairman of the PC, the Ministers of Finance, Foreign Trade,
Heavy Industry, and Agriculture. The ECCM directs and
coordinates the economic activity of the country. Its
resolutions are binding on the economic administration.
But on "key issues" it refers to the CM which is then the
decision making body. In particular the latter resolves
on the plan drafts, the basic planning methodology, the
principles governing the wage fund, financial policy,
and defines the prerogatives of the economic agencies.

The PC drafts plans based on instructions from the CM
and assigns targets to individual ministries. In particular the PC is responsible to the CM for 1) drafting of
long range, multi-year, and annual NEP's, 2) pronouncement
of opinions on the draft of the state budget, 3) development of planning methods and research on methodology, 4)
approval of major investment projects, 5) control and
reporting on the fulfilment of plans and the application
of means ensuring their implementation, 6) preparation
of analyses and reporting on the national economic situation, and 7) approval of material balances prescribed by

CHART I - <u>Administrative Structure of Key Industries</u>

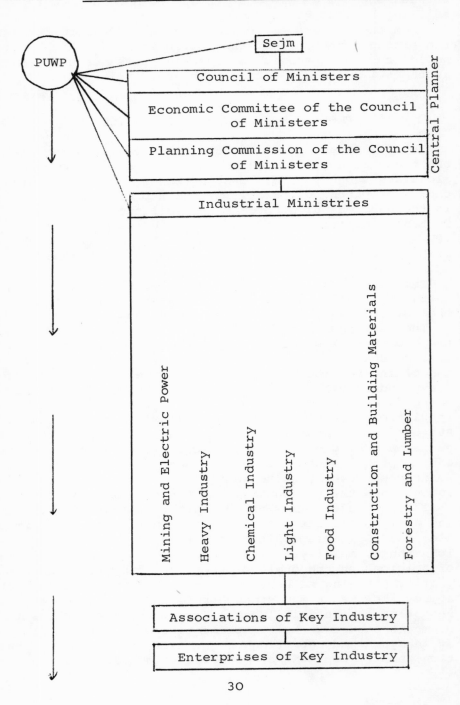

the CM, changes and reallocation of balances within the scope permitted.[113]

As shown in Chart I, immediately below the CM and its organs are the industrial ministries, an extension of the administrative apparatus. Guided by instructions received from above, the ministries control, coordinate the activity, and draft plans for the industries under their jurisdiction. In addition they formulate employment, wage, and pricing regulations for their subordinates, build, reorganize, and liquidate firms. Upon consultation with the associations and the local Party organizations they hire and fire the firms' directors. The present ministries and the industries under their jurisdiction are identified in Chart II.

Official pronouncements increasingly stress the need for enhancing the ministries' role as promoters of growth, planning, and efficiency in their branch of industry, as opposed to that of direct administrators of enterprises. But it is still common for ministries to establish output targets for a given firm bypassing the association. Similarly, the PC establishes at times production directives for enterprises bypassing both the ministry and association.[114] Ministries now perform many functions previously exercised solely by the PC. But as the vice-minister of chemical industry recently pointed out:

> Direct management of industry prevalent in ministries, numerous orders and directives limiting the subordinate units' prerogatives, and constant intrusion in their daily affairs constrain the development of economic analysis, limit initiative, and result in a decline of responsibility in subordinates.[115]

The associations are the third echelon of the pyramid. They were created in 1958 to supersede the central boards, which were mere extensions of ministries. The associations were set up as legal entities responsible for the development and output plans of their firms and accountable to the ministries for the aggregate financial results of the firms under their jurisdiction. In particular the responsibilities of the associations are to plan the development of their branch of industry, to coordinate enterprises of similar activity under the jurisdiction of different associations, ministries, or local industry,[116] to determine and distribute directive plan indexes

CHART II - The Ministries and Branches of Industry

Ministries	Branches of Industry
Mining and Electric Power	Coal, oil, salt, gas, and electric power plants
Heavy Industry	Automobiles, tractors, airplanes, motors, machine building, steel mills, non-ferrous metals, mining of iron and non-ferrous ores, fireproof materials, and metal products
Chemical Industry	Inorganic, pharmaceutical, sulfurous acid, phosphorous fertilizers, explosives, paints and lacquers, chemical synthetics, rubber, synthetic fibers, etc.
Construction and Building Materials	Cement, bricks, building supplies, etc.
Forestry and Lumber	Industries based on lumber as a raw material and production of machines and equipment for forestry
Light Industry	Textile, clothing, and leather products
Food Industry	Meat, milk, refrigeration, eggs, poultry, sugar, fats, beer, fruit, vegetables, tobacco, coffee, cosmetics, etc.

Source   W. Piotrowski, op. cit., p. 106

for the enterprises, to dispense the special funds at their disposal, to organize exchange of experiments, procurement, marketing, and cooperation between enterprises, and to supervise, control, and mediate between enterprises and the ministry.[117]

The associations are far more complex units than their precursors. They represent a larger number of firms, they embody marketing offices, research institutes, and spe-

cialized laboratories. An organizational novelty in
associations are the technical economic councils which
study and report improved methods for utilizing existing
potential and long range development programs. As a rule
these councils exist on paper only. Where they are active
their performance is far from satisfactory. A committee
composed of the firms' directors and the association's
management acts as counsel to the association. The committee discusses the industry's development plans, specialization of particular firms, policy of materials distribution, etc. It decides on the assignment of funds not
regulated centrally and the undertaking of the association's investments for all enterprises as a group. The
committee should facilitate cooperation between the
association and its firms. It has been observed that
in practice the committee's meetings have degenerated
into briefing sessions for the firms' directors.[118]
    The association's role is twofold: Theoretically it
represents the interests of the enterprises and simultaneously performs the functions of supervisor. In practice the relations of associations and enterprises have
not undergone much change since the central boards were
dissolved. Notwithstanding the official stress on long
range planning and use of economic tools in associations,
practice indicates that their paramount functions are
still the assignment of plan targets and means followed
by control of plan fulfilment in the lower units. "In
general the associations perform only the second-rate
role of intermediary links between enterprises and their
ministry."[119] The manner of transmitting indexes to firms,
so reminiscent of commands, has been aptly characterized
by Madej:

    The manner of taking decisions and transmitting
    indexes reminds one of reading out orders in front
    of a company of soldiers. Instead of arguments a
    formula is put forth: "in accordance with the order
    of the minister" which is to put weight to the tasks
    and persuade the directors of enterprises of their
    importance.[120]

Associations disregard the opinions of managers and foist
their orders on them, infringing on their prerogatives.
But a similar curtailment of associations' prerogatives
is demonstrated by ministries. In a recent interview,

Vice-Premier Woniolka, discussing the autonomy of firms
remarked that "in any event autonomy will remain a pure
formality until we break the conscious or subconscious
tendencies in associations to lead the firms by the hand."[12]

It is worth noting that the pronouncements at the
IV Congress of the PUWP held in June, 1964, indicate an
attempt at revitalizing the administrative apparatus by
investing associations with greater powers.[122] Economists
and "captains of industry" have taken their cue from
these promulgations and came up with a number of proposals
to invigorate the associations.

Their starting point is a transformation of associations into "socialist combines" with enterprises as their
component parts. The combines would be interested in
their financial results (profit) and guided by economic
calculation. But there would be no basic changes in price
formation. The contention is that such an organization
would allocate production more efficiently on the basis
of specialization, improving the process of cooperation.
The socialist combine should be development oriented.
Its investments, largely financed from profits, would be
more efficient since it will invest in the units which
will produce highest returns. Moreover, the large combine
is better suited to risk new ventures and develop foreign
trade. The latter should be stimulated (and become more
profitable) by allowing the combine to benefit from it
financially.[123]

The promoters of these changes argue that not only is
a large organization more efficient and easier to control,
but both domestically and abroad the future lies in large
organizational units.[124] Some Polish economists, however,
take the "association campaign" with a grain of salt and
see in it a manifestation of the tendency to curtail the
enterprises' autonomy.

The proposed changes have several shortcomings. Unless
more fundamental changes in planning and pricing will
follow no striking improvements are likely to materialize
because of a lack of tools for verifying optimality.[125]

                        THE PLANNING SYSTEM

The interdependence of the different levels of administration in conveying knowledge and decisions through the
chain of command is of special importance for grasping

the planning system. The communication medium between
the individual echelons is a flow of messages composed
of reported data describing a given situation flowing
upwards and directives instructing the execution of
given functions flowing downwards.[126] The process
consists of data infiltrating particular levels, transmitted by them to higher ones where decisions are made
and directives emitted to the lower levels.[127] It may be
called a transformation of data into decisions, and
decisions into directives.

The time involved in this metamorphosis is of paramount
importance and depends largely on the number of decisions
to be made centrally.[128] The central level's transformation capacity is limited, and if strained, a part of
data is transformed into decisions and decisions into
directives too late. This time element signifies that
the directive may reach the lower level when the reported
situation has ceased to exist and execution of the directive will not produce the desired effect or be harmful.

Another deficiency of the process is the impoverish-
ment of data passing through several levels. As reports
flow up through the chain of command they are aggregated,
losing their specificity in the process. Consequently
the decision and ensuing directive abstract from a
number of concrete circumstances which may be important
enough to cause the directive to produce a divergent
result from the one intended.[129] Conversely when the
directives flow downward they are disaggregated, en-
riched, embellished, and overgrown with concrete inter-
pretative instructions which may have little in common with the central planner's intention.

Furthermore the lower levels are induced to generate
systematically distorted information to attain their own
desired results. Their reports are colored and doctored
in anticipation of directives to suit their purposes.
In the aggregation and disaggregation processes there
exists a built-in mechanism which will not only impov-
erish or embellish the messages but also distort and
contaminate them in accordance with the preferences and
interests of the levels through which the messages pass.[130]
In a nutshell the sender's behavior and content of his
message are influenced by the identity of the recipient
and the use he will make of the message.

There are three basic types of economic plans in
Poland: long range plans, covering as a rule 15 to 20

years, multi-year plans, and current plans (annual and
quarterly).

The long range plan is a general program of economic
development prepared only on the higher echelons of the
administration. This plan is the first quantified form
of the projected rate of growth and transformation of
the economy in conformity with Party preferences. It
simultaneously provides a map and perspective for plans
of shorter duration. The long range plan is broad in
character, non-operational, and subject to modifications
as results of plan fulfilment are received and new
desiderata arise.[131] The long range plan formulates the
rate of growth of national income and its repartition
between accumulation and consumption. It encompasses
the major investments, the general size of output
specifying the more important materials, the expected
increase of man-power, etc. It is a classical example
of planning exclusively in physical units and where all
decisions are made at the top.

Multi-year and current plans are prepared at all
levels of the administrative structure. They formulate
in concrete terms the long range plans, specifying the
targets and means, transforming them from physical into
monetary units.

The multi-year plan is far more detailed than the
long range one. It itemizes the main production and
consumption targets and the magnitude of investments
with their detailed composition, identifying the main
objects. Its construction allows projection of balances
in physical and financial terms. It is also non-operational and subject to alterations.[132]

The annual NEP is operational and mandatory for the
units to which it is addressed. It details further the
targets specified for the given year in the multi-year
plan and assigns them as specific orders which the units
at the lower levels are bound to implement.

Apart from the length of time involved in the process,
no essential differences exist in the drafting of the
annual and multi-year plans. Our attention will focus
on a somewhat idealized construction of the annual NEP.
In practice this is a process involving much friction
and a working knowledge of the game theory.[133]

The PC initiates the work on the annual NEP early in
the year preceding the plan period. Usually in April
it emits instructions on planning methods, requiring

CHART III - The Planning Process

FUNCTIONS	Sejm	CM	PC	Ministries	Associations	Firms
1. Drafting of NEP control figures by PC			1			
2. Approval of NEP control figures by CM		2				
3. Transmission of approved NEP control figures to PC		3				
4. Transmission of control figures to ministries			4			
5. Preparation and transmission of control figures to associations				5		
6. Preparation and transmission of control figures to firms					6	
7. Drafting of projected plans and transmission to associations						7
8. Drafting of projected plans and transmission to ministries					8	
9. Drafting of projected plans and transmission to PC				9		
10. Drafting of the NEP by PC and transmission to CM			10			
11. Approval of the NEP and submission to the Sejm		11				
12. Ratification of NEP by Sejm	12					
13. Transmission of targets and		13				
14. means to all units at all			14			
15. levels in the process of				15		
16. disaggregating the NEP					16	
17. Elaboration of technical-economic plans by enterprises on the basis of targets and means allotted						17

subordinates to draft their plans applying uniform methods and forms.[134] Thereafter the PC prepares the control
figures for drafting the NEP. Simultaneously the Ministry of Finance (MF), in close contact with the PC,
drafts the specifications for the state budget. The
control figures should be issued early in the year to
allow sufficient time for the construction of the plan.
But their preparation hinges largely on current plan
fulfilment and is, therefore, delayed until results come
in for the first four or five months of the current plan.
Although the annual plan is an appropriate excerpt of the
multi-year one, it is corrected to mitigate arising
disproportions and changes in policy. The budget and
plan control figures are then submitted to the CM which
by June issues the resolution on the NEP control figures.

The first part of the resolution consists of general
data on industrial output, services, employment, and
wages. These data are not binding but guide the ministries in the preparation of plans. The second part is
mandatory and must be strictly observed in drafting
plans. It stipulates investment limits, indexes of
import, export, procurement of basic materials, employment and wages. The NEP control figures are addressed
to ministries which partition and assign them to associations which take similar steps towards firms. The process
of disaggregation is marred with an inherent flaw. The
aggregate control figures are largely unsupported by
planning information emanating from the lower echelons,
and no satisfactory method exists to disaggregate macro-
data which are not based on information from micro-units.
When drafting their plans the firms are guided by the
control figures received from associations and their own
conjectures, especially their contracts with subcontractors,
suppliers, and buyers.

Having received the firms' projected plan drafts, the
associations should subject them to scrutiny, analysis,
synchronization, coordination, correction, and aggregation.
The plan is then referred to the ministries where it
undergoes similar treatment. The ministries' plan drafts
are usually submitted to the PC at the end of August.
While the lower echelons draft their plans, the PC concentrates on collecting and analyzing data on current
plan fulfilment. It also participates in solving the
more irksome problems in the associations' and ministries'
plans. Although the associations' plans are modified by

ministries (usually upward revision of targets), by obtaining a copy of the former at the time they are submitted to the ministries, the PC keeps its finger on the pulse of the lower levels.

The PC aggregates the ministries' plans and prepares its preliminary balances. These consist of synthetic balances such as the balance of population's income and expenditures, the state's financial balance, the balance of formation and division of national income, and a number of other balances encompassing manpower, investment outlays, material balances, etc., with particular stress on the balance of payments. At this stage, i.e., around mid-September, the apparent disproportions in the preliminary balances must be mitigated by redrawing the balances and altering the plan targets.[135] This is performed in close cooperation with the MF. The state budget is a tool for implementing the targets set by the PC. Hence it must conform to these targets with a distinct priority of output over financial planning. The directive nature of the budget, the concentration, reallocation, and redistribution of funds according to the planner's preferences, the control function, siphoning off over 80 per cent of accumulation, and financing investments are among the principal functions of the budget.[136]

At the beginning of November the NEP and budget are transmitted to the CM. They are approved and forwarded by the CM to the Sejm for final ratification.

While the targets are being retouched and finalized centrally, the enterprises should elaborate their technical-economic plans. When the NEP is enacted as law, directive plan indexes are disaggregated down the chain of command. The firms must then revise their plans in accordance with the directives received. Before their plans may be finalized, the firms must present them for verification by the bank. Theoretically the enterprise ratifies its own plan which cannot involve lower targets or higher means for their execution than stipulated by the directives. A copy of the plan is then submitted to the association.

Although proposals for revitalizing planning have been heard since 1956, the authorities only now gave what seems like a seal of approval for revamping the system. The IV Congress Party resolution called for more extensive preparation of inter- and intra-industry flows, application of econometrics and optimal programming at first to segmentary and later to over-all plans.[137]

The supremacy of input-output over material balances
is incontestable as it achieves similar objectives (mainly
internal consistency), less laboriously,[138] swifter (electronic computers), and above all enables the planner to
account for direct and indirect interdependencies and
determine a more realistic set of input norms (cumulative
coefficients).[139] The Leontief-type input-output resembles
material balances casting the problem in essentially
technological terms, abstracting basically from demand
analysis and value frame, applying constant production
coefficients, eliminating the substitution effect, and
offering no criteria for choice.[140] Although it enhances
the coordination and consistency of plans,[141] input-
output does not provide a mechanism for verifying the
methods of production which are external to the system.[142]
Prices used in input-output analysis could be completely
arbitrary because they serve mainly to aggregate heterogeneous magnitudes and have no bearing on the solution.
Unless an efficiency test is applied at the time the plan
is constructed and an optimum solution reached, no effective criteria are available at the lower levels for verifying the economic rationality of production.[143]

Although so far the main efforts of Polish planners
were directed towards improving the methods of balancing,
some nevertheless claim that "the goal of planning should
not be elaboration of only internally consistent plans.
Our goal should be elaboration of an optimal plan."[144]
When the problem of optimality and efficiency of planner's
choices is accentuated, input-output must be supplemented
with linear programming which enables the planner to find
optimal solutions, i.e., a solution that maximizes the
objective function: the quantity to be maximized subject
to constraints.[145]

The question whether the obstacles facing assimilation
of new techniques will be successfully overcome in the
near future is an open one. To mention just a few constraints: the shift would curtail the Party's latitude
and freedom of maneuver in setting and resetting targets,
and convert planning methodology from gross production
to national income.[146] Lesz points out that if the sacrifice of choosing a suboptimal plan, for political
reasons, would be known, the decision makers may revert
to the optimal one recognizing that the cost is incommensurate with the political benefits.[147] One wonders whether

the proclivity to enforce Party values in planning may
not be a serious handicap against unveiling the imputed
cost of departure from the optimal solution. In addition,
ideologically the reconciliation of input-output and
especially linear programming with Marxism is a controversial issue.[148] Planning bureaucracy has a vested interest
in preserving the status quo due to passivity, predilec-
tion for established routine, lack of mathematical training, fear of replacement of planners by electronic brains,
and "voluntarism" by "determinism". The arguments that
optimality programming is superfluous and the same goal
could be attained by comparison of "say" capital, import,
and material intensity; or that the role of activity
analysis should be limited to certain phases of programming, fulfilling only auxiliary functions are still widely
propounded.[149] A serious limitation on the "invasion of
planning offices by computers" is their shortage, degree
of aggregation, quantity and quality of data to be fed
to them.[150] If the data are unreliable, use of mathematical
methods and computers would doubtless give more consistent
results but only produce spurious optimality. The problem
then is whether such results warrant the costs involved in
the application of new techniques.

Assimilation of linear programming is impeded as it
requires scarcity prices for verifying optimality. But as
we shall see there seems to be a deeply ingrained reluctance to dispose of "irrational" prices. Unless this is
remedied the goal of plan optimization is seriously impaired.

In a broader perspective it seems that Professor Nove
captured the trend of future developments in planning in
the Soviet bloc:

Meanwhile we are witnessing a flowering of mathematical
economics. Perhaps a fully fledged theory of planning,
integrally linked with linear programming and input-
output analysis, reconciled at least in words with the
Marxian dogma, is at an advanced stage of preparation...
But it is very doubtful whether such a theory will
have much that is useful to say on the definition of
objectives. It is more likely to set out the way of
finding the most effective means of carrying out the
given objectives. The determination of the basic
purposes of economic policy will doubtless remain a
matter for the political leadership.[151]

CHAPTER 2   PRICING OF PRODUCER GOODS

Prices are among the most important economic variables
that determine and condition a firm's mode of behavior.
The pricing system and prices "are among the greatest social
inventions of mankind".[1] It is through the study of the
economic units' pricing functions that we can really
grasp the mechanism of response and adjustment to economic stimuli. We attempt to evaluate and describe here the
pricing phenomenon in the state-owned industrial sector
of the Polish economy with reference to the enterprise.

The first part of the chapter is devoted to an examination of the nature of pricing within the institutional
framework of present day Poland. Particular attention is
focused on the recent developments in Polish economic
thought. Our frame of reference is Western economic
theory and not the realities of our own system. Perhaps
there is an inherent limitation in this approach,[2] but
it seems that one of the primary functions of economic
theory is to provide a norm to ascertain the cost of
deviation from the "optimum" solution.

At the time when economic growth comes to the forefront
of economists' attention, preoccupation with the scarcity
problem may become "one of the least interesting or
important attributes of a real economic system."[3] Indeed
an economic system "that at _every_ given point of time
fully utilizes its possibilities to the best advantage
may yet in the long run be inferior to a system that
does so at _no_ given point of time, because the latter's
failure to do so may be a condition for the level or
speed of long run performance."[4] Nothing in this chapter
means to minimize the importance of economic growth, and
indeed this is not the place for resolving the growth
versus choice problem. However, that the study of the
scarcity problem is not futile is emphasized by Wiles,

who recognizes that growth may sometimes conflict with
consumers' sovereignty and scarcity but it would be inadvisable to dispose completely of either. "The advantages of each must as far as possible be quantified,
and a balance struck. To correct an important and permanent misallocation of resources is in itself economic
growth; for unwanted production is not production at all."[5]
    The second part of the chapter is of a more descriptive
nature. Since our aim is to concentrate on present practices, we have not endeavored to trace in detail the evolution of the price system from the inception of the
Polish People's Republic. Our aim is more modest, attempting only to shed some light on the present state of
affairs through a more detailed examination of the 1960
price reform.

                    THE NATURE OF PRICES

    Decision making, the choice between alternative courses
of action, is the core of economics, the science of administration of scarce resources in human society. Economic
efficiency[6] can almost never be based on technological
considerations alone. To govern production (optimum combination of factors and output composition) an economic
dimension is necessary, a criterion or choice indicator,
a sufficient summary measure of all opportunities forgone. Such an indicator "cannot be derived from any
property possessed by that particular thing, but which
reflects, or in which is condensed, its significance in
view of the whole means-end structure."[7] It is the
presence of the value scale that is the differentia
specifica of the economic, as distinct from the technological, problem. As Schumpeter points out, an economic
dimension, a phenomenon basic to efficient functioning
of any society, "at all times and under all circumstances,
finds expression in coefficients of choice which are
fundamentally the same thing as prices in capitalist
society."[8] To select between alternatives an economic
unit must have at its disposal reliable information: the
choice coefficients on which to base its decision. The
role of prices as signals and summary measures to convey
such information is lucidly summarized by Koopmans:

    ...price is regarded as a label, a signal, a piece

of information that is attached to the good or
service traded. This information expresses simultaneously the ultimate usefulness to consumers
of this good, and the foregone usefulness of other
goods or services that could have been produced
alternatively from the resources absorbed in making
this good. Choices about methods of production and
about amounts to be produced are based on this information; if these choices are to be good choices,
the information used has to be accurate.[9]

Indeed it is the allocative function of prices as
guides for resource allocation that renders prices indispensable for rational economic calculation. It is
particularly in solving the allocative problem that
Marxist economics is most deficient. There is virtually
no Marxist micro-economics.[10] Prices must be used in the
planning process to afford economic calculation aiming
not only at consistency but at finding optimum solutions.
The control function of prices - as a common denominator
for aggregating heterogeneous physical quantities in
value terms and performing the control and evaluative
functions, in an auditing sense - will be a serious
impediment for the use of prices as tools of economic
calculation. Even in a highly centralized economy the
questions "what, how, how much, and for whom to produce
efficiently"must be resolved on the basis of rational
prices. Three sets of data are required for a determin-
able solution of the allocative problem: 1) preference
function, which may reflect consumer or planner preferences,[11]2) choice indicator, and 3) production function. If the data under (1) and (3) are given, (2) can
be determined. Hence it is claimed that a socialist
economy can operate with rational prices without a
market in an institutional sense.[12]
    In Soviet-type economies price is a derivative of
cost.[13] The constituents of price are cost elements which
themselves are not independent variables. The production
cost of a given good cannot be said to be price determining since the constituting cost elements are determined
by prices. In these economies planners allocate productive agents and then set prices. Hence there is a basic
flaw in the system as prices cannot be set rationally
unless the productive agents were beforehand allocated
efficiently to their various uses.[14] Under such circum-

stances the <u>conditio sine qua non</u> for setting rational
prices would be that the prior allocation of productive
agents satisfies the efficiency test. However, this
condition is not fulfilled. The fundamental weakness of
an economy where the predetermined production quota and
appropriate input allocations are largely based on
physical planning is evident in the inability of economic
verification of production decisions. Without such verification there are no criteria for determining rational
costs for measuring the whole range of alternatives forgone at the margin. Without rational coefficients of
choice there can be no economic calculation:

> The Pharaohs - wrote Lord Robbins - did not need a
> price system for the erection of the pyramids. But
> at what sacrifice of other goods its products would
> be secured, at what economic, as distinct from the
> technical, efficiency it functioned, could not be
> ascertained.[15]

Rationality of economic calculation under socialism was
vigorously challenged by the "Viennese School of Anti-
socialism" and economists under their influence.[16]

ECONOMIC CALCULATION UNDER SOCIALISM

Mises, the most emphatic representative of the School,
claimed that with all its pretense of superior rationality, socialism is unworkable as under it resources cannot be efficiently allocated. With collectivist ownership of the means of production there can be no market
valuation and no rational prices and costs. Under socialism economic calculation is devoid of meaning.
The planners grope in the dark without a compass, squandering scarce resources. Their only safeguard is that
they are surrounded by a world still clinging to market
valuation. Without the help of foreign prices the planners' actions would be "aimless" and "planless". It is
only by referring to such prices that they can "calculate,
keep books, and prepare their plans."[17]
Applying Walras-Pareto tools, Barone demonstrated
that "it is obvious how fantastic those doctrines are
which imagine that production in the collectivist regime
would be ordered in a manner substantially different from

that of 'anarchist' production."[18] As a result Hayek and
Robbins did not **argue** that it is within the realm of
theoretical possibility to assign rational valuation to
factors, but questioned its practicability. Robbins
stressed that the time involved in gathering data, drawing
up, and solving the "millions of equations" renders the
information on which the equations are based obsolete.
Expectations to discover the relative sacrifices of alternatives and "means of adjusting production to meet the
preferences of consumers" are futile.[19] Hayek accentuated
the role of the price mechanism for communicating information swiftly and insisted that complete knowledge of all
pertinent data will not be available to the central
planner.[20]

Gathering hints from earlier contributions, Lange
refuted the argument that it is not within the domain of
practical possibility to "solve the equations" under
socialism. Lange's competitive solution[21] demonstrated
that socialism "can escape the irrationality which is
predicted of it if, but only if, it closely imitates the
mechanism of the competitive market and consents to be
ruled by the values which this market affirms."[22]

Performing the function of the market, Lange's Central
Planning Board (CPB) can achieve rational prices by "trial
and error". The crux of the problem is a confusion of
what is meant by prices and markets. Lange argued that
prices as "indices of the terms on which alternatives are
offered" are indispensable for rational resource allocation
Prices do not have to be concrete exchange ratios resulting from bargaining on a real market. It would suffice
if they were magnitudes calculated by the CPB,[23] which
may initially be chosen at random but actually the trial
and error process would proceed on the basis of the prices
historically given until demand is equated with supply.
Price setting à tâtonnements by the CPB entails prices
as constant parameters for managers.[24]

The CPB imposes rules on managers: to combine factors of production so as to produce at the lowest possible costs and to expand production or investments
until marginal costs equal prices.[25] The rate of investments is determined by the CPB to eliminate fluctuations
and foster growth. The distribution of capital among
firms relies on the interest rate which balances availability and demand for capital.[26]

Lange maintained that economic equilibrium is deter-

minable under socialism, that the only equations to be
solved are those of managers of production and consumers,
similar to those under capitalism, that Hayek and Robbins
"solve" at least hundreds of these equations daily every-
time they buy something, and that there is not the slight-
est reason why under socialism rational prices of producer
goods and means of production cannot be determined:

> The Central Planning Board has a much wider know-
> ledge of what is going on in the whole economic
> system than any private entrepreneur can ever have,
> and consequently, may be able to reach the right
> equilibrium prices by a much shorter series of
> successive trials than a competitive market actually
> does. The argument that in a socialist economy the
> accounting prices of capital goods and of productive
> resources in public ownership cannot be determined
> objectively, either because this is theoretically
> impossible, or because there is no adequate trial
> and error procedure available, cannot be maintained.[27]

In his rebuttal Hayek, _inter alia_, argued that the
tâtonnement process is inferior to a genuine market as
far as rapidity and completeness of the adjustment is
concerned. Such a market is handicapped by the absence
of price competition, and insufficient differentiation
of prices according to quality of goods and circumstances
of time and place. The actual mechanism for implementing
equilibrium cannot even "distantly approach" the efficiency of real markets where the required adjustments result
from "spontaneous action of the persons immediately
concerned."[28]

A criticism was also launched by the Western advocates of central planning. As Dobb pointed out, the
competitive solution implies vesting managers of firms
with investment and output decisions, as distinct from
central decisions on these matters. Indeed the Lange
solution places "severe limitations on the type of
economic mechanism which a socialist economy could
employ if it was to remain rational",[29]and undermines
the central planner's powers and control. Here seems to
lie the reason for unacceptability of this solution to
the central planner. Sweezy views Lange's CPB not as a
planning agency but as a price fixing one. Such a system
"reproduces some of the worst features of capitalism and

fails to take advantage of the constructive possibilities of economic planning."[30]

The pricing controversy under socialism is still
very much alive although geographically it has moved
eastward. Socialist planning has been a reality in the
Soviet Union for over forty years and in Eastern Europe
for almost two decades. Although Mises' gloomy arguments on the impossibility of economic calculation under
socialism were theoretically refuted, practice has yet
to show conclusively whether a socialist economy can
solve the allocative problem more efficiently, or as
efficiently, as a capitalist economy. It seems to be
an irrefutable fact that centrally planned socialist
economies do function. They are neither "aimless" nor
"planless" and "complete chaos" does not prevail. But
what is the economic cost of their functioning? Granted
that the socialist system can function, the next question is whether it can function more efficiently than
our market economy. The question raised by Hayek -
which system is more efficient? - has yet to be answered.
The preoccupation of many Polish economists with the
problem of economic calculation in socialism tesifies
to the relevancy of the subject today.[31]

THE POLISH PRICE CONTROVERSY

As mentioned in the previous chapter, it was left up
to the once orthodox Marxists to strike the first serious blow at the irrationality of economic calculation
in a command economy and seek remedy in a model reminiscent in many respects of the market solution once advocated by Lange. In his address to the 1956 congress
of economists Brus pointed to the relevance of Lange's
prewar model to present day Poland:

In particular, it seems to me the solutions proposed
by Oscar Lange in his work entitled On the Economic
Theory of Socialism are worthy of note today. Not
because I agree with all of the author's solutions,
and in particular with the theoretical methodological
foundations of his conceptions; on the contrary, I
believe particularly that rejection of the theory of
marginal utility and the basing of the whole reasoning on the Marxist theory of value can lead to

positive results. Nevertheless, the very conception
of an economic mechanism advanced by Lange is worthy
of careful study, and many elements of it should be
applied.[32]

During the Polish model discussion one of the main subjects of controversy was the price system which had
proven so inadequate and its reforms so futile. Proposals were advanced running the gamut from free market
price determination [33] to those propounded by the adherents to the status quo. The outright "revisionists"
were few, but the adherents to the status quo were not
numerous either. The majority of economists vacillated
between the two extremes.

Kurowski, the outstanding spokesman for the value-
men, candidly believed that if the all powerful forces
of supply and demand be let loose, they would be the
ultimate cure for all ills plaguing the Polish economy:

> So that the interest of the enterprise, expressed in
> its aim towards profit, should remain in accordance
> with the social interests, prices, being parameters
> of the enterprise's activity, must express the so-
> cial needs and actual possibilities of their ful-
> filment. This means that prices of goods should be
> determined by the market, as a result of the law of
> demand and supply, which in the long run will ensure
> their proportionality to the cost of production.
> Acting within the parameters of market prices and
> aiming at profit, enterprises, whether steel mills
> or button producers, should be the only bodies
> undertaking the decisions what and how much to
> produce.[34]

Brzeski, whose views gravitated around Kurowski's,
stressed that a modern state must use instruments of economic policy to mitigate the maladjustments of a market
economy. He considered the state's command over resources
advantageous, enabling central determination of investments which is superior to influencing them by manipulating the rate of interest. He pointed out that
prices "if they are to serve the directors of the e-
conomy as an infallible thermometer, must be formed on
the market." For economic calculation prices must be
treated as parameters reflecting current scarcity

relations, hence they must be continuously variable.[35]

Another leading value-man, Popkiewicz, unequivocally proclaimed market prices as the regulators and stimuli for output adjustment. He recognized, however, a wider scope of economic action by planning organs such as countercyclical policy, mitigating monopolistic practices, etc. The state's interference should not be abused, and should revert to tools of economic policy such as credit, formation of reserves, subsidies, formation of new firms, regulation of monetary circulation, investments, etc. But it is only the market that can transmit signals on the direction, structure, tempo, and localization of production and investments to firms and authorities. All other criteria are fictitious and untenable for economic decision making as they do not rest on the scientific foundations of economics. Popkiewicz particularly attacked the Stalinist concept of "higher social profit-ability" (supremacy of voluntarism). He stated that this allegedly superior concept was the most harmful and disastrous principle of Polish economic policy and a negation of any economic calculation. It enabled the undertaking of illogical and economically unsound decisions only because "someone" deemed them "socially beneficial". According to Popkiewicz, production should be undertaken and its composition determined by consumers' preferences. He grants that production should also in-fluence consumers' preferences but only through the market. He proposes that the firms' profitability - distinguishing economic profitability from that set by bureaucrats - should be based on the rate of profit determined on the market. It is hard to disagree that "not bureaucratic commands but a clear-cut economic cal-culation should decide the direction, tempo, and scope of the most desirable undertakings for society and employees of a firm. Calculation should always be per-formed before a decision is made and not after."[36]

It is obvious that in his ardent desire to liberate the economy from oppressive centralization, Kurowski did not delve on the possibility of monopolistic misalloca-tions.[37] Price fixing has excellent potential in Poland where production of basic producer goods is centered in a few large firms. The value-men were commonly criticized for basing their proposals on Western economic thought without due consideration for its modern developments:

This would mean to compare our model of socialism
with the model of capitalism, though not modern
capitalism but capitalism of a hundred years ago,
pre-monopoly, competitive capitalism. I would
define such viewpoints as utopia, as a utopia of a
reactionary character at that. They disregard the
entire process of concentration and centralization
of capital which took place in the course of the
past 100 years, as well as the technical and
organizational achievements during the monopolist
stage of capitalism.[38]

Jedrychowski did not perceive that in economics the model
of perfect competition is used not as a description of
an actual economic reality but as a standard facilitating
evaluation of the cost of deviation from the norm.
     The vice-chairman of the PC, Adam Wang, clearly ex-
pressed the feeling of the adherents to the status quo:

Personally I am not a follower of a free interplay
of prices with demand and supply. It seems to me
that such an interplay would harm the socialized
and private buyer since prices would tend to increase... It is possible that after some time when
production will reach a high enough level so that
the national economy will dispose of sufficient
commodities my reservations will lose their importance.[39]

Wang was obviously alarmed by the sharp price fluctuations
which might result should prices be determined by market
forces. In his opinion the economy would be faced with
an accelerated increase in prices and ever increasing
inflationary pressures. He shared with other high officials of the PC a fear of the elasticity of prices. The
planners' preoccupation with the control function of
prices obliterated for them the function of prices as e-
conomic stimuli. Jedrychowski formulated the official
view in these words:

The freedom of enterprises to fix prices for goods
is incompatible with our conditions. We have no
intention of giving such liberty to socialist establishments, for it is incorrect that they themselves
should set the prices for the goods they produce.
This would inevitably bring about a general rise in

prices and maintenance costs. It is possible that
price fixing could be decentralized in regards, for
instance, to establishments of a local character -
or to work cooperatives, that in these cases it might
be feasible to resort only to less rigid price control, accepting the principle of basing prices on
the calculation of cost plus a certain percentage of
profit. However, prices of basic articles that
affect the costs of capital investments, the costs
of maintenance, or production costs in important
branches of industry should be fixed by the state.[40]

At that time Lange explicitly stated that prices should
not be set by individual firms. This function should be
performed by the responsible state organ. Only in exceptional cases in small-scale industry, either private or
socialized, where a number of competitive firms exist,
prices may be formed on the market. But even in such
cases control by the state is essential.[41]

Brus attempted to lay the foundations of a price
system ensuring profitability to producers and permitting
rational allocation of resources. He started out from
the principle that economic activity rests on rational
selection of alternatives to attain maximum ends with
given means or given ends with minimum means. This
principle should govern socialist as well as capitalist
economies. It should be even more applicable to the
former where decisions are made not only at the risk of
an individual firm but at that of the entire economy.
Consequently, economic calculation on the central level
"if it is to be rational, cannot operate with an arbitrary price structure but only with a structure which
actually exists in the complicated conglomeration of
relations between objects of economic activity influencing their choices."[42] The necessity of gearing
economic activity to market stimuli and the recognition
that both demand and supply are price determining were
clearly stated by Brus:

The basic requirement of a price structure is the
reflection of exchange conditions (the relation
between the size of production and requirements) in
both consumers' and producers' prices. Generally
speaking, this denotes the necessity of observing
a strict harmony between the price structure and

all economic conditions including the degree of
scarcity of a good. A deviation of the price structure from economic conditions is inadmissible in a
decentralized model.[43]

In a socialist economy the plan indicates for a number
of years the structural developments of the producing apparatus. Quantities of producer goods are predetermined
and should not be subject to considerable change. Thus
scarcity and abundance are to an extent determined by
the plan. By allocating and distributing supplies the
central planner operates with the scarcity and abundance
embodied in the plan. Where planning is conducted mainly
in physical terms prices become arbitrary devices since
planners can make them what they need them to be to
promote plan fulfilment.[44] In a relatively decentralized
economy producers' prices should reflect the relative
scarcities enabling the planner to influence the producers' behavior through the price mechanism and synchroniz-
ing economic calculation on the central level with that
on the lower ones. A price deviating from cost because
of the relative deficit or surplus of that good is a
translation of central preferences into a language under-
standable to firms. Consequently, relative scarcities
of particular producer goods cease to be the central
level's "secret" and become also apparent at the lower
ones. When prices reflect the scarcity relations at
large, erroneous solutions even on the central level
are counteracted and the divergence of interests between
firms and the national economy is minimized.[45]
The mechanism of economic impulses to be generated in
a socialist economy and transmitted to economic agents
was conceived by Brus as follows:

If the market equilibrium price shapes up higher than
the average production price for the commodity (and
hence gives higher accumulation than average) this is
a sign that the demand for the given commodity exceeds
supply. In the reverse case the supply exceeds the
demand. On this basis the planning organs can decide
to increase or reduce production of a given commodity,
passing this decision to the appropriate producer.
In this way the planning organs can ensure balanced
exchange and bring prices to the level of value...
The process of consumption reacting on production,

to adapt the production structure to that of consumers' requirements, must take place through the medium
of the market by transmitting market impulses to
production, with due account for the corrections
mentioned above.[46]

The well known argument of elasticity of production to
the changes in quantities demanded, or demand, is presented by Brus. The responsiveness and adjustment of
supply to the variations in demand are accomplished without minute sanctions of output composition by the central
planner. In a command economy the process of adjusting
supply to changes in demand is too rigid. It is impossible
to expect from the planner correct decisions in respect
to the multiplicity of products which constitute the
detailed structure of demand and supply.[47]

With a given hierarchic structure of economic units
and criteria for evaluating their adherence to the plan,
in the event of conflicts between the plan and buyers'
demand the plan will reign supreme and demand will be
disregarded. In view of permanent shortages the seller
virtually dominates the buyer. But if production is
undertaken in response to market forces, the firm, interested in maximizing profit as the criterion for evaluating its performance, will produce a product mix that
will satisfy the buyers. The rate of profit on the various products will guide the firm in its product mix
policy with the flow of production adjusting itself to
economic stimuli. The firms, which would adapt themselves
faster, produce more efficiently, and in accordance with
buyers' preferences, will grow and expand. Non-adaptable
enterprises will decline and perish.[48]

Not only were some of the PC officials apprehensive
about the responsiveness of firms to market stimuli, but
the distinguished economist Kalecki also questioned the
feasibility of a price system leading to rational allocation of resources replacing central distribution of materials. According to him, the producers' speed of adjustment to the alteration in prices will not be sufficient
to overcome bottlenecks. He contends that substantial
and frequent price changes would be necessary to induce
the desired effect on the supplier's part. This process
could be reached only by trial and error. Kalecki feels
that such a method is not very practical. According to
him the system of central allocation is simpler, more

efficient and effective.[49] It is obvious that Kalecki
considers only the expediency of the central planning
functions. Indeed the use of command makes for a more
expedient method of administrating than the slow process
of adjustment by trial and error. But there is yet
another side to this coin. It is the misallocation of
resources resulting from administrating the economy by
commands, as distinct from the benefits flowing from the
allocative function of a market economy,[50] as imperfect
as it may prove in practice. Kalecki, the distinguished
student of business cycles, rightly sees the dangers and
maladjustments of a market economy. It seems, however,
that he underestimates its advantages.

In addition to elasticity and adaptability of production to demand, the second argument presented by Brus,
in favor of the market solution, is the assertion that
a more efficient utilization of available resources will
result. Brus sees the mainspring for cost minimization
in steering the firms' efforts towards maximization of
profits, thereby creating material incentives for cost
reduction. The performance criterion is no longer comparison of activity with the plan targets resulting in pressure by firms to receive relatively low indexes. The
tendency to conceal reserves is then counteracted by the
tendency to exploit reserves to attain maximum profit.
Since it is interested in reducing costs, management
will endeavor to use resources economically, improve
organization of production processes, introduce new
techniques, etc. Vested with greater autonomy, management will attempt to adapt the cost-reducing devices to
its particular conditions. The enterprise will be allowed
and induced to combine inputs in a most efficient manner
so as to substitute them should changes in relative prices
occur. Profit will be the sole performance criterion.
Cost reduction or increase of production per se will no
longer be tests for assessing performance.[51] Output which
cannot be realized at a profit will be eventually discontinued, adapting product mix to buyers' preferences.

Brus sees the benefits resulting from a more balanced
growth of the individual branches of industry and firms
as yet another argument in favor of the market solution.
The rate and direction of investments are decided by the
central planner at the time of plan adoption as dictated
by the major proportions of the plan. However, at the
executing stage possible bottlenecks or disproportions

must be mitigated. If enterprises could react to market
signals, they would mitigate the situation by using their
initiative in carrying out their own investment programs.[52]
Such actions would be far swifter than if they were to go
through the bureaucratic machinery of the central authorities.[53] In a command economy the recurring disproportions
during the realization of plans do not stem only from the
necessity of implementing main priorities but also from
the lack of responsiveness of production agents to market
impulses.

Since under the market solution the firm would be
granted a relatively great deal of autonomy, the central
planner would be released from the minute tasks of undertaking innumerable decisions of an administrative nature
every day. He could then concentrate on major issues of
long range planning and economic analysis.

According to Brus, the market solution asserts strict
compatibility between prices and the underlying economic
forces. Prices may be used as guides for economic decisions since they do reflect the terms at which alternatives are offered, whereas without a market mechanism
prices are arbitrarily set and do not reflect scarcity.[54]
But is it possible for the central planner alone to
construct prices reflecting the relative scarcities of
all producer goods?, asks Brus. He considers the question
particularly pertinent in view of the lack of widespread
application and refinements of mathematical methods in
planning in general and in price planning in particular.[55]
It seems that an analysis of substitution relations
conducted exclusively at the central level would be doomed
to failure. Methods which the central planner may find
helpful in establishing scarcity prices for basic raw
materials may prove to be quite impractical for setting
prices for articles of lesser importance. But when enterprises have relative autonomy, when profit maximization
is their goal, and no factors of production are allowed
to them free of charge, a market for producer goods comes
into being. Then the relations between supply and demand
for producer goods are not hypothetically calculated in
the planner's office. They are concrete and tangible,
easily translated into the language of prices. Brus
concedes that it is not a market in the full meaning of
the term since the structure and general size of the
producing apparatus and basic elements of demand are
determined by central decisions. One of the important

features of such a market is that price relations of the
basic factors of production are established centrally.
Nevertheless such a market may positively influence the
formation of scarcity prices of the non-strategic inputs.

The formula "prices are independent of the enterprise"
does not aim at depriving the firms from influencing
price formation. Its aim is to exclude possibilities of
price manipulation by firms in their aim at profit maximization. Brus admits that not in all circumstances
and in relation to all products is it strictly necessary
to have prices and price changes shaped exclusively by
the State Price Commission (SPC). In some cases it may
be sufficient to control the applications for price
changes submitted by the firms. In other cases it may
be sufficient to set maximum or minimum prices, the
rate of turnover tax, etc. In cases where competitive
conditions eliminate the possibility of monopolistic
influences on prices, even control may be unnecessary.
But in many cases, particularly for basic producer and
consumer goods, only direct price setting by the SPC
can insure the realization of the parametric function
of prices. Generally speaking, the state has at its
disposal a variety of means and tools with which it may
control the price structure and its dynamics.[56]

It is unavoidable that Brus' socialist market solution
should follow the Mises-Hayek-Lange debate since it is
partially a derivative of Lange's model. But to comprehend
the more specific issues raised during the Polish price
controversy, it may perhaps be instructive to revert to
the very foundations that were challenged: the deep
rooted belief in the dual price system.

                    THE DUAL PRICE SYSTEM

In Poland, as in other Soviet-type economies, the price
system rests on separation of producers' and consumers'
prices, the functions of which are considered to be
qualitatively different. Producers' prices were designed
to serve mainly as calculatory and financial devices,
constituting above all instruments for aggregating
physical magnitudes and controlling execution of plans.
Consumers' prices were designed to perform a rationing
function allocating what has been produced among consumers.
Consumers are normally free to spend their income as

they choose. The wage system and differentials play an
important role as production incentives.[57] The income
earned entitles the worker to spend it as he chooses.
But his choice is limited to the commodities which are
produced. Since the workers' real income and their
productivity depend on the prices of consumer goods, the
relationship between the aggregate wage fund and the
aggregate and structure of consumer goods produced is
of paramount importance.

Consumers' prices are to achieve equilibrium between
aggregate planned expenditures on individual consumption,
largely a function of the total wage fund, and planned
output (and imports) of consumer goods. The objective is
not only to equate aggregate supply with aggregate demand,
but the structure of relative prices should be so devised
as to equate consumers' demand with the available supply
of each consumer good. Hence, in principle, the state
has to set such relative retail price ratios as to equate
supply and demand for each commodity reckoning with substitution, complementarity, and income effects. For the
system to be efficient it must embody an equilibrating
mechanism with flexible prices should any of the magnitudes diverge from the plan. In theory excess demand
is a signal for an upward price adjustment discouraging
consumption and encouraging production. And in practice?
Retail prices are seldom changed. They are not designed
to reckon the interdependencies of related products and
largely aim at balancing total supply with total demand.
Even if prices were originally set to balance supply and
demand for a commodity, they are now obsolete in view of
the shift parameters. Hence disequilibrium prevails for
particular goods.

By stabilizing prices for necessities the state aims
at counteracting inflation. The stability of consumers'
prices is considered one of the basic aims, since upward
movements have direct repercussions on wage levels and
structure, rendering cost calculation, planning, and
auditing intricate and arduous. Price stability, in
such conditions, induces increased consumption and
discourages production of deficit products.

Viewing the entire socialist industry as a gigantic
combine of successive production phases, Turetski, as
far back as 1929, pointed out that "the prices of producer goods, under those circumstances, maintain only a
calculatory, purely conventional meaning."[58] The role

of producers' prices as tools facilitating accounting
calculation was emphasized by Stalin:

> Why... do we speak of the value of means of production,
> their cost of production, their price, etc.? ...this
> is needed for purposes of calculation and settlement,
> for determining whether enterprises are paying or run-
> ning at a loss, for checking and controlling the
> enterprises.[59]

The function of producers' prices is closely tied in
with business calculation.[60] The necessity of enforcing
stringent control over the firm's activity has given
rise to the phenomenon of business calculation. The
budget constraint is imposed on the enterprise. It
induces economy by requiring the firm to carry out operations within the state-determined targets, covering
its expenditures from its receipts. The latter should
not exceed the payments, depriving the firm of surplus
funds which it might use for unplanned ventures. This
is one of the reasons for setting producers' prices at
costs plus only a slight margin of profit.

Prices of consumer goods include not only their own
cost of production and accumulation, but also the accumulation of producer goods used in their production.
The total accumulation (surplus product) is realized
almost entirely in the prices of consumer goods which
considerably exceed costs, whereas the prices of producer goods gravitate around, and often below, costs. In
the past the disparity between those two in the U.S.S.R.
was such that Turetski reported in 1959 that a crude
estimate by Soviet economists indicated that should the
prices of producer goods reflect value,[61] they would
have to be doubled.[62]

While prices of consumer goods ought to balance supply
and demand, this is deemed unnecessary for prices of
producer goods since they can only be procured by socialized firms on the basis of their plans and no real market for producer goods exists.[63] The major producer goods
are distributed centrally on the basis of the material
and technical procurement plans.

In principle producers' prices are set on the planned
average production costs of a branch of industry producing a given good. In Fiszel's words:

> The law of value requires the basis for the proportions
> of prices of means of production to be the socially
> necessary labor inputs for production of specific
> products, expressed in the average cost of production.
> This signifies that prices of specific goods should
> generally remain in the same ratios as costs.[64]

Deviations of prices from costs are sanctioned to allow
for the relative technical "use value",[65] to enhance or
limit usage in view of relative shortages or surpluses,
or to alleviate the balance of payments and other policy
reasons. At times the majority of producers' prices fall
below costs and the firms must be subsidized by the state.
The dual level of prices often features deficits of many
producer goods, whereas consumer goods may be exceedingly
profitable. One of the reasons for deficits is the increase in wages unwarranted by an increase in labor
productivity. This results in higher costs exceeding
the meager profit. Wage increases occur between price
changes. When prices are changed and profitability
restored another increase in wages causes the return of
deficits. For reasons of control and financial expediency,
deficits tend to be focused on materials which originate
in the early stages of the production phase (minerals,
raw materials, etc.). Planning and financial control are
facilitated by concentrating subsidies on fewer items of
major importance. The infrequency of price changes and
the recurring shifts in the production function, quality
of inputs used, changing wage level and structure, as
well as many other factors aggravate deficits.
    The obsoleteness of prices is intensified with time.
Demands for a price reform increase but the planner
resists since any price reform reduces his control over
the firms, necessitates recalculation of plans for comparability purposes, and involves innumerable repercussions as price changes are interdependent.[66] During the
ensuing price reform, prices are set up allowing only a
meager margin of profit on planned costs. Planned cost
is usually based on overoptimistic assumptions as to the
increase in labor productivity. In view of an intensive
exploitation of resources and the accomplishment of increased output through conversion of peasants into industrial workers, undue overtime, etc., labor productivity
falls short of expectations. Since the wage rate is the
least stable variable, its proposed changes are kept

secret even from the price fixing officials to avoid un-
rest and speculation on the consumer market.

In Poland the divergence between costs and prices of
producer goods markedly increased during the SYP. Prices
of producer goods, however, remained virtually unchanged.
Tracing the history of pricing in the U.S.S.R., Kondrashev
pointed out that already during the first Soviet FYP costs
exceeded prices notwithstanding the restriction on money
wages through payments in kind. The 1936 price reform
did not produce the desired results. Heavy industry
suffered deficits after a year due to increased costs.
This was followed by annually increasing deficits. The
prices remained unchanged until 1941 regardless of marked
increases in costs. Kondrashev's conclusion is most
instructive pointing to the similarity with the Polish
pre-1960 experience:

> During several revisions of producers' prices the
> planning authorities have committed one and the
> same error: disregarding the future they predetermined
> too low a level of costs, consequently, at the same
> time, the planned price.[67]

The foremost argument in favor of low producers' prices
is that they stimulate technical progress by reducing the
relative cost of capital assets.[68] The second argument
is that low producers' prices facilitate economic calculation since they confront only a part of value added by
labor (excluding surplus product) with only a part of
labor embodied in the means of production.[69] The third
argument maintains that low prices facilitate planning
and levying turnover tax by concentrating the bulk of
accumulation in relatively few industries.[70] It seems
that here again financial expediency outweighs economic
arguments.

Contrary to claims that low producers' prices facilitate economic calculation, the opposite may be claimed:
the dual price system distorts calculation. The artificially reduced price level of producer goods in relation
to consumer goods hampers the analysis of processes in
the national economy. The share of the branches of industry producing producer goods is actually greater, and
that of light and food industries lower than represented
by the national income calculated at prices based on
costs. The parts of national income diverted to con-

sumption and accumulation are similarly distorted. In
comparison with total output produced, the part of output consumed is reported larger than it actually is.
The dual price system hampers calculation of economic
efficiency in the planning and analysis of relative
efficiency of investments. Since producers' prices are
low, the share of material inputs in total costs appears
to be low, facilitating the introduction of technical
improvements of actually low efficiency but resulting
in considerable savings on wage payments. The reasoning
that low prices of capital assets foster technical progress rests on fallacious premises. The firm is largely
indifferent to the cost of capital goods since the planner distributes investments among enterprises with the
monetary equivalent allotted from the state funds. No
matter what price the state imputes to the capital asset
the monetary equivalent is paid out. As a result of low
prices of capital assets smaller depreciation charges
will mean lower costs to the firms, lowering simultaneously the price of the product based on cost.[71] Furthermore, low producers' prices apply also to material inputs,
which has very little to do with technical progress but
much to do with waste,[72] as management tends to substitute
materials for labor whenever possible. Since some of the
basic raw materials are imported, or may be exported,
the ensuing harm to the economy is enormous.

Producers' prices are deficient as coeffcients of choice
distort cost calculations, are not summaries of alternatives forgone at the margin, abstract from current
scarcity relations, and the supply or demand for an
input **is largely not a function** of its price. In allocating producer goods and eradicating shortages, the
central planner relies on "balancing" conducted mainly
in physical units without reverting to the allocative
function of prices.

Recently Wakar and Zielinski concentrated on the
question of the present system of allocating resources,
and on improving the efficiency of this system with the
handicap of irrational prices. They emphatically point
out that effective functioning of the economy does not
depend primarily on the degree of decentralization but
on the types of economic calculation adopted, distinguishing, in pure form,[73] direct and indirect (or market-
type) calculations.[74] Zielinski maintains that there
are three alternative ways of achieving rational prices:

1) determination by free interplay of supply and demand,
2) Lange's trial and error solution, and 3) shadow prices.
In his view (1) is unacceptable due to deficiency of
market prices for choosing optimal investments, market
failures, etc.; (3) would be more compatible with the
present institutional framework than (2) and more acceptable to the central planner as it would not necessarily
require decentralization of decision making and could
be used in conjunction with commands.[75] The type of e-
conomic calculation adopted prejudges whether value
parameters or commands are the most suitable tools for
fulfilling the plan.

Under the prevailing method of direct calculation,
the central planner largely reckons and coordinates
directly in physical magnitudes (hence the name).
Prices perform, or ought to perform, the aggregation
function only, and there is no mechanism for verifying
the technical production coefficients. Hence transmission of minute commands is the only logical solution.
The central planner basically operates with three sets
of data: 1) the available capital, human, and natural
resources, 2) the desired output, reflecting his preferences, and 3) technical input coefficients as independent structural constants. The transformation of
(1) into (2) is constrained by the size of (3). At
the stage of plan construction what has been "chosen
in natura must, in turn, be chosen by the means of
prices." The planner sets prices, wages, interest, etc.
but he is not guided by them, and reaches his own
solutions without reverting to prices as coefficients
of choice. The aim is to produce an internally consistent plan, but the problem of economic efficiency
of production is almost disregarded. The methods of
production are chosen on the basis of prevailing techniques or "progressive engineering" mechanically trans-
planted from more advanced countries. Since the substitution effect is eliminated in plan construction,
it should logically be eliminated in plan implementation. Passive prices perform this function admirably.
Activating prices would bring about factors' substitution, therefore alterations in technical coefficients
with the inevitable consequence of demolishing the
laboriously achieved internal consistency of the plan.
At the executing stage of the plan prices, as a con-
stituent part of the premium system (discussed in

Chapter V), do influence managerial behavior. Hence
they are called to perform a function for which they
were not designed. This causes undesirable effects
which bring about, _inter alia_, bottlenecks and disproportions that must be mitigated by central commands and
allocations restraining managerial actions.

From the fundamental weakness of direct calculation
it would follow that this type of calculation should be
abandoned, or if retained, practical consequences must
be drawn from its very nature. The plan should be
executed by a conglomeration of integrated minute commands. Prices that were not designed for transmitting
information must not be activated to perform such a role.
Hence the role of prices in plan execution is strictly
defined by the nature of economic calculation employed
in planning. Indeed the question may be raised: Should
functions other than accounting be assigned to producers' prices, and does not the central planner defeat
his own purpose by activating prices?

The dual price system has not been abolished in
practice. However, Polish economists have dared to
question its basic tenets. As we have pointed out, the
question whether prices are to be set by the state or by
an interplay of market forces was heatedly debated
during the 1957-58 price controversy. But the debate
did not end there. It was obvious, even to the stanchest
supporters of a state controlled price system, that the
state's price setting methods should be modified. The
three salient features of the Polish price controversy
were: the use of marginal costing in calculating the
point of departure price, the inclusion of interest and
rent as cost elements, and the pricing of basic raw
materials in relation to world market prices. The
significance of the controversy that follows is the
ferment it created in Marxist economic thought, even
though it had little bearing in practice.

Of all issues debated none was more strongly
attacked and defended than the principle that the average production cost constitutes the "most favorable
basis" for the formation of point of departure prices.

THE POINT OF DEPARTURE PRICE

The theory of price is one of the most neglected

fields of the "economic theory of socialism" in Soviet-
type economies.[76] The Soviet price debate of the mid-
1950's was mainly concerned with the problem at which
stage of production surplus product is realized.[77] This
issue was not the center of gravity in the Polish discussion which raised the problem of an appropriate construction of the point of departure price, a calculated
magnitude constituting the initial basis in price formation and relating it to costs.[78] The actual price may
deviate from the point of departure price under the
influence of market conditions and the state's political
and economic preferences. The main issue here is whether
average or marginal costs constitute the point of departure price.[79] It is the introduction of the marginal cost
concept as a point of departure for price formation that
distinguishes the Polish discussion and renders it unique.[80]

The Theses on Price Formation, an attempt to reach a
compromise between divergent views, submitted to the
Economic Council at the end of 1957 but never officially
approved by it, defined marginal cost as the average
variable cost of the group of most expensive producers
producing a substantial share of total output of a given
good.[81] Undoubtedly such an approach incorporates elements
of marginal calculation, but it does not take full
cognizance of its analytical framework. The basis for
price formation is not the heretofore average cost of
total output but the magnitude defined by the average
conditions of a wide range of production falling into
the group of the most expensive producers.[82] The advoca-
tion to classify costs into fixed and variable and
recognition of the functional dependence between the
increase in costs and the flow of production deserve
particular emphasis. It should be borne in mind that
the reasoning of the Polish "marginalists" is conducted
on the scale of the entire output of a good and not on
that of an individual producer. The size of production
is not analyzed within the enterprise but within a
branch of industry witn analysis independent of the
given cost curve within the firm.

The Theses formulated that the point of departure
price should not be equal to the variable cost of the
more expensive producers but only proportional to it.
A uniform percentage increase for all products should
be added covering fixed costs (including interest,
rent, etc.) and a percentage of profit.[83] The construc-

tion of the mark-up gives rise to several solutions and various interpretations. However, it does not seem to be overly relevant as we are concerned here with a short run where fixed costs are not price determining but quasi-rent price determined.

The main arguments in favor of marginal costing were summarized by Brus as follows:[84] 1) Production cost differentials resulting from "unequal objective production conditions", particularly due to differences in capital-labor ratios, must be considered. In forming a workable price structure, short run conditions (where the producing apparatus, including the new factories initiating production during that period, is given) should be considered. 2) The price structure should afford buyers correct choice criteria among the appropriate quantities of individual products. Hence price formation should be guided by the quantitative relations corresponding to the opportunities of transformation and reallocation in the economy. 3) In the short run there is generally no reallocation of the entire output of a given good for that of another. The actual alternative is usually not product A or product B, but more of product A and less of B, or vice-versa. Basing price ratios on average costs would not reflect the actual relations of reallocation. Since possible reallocations would pertain only to a part of output, the relations of reallocation would be better reflected in the cost relations of the more expensive producers of A and B. Of course, this assumes that extra production would be added to or cut from production in the least efficient plant. The savings in the use of a unit of A would signify the release of not an average cost outlay, but the release of a cost outlay in the marginal group.[85] In other words, for rational economic calculation, the marginal rate of substitution or transformation is needed since the average rate may conceal the rate and direction of change of factors' productivity in alternative uses.

Jan Lipinski correctly argues that excess capacity should only appear in firms which are relatively inefficient and expensive to run. Idle capacity in the more efficient enterprises with simultaneous use of full capacity in the less efficient ones testifies to irrational distribution of production tasks among firms, at cross purposes with cost minimization.[86]

According to Brus, a very important feature of marginal cost pricing is that such a price is a measure of
maximum limits of permissible inputs, given the demand
function.[87] The price based on marginal cost transmits
in a sense the message that it is profitable to expand
production only up to the point where marginal cost is
equal to price. The idea is to weigh the increase of
costs with the increase in revenue. Average cost cannot perform such a function.

Price formation on the costs of expensive producers
is much more meaningful than on average costs of total
output. It indicates a remarkable tendency to grasp the
economic problem and free economic thought of dogmatic
prejudice. The Western economist observing the phenomenon
should not be too critical of the crudity in the Polish
concept of marginal analysis, but appreciate the dia-
metric change in the approach to the problem. Since
marginal costing - even in this crude form - was found
unacceptable by the state and the orthodox Marxists, it
does not warrant elaborate discussion on the refinements
of the tools of analysis.

There is, however, an inherent limitation in this
approach as its proponents oppose frequent price changes.
Jan Lipinski writes:

It would not be advisable to ensure complete price
flexibility in a socialist economy even were this
technically possible. Too frequent revisions of
producers' prices would encroach on the stability
of a basis for business calculation in the enterprise
due to uncertainty... Similarly, in case of consumer
goods... too frequent fluctuations of prices would
have detrimental effects on the division of real
income among different groups of population... If
a given product is produced by one enterprise, the
latter might easily exploit its quasi-monopolistic
position given flexible prices.[89]

This is a serious handicap since the underlying conditions
of the cost function may alter while prices remain constant.
Such prices will not reflect future scarcities becoming
obsolete. Economic calculation will become irrational,
and the evaluation of relative efficiency of investments
particularly hindered. For prices to reflect actual
scarcities both demand and supply must mirror the current

state of needs and possibilities.

It seems that for doctrinal reasons the "marginalists" refrain from an application of modified marginal calculus to the cost function within the firm, negating the law of eventually diminishing marginal productivity. An enterprise producing a small amount of a good at high costs would not affect the point of departure price. Even in more "practical" terms, it would seem that the range of output reckoned as marginal would be much too wide to be meaningful for efficient allocation.

The Polish "marginalists" as well as their critics, often confuse the movement along a cost curve with the shift of the parameters of cost function. But this "sin" seems to be a rather common one, even among their Western confreres.

After publication of the Theses on Price Formation, a conference on price theory was called for mid-March, 1958, by the Economic Institute of the Polish Academy of Sciences. Its director, B. Minc, was the leading oponent of marginal costing.[90] He raised the problem that the concept of the point of departure price formulated by the "marginalists" was a negation of Marxist principles of economic theory. He referred once again to his favorite quotation from Marx where the latter criticized Storch's assertion that costs of the marginal firms operating under the most favorable conditions constitute a basis for pricing, and Marx's criticism of Ricardo's position that costs of the firm operating under the most unfavorable conditions constitute the basis for prices. According to Minc, Marx maintained that such a solution would contradict the law of value and cause permanent disproportions between purchasing power and the sum of prices of commodities on the market. After a long dissertation on the pitfalls of "bourgeois" economics, Minc immediately applied Marx's arguments to present day Poland. Among others, he asserted that the social function of marginal costing as a basis for pricing in a capitalist society is the justification for high prices, low wages, and low taxes.[91]

In answer to Minc's arguments, stretching Marxist theory to fit his own concepts, Brus acknowledged Marx's formulation of the "socially necessary" cost in agriculture as the one of the less fertile lands, and in industry as the average and not the marginal cost.

According to Brus, Marx's position regarding industry
was such because he presupposed that land cannot be
substantially improved, but through investments the conditions under which firms operate may be equalized.
However, since investments are circumscribed by the
availability of resources, and not distributed evenly
to all enterprises, the same situation that applies to
land may fit industry:

> If a substantial part of output indispensable to
> cover demand has to be produced in conditions
> worse than average, then abstraction of this fact,
> when solving the problem of a basis for the point
> of departure price, would be contrary to the prin-
> ciples of economic calculation. This calculation
> must consider the magnitude reached by a unit of
> input when production reaches sizes indispensable
> to satisfy demand. Such input... is of a social-
> ly necessary nature, in a sense analogous to the
> one accepted by Marx in analyzing the value of
> agricultural products.[92]

In addition Minc questioned the suitability of
prices based on short run marginal costs for calculating
the efficiency of investments. However, as Brus re-
joined, this deficiency is not only peculiar to this
type of a price system but is inherent in all systems
reflecting current economic conditions and not future
ones. For investment calculation it is necessary to
take into account, besides current prices, specific
factors and variables applicable to the case in point
so as to arrive at a decision regarding relative efficiency.[93]

In his concluding remarks Minc questioned Jan Lipinski's
contention that idle capacity should occur in the least
efficient firms. According to Minc, under dynamic
conditions, reserves exist in enterprises working under
the most favorable circumstances (new plants) and in
stagnation the opposite is true. Lipinski defended his
stand by stressing that when the short run is considered
only capacity of existing enterprises is of interest, as
it is only on such capacity that reallocation of production depends. In an efficient economy such capacity
should occur in the least efficient firms.[94]

The official attitude towards marginal cost pricing

was indicated at the conference when the chairman of the
SPC, J. Struminski, interpreted it as only a supplementary
form of analysis which could be used for evaluating efficiency of investments and comparative advantages in
foreign trade, but could not become the basis for pricing.[9]
   Economic calculation in Soviet-type economies is not
only inhibited by a rejection of marginal calculus, but
also by the inherent limitations of the cost concept.
In the pincers of the labor theory of value, the problems connected with the time structure and roundaboutness
of production processes and with the limited availability
of natural resources and their inelasticity to variations in demand for them (rent) cause perturbing difficulties. The picture of the Polish intellectual
ferment underlying the broad issues of pricing would not
be complete without mentioning the revolutionary - within the framework of Polish Marxist thought - contribution made by Henryk Fiszel.

                        INTEREST AND RENT

   Profit as an indicator of efficiency or waste in
performance would be meaningful only if all cost elements
are reckoned, otherwise spurious results will be indicated.
In Poland utilization of fixed and working capital (apart
from bank loans) is not reflected in costs. The distribution of fixed and working capital without charge results
in the firms' indifference to economical use of these
resources. In an article published in May,1956; by the
official theoretical monthly of the PUWP, Fiszel suggests:

   The relationship between the state budget and the
   industrial enterprise should be fundamentally changed
   and shaped rather on "commercial" principles. The
   firm does not obtain the means of production free of
   charge, but in the form of credit. The budget plays
   the role of an institution granting credit for which
   the firm pays interest according to the set rate.[96]

Such interest levied on all fixed and working capital in
a firm should constitute cost elements reflected in
prices.[97] Deploring the infantile attempt to adhere to
Marxist dogma without an awareness of actual conditions,[98]
Fiszel continues:

Since we have taken the legitimate stand that the
law of value is in operation here, we have to deduce
the resulting consequences. We cannot stop halfway.
This is why it is necessary to apply interest to the
whole extent. Thus in circumstances where the
entire record of input is expressed in terms of value
it is not possible to apply other measurements to the
effectiveness of exploitation of resources but with
interest expressed in zlotys.[99]

Fiszel rightly points out that interest as an economic
category is not only justified at the enterprise level,
but also in evaluating various branches of industry
where different amounts of fixed and working capital are
used per unit of output. The same is true of different
firms within a branch of industry.[100] Disregard of capital
intensity distorts cost calculations and the effect is
transmitted to prices. Hence in the future, "the price
will have to recompense the firms not only for costs in
sensu stricto but also for interest paid for 'loaned
means'."[101]

Heeding his own advice Fiszel does not stop halfway.
He develops his "revolutionary" thought further by pro-
pounding that agricultural producers, industrial, and
mining concerns should pay rent on land to the state.
According to Fiszel the time is ripe for reactivating
the economic category of rent and applying it fully in
a socialist economy. Without absolute and differential
rent economic calculation is distorted. Abstracting
from rent in the socialist sector results in land and
its natural resources having no price tag, and hence
their exclusion from the firms' assets. Since land
exists in limited quantity in relation to demand for it,
and has alternative uses, to treat it as a non-economic
good is irrational. Rent should be included in costs
and hence in prices:

Value... in the form of rent should be transferred
to the product and charged to the cost of production.
Without such an element of cost, the foundations for
economic calculation vanish. Thus if land given out
to administration by state agricultural farms does
not cost anything, stimuli for a rational exploitation
do not act. The enterprise does not bear any losses
even if the land lies fallow. The difference between

fertile and less fertile land is obliterated, since
the former and the latter do not cost anything.
This state of affairs does not lead to intensified
production.[102]

The price of land should be reckoned in choosing an
investment variant and location. Industrial enterprises
should pay rent on the amount of land they occupy, influencing potential savings of land when building firms,
and discouraging them from keeping unused land surrounding their buildings. This rent should also reflect the
potential agricultural uses of land to recompense the
state for forgoing the income which could be derived
from agricultural uses. Furthermore, the extraction industry should pay rent proportionate to yields. It is
inconceivable that deposits of coal, iron, oil, etc.
should have no price. Rent should be set not a posteriori but a priori as only then would it be a meaningful category in economic calculation. Fiszel stresses
the importance of geological factors that must be considered when establishing rent on mineral deposits.
Differential rent would largely equalize the great discrepancies in production costs of the extraction industry.
    In his criticism of Fiszel's proposals Minc reverted
once again to his arsenal of Marxist theory. He reasserted that interest and rent are part of surplus product and
as such cannot constitute cost elements.[104]Needless to
say if one asserts, and does not question, that interest
and rent are part of surplus product - then by definition
they are not costs. The argument is logical but based
on false premises since if land has alternative uses it
becomes a price determining cost. Minc's argument
follows from limiting assumptions. He eliminates the
market by definition, then contends that prices of land
and capital would be set arbitrarily, hence would be
fictitious. Rent and interest based on such prices
would distort costs and consequently prices. This must
be so since rent and interest, according to Minc, do not
constitute cost elements in the first place.
    Although the Theses on Price Formation upheld Fiszel's
proposals on rent and interest, as in the case of most of
its recommendations, these were not implemented in
practice.
    At present we are witnessing a renewed discussion on
interest with good prospects for practical implementation.

Conceding the advisability of levying interest some
writers still propound that it should not constitute a
cost element but a direct charge against profit, whereas others strongly stress its features as a cost element.[106] The majority of economists recognize that
levying interest would induce more efficient utilization
of capital assets imposing on management the consideration
of capital as an economic good. It would permit cost
comparisons among firms endowed with modern and backward equipment and among industries of different capital
and labor intensity. The cost so determined would be
more meaningful for price formation.[107] Although the
question of interest's place in socialist economic
theory remains unsettled,[108] the debate's center of
gravity has shifted to a search for a satisfactory
variant of computation as mentioned in Chapter IV,
where the recent proposals for revitalizing the financial
system are discussed.

   The problem of rent has not been entirely forgotten
either. It creeps up whenever economic calculation and
rational allocation of resources are discussed.[109]
Very recently Fiszel wrote that seven years ago when he
first tackled the problem he did not visualize that its
disregard would continue hampering economic calculation
for so long. Nevertheless, he seems optimistic that at
this time no one really needs to be convinced about its
urgency. He proposes to shift the discussion to the
problem of land valuation to help the implementation of
differential rent in practice.[110]

   In addition to suggesting marginal costing for the
point of departure price and rehabilitating interest and
rent, the Polish price discussion cast another stone at
accepted dogma by proposing that basic raw materials
should be priced in relation to world market prices and
not on average costs.

                  PRICES OF BASIC RAW MATERIALS

   One may agree with Fiszel's criticisms of existing
pricing on the grounds of the inherent deficiencies of
cost computation and that export calculations must
reckon with costs at the margin rather than average
costs which may be misleading. He correctly conceived
that basically export decisions hinge on incremental out-

put and the latter's costs are generally higher than
those of goods for the domestic market. Ignoring the
law of variable proportions Fiszel visualizes initiation of additional shifts, special quality and packing
requirements for export production, etc. This would
result in higher incremental costs than those for
domestic purposes.[111]

It would be misleading to calculate export profitability on the basis of average cost. But the deficiency in pricing of raw materials does not rest only
on a fallacious determination of domestic costs but on
the disregard of comparative costs, demand, and scarcity relations on the world market.

A unique feature of the controversy was the redis-
covery by some Polish economists of the theory of comparative advantages and the ensuing benefits of international trade.[112] Although the arguments presented are
well established in Western economics, they are a novelty in a system where prices are deemed to reflect domestic
costs. A great emphasis was placed on demand factors
of the world market, indicating a recognition that both
demand and supply are price determining. Hence the
principle of equating economical use, efficiency, and
sacrifice with the average cost of a given raw material
was undermined.

In Soviet-type economies prices largely abstract
from the movements of the world market. Consequently
domestic prices of raw materials reflect neither the
advantages to be gained from the international division
of labor, nor the cost of raw materials and the relative
exchange ratio between them in terms of comparative costs
and advantages of "indirect production" on the world
market. As Zachariasz stressed in his pioneering article,
in view of the significance of raw materials for the
economy, scarcity, high dependence on foreign trade, and
chronic perturbations in the balance of payments "when
establishing transfer prices, abstraction from prices
realized or that could have been realized in our foreign
trade, must have led to distortion of economic calculation."[113]

Zachariasz rightly stated that the pricing problem
of raw materials should be viewed both from the standpoint of the level of prices of raw materials (in relation to other factors of production) and the relative
price ratios within the group of raw materials. Referring

to existing prices he showed their irrationality in
terms of benefits flowing from international exchange.
He illustrated his arguments with a table where according
to the prices prevailing in Poland alternative physical
quantities of different raw materials could be obtained
at the same monetary expenditure.[114] If guided by domestic
prices the planners or firms would be financially indifferent to the relative savings of alternative raw materials.
But from the over-all viewpoint the profit derived from
alternative savings varies according to opportunities in
foreign trade. For example, given the existing prices,
a greater emphasis would be placed on the savings of 1
ton of cement priced at 238 zl. than 1 ton of coal
priced at 145 zl. The irrationality of the system is
apparent when one considers that 1 ton of coal saved
would produce at the very least $21, whereas 1 ton of
cement saved would produce about $11.

The disregard of world prices is not only devastating
for the calculation of substitution of alternative raw
materials. It also has detrimental effects on the calculation of investments' efficiency and choice of technological and construction variants due to the comparatively low prices of raw materials and price ratios
which do not reflect relative scarcities. For example,
if a given technological variant would allow a steel
mill to save 300 zl. on wages, simultaneously increasing
the use of coke by 800 kg. at the domestic price of
240 zl., the mill would show 60 zl. financial savings.
In reality the value added by labor could be converted
into about $11 on the world market, whereas the 800
kg. of coke could easily bring about $22.[115]

Kalecki and Polaczek, of the PC, pursued the idea
that domestic prices of basic raw materials should
correspond to the relations and level of world prices.
Since both prices on the world market and the rate of
exchange or conversion of Polish currency into "world
currency" (in all discussions the U.S. dollar is taken
as the representative currency) are necessary, Kalecki
and Polaczek, inter alia, elaborate on the determination of the general exchange rate of the Polish zloty
to foreign currency.[116]

The Theses on Price Formation supported the argument
that basic raw materials should be priced in relation to
world market prices. This engendered more controversy.
Fiszel attempted to prove that prices of raw materials

set in relation to world market prices and not to domestic
costs might result in waste of "social labor".[117] What
Fiszel, however, did not conceive was that the existence
of international trade alters the advantages derived
from particular directions in the utilization of "social
labor". In the polemic that ensued Kalecki replied to
Fiszel's arguments and showed that Fiszel's conclusions
were based on imprecisions and limiting assumptions.
Although Kalecki considered Fiszel's argument refuted,
he conceded that in basing prices of raw materials on
world market prices, it is necessary to reckon with the
repercussions such prices may have on investment efficiency calculations and the difficulties that may be
encountered in importing or exporting certain goods.[118]

Furthermore, Fiszel stressed the inherent difficulties
arising from sharp fluctuations on the world market.
Shortly after prices of basic raw materials would be set
they would become obsolete to the movements on the world
market. It is impossible, contended Fiszel, to alter
prices continuously since price stability is a necessity
wherever the state participates directly in price formation. He was joined by B. Minc who stated that neither
the fluctuation of domestic prices according to world
market fluctuations nor their obsolescence would be a
satisfactory solution.[119]

Once again we encounter the contradiction between
the accounting and allocative functions of prices. It
should be noted that neither Zachariasz, Kalecki, nor
Polaczek advocated a mechanical transposition of world
prices into the Polish domestic price structure.
Polaczek stipulated that fluctuations of world prices
do not necessarily entail permanent manipulation of
domestic prices:

> Certain typical relations in a given period of
> time should be grasped and then corrected if
> necessary within two or three year periods. More-
> over, it should be remembered that changes in world
> price levels do not necessarily indicate strong
> changes in price relations. And only the latter
> are of interest to us.[120]

Similarly Kalecki pointed out that "it does not follow
from the fact that domestic prices of raw materials cannot reproduce adequately the movements of world prices

that they should be completely ignored."[121] Zachariasz
foresaw the future trend of criticism. He was most
emphatic in stating that world prices would be only a
starting point in price setting. Due weight should be
given to export or import possibilities of particular
raw materials, actual and forecast trade conditions of
these transactions, and temporary fluctuations on the
world market.[122]

In addition the requirements of economic policy would
dictate the deviations of domestic from world prices due
to the dependence of import on export to secure the
means of payment. Similarly relative scarcity or abundance on the domestic market might dictate an increase
or decrease in domestic prices in relation to the world
market to stimulate the desired economic effect.
Kalecki and Polaczek anticipated the necessity of occa-
sional deviations of domestic from world prices. This
would particularly apply to raw materials subject to
exchange between town and country, or those affecting
the distribution of national income.[123]

The argument of infancy of the Polish industry was
advanced by Rzedowski and Fiszel. According to
Rzedowski, Poland may benefit from a high degree of
industrialization only if she would develop basic processing industries. It would be more advantageous in the
long run to export processed goods rather than revert
to the temporary advantages derived from the international division of labor.[124] It should be pointed out
that Poland has not yet succeeded in reorienting its
foreign trade towards export of processed goods at the
expense of raw materials.

As most of the issues raised during the controversy,
the contention that world prices should guide setting of
domestic prices for raw materials was not implemented in
practice. However, it must have left an intellectual
imprint on economic thought. Perhaps in the future
someone may once again ponder on this statement by
Zachariasz:

Under conditions of a seriously developed foreign
trade (and especially under conditions of a taut
balance of payments) savings of individual raw
materials are not decided by our own cost of production but rather by how much we can get for them.
To translate it into theoretical language the rela-

tions and level of prices of raw materials should
correspond to the actual exchange value.[125]

Whoever analyzes this statement in the future will perhaps
be working under more favorable circumstances for implementing it in practice.

THE POLISH PRICE TERMINOLOGY

Before examining the price structure that emerged in 19
it would be helpful at this stage to introduce the
various types of prices and their construction. This
material might prove useful for an understanding of the
salient features of the price structure which shall
then follow.

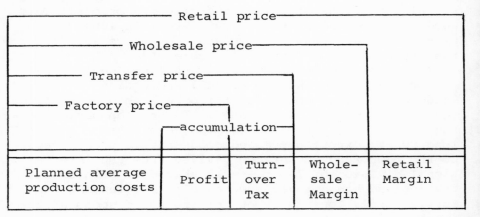

Planned average production costs	Profit	Turn-over Tax	Whole-sale Margin	Retail Margin

Factory price is essentially the average (total) planned cost of production for a branch of industry producing
a given good plus a small profit margin gravitating around
5 per cent and calculated as a percentage of cost. The
factory price is uniform for all producers, and mainly
used as a calculatory device to establish the amount of
turnover tax, the amount of profit, and for purposes of
settlement with the budget. Its function as an economic
incentive for influencing variation and composition of
output through a differentiated rate of profit is increasingly stressed.

Turnover tax is a form of sales tax, imposed mainly
on consumer goods and levied at the time the commodity

is transferred from the producer to the wholesaler.
Essentially it is the difference between the factory
price of a product and its transfer price. It is collected from the producers by the state budget. It constitutes
by far the largest source of the state's income.

Transfer price is the price at which producers sell
their products -- whether consumer or producer goods --
to the wholesale trade centrals or a socialized industrial enterprise. In case of most consumer goods the
transfer price equals factory price plus turnover tax.
In case of the majority of producer goods the transfer
price equals the factory price.

Accumulation (financial) is the excess resulting from
the sale of goods and services less the attributable
cost of production computed by the accountant. Generally
in case of producer goods accumulation is equal to profit.
In case of consumer goods accumulation equals profit plus
turnover tax.

Wholesale price is essentially equal to the transfer
price of a good plus a markup to cover the cost of
distribution and small profit margin of a trade central.

Retail price is essentially equal to the wholesale
price plus a markup to cover the cost of distribution
and a small profit margin for the retail outlet.

Constant price was based on the 1937-38 wholesale
price. It was used from 1945 to 1955 to measure national
income and output for planning purposes.

Comparable price superseded the constant price in
1956 for the computation of national income and for
planning purposes. The comparable price is constant for
a period of approximately five years (the duration of
a FYP). It is equal to the factory price of a good as
of the first year of the plan.

Settlement price is mainly used as a tool of financial
settlement between the producer and his supervisory unit.
It is based on the individual production costs of a good
in a particular firm or group of firms. The settlement
price may be lower, higher, or equal to the factory
price. The difference, if any, is transferred to, or
extracted from, the firm by the association.

After this brief review of pricing terminology, let
us now turn to a more detailed exposition of the basic
price concepts forming the skeleton of producers'
prices in Poland, focusing on factory prices which
are the cornerstone for producers' price formation.

FACTORY PRICES

From their very inception (1954) factory prices were
mainly used for computing turnover tax and settlement
between producers and foreign trade centrals.[126] The
ministries were to set factory prices on the basis of
planned average production costs in a branch of industry
plus a markup not exceeding 5 per cent of costs.
Factory prices were to be equal to transfer prices less
turnover tax, or in the absence of the latter, coincide
with transfer prices whether or not they covered costs
plus markup. Not only did factory prices not ensure
profit, but they maintained deficits.[127] With the
aim of enhancing the usefulness of factory prices their
1960 reform featured: 1) Factory prices are always
equal to average cost plus profit, irrespective of the
level of the corresponding transfer prices, thus ensuring profit to the producers,[128] 2) The precentage of
profit may be calculated either on total costs, costs
of processing, direct labor, or transfer price.[129]
3) The rate of profit may be set so as to promote or
curtail production. 4) The factory price may be changed
once a year when profit exceeds the upper limit imposed,[130]
or when transfer prices of inputs are increased.[131]
        The most recent regulations governing factory prices
reinforce their influence on product mix by allowing
wider variations of the rate of profit to encourage or
discourage flow and composition of output. For example,
to promote production of goods "of substantially improved
technical attributes, construction, or quality" their
factory prices may include up to 50 per cent profit for
the first year or, in exceptional cases, for two years.
The upper limit of profit for producer goods was specified
as 10 per cent, leaving the PC in conjunction with the
MF and SPC the prerogative of manipulating the upper
limit. This revision also condones levying turnover tax
when the factory prices of producer goods are lower than
the corresponding transfer prices.[132]
        The revisions of official regulations indicate that the
trend is to vest factory prices with an economic incentive
function. This issue has been raised on several occasions
in literature before the first shaky steps were taken in
the 1960's to attack the problem. Of late it is increasingly stressed that factory prices should perform three main

functions: 1) to serve as economic incentives, 2) to
measure output and 3) to serve as tools for financial
calculations and settlements with the budget and foreign
trade centrals.[133]

In a nutshell the argument for factory prices to perform the incentive function is: if some choice is left
to the firms (or associations) the planner needs a tool
for influencing his subordinates. Transfer prices could
not serve as such a tool because their increase or reduction to discourage or encourage quantity demanded, would,
ceteris paribus, promote or curtail quantity produced.
This may not be the result intended by the planner.
Transfer prices, primarily designed to influence the
buyer, often deviate from average costs to take into
account the technical relationship of substitutes, policy
considerations to restrict or enhance the use of a
particular factor due to its relative scarcity, relation
to import prices, price ratios on foreign markets, and
other considerations deemed beneficial for policy reasons.
Consequently, when revenue is reckoned in transfer prices,
the rate of accumulation or deficit varies substantially,
and not necessarily in the same direction as the state
intends to influence the producer. Hence factory prices
are required to influence the producers' product mix
in the direction desired by the state.

As early as 1960 Stankiewicz proposed the use of
factory prices with a uniform rate of profit neutralizing
the producers' behavior towards assortments, rendering
them all equally attractive to produce.[134] Lately Kalecki
went a step further. He suggested varying the rate of
profit for different branches of industry or large groups
of products according to central preferences. This would
still leave the enterprises of those branches neutral
towards their product mix since the rate of profit
would remain uniform for the goods produced in that branch.
Furthermore, through an appropriate determination of
factory prices, it is possible, when desired, to
influence the producers' output composition and flow by
varying the rate of profit on individual goods to stimulate or contract production.[135]

Hence the pricing system rests on the separation of
the prices for the buyer (transfer price), for whom they
constitute elements of costs of production and investments, from the prices for the producer (factory prices),
for whom they constitute revenue covering production

costs and profit. Consequently "if the main purpose of
transfer prices is to shape demand... the purpose of
factory prices is to form a basis for a possibly objective evaluation of activity of enterprises and associations, as well as limit the restraints in adaptation
of production to needs."[136]

Transfer prices which include widely divergent rates
of accumulation or deficit are heterogeneous and do not
present a clear picture of the cost of total output.
The rationale behind the second function of factory
prices, i.e., output measurement, is to have a uniform
standard for measuring production based on supply conditions only. Such a standard can be obtained only by
eliminating the influence of demand conditions from
transfer prices.[137]

Factory prices perform their third function in facilitating levy of turnover tax, the difference between
the factory price and the corresponding transfer price.
They are the basis for budget subsidies when transfer
prices fall below average costs plus profit. They are
also the prices at which producers sell their goods to
the foreign trade centrals. The third group of functions
is the one for which factory prices were primarily
designed and is still the one for which they are most
commonly used.[138]

How well do factory prices perform these three functions simultaneously? Firstly, let us consider the
problem of the upper limit of profit in factory prices.
When the rate of profit actually attained exceeds the
upper limit allowed, a new lower factory price is set.
The lowering of the factory price was considered a
necessity to keep enterprises on a budget constraint and
to prompt them into a constant "fight and struggle for
cost reduction". This stand is highly questionable.
Given the existing price system, the firm will not be
interested in cost reduction that will provoke a reduction of the factory price jeopardizing profit. This
would be so because the new rate of profit would be
lower than the one actually attained, since it is the
excess of the actual rate of profit over the allowed
limit that has brought about the decrease in factory
price. Reduction of costs, if followed by a proportionate
reduction in the factory price, would simply mean a
transfer of the enterprise's savings to the state budget
at the detriment of the producer who will be entitled

to a smaller amount of profit than he otherwise would
had the factory price not been decreased. Analyzing
the responses received Dudzinski writes:

> Lately enterprises and associations repeatedly claim
> that the principle of decreasing factory prices min-
> imizes their interest in cost reduction. Since
> every year as costs are reduced the factory price is
> to be reduced to a level safeguarding the stable 5
> to 7 per cent margin of profit, the enterprise's
> efforts to increase profit in this manner are turned
> against it. The principle of a yearly limitation
> of profit through factory prices cannot be reconciled
> with that of interesting enterprises and associations
> with the economic results of their activity.[139]

Firms will report relatively high profits only when they
are "conservative" in cost reduction. It is advantageous
for them to reduce costs only up to the point beyond
which factory prices would be reduced. But the firms
are guided by a range rather than a point. They assume
a safety margin and as a precautionary measure are not
interested in cost reduction that will endanger the
safety margin.[140]
    Nevertheless the prevailing current practice largely
counteracts the built-in tendency against cost reduction
beyond a given point. The firm's performance is primarily
judged on accumulation, the difference between transfer
price and respective cost. Since the enterprise is
evaluated on the basis of the transfer price rather than
the factory price, the latter does not perform in practice
its role of economic incentive.[141]
    The claim that factory prices measure output in homo-
geneous terms adequately since they reflect cost of production with uniform rates of profit and show the relative
contribution of each output, firm, or branch of industry
to total output, stems from the reasoning that "when a
dual price system is maintained prices of the means of
production and means of consumption can be reduced to
a 'common denominator' only if factory prices are used."[142]
This reasoning seems to be sensible enough since transfer
prices of producer and consumer goods are incomparable
magnitudes. Yet it seems questionable whether output
and relative contribution to output can be measured by
reverting solely to supply prices. The fact that out-

put was produced and cost incurred is not sufficient
evidence that a contribution which will benefit society
has been made as it lacks the buyer's seal of approval.
Notwithstanding this criticism, the cost data on which
factory prices are based are not indications of true
cost. Barring the limitations of cost data, discussed
in the following chapter, it is generally admitted that
the cost data used as a basis for factory prices during
the 1960 reform were the crudest of approximations.

When establishing factory prices, costs were calculated
by using precomputed indexes established centrally on the
basis of general and very rough computations. The factory
price catalogs were prepared hastily using 1958 and
partly 1959 costs.[143] It is not surprising that after
the reform the rate of profit on many items proved to
be very high and in most cases varied considerably.
Sztyber reports that the 1962 actual rates ranged from
deficits to profits exceeding 30 per cent.[144] For
example, the estimated and reported rates of profit in
1960 for the several branches of light industry were:
cotton industry 6.3 and 11.6, wool 1.9 and 8.3, silk
4.2 and 7.7, felt 3.6 and 14.9, button and haberdashery
3.8 and 13.4, and leather industry 4.3 and 6.9 per cent.[14]
In many cases the rate of profit, depending on the
assortment and the branch of industry, exceeded 10 per
cent by 1961. In the chemical and heavy industries it
gravitated around 12 to 20 per cent. In the machine
building industry by 1961 70 per cent of total output
had factory prices with a rate of profit exceeding 10
per cent, 10 per cent of output was unprofitable, whereas
only 20 per cent of output was profitable in the range
of 5 to 7 per cent.[146] Although the profit included in
factory prices as a result of their 1960 revision is
greatly differentiated "in a majority of cases it is
largely accidental and exhibits no correlation to existing preferences (from the market, technical progress,
export, etc., standpoints)."[147]

It is especially in view of the practical difficulties
in cost determination that Struminski attacks the proposals aiming at reinforcing the use of factory prices.
As a result of this deficiency the actual profit realized
departs from the postulated rate of profit rendering
central manipulation of this rate futile. If factory
prices remain constant for a number of years their
shortcomings are magnified. But their annual revision

on a large scale cannot, according to Struminski, be
accomplished accurately. Hence the usefulness of factory
prices as economic incentives and to aggregate output
collapses.[148]

A price which reflects supply conditions only, based
on a fallacious definition and computation of costs,
cannot perform satisfactorily the function of economic
incentive, and it is even doubtful whether it performs
the function of aggregating output adequately. If
factory prices are to function as economic incentives
the rates of profit must be differentiated. But if
they are to serve as tools for aggregating output the
rates of profit should be uniform. Hence factory
prices cannot simultaneously be economic incentives and
tools for measuring output given their present formation.

Until now the factory price system has fulfilled
primarily the settlement functions. In view of the
limited role and functions of these prices it was
concluded that keeping this system exclusively for
settlement purposes cannot be substantiated since it is
extremely labor consuming. Recently a commission under
the chairmanship of M. Kalecki was called by the chairman of the PC to study and report on the uses of factory
prices in planning and the financial system. In a nutshell the proposals, which are now being considered,
were:

1) To relate the incentive system to profit instead
of accumulation rendering producers sensitive to factory
prices. The latter will be employed, together with the
rate of profit therein, to stimulate or contract flow of
production. Transfer prices will be used to induce or
discourage buyers' demand. For example, to promote
technical progress transfer prices of newly produced
goods could include low turnover tax, or none at all,
and factory prices include a high rate of profit to
promote both demand and production. The turnover tax
on outdated products could be raised and factory prices
decreased to discourage both demand and output. This
would be equivalent to introducing separate prices for
buyers and producers. It is claimed that under conditions
of a more or less deeply ingrained sellers' market,
separate prices for buyers and sellers are preferable.
Kalecki argues that in cases of increased demand for a
particular good a price exceeding average cost would have
to be set to limit usage. However, it does not follow

that the same price should regulate the producers' behavior because they may be operating at full capacity and the additional cost would be prohibitive. Moreover, there may not be sufficient reasons for investment expenditures as costs may be incommensurate with returns.[149]

2) Factory prices should also be used to aggregate output. The turnover tax included in transfer prices being widely differentiated, aggregation in transfer prices affords management a wider field for product mix manipulations. Furthermore, factory prices should be the basis for calculating cost reduction when the latter is computed as the share of costs in value of total output. In this case again factory prices, where the rate of profit is less differentiated, narrow down management's field of manipulation.

3) Due to the importance of the size and relations of the rates of profit on different products, the following principles should be observed when establishing those rates: a) The standard rates of profit should vary for different branches of industry or large product groups in view of central preferences to promote increase of output or cost reduction. The magnitude of profit increments (z) in relation to costs depends on: cost reduction (k) and increase of output (p). With a given rate of profit (m), this may be represented as:

$$z = k + pm$$

Consequently, the higher the rate of profit, the greater is the influence exerted on the increment of profit by increase of output, and a smaller influence by cost reduction. Where increase of production is preferred the rate of profit should be higher. Conversely, where cost reduction is the target, the rate of profit should be lower. For example,if in the textile industry premiums are based on accumulation, the increase of production is rewarded more than cost reduction. The situation should be reversed. This industry suffers from shortages of imported materials and incentives for savings of materials are needed. Hence the rate of profit should be lower than the accumulation to stimulate cost reduction.[150] b) The rate of profit in factory prices should be increased to promote production of goods in short supply and decreased to curtail the output in cases of oversupply. c) To discourage production of material

intensive goods, the rate of profit should be set on
value added (or a standard approximating value added by
eliminating material costs from total costs). d) Factory
prices should not, as a rule, be subject to change during
a FYP as a result of cost reduction. This should induce
enterprises to reduce costs since they will benefit from
such action.

4) Factory prices should still serve for computing
the turnover tax due the state budget as well as the
amount of subsidy owed an enterprise in cases where the
factory price is higher than the transfer price.

5) When transfer prices are changed during the course
of a FYP, the factory prices should be recalculated to
allow for the increased production costs.

6) In view of the limited scope foreseen for the 1965
revision of producers' prices new factory prices could
be introduced simultaneously or one year later. When
calculating the new factory prices the planned cost
reductions should be considered. If a substantial
revision of transfer prices should take place in the
future, the factory prices should be changed only one
or two years later to afford full cognizance of the
mutual interdependence of prices and costs.[151]

The IV Congress of the PUWP reiterated the stability
and rigidity of transfer prices, acknowledging simultaneously the need for flexibility. It promulgated that
the flexibility element could be introduced through a
wider application of factory prices. However, the process
of revising factory prices has in itself a built-in
rigidity. The adjustments of output to stimuli introduced by factory prices and the required adaptation
feature most of the shortcomings that Hayek so clearly
conceived. Without questioning the nature of profit
determined, it is doubtful whether a markup on cost
fallaciously determined is a measure of some significance
since cost reduction may be achieved, inter alia, at
the expense of capital intensive processes for which no
cost is imputed. Scrutinizing the proposal and Kalecki's
arguments, the deficiency of computations based on
average instead of marginal costs becomes more apparent,
and indeed the sacrifice for not following a sort of
Lange-Lerner Rule is evident.

Apart from all other limitations and deficiencies,
one may have strong reservations about a wide use of
factory prices since they undoubtedly widen the rift

between the producer and the market for his products.
The producer is rendered insensitive to any stimuli but
those originating within the four walls of the PC, or
those inadvertently created by calculatory errors which
may be undesirable from both the consumers' and planner's
standpoints.

Factory prices are the basis for the formation of
comparable prices. However, before examining the latter
to gain perspective, we should revert briefly to constant prices which from 1945 to 1955 held the role
presently allotted to comparable prices.

CONSTANT AND COMPARABLE PRICES

The primary functions of constant prices were to
measure national income, investment expenditures, and
the value of production.[152] Here they will be examined
primarily from the standpoint of their suitability for
measuring a firm's output, to indicate the degree of
plan fulfilment, thereby evaluating the firm's performance. As such, constant prices influenced to a large
extent whatever production decisions (manipulations of
assortments) the enterprises made.

Prior to 1949 constant prices were based on the
individual 1937-38 prices. They varied considerably
on identical goods produced by firms subjected to different central boards. Each industry aimed at the
most advantageous structure of constant prices. For
example, the metallurgical industry set constant prices
on its 1937 prices without deducting prewar discriminatory discounts. The constant price for all grades
of coal was set on the 1937 price of the best grade.
The industries which had been cartelized had the
advantage of a more favorable price structure.[153]

On March 15, 1949 the ECCM directed the SCEP to
prepare a uniform catalog of constant prices to be
based on the average 1937 wholesale prices eliminating
the discriminatory discounts. But the new catalog was
far from adequate. For example, it detailed prices for
almost all goods produced by one industry, whereas in
others large groups of products were aggregated under
one price. New products not listed in the 1949 catalog
had their prices set on the basis of comparison with a
product listed and produced by similar technological

processes. The ratio of constant prices was set proportionately to that of transfer prices.[154] In practice the
transfer price of the new product was usually computed
on the initial production costs without discounting
future cost reductions when a larger volume would be
produced obtaining a higher constant price for the new
product.[155]

Since production plan fulfilment was management's
main consideration two manipulation trends were detected:
management strove to manufacture mostly products that
had favorable constant prices assuring a high plan fulfilment with minimum inputs, and tended to boost the constant prices for products not listed in the catalog.
The first tendency may be illustrated with an example
submitted by W. Budzinski, the director of the planning
section of the Central Board of Heavy Machine Building,
Boilers and Turbines Division:

> One of the enterprises under the jurisdiction of our
> central board produces two basic assortments - pipe-
> line boilers and upright boilers. The constant
> price of one ton of pipeline boilers is 2,800 zl.,
> whereas that of upright boilers (calculated in one
> ton) is 3,000 zl. To produce one ton of pipeline
> boilers 40 manhours of labor are required, and for
> one ton of upright boilers approximately 600 man-
> hours of labor. Thus one manhour of labor on pipe-
> line boilers gives the enterprise a value of 70 zl.
> in constant prices and with the upright boilers 5 zl.
> Hence it is not surprising that the firm is in-
> terested in the production of the more favorable
> assortment (pipeline boilers), whereas the production
> of the unprofitable upright boilers is constrained
> with farfetched "objective difficulties".[156]

The second tendency reached at times astounding
proportions. The grinding wheel factory in Grodzisko
Mazowieckie had a constant price set for one kilogram of
plain grinding wheels at 4,128 zl. with the corresponding
transfer price being 374 zl. The ratio of the transfer
to the constant price was 1:11. Other types of grinding
wheels produced by this factory had much lower ratios.
Therefore, whenever the production plan fulfilment was
threatened the enterprise abandoned the production of
the required assortment and produced plain grinding

wheels. It always fulfilled its production plan in this
manner.[157]

Use of constant prices for measuring plan fulfilment
greatly distorted the firms' and industries' shares in
output. The ratios of constant to transfer prices in
several basic industries were: ferrous metallurgy 1:3.35,
mining 1:3.75, machine building 1:2.80, and chemical 1:
2.20.[158] It was impossible to evaluate the relative contribution to output by branches of industry or even to
state whether, for example, the mining industry's contribution was better than that of the chemical industry.

Constant prices were based on completely anachronic
scarcity relations and were crude calculatory devices.
The perturbing difficulties of adding new products to
the catalog and maintaining "unchanged relationships"
caused additional difficulties. Arbitrary use of those
prices by the firms' planners and statisticians was
common.

At the beginning of 1956 comparable prices were introduced to perform the role heretofore assigned to constant
prices. The aim was to have better weights to measure
the dynamics of output.[159] The July, 1955, resolution
proclaimed that essentially factory prices are the
basis for the formation of comparable prices with
deviations allowed when the former fall below average
costs plus profit. In such cases comparable prices
cover costs plus profit. This was especially applicable
from 1956 to 1960 when factory prices of many goods
fell below costs. But it lost its applicability with
the 1960 reform of factory prices. The basic difference
between factory and comparable prices is that the former
may be changed from year to year, whereas the latter
remain constant for the duration of a FYP. Thus comparable prices for the 1956-60 FYP were basically
factory prices as of January 1, 1956, and those for the
current FYP (1961-65) are factory prices as of July 1,
1960.[160]

Comparable prices for new products are established
on the basis of their factory prices corrected by a
coefficient expressing the relation between the comparable
price and the actual factory price of the product most
similar to the newly produced one. In cases where comparison of the new product with an existing one is
impossible the comparable price of the new product is
set on the basis of the average cost corrected by a

centrally established coefficient corresponding to changes in prices of the more important inputs.[161]

The superiority of comparable over constant prices is the former's closer reflection of costs. At least they reflect cost ratios recently determined indicating current production conditions, whereas constant prices were based on obsolete price ratios prevailing under the different economic conditions of prewar Poland. But it is in measuring output that comparable prices, together with transfer and constant prices for that matter, meet with their greatest failures. Measuring output in comparable prices still induces firms to manipulate the assortment plan to produce more material intensive output avoiding the labor intensive one. When faced with a choice whether to produce a good from cheaper or more expensive materials, management will always lean to the latter as the higher cost of materials will automatically raise the comparable price inflating the output plan.[162] For example, the boiler manufacturing plant in Sosnowiec produces coil heaters for boilers. Coil heaters for the low pressure boilers are manufactured from carbon steel, whereas the identical heaters for high pressure boilers are manufactured from chromemoly steel. Chromemoly steel is a far more expensive material than carbon steel, but the labor input for both coil heaters is the same. Assuming that the output plan is based on given quantities of both types of coil heaters, should the firm produce ten more chromemoly heaters and ten less carbon steel ones, it will undoubtedly overfulfil its output plan.[163]

It would seem that comparable prices for measuring the firm's dynamics of production cannot perform satisfactorily since for evaluating contribution to output only value added is the relevant data. In addition, comparable prices suffer, of course, from the same shortcomings as factory prices from which they are derived.

SETTLEMENT PRICES

In some industries considerable variations in geological and technical conditions of different firms result in substantial cost differentials. These are often the product of fallacious cost determination which

abstracts from differential rent, interest on capital,
and is due to improper valuation of capital assets.[164]
In such cases, in practice only in the coal and electric
power industries,[165] a settlement price is used . This
is nothing else but a factory price based on the planned <u>individual</u> cost of production in a particular firm,
or the average cost in a group of enterprises working
under similar conditions. Not to favor high cost firms
the profit included in the settlement price is not a
percentage of costs, but a fixed amount.[166]

The settlement price refers generally to a price
received by the producer as a result of settlement with
the association. This price may be higher or lower
than the price paid by the buyer.[167] The methodological
premises for settlement prices are basically the same
as for factory prices and this concept suffers from
similar shortcomings. It should be stressed that
widespread application of settlement prices may nullify
cost reduction drives as the settlement price based
on the individual cost of production would sanction in
many cases technical inefficiency, poor management, and
cost planning allowing a wide safety margin. Moreover,
basing a price on the individual costs further widens
the gap between the producer and the market for his
product. The producer who always receives a price
covering his costs is rendered almost totally insensitive
to buyers' preferences.

Having discussed at some length the various types of
prices for the producer, the next logical step is to
examine the price for the buyer: the transfer price.
At this point the reader should be warned once again
that no such clear-cut line of demarcation can be drawn
between the prices for producers and buyers. It must
be borne in mind that the firm's activity is also judged
in terms of transfer prices rendering them of interest
to the producer. Before proceeding with the several
changes of the uniform transfer prices - to which the
Poles attribute the high sounding name of "price reforms"
it might be advisable to glance at the calculation of
prices for non-typical products.

PRICING OF NON-TYPICAL PRODUCTS

A non-typical product is basically one which cannot

be found in the effective price catalog. The production
of these goods is non-repetitive and executed on order,
according to individual technical specifications. In
particular, the producer qualifies a good as non-typical
when one of the three following factors enters into the
processing of a given order: 1) when the chief engineer
and designer have to carry out additional work leading
to the application of different technological processes
or designs, 2) introduction of additional operations or
use of different materials, and 3) manufacture of such
products in uneconomical quantities.[168]
    Prices of non-typical products are calculated by the
producer on the basis of his planned production costs
plus a planned rate of profit equal to the one realized
on similar typical products. When the firm shows a
deficit on the similar typical product, it should reduce
its planned cost of the non-typical product accordingly.[169]
It is interesting to note, however, that the most often
encountered practice was addition of 5 per cent profit
to the planned cost notwithstanding the losses sustained
on the similar typical products.[170] The 1963 amendment
to the regulation governing price calculation for non-
typical products formulated the basis of those prices as
the planned production costs of the individual producer
increased by a planned percentage of profit corresponding
to the one earned on a similar typical product not
exceeding the firm's average rate of profit. When the
firm suffers a loss on the similar typical product, the
rate of profit included in the price of the non-typical
product should not exceed 5 per cent. If the actual
rate of profit realized on the non-typical products
exceeds the allowed profit by over 3 per cent of costs,
the excess will be confiscated by the state.[171] This
seems to be one of the most important steps taken to
discourage producers from favoring non-typical production and allowing a wide margin of tolerance in cost
planning.[172]
    The individual setting of prices for non-typical
products causes many problems for the central planner.
Since these prices are calculated on individual costs
they vary greatly on similar goods produced by different
enterprises undermining largely the price uniformity
that the central planner strives so hard to maintain.
Furthermore, the pricing on planned individual costs
lacks cost reduction stimuli, for profit will be realized

as long as the firm plans costs allowing a wide safety
margin. What is more, the higher the planned cost the
more inflated the value of output. The very existence
of non-typical products offers a wide field for manipulation and is an available device for undermining the
planner's targets.[173]

So far we have examined the skeleton of producers'
prices, acquainted the reader with the basic terminology
and techniques used, and some of the issues involved.
Further insight into the pricing of producer goods may
be gained by tracing the evolution of the pricing system
with special attention to present developments.

SOME ASPECTS OF PRE-1956 PRICES

Initially the price system which took shape after
the war was an amalgam of state controlled and flexible
market prices. By April, 1945, the state specified stable
prices for a majority of products manufactured by state-
owned enterprises as equal to 1939 prices multiplied by
a coefficient of six. On the free market prices were
incomparably higher.[174] Of course, stable prices were
far from reflecting actual scarcities.

By mid-1946 a system of settlement prices, covering
individual production costs plus a margin of profit, was
introduced for individual state-owned firms or groups.
In principle, trade centrals were the only buyers,
purchasing industrial products at their settlement prices
and reselling them at uniform stable prices. The trade
centrals added a profit margin and turnover tax (from
1 to 10 per cent) to the firm's settlement price and
settled the price differentials between that price and
the stable price with a central price account at the
NPB.[175]

Basic raw materials were sold primarily at stable
prices. Limited quotas were marketed at commercial
prices which fluctuated with the market or were regulated
where the state sector was the sole producer. State firms
were allotted rationed materials at stable prices and
additional quantites required had to be procured at
commercial prices. The private and cooperative enterprises were allowed to purchase their supplies at
stable prices only when fulfilling an order for a
state-owned firm. Otherwise they were charged com-

mercial prices for their purchases. Seventy-five per
cent of the difference between the commercial and stable
prices was retained by the firm to finance working
capital and the residue transferred to a common fund.[176]
     To enable the state firms to finance their operations,
producers' prices were revised. The solution adopted
at the beginning of 1948 featured "factory settlement
prices" paid to the producers by the trade centrals.
These prices consisted of individual planned costs of
production composed of production expenses, depreciation,
and fringe benefits plus a profit margin calculated as
a percentage of planned costs (usually 10 per cent).[177]
In practice the factory settlement prices were established
individually for each producer and for each product.[178]
These prices were approved by the central boards in
conjunction with the NPB. In principle they were to be
stable for a year, but the central boards jointly with
the NPB were authorized to alter them during the course
of the year to counterbalance adverse economic or
technical conditions.
     The trade centrals added a small turnover tax plus
various margins covering their expenses and profits to
the factory settlement price obtaining thus the "transfer settlement price". The trade centrals sold these
products to the industrial buyer at the uniform "effective
price" covering average production costs of the industry,
taxes, and markups. At the end of every month the trade
centrals settled the positive and negative differences
between the effective prices and the transfer settlement
prices with the price differential account of the Ministry
of Industry and Trade at the NPB. The final step was
taken by the Ministry of Industry and Trade which settled
with the budget on the basis of the financial results
of the trade centrals under its jurisdiction.[179] The
trade centrals functioned as intermediaries between
the producers and buyers, but did not exert any influence
on producers to adjust their production flow to market
demand.
     The system was a serious impediment on cost reduction.[180]
Planned cost being a projection of actual costs, there
was little incentive for managers to report substantial
cost savings, thereby endangering future profits. The
simplest solution was to plan costs with a wide safety
margin, reaping higher profits as a percentage of
inflated costs, remaining reasonably within the costs

planned.[181]

In preparation for the SYP major changes in pricing were envisaged. The reforms were gradual. In 1950 a uniform cost accounting system was introduced into all enterprises.[182] Large enterprises incorporating several plants were broken up into several firms set up as legal entities. Trade centrals became wholesalers of industrial products, distributing them to retailers. The firms were to effect their purchases and sales with one another directly.

The transfer of goods and services was to be carried out at uniform transfer prices, based on the planned average (total) cost of production plus a planned profit gravitating around 5 per cent of costs.[183] In practice, however, the transfer prices were deliberately set below the average costs.[184] The transfer prices of consumer goods included uniform turnover tax. In time this became a major tool for extracting accumulation from firms. But where cost divergencies were excessive the system was supplemented with settlement prices designed both for subsidizing deficits and extracting accumulation.[185] The change over to prices based on average production costs in a branch of industry magnified the problem of deficit enterprises.[186] The latter were to receive a fixed planned subsidy. Overfulfilment of deficit assortments would not entail increased subsidies.[187] However, in time even above plan deficits, which were not supposed to be subsidized, were so in practice.[188]

The 1950 reform of producers' prices aimed at reducing the over-all volume of subsidies.[189] Prices of steel, building materials, and heavy machinery were considerably increased. On January 1, 1951, however, the prices of these goods were again reduced. This rendered most processing industries profitable, whereas the producers of raw materials, semi-fabricates, and investment goods suffered deficits and were heavily subsidized.[190] The aim was to concentrate subsidies in a few key industries. The cut in prices was dictated by the doctrinal assertion that low prices of investment goods favor industrialization, low prices of material inputs entail low production costs, and generally low prices of producer goods are a potent tool in the struggle for cost reduction:

Instead of extracting accumulation from the machine building industry which may then be intended for invest-

ment purposes, it is much simpler to reduce the prices
of these machines as well as the amount of investment
expenditures... Reduction of prices of procurement
and investment goods... means a further reduction of
costs of all products and services in whose production
these goods are used. Reduction of prices of procurement goods has still another, even though indirect,
nevertheless important significance. It fortifies a
pressure on production costs... and ensures a correct
level of profitability mobilizing further effort
towards... an increased struggle for economical use
of material and financial inputs.[191]

Needless to say practice did not reflect the postulated
struggle for an economical use of materials. Waste of
materials was more and more apparent.[192] The envisaged
cost reductions did not materialize. Deficits rose at
an accelerated rate rendering a price reform indispensable.
    Basically the 1953 reform was limited to material
inputs with little or no effect on the prices of capital
goods. The prices of coal were raised by an average of
33 per cent and differentiated according to use value.
Prices of basic rolled steel products were increased by
an average of 40 per cent, prices of pipes and fittings
by approximately 25 per cent, and high grade steel by
8 to 20 per cent. Prices of iron ore were worked out
on the principle that production costs of pig iron must
be the same no matter what quality of ore is used. Prices
of steel scrap were raised in proportion to prices of pig
iron. However, the extent of price adjustments was
constrained by the postulated cost reductions. Deficits
were only mitigated but not eradicated.[193]
    On January 3, 1953 the rationing of consumer goods
was revoked, followed by a considerable increase of
consumer goods prices and wages. On the average prices
increased by 43 and wages by 35 per cent.[194] As a result
two days after the new producers' prices became effective,
they were already more than obsolete. Because of this
a far greater number of industries than originally
envisaged by the planners suffered deficits and had to
be subsidized.[195]
    For example, in the coal industry prior to 1956 only
one of the eighty mines was profitable. The majority of
mines suffered losses from 21 to 60 per cent.[196]
Similarly in the steel industry all the basic steel mills

were unprofitable with the exception of a handful of
mills where the processing of steel was dominant.   The
situation in the building materials industry was not
much better.[197]

In deficit enterprises interest in cost reduction is
minimized, indifference towards financial results develops,
and the budget constraint is weakened as in any case
losses will be covered by the state.

With time the discrepancy between prices and costs
increased.   For example, by 1955 the average production
costs of coal had increased by 65 per cent in relation
to the average costs in 1952.   The transfer price of coal
during that period was not subject to change.[198]

Pricing of basic raw materials below costs caused
artificially lowered costs in firms using them.   Similarly prices of products manufactured by those firms
influenced costs in enterprises using these semi-fabricates.   For example, the low price of coal entailed low
production costs of smelting coke, which in turn lowered
the costs of steel, which lowered the costs of tools and
machines.   The low prices of machines, resulting indirectly from the low prices of coal, once again lowered
the costs of coal, where machinery was necessary in the
production process.   Hence a result was transformed
into a cause and the cycle completed.   Considering the
interdependence between the individual branches of
industry, it was impossible to reckon the actual costs
(granted the basic conceptual flaws) of individual
products or the entire output.   Prices were completely
outdated and the need for a general reform of producers'
prices was again flagrantly apparent.

THE 1956 PRICE REFORM

The 1956 reform of producers' prices was the most
ambitious in scope up to that time.   Its goals were to
raise the prices of raw materials to reflect the average
cost of production, entailing an increase in the prices
of semi-fabricates and finished producer goods, and to
differentiate prices according to technical substitution.[199]

At the time of the reform consumers feared that the
price increases will necessarily entail a general price
increase of consumer goods.   Such was not the case.[200]

The concept of the dual price system was reiterated by
Augustowski who asserted that changes in the prices of
producer goods, as objects of intra-transfers in the
socialist sector, cannot by their very nature cause
changes in the prices of consumer goods because they do
not alter any of the basic factors on which price formation of retail prices depends:

> Two basic factors decide about the level of retail
> prices: the size of monetary income of the population
> and the size of the goods and services designated for
> personal consumption. The alteration of prices of
> procurement and investment goods by itself cannot
> have an influence on the level of prices of consumer
> goods. A change in prices of procurement and invest-
> ment goods does not influence the total income of the
> population nor the size of production designated for
> consumption.[201]

Notwithstanding the general criticism of the separation
of producers' and consumers' "markets", it seems that
Augustowski does not reckon with anticipation of future
price changes as an important parameter of the demand
function. The anticipation of future price changes of
consumer goods, prevalent then in Poland, would by itself
shift the demand function for consumer goods causing
shortages even if the income of the consumers and flow
of production remained unaltered.

A primary undertaking of the reform was to increase
the prices of coal. In 1956 the price of coal was raised
on the average by 80 per cent, i.e., to 120 zl. per ton.[202]
Waste of coal had not been only a factor of its low
prices but also lack of differentiation according to
quality, a problem which the reform attempted to remedy.

Electricity tariffs which had been in use since 1949
varied between 0.036 and 0.13 per kw-hr, the greater
the volume used the lower the tariff inducing larger
use. The 1956 reform established a uniform price of
0.13 zl. per kw-hr aiming at reflecting average costs
of power in those tariffs.[203]

The basis for pricing some rolled steel products was
changed from weight to length inducing steel mills to
adhere to negative weight tolerances, thereby saving on
use of raw materials.[204] Preoccupied with the technocratic notion of efficiency, attempts were made to dif-

ferentiate prices according to technical use value. For
example, steel scrap and pig iron were assigned uniform
prices, whereas prior to the reform they had been priced
at 434 and 745 zl. respectively.[205]

Notwithstanding the substantial variations in world
market prices of imported non-ferrous metals, their
transfer prices remained virtually unchanged since 1948.
These prices reflected neither cost of import, price
ratios on the world market, nor even domestic costs.
To counteract waste and reduce import the new prices of
these goods were to take technological substitution
into account. The price of zinc, a domestic product,
was based on average production costs. Price relations
of other non-ferrous metals were based partly on cost of
import and partly on domestic prices in the Soviet Union.[206]

Prior to 1956 prices of building materials hindered
the use of substitutes and prefabricates in the construction industry.[207] Table 1 indicates the old and new
prices of construction materials in relation to pine.

Table 1 - <u>1955-56 Prices of Pine Boards and Substitutes</u>

Name of material	1955 prices zl. per 1 m^2	Index	1956 prices zl. per 1 m^2	Index
Pine boards, 25 mm thick, Class V	5.03	100	10.37	100
Hard Pilsen plates, 4 mm thick, Class I	6.50	129	7.09	68
Hard Pilsen plates, 4 mm thick, Class II	5.96	118	6.50	63
Reed plates 35 mm thick	13.10	260	13.10	126
Reed plates 50 mm thick	15.25	303	15.25	147
Reed plates 70 mm thick	20.40	406	20.40	197

<u>Source</u> Z. Wit and S. Szajko, in <u>Z zagadnien</u>..., pp.95-6

Regardless of the scarcity of pine and lumber in general,
the pre-reform prices hampered the use of substitutes.
The case in point are Pilsen and reed plates. Pilsen
plates are produced from lumber by-products and cuttings,
hence from substandard materials. However, their tech-

nological use value exceeds that of pine boards. Given
the scarcity of lumber it would be desirable to induce
building planners to substitute Pilsen plates for pine
boards. Prior to the 1956 reform "moral suasion" was
used to promote "proper" use of resources. Unfortunately
it was not backed by proper indices to guide choice.
Even after the reform the prices of reed plates were still
out of proportion as substitute materials.

As a result of the reform the cost composition was
changed with the relative share of material costs increased and labor costs reduced as illustrated in Table
2.

Table 2 - <u>1951-56 Structure of Cost Elements in Industry</u>

Cost elements	1951	1952	1953	1954	1955	1956*
Materials	70.6	65.2	64.0	62.9	65.0	70.0
Labor	18.6	21.9	25.8	26.5	24.0	19.0
Depreciation	3.1	3.7	3.1	3.1	3.0	5.7
Others	7.7	9.2	7.1	7.5	8.0	5.3

*Planned

<u>Source</u> H. Fiszel, <u>Prawo wartosci</u>..., pp.114 and 127

Data for particular industries confirm the over-all conclusions that can be reached after an examination of the
statistics presented for the industry as a whole.[208]
One of the aims of the reform was to cut down deficits
and the ensuing subsidies. To evaluate the repercussions
of the 1956 reform on the enterprises' profitability the
Institute of Economic Analysis of the PC analyzed data
gathered by the Central Statistical Office (CSO) for the
years immediately preceeding and succeeding the reform.[209]
The investigation revealed that in 1956 the rate of profit
was 1.4 per cent in state owned key industry compared to
the rate of deficit of 1.6 per cent in 1955, pointing only
to a slight improvement.[210] The rates for the two consecutive years according to industries were as shown in Table
3. Although deficits were not eliminated in coal mining
they fell by 18 per cent. Metallurgy registered a 13 per
cent shift extricating itself from the deficit industries.
The chemical industry moved in the opposite direction
due to the low prices of synthetics (to induce substitu-

Table 3 -   1955-56 Rates of Profit or Deficit in Some
            Branches of Industry

Industries	Years	Rate of profit %	Rate of deficit %
Electric power	1955	2.6	
	1956	7.5	
Coal mining	1955		36.9
	1956		18.7
Petroleum	1955	0.3	
	1956	6.6	
Metallurgy	1955		10.4
	1956	2.7	
Machine building	1955	2.7	
	1956	5.2	
Chemical	1955	2.8	
	1956		2.4
Building materials	1955		9.5
	1956		9.2
Forestry and lumber	1955	0.4	
	1956	6.9	
Light industry	1955	7.7	
	1956	7.2	
Food industry	1955	2.8	
	1956	0.8	
Small-scale	1955	13.4	
	1956	13.1	
Total	1955		1.6
	1956	1.4	

Source Z. Madej, GP, no. 12, 1957, p.2

tion) and high costs of newly built plants. The increased
prices of lumber reflected favorably on the results of
this industry.

The number, distribution, and shift of profitable and
deficit enterprises among the different branches of industry is illustrated in Table 4. In coal mining, metallurgy,
and machine building a substantial decrease in the number
of deficit enterprises was registered. In the building
materials, food, and chemical industries the number of
deficit enterprises markedly increased. These data are
comparable to the general rate of profit and deficit for

Table 4 - <u>1955-56 Profitable and Deficit Enterprises</u>

Industries	Year	Total no. of firms	Including enterprises			
			Deficit	%	Profitable	%
Electric power	1955	88	5	5.5	83	94.5
	1956	93	4	4.2	89	95.8
Coal mining	1955	119	92	77.3	27	32.7
	1956	127	80	63.0	47	37.0
Metallurgy	1955	149	84	56.3	65	43.7
	1956	151	64	40.0	87	60.0
Machine building	1955	276	119	43.1	157	56.9
	1956	285	91	39.9	194	60.1
Chemical	1955	123	50	40.6	73	59.4
	1956	130	64	49.2	66	50.8
Building mat.	1955	218	131	60.0	87	40.0
	1956	226	150	66.3	76	33.7
Forestry	1955	205	87	42.4	118	57.6
	1956	206	47	23.8	159	77.2
Light industry	1955	427	92	21.5	335	78.5
	1956	429	86	20.0	343	80.0
Food industry	1955	511	192	37.5	319	62.5
	1956	518	245	47.1	273	52.9
Small-scale	1955	157	37	23.5	120	76.5
	1956	169	41	24.2	128	75.8
Others	1955	308	109	35.4	199	64.6
	1956	319	117	38.0	196	62.0
Entire industry	1955	2581	998	38.6	1583	61.4
	1956	2647	989	37.2	1658	62.8

<u>Source</u>   Z. Madej, <u>GP</u>, no.12, 1957, p.3

the particular industries.

The data presented are a good illustration of the financial results of the reform and the relative shifts in profitability among branches of industry. However, too great weight should not be attributed to the revelations as they are only an indication of the progress made. For economic calculation, appraisal, and evaluation we need prices and costs which do reflect current scarcity relations. The residue - profit or loss - has little meaning as long as prices and costs are products of a faulty price system and structure. One wonders what is the economic implication of a shift of a branch

of industry, or enterprise within it, from deficit to
profitable when the line of demarcation has little
significance. How meaningful is a rate of profit on
costs which abstract from opportunity and imputed costs?

THE AFTERMATH OF THE 1956 REFORM

The failures of the 1956 price reform were evident
shortly after the inception of the new prices.[211] In
general the 1956 reform was directed against the doctrinal assertion that low prices of producer goods favor
economic progress. However, the revision of this tenet
was superficial. It was admitted that low prices of
material inputs induce waste rather than progress. But
in the case of capital goods the old thesis still had
strong roots.[212]

By the very nature of the economic phenomenon, there
is an interdependence of economic quantities; as Cournot
so clearly conceived,"in reality the economic system is
a whole of which all the parts are connected and react
on each other."[213] Prices and costs are interdependent
and every price reform has to cope with this problem. But
as application of mathematical techniques and computers
had not yet come of age in Soviet-type economies, the
1956 reform was conducted without due weight given to
the interdependence of prices.[214] Prices of producer
goods failed to reflect even the average production costs.

The fact that cost is only one of the determinants of
price was clearly manifest in case of the low prices of
lumber. Not only due to complete disregard of differential
rent and charge for capital in the long process of gestation, but mainly because scarcity of lumber was ignored.

The reform which was to take effect on January 1, 1955,
but was implemented one year later, was based on cost
data for 1953 and 1954. By 1956 these costs were already
outdated and became increasingly irrelevant as time went
by. The postulated future cost reductions were soon
proven unfounded.

The period between 1956 and 1959 featured a strong
upward movement of wages. By 1959 the nominal wages in
industry were 48 per cent higher than in 1955.[215]The
average monthly wage during that period rose by 50.6 per
cent. The rates of increase in the more important indus-

tries were: electric power 62.4, fuels and petroleum
57.2, ferrous metallurgy 48.2, non-ferrous metallurgy
48.4, machine building 48.1, chemicals 47.0 per cent.[216]
   It should be remembered that prices of producer goods
are not altered only as a result of general price reforms,
but also by sporadic interim price revisions of selected
goods. On January 1, 1957 the prices of lumber were
raised by about 200 per cent. This increase was motivated
as an incentive to save on lumber in view of its relative
scarcity. In this connection the new prices of lumber
seemed to have fulfilled their purpose.[217] But the
savings were also influenced by stricter rationing.
   Simultaneously the prices of cement were increased
to render the cement industry profitable in anticipation
of the impending price changes in coal, electricity, and
transportation. The latter were, however, delayed.
When setting the new prices the relations between the
grades of cement were altered. Whereas the 1956 price
relations adhered closely to the use value concept, the

Table 5 - <u>1956-57 Price, Cost and Use Value Relations
          of Cement</u>

Cement	1956 zl/ton			1957 zl/ton			Compression Resistance Index*	Substitu- tion Coefficient*
	Average Cost	Price	Price Index *	Average Cost	Price	Price Index *		
Masons 150	261	102	60	269	240	71	60	73
Construction 250	178	155	91	204	320	94	100	93
Metallurgical 250	185	170	100	272	340	100	100	100
Portland 250	198	170	100	220	340	100	100	100
Portland 350	200	238	140	227	410	120	140	128
Paving 350	197	261	153	222	450	132	140	-
Quick-setting 400	526	323	190	527	470	138	160	140

* In all cases Portland Cement 250 = 100

<u>Source</u> A.Plocica, Podstawy cen..., pp. 166-8

1957 revision was a departure from this, attempting to
mitigate deficits on the lower grades, as illustrated

in Table 5.

While during the period 1956 to 1959 prices of some
producer goods (lumber, paper, and building materials)
were raised,[218] the majority of producers' prices
remained virtually unchanged. A typical example is
once again the coal industry where Table 6 illustrates
the costs and prices of coal.

Table 6 -   1950-59 Average Prices and Costs of Coal

Year	Cost in zl. per ton	Price in zl. per ton	Ratio of price to cost %
1950	62.14	53.22	85
1951	62.22	54.82	88
1952	73.82	57.34	78
1953	102.41	74.88	71
1954	110.86	73.45	66
1955	120.39	72.35	60
1956	163.18	128.25	79
1957	222.49	128.91	58
1958	225.26	128.84	57
1959	236.01	128.98	55

Source   J. Zachariasz, GP, No.6, 1960, p.3

The 1956 average price of coal was 128.25 zl., an increase
of about 80 per cent. Since the average production cost
was 120.39 zl., the average 1956 price was to reflect
costs and ensure a meager profitability in the coal industry as a whole. Nevertheless by 1957 a 7 billion zl.
deficit arose in the coal industry.[219] In the first year
it was in force the 1956 price covered only 79 per cent
of costs and in 1958 barely 57 per cent. One of the
reasons for increased costs in the coal industry was
the upward pressure on wages resulting in an increase
of the average monthly wage from 1727 zl. in 1955 to
2701 zl. in 1959. This was aggravated by the increased
prices of lumber, a steadily declining labor productivity,
and increasing use of materials.[220]

Although the scope of the 1956 reform was broader than
that of its predecessors it is significant that it met

with an almost identical fate. Granted the average cost
of production as a basis for price setting, a few months
after their introduction the 1956 prices ceased to represent costs. Once again cost of materials was greatly
understated and artificially lowered in relation to
labor costs, inducing waste of materials.[221] It was
apparent that a general price reform was long overdue.

THE 1960 REFORM OF PRODUCERS' PRICES

By 1960 the time was ripe for a general revision of
producers' prices, particularly in view of preparations
for the forthcoming FYP (1961-65). The preparations for
this reform were already started at the SPC in 1957.
According to resolution 497 of the CM the reform aimed
"at ensuring correct proportions between the cost of
raw materials, materials, and other elements of production costs as well as correct proportions between
prices of material inputs, and at creating conditions
for specific branches of industry to attain full recovery
of costs and an appropriate profit."[222] The main goal
of the reform was to annihilate deficits in the production of material inputs and investment goods. It was
claimed that this would ensure adequate economic calculation, especially for investment decisions.[223] The increase of prices of raw materials in short supply was
to promote their economical use. More adequate price
relations of substitute products were to induce firms
to replace raw materials in short supply by those more
readily available.[224]

The price reform became effective on July 1, 1960.
Viewing it in the light of past experience Siemiatkowski
rightly emphasized its scope: "Our economy has never
experienced such a far reaching reform."[225] Unfortunately
it was far reaching only in its quantitative effect. It
was not "revolutionary" in a methodological sense as
basically it did not implement even the compromised
recommendations of the Theses on Price Formation.

The reform pertained to prices of producer goods in
all branches of industry, but in principle did not
embrace prices of consumer goods as illustrated in
Table 7. Among the most important products affected
were coal, coke, ores, building materials, quicklime,
plaster of Paris, lumber, cotton, flax, jute, sisal,

Table 7 - <u>1956-61 Index of Price Increases</u>

Description	Index 1956 = 100					
	1957	1958	1959	1-6 1960	7-12 1960	1961
Industrial output	108	108	112	113	126	126
Producer goods	113	119	124	124	156	155
Machinery included	103	102	101	105	126	120
Consumer goods	107	104	106	109	110	109
Fuels industry	100	104	139	136	204	-
Ferrous metallurgy	100	102	102	101	166	-
Non-ferrous "	100	101	101	100	167	-
Building materials	150	148	154	148	191	-
Lumber industry	191	195	195	202	208	-
Paper "	198	204	203	214	215	-

<u>Source</u> A. Plocica, <u>Podstawy cen</u>..., pp.95 and 97

manilla, leather, oil seeds, electric power, gas, railway
tariffs, ship and truck transportation, steel and iron
products, non-ferrous metals, machines and equipment,
chemicals, paper, and some products of the light and food
industries. The scope of the reform was such that nearly 160 new price catalogs were issued, each incorporating
ten to twenty thousand items.[226] The preparations for the
reform lasted for over two years enrolling the participation of numerous employees from all levels of administration. One of the features of the reform which complicated
its preparation, simultaneously distinguishing it from
its predecessors, was the balancing of mutually interdependent changes in the prices of raw materials, semi-
fabricates, finished products, and services to account
for the chain reaction of prices. With the inevitable
changes in assumptions of relative price movements,
stemming from the ever more detailed elaborations, the
need arose for further even more complicated calculations
of all interdependent prices. This was an arduous task
with the skill and resources at hand. In the words of
one of the originators of the reform:

The execution of a general price reform was a difficult
and complicated business. Not everybody realizes the

scope of difficulties, even if only technical, which
had to be overcome in this connection. For example,
the reform necessitated the calculation of approximately half a million items in the price catalogs.
An additional difficulty lay in the fact that due
to the interdependence the calculation of individual
prices depended on the magnitude of other prices,
which in turn could not be assessed without a knowledge of the former... A price reform also entails
changes of the most important plan indexes (value
of production, production costs, financial results,
etc.,) which necessitates complicated calculations,
creating dangers of unconscious or tendentious
distortions.[227]

A price reform of such magnitude involves a recalculation of past, present, and projected NEP's at the new
prevailing prices to afford comparative data.   Such
far reaching revisions cause many problems and difficulties.[228]

The 1960 price reform did not break away from the
dual price system, nor did it abandon the principle
of a minimal margin of profit. In principle the new
prices were to cover the planned average (total) costs
of the producers of a given good, increased by a planned 5 per cent profit. The cost data were based on
the period prior to the reform with allowances for
projected cost reduction. Profit was to increase as
a result of cost reduction.[229]

However, many exceptions were made to the general
pricing rules. Prices of ferrous metallurgy products
and cotton yarn were set on the average costs of the
more expensive producers to ensure profitability in a
majority of enterprises. Prices of steel mill products
were set on the average costs of the older mills,
abstracting from costs of the Nowa Huta mills, the
largest and newest complex of steel mills in Poland.[230]
In the cotton industry, where a considerable number of
mills are equipped with old machinery and use backward
techniques, prices of cotton yarn were set on the average
costs of those expensive producers.[231]

In specific cases prices were set on the average costs
of the preponderant producers. For instance, prices of
caustic soda were set on the average costs of the firms
in Cracow and Matwach since other enterprises had just

started production. Prices of ammonia, nitric acid, and
other nitrogen products were based on the costs of the
enterprise in Kedzierzyn, their largest producer.[232]

It was impossible to base transfer prices of all machinery on average costs since a great number of these
goods are produced in highly specialized enterprises
where only one or two firms produce identical goods.
Transfer prices were, therefore, based in such a manner
as to ensure profitability to the individual producers.[233]

To encourage the use of newly developed substitutes,
their prices were not set on their average costs but
in relation to the prices of inputs they were to replace.
A case in point is the price of synthetic fibers which
is lower than that of natural fibers although the entire
synthetic fiber industry shows a deficit.[234]

Prices of products which are mostly imported were set
in relation to the cost of import. Two cases in point
are iron ore and synthetic rubber. The transfer prices
of zinc, a domestic and exportable good, were established
on the average cost of production plus a slight profit
margin.   Prices of the other non-ferrous metals (largely
imported) were set on the basis of world market prices,
in relation to the domestic price of zinc. For example,
domestic production costs of copper are seven times
those of zinc, whereas on the world market the price of
copper is roughly 2.7 times that of zinc. Under these
circumstances the price of copper was set at 3.5 times
that of zinc, covering only 50 per cent of the average
domestic production costs of copper.[235]

The price of coal has a rather interesting aspect.
Although it was set on the average cost of production,
it should be pointed out that world market prices of
coal were used as a frame of reference in the calculation of the domestic price.[236] As a result prices of
coal were increased on the average by 150 per cent.[237]

Railway tariffs were most outdated contributing to
the misuse of transportation and recurring bottlenecks.
Freight charges were only a fractional element of total
costs.[238] Whereas there was a great shortage of railway
cars, entire freight trains loaded with gravel, bricks,
and sand were moved from one end of the country to the
other. The general increase of freight tariffs was
over 70 per cent, whereas the total revision of railway tariffs approximated 80 per cent.[239] The changes
in freight tariffs on the more important products are

presented in Table 8.

Table 8 - <u>1960 Revision of Freight Tariffs on Selected</u>
          <u>Producer Goods</u>

Products	Zl. 1 ton/100 km.	
	1959	1960
Coke	13.40	33.90
Rye	27.60	50.80
Potatoes	14.80	33.90
Sugar beets (raw)	15.60	42.40
Stones	11.80	28.30
Sand and gravel	13.40	28.30
Iron ore	14.80	33.90
Crude oil	27.60	62.40
Phosphorous fertilizers	17.00	50.80
Nitrous fertilizers	21.70	50.80
Lumber	14.00	42.40
Mine lumber	12.80	42.40
Iron and structural steel	31.50	50.80
Pit coal	12.80	28.30

<u>Source</u>   S. Pozniak, <u>GP</u>, No.8-9, 1960, p.26

Since most products are priced f.o.b. destination, the
revised tariffs intend to induce suppliers to sell their
products in their area aiming at reducing the potential
squandering of railway transportation.

Regardless of the shortage of water for industrial
uses, the low water tariffs of 0.8 zl. per cubic meter,
with a production cost of 1.3 zl. did not induce economical
use of water, nor did they stimulate the carrying out of
such investment variants which would economize on its use.
As a result of the reform water tariffs were raised
considerably.[240]

Building materials were highly underpriced and in
great shortage. The price of bricks covered only 55
per cent of costs and the price of cement 83 per cent.
These prices were increased in 1957. During the 1960
reform the revision was not substantial averaging about
25 per cent.[241] The new prices of building lime, illustrated in Table 9, reflect the average costs of production and ratio of those costs between the different

Table 9 - <u>Price Increases and Relations of Building Lime</u>

Qualities of Lime	1 9 5 6		1 9 6 0	
	Price zl/t	Price Index*	Price zl/t	Price Index*
Quicklime				
Grade I (95% CaO + MgO)	285	108	350	111
" II (88% " ")	264	100	315	100
" III (80% " ")	240	90	260	83
Industrial ground lime				
Grade I (95% CaO + MgO)	356	108	405	104
" II (88% " ")	330	100	390	100
" III (80% " ")	300	90	360	92
Slack lime				
Grade I (72% CaO + MgO)	371	108	430	109
" II (68% " ")	342	100	395	100
Ground lime (Smirnov)	300	100	360	100
Lean lime	371	100	455	100

* In all cases Grade II = 100

Source　A. Plocica, <u>Podstawy cen</u>..., p. 171

types of lime. The prices of the grades of each type of
lime were differentiated according to use value (CaO +
MgO content) and not according to costs. This widened
the gap between superior and inferior grades.

Prices of building materials were changed from f.o.b.
destination to f.o.b. source of supply to mitigate
abuses of hauling facilities.[242] Products available
locally were often ordered from distant suppliers as the
hauling charges were incurred by the producer. Exclusion
of freight charges from prices of building materials
should induce buyers to take advantage of the sources of
supply in their area (provided the materials are availabl
there!).

As the majority of power plants are thermal, the price
increases of coal resulted in substantial alterations of
electricity tariffs. The tariff was increased on the
average by 75 per cent. Differential rates for electricity were applied with peak hour rates considerably
exceeding slack hour rates inducing enterprises to operat
night shifts. It has been estimated that if firms take

advantage of the reduced rates, on the average, payment
for electricity during the next few years will drop by
approximately 3 per cent annually.[243]
   The average price increases on selected producer goods
and services are illustrated in Table 10.

Table 10 - 1960 Increases of Some Producers' Prices

Name of Product	Average price increase 1959 = 100
Pit coal	127.9
Lignite	302.0
Pit coal briquettes	94.7
Crude oil	144.4
Iron ore	185.2
Non-ferrous ores	227.5
Steel	171.5
Rolled steel products	164.6
Processed non-ferrous metals	159.0
Machines and electrical equipment	115.3
Sulfuric acid	166.4
Calcinated soda (98%)	188.7
Commercial carbide	275.5
Cement	126.1
Quicklime	117.5
Bricks	112.9
Cotton yarn	129.1
Worsted yarn	105.9
Rayon yarn	223.0
Railway tariffs	180.0
Electricity tariffs	175.0

Sources   M. Krol, GP, No. 1, 1961, p.35, J. Struminski,
          GP, No.1, 1962, p.8, J. Zachariasz, GP, No.6,
          1960, p.2, and A. Plocica, Podstawy cen..., p.98

   Price increases of raw materials were more pronounced
than those of semi-fabricates and finished products.
Where cost of processing is more prominent than cost of
materials, price increases were less manifest. For
example, in the machine building industry where the
average price increase was 15.3 per cent, the rate of

increase on various products was: electrical machines
26 per cent, machine tools 12, textile machines 6, heavy
machinery 28, rolling stock 23, and shipbuilding 20 per
cent.[244] The prices of machine tools, which require
relatively less material and more labor than heavy
machinery, were increased only by 12 per cent, whereas
prices of heavy machinery went up by 28 per cent.

After the reform the share of material costs in total
industrial costs of production increased in relation to
the share of labor costs, as shown in Table 11.

Table 11 - Industry's Labor and Material Costs 1958-61

| Branches of Industry | In percentages of total costs | | | | | |
| | Material costs | | | Labor costs | | |
	1958	1959	1961	1958	1959	1961
Electric power	57.7	62.5	67.4	42.3	37.5	32.6
Fuels	69.6	55.8	53.6	30.4	44.2	46.4
Ferrous metallurgy	75.0	81.6	78.2	25.0	18.4	21.8
Non-ferrous "	80.1	86.4	77.3	19.9	13.6	22.7
Machine building	56.7	54.1	61.4	43.3	45.9	38.6
Electrical machines	-	58.1	62.3	-	41.9	37.7
Automotive	-	60.8	65.2	-	39.2	34.8
Metals	-	52.2	58.1	-	47.8	41.9
Chemicals	66.0	71.6	70.3	34.0	28.4	29.7
Rubber	59.2	57.0	61.1	40.8	43.0	38.9
Building materials	43.3	53.0	57.6	56.6	47.0	42.4
Glass	-	33.3	45.3	-	66.7	54.7
China and pottery	-	37.8	42.1	-	62.2	57.9
Lumber	74.4	73.1	71.8	25.6	26.9	28.2
Paper	71.3	73.0	68.8	28.7	27.0	31.2
Printing	56.6	59.0	57.6	43.5	41.0	42.4
Textile	56.3	60.9	61.5	43.7	39.1	38.5
Clothing	74.7	76.6	76.7	25.3	23.4	23.3
Leather and shoes	52.1	56.1	58.9	47.9	43.9	41.1
Food	69.1	69.4	72.9	30.9	30.6	27.1
Salt	26.3	37.7	44.7	73.7	62.3	55.3
Others	61.6	61.3	69.5	38.4	38.7	30.5
Total	-	65.2	67.0	-	34.8	33.0

Sources   CSO typewritten material, 1963, RS 1960, p.92
          and RS 1959, p.86

However, since price increases of coal and electric power

went into effect on January 1, 1959 the proportions are
slightly distorted here. During the period of transition
the industries were receiving subsidies amounting to the
difference between the old and new prices of coal and
power.

Prior to 1960 the contribution of various producer
and consumer goods' producers to total output was badly
distorted. The shift in contribution, according to
official computations, is indicated in Table 12.

Table 12 - 1960 Percentage Contribution of Individual
           Branches of Industry to Total Output

Branches of Industry	In 1956 comparable prices	In 1960 comparable prices
Total	100	100
Electric power	1.8	2.1
Fuels	5.5	9.5
Ferrous metallurgy	7.1	8.6
Non-ferrous "	1.9	2.3
Machine building and metal processing	22.2	19.7
Machine building	6.0	5.5
Electrical machines	4.1	3.4
Automotive	7.6	6.7
Metal processing	4.5	4.1
Chemical	6.4	6.4
Rubber	1.0	1.0
Building materials	2.3	3.2
Glass	0.5	0.5
China and pottery	0.3	0.2
Lumber	3.0	4.2
Paper	1.2	1.6
Printing	0.6	0.6
Textile	12.4	9.8
Clothing	2.6	2.6
Leather and shoes	2.6	2.5
Food	28.0	24.3
Salt	-	0.1
Others	0.7	0.8

Source   J. Kowalewski, GP, No.1, 1962, p.13

It is significant that the contribution of fuels, ferrous and non-ferrous metals, power, building materials,
lumber, etc. increased, whereas that of industries processing these materials declined.

Viewing the reform from the standpoint of the producers' financial results, it seems that its objectives
were largely accomplished.[245] As a rule the actual rates
of profit exceeded what was deemed the desirable level
(about 5 per cent), and are greatly differentiated, as
can be seen from Table 13. Obviously when planning
production costs, based on the 1957 and 1958 actual costs,
the responsible units, whether enterprises, associations,
or ministries, must have allowed a considerable margin
of tolerance to ensure profitability. During the following years many new products were introduced. Those prices
are usually set on the planned costs submitted by the
firm and approved by the association and ministry. "Prices
of those goods, in many cases, were set at a too high
level. Sometimes, as it seems, because the firms lacked
discernment, most often, however, in pursuit of profit."[2]

It is evident from the data that the gap between the
levels of consumers' and producers' prices seems to have
been narrowed by the reform. Table 14 indicates that
realized accumulation in 1962 and 1963 and the planned
one for 1964 and 1965 demonstrate a gradual weakening
of the gap. Although the trend seems to be towards a
rapprochement between the two levels,[247] it does not
strike at the core of the dual price system and does
not destroy its very premises - the separation of
producers' and consumers' markets. The main reasons
for the divergence in the reported rates of accumulation for 1961 and 1962 are the introduction of new
depreciation charges in 1962 and price reductions of
some goods.[248]

Pricing policy contributes to losses on some products
which must be covered by subsidies from the state budget.
Three types of deficits may be distinguished, namely,
those caused by the difference between the individual
production costs and the transfer prices, deficits
caused by the difference between the transfer price
and retail price (retail price being smaller) those
are the "negative budget differences", and finally
deficits resulting from the difference between the
transfer price and the factory price.

In 1960 approximately 6000 products of key industry

Table 13 - Rate of Accumulation in Associations of Producer and Consumer Goods Industries 1961-62 *

Associations	Rate %		Associations	Rate %		Associations	Rate %	
	1961	1962		1961	1962		1961	1962
MINING-METALS.			BUILDING MAT.			Brewing	34.5	50.1
Pit Coal	15.3	10.1	Concrete	26.2	11.0	LIGHT INDUSTRY		
Lignite	28.5	17.6	Cement	16.6	13.5	Cotton	18.9	18.3
Petroleum	93.0	58.4	Bricks	41.4	48.7	Cotton – North	94.0	77.6
Electricity	10.6	20.4	Ceramics	10.0	-0.4	Wool mills	12.2	12.4
Iron Ore	-45.7	-41.4	Aggregate and mineral raw mat.	30.7	16.5	Linen	-7.5	-8.1
Chemical	25.4	10.3	Insulation	22.1	26.7	Clothing	-0.3	2.6
Steel & Iron	12.4	9.5	Hardware	24.6	24.7	Silk	45.1	43.7
Non-ferrous metals	10.2	12.6	Lime & plaster	-5.0	-8.5	Women's apparel	60.2	69.1
MACHINE BUILD.			FOOD INDUSTRY			Felt	18.2	17.4
Heavy Machines	13.4	14.0	Meat	4.8	4.9	Leather	36.9	39.0
Construction "	27.8	22.0	Eggs & poultry	4.2	3.3	OTHERS		
Textile "	29.1	27.3	Sugar	12.6	35.1	Furniture	19.1	15.4
Electrical "	24.2	30.0	Potatoes	11.7	8.5	Folding "	-2.7	0.9
Mining "	20.1	-	Oil	19.1	9.6	China	27.7	18.9
Forestry "	16.6	14.5	Concentrates	12.9	10.6			
Food "	12.7	11.9	Vegetables and fruit	12.2	-			
Chemical "	18.3	13.9	Confectionary	30.5	29.6			
Machine Tools	24.6	28.4						

* Accumulation on producer goods largely coincides with profit, whereas its constituents are profit and turnover tax in consumer goods industries.

Source A. Plocica, Podstawy cen..., pp. 100-1

117

Table 14 - 1962-65 Rates of Accumulation and Profit

| Industries | Rates in percentages | | | | | |
| | Profit | | Accumula-tion | | Accumula-tion* | |
	1962	1963	1962	1963	1964	1965
Total	10.7	9.4	21.4	20.8	26.5	28.5
Mining & Electricity	11.8	10.5	7.3	9.6	27.0	22.8
Heavy Industry	14.7	11.9	16.2	14.4	26.1	29.3
Construction and Building Materials	12.8	7.8	21.7	17.0	32.6	35.1
Chemical Industry	18.1	16.4	28.6	30.3	38.5	43.8
Light Industry	7.2	7.2	31.1	31.4	35.6	37.5
Food Industry	3.9	3.9	29.7	28.4	35.6	35.3

*Planned

Sources   J. Struminski, GP, No.5, 1964, p.20 and A. Plocic
          Podstawy cen..., p.103

showed losses caused by the difference between transfer
prices and individual production costs. Total deficits
on this account approximated 5.5 billion zl. In addition
a 5.6 billion zl. deficit was incurred from negative
budget differences. The result was 11.1 billion zl.
deficit.[249] Table 15 itemizes the negative budget
differences.
     The case of coal for the consumers' market merits
particular attention and its history should be traced
in a nutshell. Until 1953 the same price of coal for
industrial and household uses prevailed. Already by
1949 the price of coal did not cover costs. The industry
suffered large losses and was heavily subsidized. In
1953 the price of industrial coal was raised without
ensuring profitability. During the 1953 increase of
consumers' prices and abolition of rationing the consumers' price of coal was raised to 300 zl. Coal of
the same quality was sold to industry for 93 zl. per
ton. In 1955 the consumers' price was reduced to 250 zl.
and less a 10 per cent trade margin produced 225 zl.
per ton. This price exceeded costs and the "positive
budget difference" was paid into the state budget. On
the other hand, the coal industry received large subsidies on every and each ton of coal sold to industry.

Table 15 - <u>1960 Negative Budget Differences</u>

Products	Deficits billions/zl.
Coal as a consumer good	2.3
Electricity as a consumer good	0.8
Coke and metal products as consumer goods	0.4
Wool and flax procured from domestic producers	1.3
Oil seeds procured from domestic producers	0.3
Clothing	0.4
Others	0.1
Total	5.6

<u>Source</u>   T. Kierczynski, <u>Przedsiebiorstwa deficytowe</u>...,
          p.122

The situation was not improved by the 1956 reform. It
was steadily aggravated annually up to the 1960 reform
of producers' prices. From 1955 the consumers' price
of coal did not change. By 1958 it was already equal
to cost and by 1959 the positive budget difference was
transformed into a negative one. By 1960 the price
of industrial coal of the quality used for household
purposes was raised to 415 zl. per ton. Since the
consumers' price of coal was not subject to change
the state subsidized each ton of coal sold to consumers
by 190 zl. (415 less 225).[250] A similar situation where
transfer prices exceed retail prices existed in electricity, coke, and metallurgical products.

    On April 1, 1963 the prices of coal, fuels, and
electricity sold to consumers were considerably increased. The retail price of coal was raised from
250 zl. to 500 zl. per ton, thus exceeding the transfer
price by 85 zl. Whereas the average cost of 1 kw-hr of
electricity for the city population was .67, the price
was .41 zl. This price has been raised to .90 zl. The
average cost of kw-hr of electricity for the rural
population was .99 and the price was .82 zl. This price
was raised to 1.20 zl.[251]

    The state purchases wool, flax, and oil seeds from
the domestic producers (usually private farmers) at
prices which would induce the farmers to produce them.[252]

Since these products' main source of supply is from import
the actual transfer price must be based on the cost of
import which is lower than the domestic procurement cost.

In the clothing industry the negative budget difference
occur when textiles are purchased at wholesale prices
less a discount. The latter is paid to the clothing
producers directly from the budget as a negative budget
difference. The reason behind this procedure is to
maintain uniform transfer prices in the textile industry.[253]

The third group of deficits, occurring when the
factory prices exceed transfer prices, amounted to 24.6
billion zl. in 1960.[254] Eighty per cent of deficits incurred in this category are centered on eleven products,
as shown in Table 16.

Table 16 - The Main Deficit Products in 1960

Name of Product	Deficits as % of trans- fer prices
Iron ore and non-ferrous metals	75
Tractors	36
Agricultural implements	19
Fertilizers	41
Rubber	126
Feed mixtures	33
Children's shoes	33
Cotton textiles	32
Linen textiles	36
Wool textiles	7.5
Synthetic fibers	22

Source T. Kierczynski, Przedsiebiorstwa deficytowe...,
        p. 125

With the present prices and costs, mining of iron,
copper, and zinc ores, aluminum oxide, phosphorite,
gipsum, and sulfur depends heavily on state subsidies.
The largest deficits are incurred in connection with the
exploitation of iron and copper ore deposits.

In 1961 domestic production of iron ore covered about
23 per cent of requirements.[255] Because of the share of
import the prices of iron ore are based on the cost of

import. The reasons for the high cost of domestic iron
ore excavation are the difficult and disadvantageous
geological conditions of the deposits and poor quality
of yields.[256] Table 17 represents the iron and silicon
oxide content of domestic iron ore compared to the
imported product. Domestic iron ore is considerably

Table 17 - 1960 Prices of Domestic and Imported Iron
           Ore According to Content

Type of Iron Ore	Origin	Content Fe %	Content SiO_2 %	Transfer price zl/ton
Krivoi Rog	U.S.S.R.	56.5	15.0	487
Kuruna	Sweden	66.0	2.5	742
Hainan	China	60.0	9.0	552
Santa Barbara	Brazil	60.0	4.0	653
Laczyca A + B	Poland	23.0	9.5	203
Malice	"	34.0	10.5	290
Edward	"	27.0	20.5	61
Sintered ore	"	31 - 44	16.2	339

Source   Ministry of Heavy Industry, Price Catalog,
         No.22-z/60, pp.13 and 30

inferior to the imported product and priced accordingly.
However, costs of these low grade ores greatly exceed
their post reform transfer prices.[257] The rate of deficit
in the Association of Iron Ore Mining was 45.7 per cent
in 1961 and 41.4 per cent in 1962, as shown in Table 13.
For similar reasons considerable deficits are also incurred in the mining of copper ore.
     In the machine building industry the largest losses
stem from production of automotive equipment.[258] In
particular these deficits result from transfer prices
of tractors lower than their factory prices to encourage
investments by agricultural producers.[259] Deficits in
the machine tool industry are mainly centered on the
production of obsolete and backward equipment featuring
rather high costs of production. However, the prices of
such tools were set in relation to the prices of the
more modern tools of a similar nature. Therefore, costs
of the backward tools exceed their transfer prices
resulting in deficits on 17 per cent of this industry's

output.[260]

In the chemical industry the greatest deficit is incurred in the production of synthetic rubber. All natural rubber is imported and so is a large part of
synthetic rubber. The first Polish synthetic rubber
plant in the chemical combine at Oswiecim started production by the middle of 1959. The basic semi-fabricate
used in the production of synthetic rubber is butadiene
which, according to plan, was to be manufactured from
ethyl alcohol, produced on a carbide base. However,
the construction of the plant to produce ethyl alcohol
was greatly delayed and synthetic rubber had to be
produced on alcohol. This increased costs immediately.
While the most efficient and cheapest production of
butadiene is in petrochemical processing, the petrochemical combine in Plock will be only partly operative
in 1965.[261] Although the production costs of synthetic
rubber far exceed the transfer price, an increase was
inadvisable since the price had to remain in relation to
that of imported rubber. Since the use value of natural
rubber is higher, the price of synthetic rubber was set
lower. Prices of synthetic rubber have been established
in relation to the prices of imported synthetic rubber.
Thus the price of natural rubber ($R.S.S._1$) is 28,200 zl.
and that of synthetic rubber (Buna S_2) is 22,100 zl.
per ton.[262]

Another important deficit product of the chemical
industry are fertilizers with prices set below costs
to promote their use in agriculture. The reform aggravated the situation since prices of fertilizers were
not changed, whereas those of material inputs rose
considerably.[263]

Deficits incurred in the production of synthetic
fibers result from their prices which are kept lower
than those of cotton and wool yarns.[264] Simultaneously
costs are high in this "infant" industry. Such a policy
aims at substituting synthetic fibers for cotton and
wool yarn derived from imported raw materials.

The building materials industry suffers losses in
connection with certain grades of cement, quicklime,
plaster of Paris, fiberglass, and glass wool. As a
binding material plaster of Paris has a much lower use
value than cement or quicklime. But because the production of cement does not, at present, satisfy requirements,
it was considered necessary to stimulate the use of

plaster of Paris by decreasing the transfer price despite
high costs.   Production costs of fiberglass are higher
than those of steel wool.   However, the price of fiberglass was set below that of steel wool.   The motivation
behind this move was to promote use of fiberglass   and
save steel wool which is a profitable export item.
Glass wool replaces cork as an insulating material.
Cork is an imported item priced slightly above glass
wool to reduce its import and widen the use of glass
wool.   The price of cork could not be raised in excess
of production costs of glass wool because it would then
be out of line with prices of other building materials.[265]
     Generally textiles are profitable, some even highly
profitable.   For instance, the 1960 plan indicated a
rate of accumulation of 76.2 per cent on the wool textiles
manufactured in Lodz, 134 per cent on those manufactured
in Bielsko, 63 per cent on silk and 10.8 per cent on
cotton, while 40 per cent of cotton textiles were unprofitable.[266]   The 1962 results indicated an average
rate of accumulation of 118 per cent on wool textiles,
18 per cent on cotton textiles, and 47 per cent on silk.[267]
The state is reluctant to reduce prices of textiles as
it fears that the increased purchasing power of the consumers will be applied not towards increased purchases
of textiles at reduced prices but rather towards increased purchases of foodstuffs whose shortages are felt
on the market.[268]   It seems that the "bourgeois" concept
of Allen-Hicks-Slutsky regarding the separation of the
income and substitution effects of price change is con-
sciously applied here.   But the textile industry has its
share of deficits.   The largest losses are incurred in
connection with production of cotton, wool, and linen
fabrics.   The losses on cotton and wool fabrics are
incurred on goods priced below costs for social reasons.[269]
Deficits incurred in the production of linen fabrics
result from developing domestic production of linen
using a domestic raw material (flax) to substitute for
cotton textiles produced on an imported one.
     Although the clothing and shoe industries are
generally profitable, deficits in those industries occur
mainly in the production of children's shoes and clothing.[270]
     Although the 1960 reform did not depart from the dual
price system and average costing, did not basically
reckon with price ratios prevailing on the world market,
and most important did not reflect current economic

scarcities, it was an undertaking of great magnitude.
It is generally recognized that over-all the reform
came closer than any of its precursors to reflecting
the average production costs in producers' prices,
strengthened financial discipline in the struggle
against squandering, differentiated prices of substitute
goods, and took cognizance of world market prices, especially on imported goods. The reform eradicated, or
mitigated, deficits in most industries. The existing
deficits are dictated by reasons of economic policy,
and in many cases are justified given the basic premises
of the present system. The reform should also be credited
for drawing closer together the levels of producers' and
consumers' prices.

The reform sanctioned the stability of prices at
least for the duration of a number of years. The stability of prices is considered as a conditio sine qua non
for effective planning. This renders any price reform
obsolete not long after - in some cases even at the time
of - its implementation. Price stability may mean in
practice absence of fundamental revisions for a duration
of five to eight years.[271] It should be remembered that
over two years are required to prepare a reform embracing
the majority of producer goods. The revised prices, which
in principle should remain stable for a period of five
years, are determined, in most cases, two years before
their introduction, based on statistical cost data of
the preceding year. Hence many prices are obsolete at
the outset. The changes that are taking place in the
methods of production and many other shift parameters,
as well as changing scarcity relationships, undermine a
price reform from the very moment new prices come into
effect. Even assuming that the reform would accomplish
satisfactorily the purposes for which it has been undertaken and provide rational prices it is immediately and
mercilessly defeated by its obsoleteness.

The inadequacy of anachronic prices is well recognized
in Poland among leading officials, as illustrated by
Vice-Premier Szyr's recent comment:

It is being said that planning "cannot endure"
frequent price changes of producer goods. But can
economic life endure the stability of improperly
set prices? It may be deduced from some arguments
that technical difficulties of statistical and plan

calculations justify maintaining a situation contrary
to economic needs. Economic considerations dictate
that a more flexible price policy should be applied
in some areas of producer goods.[272]

But there are no signs on the horizon indicating the
approach of sweeping changes in the price system.[273]
Granting the necessity for more price flexibility, the
IV Party Congress nevertheless reiterated the need for
price stability. The resolution proclaims introduction
of the flexibility element through a wider application
of factory prices changed periodically with the aid of
turnover tax levied on producer goods.[274] Notwithstanding
the disincentive involved in lowering the factory price
the bureaucratic machinery conducting such revisions
will interfere with their impetus and hamper them from
producing the desired effect at the time required.
    In conclusion, after an examination of the skeleton
of the pricing system and the reforms of producers'
prices, it is again apparent that the alterations in
buyers' demand are not determining factors on the firms'
output composition. The enterprises produce such an
assortment which will enable them to fulfil and overfulfil the predetermined plan targets. In such a system
the producer is secured the price of his product based
on alleged supply conditions only and he does not have
to adhere to buyers' preferences. The system lacks a
mechanism for the transmission of market impulses to
producers and features a built-in inelasticity of
response on the part of the firm - increase or curtailment of the flow of production or alteration of product
mix - as a result of changes in the structure of demand.[275]
The system also lacks the speed of adjustment which is
required not only for production to be carried out
according to plan, but carried out in such assortment as
to reflect buyers' preferences.
    It would not be sufficient, however, to recognize that
both demand and supply determine price and abolish a dual
price system in order that economic activity be guided
by rational prices. Economic decisions are taken at the
margin and rational allocation of resources has to be
guided by marginal calculus of the theory of the firm,
and not by an average quantity. It is to the great
credit of some Polish economists that they were the
first among Marxists to proclaim the value of the mar-

ginal approach to economic problems. Their recommendations, as we have seen, were not implemented but the
ferment created by their ideas may contribute to a
sounder approach to economic problems. Perhaps the
oponents of marginal costing in Soviet-type economies
will some day accept these words of Professor Schumpeter:

> The marginal principle per se is a tool of analysis,
> the use of which imposes itself as soon as analysis
> comes of age. Marx would have used it as a matter
> of course if he had been born fifty years later.
> It can no more serve to characterize a school of
> economics than the use of the calculus can serve to
> characterize a scientific school or group in math-
> ematics or physics. To this day, the very use of
> the term Marginalism is indicative of erroneous
> conceptions of the nature of the principle. A
> fortiori, it cannot have any bearing upon policy or
> social philosophy; this is perfectly understood in
> England, where no radical or socialist takes offense
> at it. It is only the political or ethical inter-
> pretation that is put upon the results of marginal
> analysis which can have such a bearing.[276]

CHAPTER **3** COST DETERMINATION
IN THE
ENTERPRISE

According to the Marxist theory of value the average
cost of production is the point of departure for pricing.
In the case of producer goods in Poland the process of
market valuation - imputation of value to the factors
of production - was partly "supplanted" by cost accountants. They determine costs which are then converted into
prices, subject to policy adjustments. Hence the question of paramount importance is the content of the cost
data determined according to the uniform standards of
costing officially adopted for the public sector of the
economy. The answer to this question constitutes the
subject of this chapter. It has been attempted as much
as possible to discuss the actual practices followed.
From the scant material available it is impossible to
judge the quantitative effect of cost distortions. One
can only infer the magnitude of malpractices from the
frequency and tone of complaints.
The accuracy of cost data depends on the cost concepts adopted, the allocation of costs between accounting periods, "process of matching costs with revenue,"
the classification and allocation of costs within an
accounting period to the cost segments responsible for
their incurrence, and on allocation of costs to the
products (objects of activity) to determine the cost
per unit of output. The usefulness of cost data so
determined is constrained by the scientific validity
of the cost concepts used, the limiting assumptions,
reliability of accounting tools, and consistency of
their application.

THE NATURE OF COSTS

In Polish accounting, as elsewhere, costs are usually
measured by the sacrifice actually made in terms of dis-
bursement of funds, exchange of assets, or incurrence of
liabilities. Only those costs which will cause ultimate-
ly a diminution of the firm's resources and are identifiable in terms of money are sanctioned by the accountant.[1]
The amount actually paid is felt to constitute the best
available objective evidence as to the economic significance of a factor acquired by the firm, and, therefore,
constitutes the basis for the accountant's recognition
of costs. Poland's leading accountants write:

> The principle of valuation of all assets according to
> actual cost has been adopted in socialist accounting.
> Consequently valuation is in accordance with the
> historical cost actually incurred (price actually
> paid).[2]

Costs pertain only to the explicit monetary sacrifices
made by the enterprise, with implicit costs disregarded.
The explicit costs depend on the quantities of factors
of production used and their respective prices. The
latter, in turn, depend on the content and validity
of the official cost directives and policy of price
determination.

Faithful to the Marxist version of the labor theory
of value, differential rent and interest on long term
capital are not collected and, therefore, do not constitute price determining costs. The labor value theory
attributes the entire product to the productivity of
labor rather than to the joint and complementary productivity of several production factors. The Marxists'
negation of the cost of capital, rent, depletion,[3] and
return to entrepreneurial ability is the basic flaw in
their cost concept. Even if accounting data would
provide no other distortion, the omission of interest,
absolute and differential rent, and other imputed costs
would result in misleading cost data for economic calculation.

Furthermore historical costs do not provide relevant
data for economic calculation at the micro and macro
levels. Data about opportunities forgone are necessary

for a proper evaluation of what a given product costs.
The cost of any factor of production engaged in the production of any commodity a is the maximum amount of product
that the factor will produce of any other commodity
b,c,...n.   The more valuable the alternative product
b,c,...n of a given factor of production, the greater
will be its cost in producing product a.   The cost of
getting something is the sacrifice of alternatives.[4]
The opportunity cost concept always refers to a comparison between the policy chosen and those rejected.   The
sacrificed alternatives are never registered in the
accountant's records since he deals with actual not
hypothetical events.   The appraisal of economic performance cannot be based only on what decisions were made,
but can only be evaluated in the light of alternative
choices which were rejected or not considered.   It is
the decision in the light of those alternatives that
constitutes the crucial cost consideration.

   The shortcomings of cost concepts are not the only
constraint imposed on cost accounting in Poland.   The
control function that cost accounting is to perform in
industry is another factor which greatly limits the
validity of cost accounting data for economic calculation.

OBJECTIVES OF COST ACCOUNTING

   To understand the limitations of cost accounting it
should be remembered that it was developed in a market
economy mainly as an aid to management in exercising the
control function: the measurement of conformity to management's decisions.   It is only fairly recently that
it has been recognized that cost accounting should guide
management in decision making.

   The two main objectives of cost accounting, the control
and decision making, are often conflicting ones as different cost concepts and tools of analysis are required
for these separate tasks.[5] Cost accounting as a tool of
control is more efficient if historical basis of valuation are adopted since historical cost is an objective
and easily ascertainable magnitude.   However, historical
cost used as a guide for decision making may be misleading as it does not provide guidance in the light of
present opportunities and does not reflect present
scarcity relationships.   Referring to a market economy

Mises made the following statement - which seems to apply to present day Poland as well:

> Attempts to establish cost accounts on an "impartial"
> basis are doomed to failure. Calculating costs is a
> mental tool of action, the purposive design to make
> the best of the available means for an improvement
> of future conditions. It is necessarily volitional
> not factual. In the hands of an indifferent umpire
> it changes its character entirely. The umpire does
> not look forward to the future. He looks backward
> to the dead past, and to rigid rules which are use-
> less for real life action.[6]

In Poland, as in other Soviet-type economies,[7]cost
accounting has not been redesigned to supply data for
decision making purposes. It is indeed a paradox and
irony of history that in a system where costs are the
very foundation for the valuation of commodities, the
control function still plays the leading role and the
same costs are used as "coefficients of economic choice".
It is unfortunate that Lenin in this often quoted
passage - "accounting and control are the chief things
necessary for the smooth and correct functioning of
the first phase of the communist society"[8] - exalted
the control function of accounting.

However, one should bear in mind that the control
function has different tasks to accomplish in Soviet-
type and market economies. In our system the foremost
purpose of control is to measure the efficiency of
factors of production employed within a firm. In Soviet-
type economies the problem of paramount importance is
the accountability to and the control of the firm by
the supervisory units. Still cost data are necessary
for internal purposes of the firm to control the individual segments. But the very design of cost accounting is directed towards external reporting to
superiors.[9]

Since the firm's management will be evaluated on the
basis of the reported data there is a built-in tendency
to manipulate reports to reflect favorably on the performance of the firm. Even if cost data would be conceptual-
ly sound and able to provide reliable information for
decision making, one would have to isolate actual data
from the reported ones.

Each socialist firm submits data to its superiors to guide them in economic calculations. It would seem that the validity of the concepts used in cost determination is of much greater importance in a socialist than in a capitalist economy. Any fallacy in concept or inaccuracy in practice have far reaching repercussions in the socialist economy since there is no market mechanism to correct them. The cumulative effect may contribute to a fallacious allocation of resources on a national scale.

To have cost data perform the control function over enterprises cost accounting procedures had to be standardized. Only a uniform system of cost computation, classification, and recording could afford the planners the comparability of cost data they required. The standardization process passed through several phases identifiable with the prevailing degree of centralization. At first the "uniform plan of accounts" was flexible and afforded a wide latitude for adaptation by particular enterprises. During the SYP period it was petrified by drawing largely on the Soviet experience. By 1960 it was again revised to conform to requirements of particular industries without impairing uniformity of accounting data.[10]

In accordance with regulation no. 21 of the chairman of the PC and the Minister of Finance, dated April 12, 1960, an Instruction Manual on the principles of cost calculation in industrial enterprises was issued. According to the Instruction Manual, the planning, recording, calculation, and analysis of costs should provide correct quantitative data indispensable for a) the documentation of the firm's tasks in the field of costs and cost reduction and efficient management of the enterprise; b) the determination of correct results of the enterprise's activity in total output and the production of particular products; c) the evaluation of tasks assigned to departments within the enterprise; and d) to facilitate decisions pertaining to price setting, evaluation of the efficiency of contemplated investments, evaluation of projected product mix changes, and introduction of new products as well as profitability of products intended for export.[11] It is doubtful that cost data determined by the accountant may serve all purposes outlined in the Instruction Manual. It is even doubtful that it may serve one or two of these purposes infallibly.

Notwithstanding the uniformity of accounting, there

are deviations in practice from the uniform standards.
Malpractices and fraud are common.[12] Therefore, all accounting records are subject to internal and external
audits. According to resolution No. 87 of the CM, accounting data should be internally controlled. The very limitation of such an audit is that it is internally performed
and does not preclude reporting of distorted figures
according to managerial preferences.[13] With reference to
external audits, a decree of the CM empowered the
Superior Control Organ to verify the firms' accounting
data. The Superior Control Organ performs the verification of transactions mainly reverting to accounting
records as evidence. If necessary the external auditor
is authorized to verify the physical existence of the
asset and confront witnesses.[14] Audits are only a
deterrent against fraudulent activities which are frequently aired in the press. Even efficient control can only
verify the conformity of accounting entries to the
accepted standards and regulations. If the conceptual
framework on which the regulations are based is erroneous, the audit will not disclose the shortcomings of
the accounting data.
    Now that we have indicated the objectives of cost
accounting our next step will be to examine how costs
are determined according to the accounting precepts.
This brings us to the examination of inter-temporal
allocations of expenditures as a first step in tracing
the determination of costs per unit of output. The perplexing problem of determining periodic consumption of
capital assets is the most important case in point.

                        FIXED ASSETS

    The allocation of costs to accounting periods is a
difficult and complex undertaking. The main task is to
correlate costs with the flow of revenue. Since many
resources render a flow of services over a period exceeding a single accounting period, a satisfactory basis
must be found to allocate such costs among accounting
periods. Furthermore, it is the period during which
resources render services that is relevant and not when
payment for such resources is made. Consequently it
becomes necessary to apportion costs and delete to
future accounting periods, or accrue costs for which

payments have not yet been made.[15]

Fixed assets are resources whose usefulness extends over several accounting periods, that are employed in the normal operations of the enterprise, and not intended for sale. Fixed assets are defined as any object of capital consumption which renders services over a period exceeding one year and whose cost at the time of acquisition exceeds 3,000 zl.[16] Fixed assets are acquired from funds specially designated for investment purposes. The rule of separating investment funds from working capital dominates Polish accounting practice.[17] An enterprise that has been endowed with fixed assets cannot dispose of them at its will.[18]

The basic characteristic of fixed assets is that the process of capital consumption is gradual. Fixed assets do not change their physical appearance impeding identification of the degree of capital consumption. Their economic usage is a function of both physical deterioration and technological and economic progress (obsolescence). The difficult task of valuation is complicated not only by the problem of determining at each stage the capital consumption deterioration due to technical wear and tear, but above all by the dynamic factors of economic growth.

In Polish practice fixed assets are classified as 1) engaged in the process of production, e.g., factory buildings, machinery used for production purposes, transportation equipment, tools, patterns, dies, and office furniture, 2) engaged in the process of distribution, e.g., warehouses, storage, etc., and 3) engaged in the so called unproductive processes, e.g., company sponsored housing and the furnishings of social and cultural establishments.[19] It is evident that this classification hinges on the Marxist definition of productive and unproductive labor.

A charge for capital consumption expressed as depreciation depends on a) the valuation of the capital asset, b) the judgment as to the resale or salvage value at the end of its useful life,[20] c) the judgment as to the future economic life of the asset, d) computation of the depreciation rate on a single asset or on a group of assets, e) the method to be used in allocating the cost of the asset to each of the accounting periods during its useful life.

In conformity with the basic concept of valuation adopted, fixed assets are valued at the original cost of

acquisition.[21] The object of accounting is to recognize,
record, and spread the original cost of the asset over
its economically useful life. To the accountant depreciation is a process of allocation not of valuation. The
fundamental limitations of this concept stem, in my view,
from the accountant's inability to grasp the opportunity
cost concept. The superiority of the replacement cost
method of valuation over the historical one is often
propounded by Polish theoretical accounting literature.
However, it is rejected on the grounds that it would
necessitate a constant revaluation of fixed assets,
creating unsurmountable difficulties in practice.[22]

In practice to obtain the cost of the capital asset,
its price is increased by the following charges: in
the case of construction costs incurred in connection
with the endowment by the state, measurement, surveying,
registration, and recording of land, costs incurred in
connection with securing blueprints and technical advice
in planning the building, the contract price (including
adjustments) due to the construction firm for materials,
labor, and overhead incurred in connection with demolishing the old building and construction of the new one,
and costs of equipment secured (e.g., elevators, etc.).
Faithful to the labor theory of value no cost is imputed
to land.[23] This results in serious distortions of investment calculations since as long as land has its alternative uses, its cost is the opportunity forgone. In
addition no interest is charged on investment funds
received from the state budget. The different costs of
capital gestation are not reflected in investment costs.
The cost of geological exploration is borne by the state
budget and excluded from the cost of the investment
project and the depreciation charges.

In case of machinery the recorded cost of equipment
is the price as per supplier's invoice. Since a great
number of machines are classified as non-typical goods,
their prices usually vary according to the magnitude of
their cost of production in the individual machine
building enterprises.[24] Machinery and equipment of the
same type may often be valued at different prices,
hampering the comparability of investment and production
costs. If the investment work was executed in the firm
the problem is whether it is to be valued at cost of
construction or cost plus a markup. The latter solution was adopted to compensate the firm for profit

forgone by engaging in the investment task and to obtain
comparable costs for projects regardless of their method
of execution.

But the comparability of costs of acquisition collapses
the moment it is realized that due to historical cost
basis of valuation the fixed asset account represents
heterogeneous amounts. Bien writes "in the accounting
of our enterprises the value of fixed assets was until
recently distorted as a result of divergent valuation."[25]
Historical costs cannot be analyzed unless they are
dated (constancy of the monetary unit cannot be reasonably assumed in the postwar Polish inflationary economy).
Both the value of the asset and depreciation thereon are
distorted if the price-cost ratio is not constant for
the period under consideration.

To offset the distorting effect the state undertook
revaluation of fixed assets on several occasions. In
the years 1946 to 1948 coefficients up to 50 for prewar currency were applied for revaluating fixed assets.
At the end of 1948 a general inventory of fixed assets
took place with a coefficient of 80 for prewar currency
applied. The 1956 price reform stipulated the necessity
for revaluating fixed assets. In the meantime, however,
increases in depreciation up to 100 per cent were authorized.[26] Full scale inventory taking and revaluation of
fixed assets was not accomplished before 1960. As a
result the value of fixed assets inventory in industry
increased by 153.8 per cent.[27] Since the inventory was
taken prior to the introduction of 1960 producers' prices
it was valued in old prices, hence understated. However,
when the new prices became effective the inventory of
fixed assets was again revalued.[28]

Notwithstanding the shortcomings of the successive
revaluations of fixed resources, the state policy of
underpricing producer goods, exclusion of rent and
interest, and the absence of a market mechanism distort
the valuation of fixed assets.

After value has been assigned to fixed assets the next
step is to distribute the value so assigned over the
economic life of the asset. It is well known that in
Soviet-type economies the economic life of the asset
is overstated.[29] The overstatement of the economic life
of the fixed assets was even admitted by B. Minc who
suggests "overamortization" as a protection against understatement of costs through depreciation.[30]

Faithful to the Stalinist dogma that no obsolescence takes place in a socialist economy, the depreciation charges were until recently greatly understated. Since Stalin became obsolete the concept of obsolescence gained respectability. In 1958 Fiszel wrote:

At long last we can abandon the false theory about the apparent non-existence of machine and equipment obsolescence in socialism, the theory which caused so much harm to our economy. It must be stated that as yet nothing has been accomplished for a practical elimination of these damages.[31]

In the post-Stalinist period in Poland, attempts were made to increase the charges for capital consumption. The upward revision of depreciation was accomplished, however, not through a reduction of the estimated economic life of the asset but essentially by upward revisions of the "value" assigned to the assets. An almost negligible allowance was made for the obsolescence factor at the time of setting the 1962 depreciation rates. In revising the rates a crucial consideration was the estimated availability of capital assets for replacement purposes from domestic production and imports. It may be inferred that depreciation charges were understated to discourage "early" replacements.

Considerable work was done on the revision of depreciation rates which went into effect on January 1, 1962. Although the absolute amount of the depreciation charge was increased the rates were decreased from the prewar rates applied in 1946 and basically in force until 1962.[32] "The increase in depreciation charges was due to the revaluation of fixed assets and not to the change in the rates."[33]

With the data at our disposal it is extremely difficult to ascertain to what extent the depreciation charges (resulting from the new "value" of fixed assets and the new rates) represent fairly the capital consumption, even granted the methodological assumptions underlying the valuation of fixed assets. Fedak, who participated in the revision of depreciation rates, points out that in comparison to the other countries of the Soviet bloc the economic life of fixed assets adopted in Poland is shorter, therefore the depreciation rate larger.[34] Unfortunately the frame of reference is not very

revealing in view of the prevailing understatement of
capital cost allowances in Soviet-type economies.

After value has been assigned to the fixed asset, its
economic life estimated, and the depreciation rate established, a decision must be made whether the rate should
be applied to a single asset or a group of assets. In
Poland depreciation is computed on a group or pool of
assets.[35] The application of undifferentiated rate of
depreciation on a group of assets is to a large extent
an inaccurate device; the groups are very broad and
incorporate a multitude of different assets of heterogeneous economic life. Depreciation so computed presupposes the time distribution of fixed assets. Any
deviation from the assumed condition would result in a
divergent life of specific assets from the postulated
average. Therefore, there are many assets still in
use but depreciated on the books.[36]

There was a considerable controversy in Polish accounting literature whether or not depreciation should
be charged against totally depreciated assets.[37]For the
purposes of comparable data it was resolved to adopt
the method of charging depreciation to fully amortized.
assets.[38]

The size of depreciation for a given year depends,
of course, on whether a uniform or differentiated rate
is used. The straight line method for allocating depreciation to an accounting period was generally adopted
in practice. The only exception to this rule is transportation equipment where depreciation is computed on
usage basis.[39] The straight line method assumes that
time and intensity of exploitation are identical in
each and every period. The major advantage of this
method is its simplicity. Its main drawback is its
disregard of the declining economic and technical
productivity taking place as the asset ages.

The "Depreciation Table" illustrated in the Concise
Accounting Encyclopedia indicates two columns for depreciation charges: total depreciation and the provision
for capital repairs. Capital repairs constitute approximately 30 per cent of the depreciation rate of buildings, 43 per cent of machines, and 63 per cent of transportation equipment.[40] In other words, if N is the
original cost of the pool of fixed assets, R the estimated cost of capital repairs which are to be incurred
to preserve the fixed asset pool for n years, the

annual depreciation rate A may be calculated as follows:

$$A = \frac{N + R}{n}$$

This procedure presupposes that capital repairs start
from the date the object is put into operation, not
when an actual repair is performed. In case of a new
object the distortion may be substantial. It does not
seem reasonable that earlier years should bear the charges
for capital repairs in later years. Financing capital
repairs from investment funds has still another repercus-
sion. It induces management to abuse capital goods at
their disposal. Current repairs (financed from working
capital) are often avoided and when faced with total
breakdown capital repairs are performed. A well in-
formed Polish economist writes:

> Enterprises avoid as much as possible the execution
> of current repairs pulling them up to the category
> of capital repairs. In such a manner they "economize"
> on costs and attain higher profitability. According
> to the existing regulations, capital repairs include
> all repairs whose cost exceeds 30 per cent of the
> value of the asset. In this connection everything
> is done to exceed this artificial limit. In some
> enterprises - as we are informed - good parts of
> machines are disassembled in order to attain the
> desired 30 per cent.[41]

To reduce costs enterprises avoid performing current
repairs until it is necessary to perform capital ones.
Since the latter are financed from depreciation which
anyway is a burden on costs such a procedure is often
considered advantageous from the firms' standpoint.[42]
   Theoretically losses incurred at the time of disposal
of fixed assets represent adjustments in view of understatement of depreciation in prior years. The Polish
accounting practice has adopted the method of adjusting
the state equity account rather than treating them as
adjustments of costs. It is deemed that the production
cost of the industrial firm must not include the cost
of retirement of fixed assets.[43]
   The depreciation charge for the year depends on the
conjecture as to the economic life of the asset, expen-

ditures on capital repairs, correct estimate of scrap
value, etc. It follows that the depreciation charge
would be correct if, and only if, the assumed conditions
in the estimates are fulfilled. If they are not, as is
usually the case, the fixed asset account should have an
undepreciated balance at the time of disposal or liquidation. Or, the asset completely depreciated on the books,
may perform an economically useful function. Hence the
opportunity cost will be larger than zero.

To combat waste of capital assets depreciation is
charged as cost whether or not the asset is used, regardless of the variability in its utilization.[44] But the
future usefulness of each fixed asset depends on its
present utilization. The depreciation charge against
output should vary with the rate of flow of output.
User cost is the difference in depreciation and maintenance of unused and used assets. In Poland the accountant does not employ user cost in analysis and his data
may be misleading when user cost becomes relevant.

SOME OTHER ASPECTS OF INTER-TEMPORAL ALLOCATIONS

Inter-temporal allocations are often garbled by recording in the following period costs incurred in the
previous accounting period. Wages paid for work performed and materials purchased in a given accounting
period may not be recorded until the following period.
In practice many assets rendering a flow of services
over several accounting periods are treated as current
costs (e.g., tools, materials, prepaid expenses, etc.).[45]
Since revenue and expenses are identified with specific
periods of time when the flow of services is consumed
(accrual basis) the problem of correlating costs with
accounting periods leaves room for judgment and ambigu-
ity. The most common inter-temporal allocations refer
to costs incurred in anticipation of new production
and replacement or repair of defective products.

Costs incurred in preparation for new production
include costs of designing new products, production
processes, and special tools, preparing production equipment, training cadres, and costs of initial production.
Costs of preparation for new production do not include
costs of research or other long range undertakings, costs
of equipment required for new production, costs of geol-

ogical explorations, and experiments conducted for the
improvement of production processes.[46] It was adopted
that only costs directly attributable to a given concrete
product may be allocated between accounting periods.
Since it is difficult to foresee the extent and duration
of new production it was decided in practice to spread
these costs over accounting periods up to three years
and in exceptional cases five years.[47]

When new products are manufactured, or new technological processes introduced difficulties usually arise
entailing an increase in costs. This condition is aggravated by additional costs incurred in preparation
for new production. This problem is particularly
acute in the machine building industry where 15 to 20
per cent of total costs are attributable to preparation
for new production. To alleviate this situation firms
are prompted to strike a balance between the cost and
profitability levels by allocating costs incurred in
preparation for new production at a later date.[48]

A perplexing problem of inter-temporal cost allocation is the exchange and repair of goods sold in one
accounting period, but returned for repairs or replacement in another. As a result of the mad rush at the
end of each accounting period to fulfil the plan, it has
been noticed that defective goods are shipped out usually
at the end of the period. Apart from economic waste,
such malpractices have a distorting effect by understating costs of a given period and overstating those
of the successive ones.

When costs have been distributed and correlated
with the accounting periods, the most important task is
to establish functional relationships between them and
the flow of production.

THE MEASURE OF THE FLOW OF ACTIVITY

In Polish practice the flow of activity is measured
in three different manners: 1) product sold during the
period, regardless when production has taken place;
this method does not produce distorting effects provided
that there are no substantial changes in the flow of
production and inventories, 2) production of completed
goods during the period, whether or not sold, regardless
when production has commenced as long as it was completed

during the given period; this method may be used if there
are no substantial changes from period to period in
inventories of work in process, and 3) production of
the period equal to the total product sold, plus or
minus changes in inventories of finished goods and goods
in process; this method is used when inventories of
finished goods and work in process are substantially
altered.[49]

When applying the third method the only logical
solution is to correlate the cost of production of the
period with the total production of that period. Its
application, however, involves the difficult but inevitable process of valuating inventories of goods still
in process and finished products. The main task is to
determine the degree of completion of work in process.
This problem opens avenues to cost manipulations well
known to our accountants but probably perfected in
Soviet-type economies.[50]

But the degree of completion of a given product is
not the only variable subject to distortion. Many goods
are non-typical hence left up to the ingenuity of management to value them. Since cost reduction is one of
the performance criteria, management has a vested
interest in reporting it.[51] By inflating the cost of
non-typical products, management accomplishes its
purpose since cost of goods available for sale in a
given period less value of inflated inventory of work
in process results in an apparently lower production
cost for that period. Moreover, inflated costs of non-
typical goods afford fulfilment of the production plan
to a higher degree and larger profits as previously
discussed.

Inventory of finished goods valued at transfer prices
is assumed to satisfy the conditions of trade (packing,
delivery, etc.),[52] whereas unsold finished merchandise
does not satisfy all these requirements. Hence value of
goods on hand is inflated and additional costs, for
which no provisions are made, have to be incurred in
future accounting periods.

Production is usually undertaken in accordance with
plan specifications and producers' preferences regardless
of buyers' needs. Hence there exists a problem of valuation of unsalable inventories. In such cases the transfer price is reduced passing through innumerable bureaucratic channels.[53] But the producer still values this

inventory at the regular transfer price. Hence inventory
is inflated and costs of the period unduly understated.

After allocation of costs to an accounting period and
establishment of the flow of activity unit costs could
be calculated where there is a simple production process.
However, in most industrial firms there are several
production processes and costs are accumulated in such
a manner as to be identifiable with cost centers.

COST CENTERS

Cost accounting focuses on departments as a frame of
reference for cost accumulation, control, and analysis.
Such a cost center is viewed as a unit of responsibility
engaged in the performance of a single or group of
closely related functions. At its head is a single
person accountable for quantitative and qualitative
performance of the tasks assigned by the plan. Polish
accounting practice distinguishes between producing
departments (called basic) and service departments
(called auxiliary).[54]

A producing department is one in which labor and
machine operations are performed directly upon any part
of the product. Such a department affords correlation
of costs with products because of its direct involve-
ment in production. Contrariwise auxiliary departments
only facilitate basic production by rendering services
to the producing departments. Auxiliary production has
been defined as "services rendered or products produced
indispensable for the normal activity of basic producing
departments (e.g., transport, repairs, maintenance, power,
etc.). Auxiliary production may also be engaged in the
manufacture of tools, patterns, dies, or packaging
materials used by the producing departments, or in any
other way connected with basic production."[55] Furthermore auxiliary departments produce spare parts for
maintenance of equipment and some semi-fabricates required by the basic production departments.[56] Firms
engage in the production of those materials to remedy
the unsatisfactory procurement situation. This results
in a waste of resources since a larger volume of output could be produced if these supplies could be secured
from firms specialized in their production.

Two types of costs may be distinguished: those trace-

able to a particular center and those that are not.
Our first step then will be to examine the former:
direct costs.

DIRECT COSTS

From the cost accountant's standpoint, the fundamental problem in cost classification is the distinction
between direct and indirect costs.[57] To qualify as
direct costs cost elements must be conveniently traceable and physically identifiable with the object of
costing. Those cost elements which do not satisfy the
above requirements are classified as indirect costs.
Those two kinds of costs are separated because of the
special problem involved in determining the amount of
indirect costs chargeable to a cost center. In practice
direct costs bear a direct relationship to the commodities produced to the extent that they can be controlled
by reference to the units used in measuring the activity
of the respective operations. Hence direct costs must
be specifically traceable and identifiable with a
particular object of costing without exercising judgment as to the soundness and validity of identification. Direct costs include mainly materials entering
directly into a product, use of some special tools,
patterns, or dies necessary for its manufacture, fuel
and power for technological processes, outside services
(e.g., the dying of textiles outside the mill), wages,
and social security surcharges for labor applied directly
to a product.[58]
Although some inaccuracies may, and indeed do, occur
in case of direct costs, they seem to be generally of
smaller consequence than the inaccuracies in allocating
overhead costs; therefore, the treatment of direct costs
will be brief.
The magnitude of direct costs attributable to an
object of costing depends on the physical quantity and
price of materials used, costs ascribed to the acquisition of materials, losses incurred in connection with
deterioration, shortage, or unsuitability of materials
on hand, and the cost of direct labor used.
Since one of the determinants of the magnitude of
direct costs is the physical quantity of materials used,
it should be noted that considerable waste of this

factor of production still persists in Poland. Table 18 illustrates the substantial variance between the actual use of materials and the predetermined norms. It is based on factual data for the production of a heat transformer in one of the machine building enterprises.

Table 18 - The Actual and Predetermined Use of Materials in the Production of a Heat Transformer

Material	Norm in kg.	Actual Use in kg.	Excess	
			Kilograms	Zlotys
a	582	1,010	428	2,214
b	782	1,750	968	3,020
c	534	1,280	746	1,678
d	–	2,880	2,880	7,762
e	2,088	2,700	612	1,983
f	4,480	4,800	320	6,093
g	2,520	8,510	5,990	113,810
h	265	580	315	847
i	180	1,000	820	2,214
Total	11,431	24,510	13,079	138,793

Source   J. Matuszewicz, Rachunek kosztow..., p.90

It is obvious that great discrepancies occur between the norms and the actual use of materials, the variances being larger in many cases than the predetermined norms. Needless to say, the deviations from the norm are a reliable indicator of performance if, and only if, the norm is a realistic frame of reference. Granted that the norm does not perform this function satisfactorily, it would still seem to be a fair inference that the magnitude of deviations provides some indication of waste.

As pointed out in the preceding chapter, it is the general policy of the state to have uniform prices for identical goods to facilitate control of performance. The aim is to eliminate the price variance so that the deviation between planned and actual cost should be attributable entirely to the efficiency variance, and to afford comparability of costs between enterprises. Nevertheless, in practice there are many deviations from uniform prices. The same materials may be bought

at different prices for the following reasons: 1) In
some cases price rebates are offered for large quantities
bought.   2) The price paid may depend on the time of
acquisition, e.g., to unload the stock of coal and alleviate winter transportation problems the state offers
reduced prices of coal purchased in summer.   3) Prices
vary with the source of supply, e.g., the prices of
producer goods purchased from cooperatives are generally higher since cooperatives calculate the prices of
their products on their individual production costs.
4) Prices of some goods are not regulated by the state,
but are established on the local markets.   This is
particularly true in case of some agricultural products
and handicrafts.   5) Prices of non-typical products
vary according to the source of supply.   6) Prices of
identical domestic and imported products may be unco-
ordinated.[59]

Since in practice prices of materials do vary, it
must be decided whether costs of materials should be
recorded and inventories valued at the actual price paid
or the price stipulated in the price catalog.   The
former solution was adopted in Poland.[60]   This solution seems to be correct although it impairs comparability of cost data within the enterprise and among enterprises due to difficulties in isolating price from
efficiency variances.   Even when the price paid is
uniform, the procurement costs may vary depending on
individual conditions (distance from the railroad
station, media used for transportation, etc.).
Theoretically these costs should be charged to the
entire purchase order and allocated between cost of
goods sold, finished goods inventories, and work in
process.   In practice they are usually treated as
costs of goods sold (excluded from inventories).[61]

It is common practice to charge current production
with losses on materials used for discontinued production and those incurred on shortages and deterioration
of materials.[62]   Moreover materials are ordered in
excessive quantities (as a precautionary measure against
their possible non-availability) and charged entirely as
costs of direct materials of a given period.[63]

The prevailing method for payment of wages in Poland
is a progressive piece-rate system based on established
norms stipulating the time necessary to accomplish a
given operation.   Payment based on the progressive piece-

rate system exceeds 50 per cent of total wages in industry. The general complaint is that the norms have not
been adequately established and in most cases are obsolete
Their average fulfilment amounts to 161 per cent and 22.5
per cent of piece rate workers overfulfil these norms
by over 200 per cent.[64] Generally wages in Poland are
not a good measure of workers' productivity but may be
considered as a very crude approximation of opportunity
cost.[65]

Although wages paid for overfulfilment of the established labor norms are included in direct labor costs,
manipulations and understatements of such costs often
occur. When new time cards are issued, the workers are
not required to return immediately those covering
previous operations.[66] It seems that the loose control
over labor performed enables the transfer of direct
labor costs from one period to another. Direct labor
costs are understated because remunerations paid to
workers on a time basis are usually treated as overhead,
notwithstanding the instructions received.[67] Furthermore payment in kind (e.g., housing, training, cultural
activities) are not included in direct labor costs. The
social security surcharge (15 per cent of basic wages)
is frequently treated in industry as overhead causing
an inappropriate distribution of this substantial
burden. This procedure is even sanctioned by the Instruction Manual which states that if inclusion of the social
security surcharges proves too time consuming these
surcharges should be treated as overhead.[68] Compensation
for overtime is excluded from direct labor costs causing
severe distortions. Direct labor costs are also substantially understated by the exclusion of premiums paid to
workers. The fallacy of this treatment is beyond dispute.
The premiums are part and parcel of the supply price of
labor. Labor productivity and the labor participation
rate would fall considerably if the incentive system
would be repealed without a simultaneous raise in basic
wages.

INDIRECT COSTS

Indirect costs are incurred in connection with the
maintenance of factors of production in general production readiness. The magnitude of these costs does not

depend entirely on the type or kind of production (e.g., whether the textile mill produces linen or cotton). Indirect costs cannot be conveniently charged to specific products, jobs, or departments. Since they are not easily traceable, they can be only allocated on some predetermined basis. This type of cost is generally encountered in industry as depreciation charges, costs of materials, supplies, wages, power, and services for the maintenance and repair of equipment. In order to simplify the process of recording, it is customary in practice to treat direct supplies, such as screws, paint, nails, additional wages for overtime, social security surcharges connected with direct wages, etc., as indirect costs.

Direct costs lend themselves to precise measurement and may have a high degree of accuracy. But allocated costs must be viewed with suspicion since cost derived from allocations is no more reliable than the assumptions underlying the allocation. For control purposes, performance may be appraised by comparing direct costs incurred with predetermined norms for the volume actually produced and the variances analyzed. There is an inherent limitation in such analysis. The underlying assumption is the constancy of direct costs per unit of output which may or may not be true pending on the shape of the cost curve. Should the cost function not be linear the frame of reference is misleading. But indirect costs may be appraised only in relation to the general size of production and the causes of variances are not easily traceable.

Polish practice distinguishes two broad categories of indirect costs: departmental costs and enterprise overhead. Departmental costs are further classified into mainenance costs and departmental overhead. Maintenance costs are defined as "the part of departmental costs connected with the propulsion, maintenance, and depreciation of the producing departments' equipment. They include repairs and maintenance of machines, propulsion fuel and power, as well as depreciation."[69] Departmental overhead constitutes "the part of departmental costs connected with the organization, administration, and general servicing of production departments. These costs cover salaries of management, office personnel and general help, materials, fuel and power for general purposes (e.g., heating, lighting, cleaning), depreciation, repairs, and maintenance of buildings and equip-

ment for the general purposes of the department."[70] Therefore, indirect department costs are those costs that can
be conveniently traced to an individual department but
cannot suitably be identified with specific units of
production within the department.

By the process of elimination, those costs that do
not vary, within a range, with the flow of production
and cannot be conveniently traced to cost segments are
treated as enterprise overhead. Costs included in enterprise overhead are separated because they are incurred
jointly for the benefit of several cost centers and cannot be traced in part or in full unequivocally to any
particular one. In practice they are allocated to the
individual cost centers according to assumed relationships.

Enterprise overhead costs are subdivided into costs
of administration and general production costs. Costs
of administration mainly include salaries of managerial
staff, official trips and removal grants, office expenses,
interest on bank loans, taxes, and contributions for
financing the activity of the association. General
production costs include expenses for general facilities,
such as warehouses, laboratories, design offices,
safety measures, research, and security guards.[71]

It is common practice in Poland to treat all cost
elements not easily traceable as enterprise overhead
costs.[72] The problem is of considerable importance
since these costs represent a large proportion of total
costs and are subject to arbitrary rules of allocation.

Cost determination is further complicated by the
necessity of allocating costs of auxiliary departments
before costs attributable to any producing department
can be fully reckoned.

COSTS OF AUXILIARY DEPARTMENTS

The problem confronting the accountant is first
to determine costs of auxiliary departments and secondly the extent to which those services were used and
their equitable allocation to the users. To establish
the costs of an auxiliary department its total costs
are accumulated on the auxiliary production account.
However, in each of the following cases the elements of
total costs vary, hence their determination differs.

In the first case the auxiliary department services

the production departments and/or the general activity
of the enterprise, but does not benefit from services
rendered by others. The calculation of the costs of
services rendered by this department involves costs accumulated in this department without resorting to allocation.

In the second case the auxiliary department benefits
from services rendered by other auxiliary departments
but services only basic production departments and/or
the general activity of the enterprise. Total costs of
this department can only be determined after they have
been increased by the costs of services rendered by
others. Here the total cost of the firm's entire auxiliary production is not altered but the actual costs of
individual auxiliary departments which benefited from
services rendered by others are affected.

In the third case the auxiliary department not only
services other auxiliary departments but also benefits
from their services.   The costs of these departments
can be considered complete only when the respective
departments' costs are determined by solving simultaneous
equations since the costs of the individual auxiliary
departments are interdependent. In practice a simplified
assumption is often made that no auxiliary department
renders services to other auxiliary departments.[73] Such
a simplification usually distorts cost data. The
quantitative effect of such deformation depends on the
magnitude of the reciprocal services rendered by the
auxiliary departments, and on the significance of auxiliary production in total costs.

There are no hard and fast rules for allocating auxiliary department costs. The entire problem suffers from
the necessity of postulating arbitrary relationships,
designed to charge the production departments on some
equitable basis for services rendered by the auxiliary
departments. Allocation is usually made on **physical**
units registering consumption. However, it is sometimes very difficult to obtain data relevant to consumption by each department and obstacles may be encountered in determining a basis for the apportionment
of costs. There are usually many possibilites of
applying different bases of apportionment and the results
may diverge materially pending on the method adopted.

But the process of allocation is still not concluded.
All indirect costs which could not be traced to any

departments have been accumulated in the enterprise
overhead account and according to accounting precepts
they must be allocated to producing departments.[74]

ALLOCATION OF ENTERPRISE OVERHEAD

The use of a common denominator for allocating enterprise overhead to departments is questionable.[75]
There is no such magnitude to which all components of
overhead would be proportionate. But in practice these
common denominators are used. The fundamental problem
in selecting a common denominator is to relate overhead
to its most causal factor. The relationships are often
spurious ones: they are assumed where none exist. The
result is a distortion of cost data.

In Polish practice the most common basis for allocating
enterprise overhead is the cost added by the respective
producing departments, defined as direct labor plus
departmental costs. The reason offered for adopting such
a basis is to eliminate the distorting influence of
fluctuations in direct materials.[76]

The enterprise overhead account is composed mostly of
fixed costs. The question whether or not enterprise
overhead costs should be allocated at all to the production of the period, or treated as fixed (period) costs
(non transferable through the medium of inventory to
other accounting periods) is an open one. In my opinion
the allocation distorts cost data by assuming causal
relationships that do not exist or by introducing relationships for which there are no logical foundations.[77]
The enterprise overhead account is substantially inflated
by the very nature of the costing procedures. Hence
its allocation is of paramount importance, both on the
grounds of costing methodology and the magnitude of
the distorting quantitative effect on production costs.

After direct costs have been identified with the
flow of production (related products grouped for calculation purposes), the problem is to allocate the
departmental costs, including a share of enterprise overhead and auxiliary production costs to the production
in question.

ALLOCATION OF DEPARTMENTAL COSTS

The almost universal basis for allocating departmental
costs to output is direct labor cost.[78] Such a procedure
implies that departmental costs are proportionate to
direct labor. This is seldom the case.[79] Direct labor
cost is the product of direct labor time and the respective hourly wages of a unit of labor. Even assuming a
single causal relationship between labor time and departmental costs, whenever a change occurs in the relative
wage structure the labor cost changes entailing a
variation in the allocation of departmental costs. In
addition whenever a worker in a higher wage bracket
performs a given job instead of a worker in a lower
one, production is charged with a larger share of
departmental costs. Such a distortion is common whenever workers with different abilities to overfulfil the
work norms and increase their wages perform similar
operations on individual products. Moreover, what is
the relationship between costs of operating machinery
and direct labor costs?

Infrequently industrial enterprises with highly
mechanized production processes employ labor time or
machine time as bases for allocating departmental costs.
Such a procedure necessitates an appropriate recording
of this time for each individual production order. Since
these data are usually unreliable direct labor costs are
used. Occasionally in industries where costs are
composed mainly of direct materials the latter are used
as a basis for allocating departmental costs.[80] Even
though the total sum of departmental costs does not
vary, different results are obtained pending on the
accepted basis for allocating departmental costs.

The reason behind the allocation of departmental
costs to production is to accumulate all costs attributable to a given flow of production. The objective is to
determine cost per unit of output separately for each
product.

COSTING OF INDIVIDUAL PRODUCTS

The average total cost per unit of output is, of course,
calculated by dividing total cost by quantity. The nu-

merator, determined so far, is not the only result of
estimates, conjectures, and arbitrary assumptions. The
divisor also has to be reduced to a common denominator.
The difficult problem of weighting heterogeneous production, converting unfinished output to complete units,
and allocating joint cost must be resolved before unit
costs can be computed.

The simplest case would be the determination of unit
costs of homogeneous production without work in process.
The denominator would then be represented by the volume
of output. But there are few industrial enterprises
where at the beginning and end of the period there is
no work in process. Hence the notion of equivalent
units is used as a technique for converting unfinished
output in terms of entire units.

The total cost of the product is equal to the cost
assigned to work in process at the end of the last
period a, plus costs incurred during the period b.
This cost ($a + b$) has to be allocated to the production
completed during the period x and the work still in
process at the end of the period y. Hence:

$$a + b = x + y$$

In this equation the left side was determined and numerical values have been assigned to a and b, whereas
the right side holds two unknowns, whose determination
belongs to the tasks of cost accounting. Four methods
are used in Poland in solving this problem.[81]

1) To solve this equation precomputed costs are assigned to completed units. Total cost of finished output is determined by multiplying completed production
by the planned unit cost. Hence the cost of work in
processes is determined:

$$a + b - x = y$$

The major drawback of this solution is that the work in
process bears the total burden of the variance between
actual and planned costs. Consequently the variances
are transferred entirely to the next accounting period,
resulting in distorted cost data from period to period.
This device is often used to report non-existent reductions in costs for a given period. The quantitative
effect of the distortion depends on the magnitude and

variation of the work in process and the deviation of
actual costs from precomputed ones.

2) In this method cost of work in process at the end
of the period is established on the basis of a rough
estimate of consumption of materials and labor calculated
at planned cost. Hence:

$$x = a + b - y$$

The major drawback here is that finished output bears
the total burden of the variances between actual and
planned costs, whereas work in process is very crudely
calculated at planned costs. The firm may not be interested in reporting substantial cost reductions in a
particular period, because it will be expected to do
better in the next planned period. This method permits
cost savings to be stored for the following period and
the enterprise protects itself against increased cost
reduction targets.

3) Here an attempt is made to reduce the quantity of
work in process to a common denominator with the completed production by converting unfinished units to equivalent
production units. The right hand side of the equation
is reduced to common units to be used as a divisor for
costs accumulated on the left hand side of the equation.
Therefore, the separation of costs into those pertaining
to finished and unfinished production may be determined
proportionately to the magnitudes which served to
bring them to a common denominator. Assuming M represents
cost of direct materials per unit of output, T transformation cost (direct labor plus social security,
departmental overhead, and enterprise overhead surcharges),
A the cost of the work in process at the end of the
previous period, Y cost of the work in process at the
end of the current period, Q volume of total output
reduced to a common denominator, ATC average unit cost
may be calculated as follows:

$$ATC = M + \frac{A + T - Y}{Q}$$

The major drawback of this otherwise sound method is the
difficulty of establishing the degree of completion of
products,[82] and therefore verifying the reliability of
costing inventories. Inventories of work in process

differ from each other not only in physical quantities but also in value terms, having absorbed different amounts of costs of materials and processing. The inflation of inventories is one of the most difficult manipulations to detect.[83]

4) Costs of completed and unfinished production may be determined according to precomputed unit costs and the variances allocated to completed and work in process production with actual costs as the end result. This method would give reliable results if the variances are laboriously distributed among the completed and work in process production as well as among the products if multiple production is manufactured. If an enterprise produces similar products but differing in sizes, forms, weights, from the same raw materials, by applying the same technological operations, then production volume may still be aggregated.

Different products are reduced to the same common denominator with the assistance of coefficients forming a divisor for the sum of cost elements attributable to the cost of the heterogeneous volume of production. Thereafter by multiplying the cost of the predetermined unit of allocation by the coefficient established for individual products, the unit cost of those products is obtained.[84]

Should an enterprise manufacture in the same production process different products from different raw materials, then the cost of materials for individual products is determined directly and the following formula applied:

$$ATC = M + \frac{A + T - Y}{Q_w} \cdot X_r$$

where the same use of terms is made as in the formula on page 153 and Q_w represents the sum of the weighted volume of production and r the coefficient for the conversion of a specific product (included in the weighting).

Coefficients employed in conversion are relative weights enabling the reduction of different products to a common denominator. The coefficients may be weight, thickness, capacity, time involved in processing, content of the "active substance" (e.g., iron in iron ore), planned costs, or prices of individual products, and index of quality. The conflicting objective of this type of allocation is the choice of such coefficients

which would correctly reflect mutual relationships of
costs for similar products and that could be easily
computed. When the cost of raw materials dominates in
total cost, coefficients are established on magnitudes
characterizing the use of this material, weight, thickness, surface, etc. Disregard of the cost of processing
is not considered a grave error in such cases. If materials used in production are priced differently the
coefficient may be established on the relation between
the prices of materials. In industries where costs of
processing prevail coefficients are established on
labor inputs.

In most industries employing this method costs of
materials and processing must be considered when establishing the coefficients. Since the determination of a
physical unit, proportional to the accruement of total
costs, is usually difficult, the coefficients are established on the basis of planned allocation based on norms,
determined separately for individual related products.
The accuracy of costs so computed depends on the reliability of the coefficients used. In case of non-typical
goods or new production line, the coefficients will be
set to suit the objectives of management.

The calculation of cost per unit of output is further
complicated by the phenomenon of joint costs which,
according to the accountant, must somehow be allocated
to the resulting products.

ALLOCATION OF JOINT COSTS

In many industries one product cannot be produced
without the simultaneous emergence of others creating
the phenomenon of joint costs. Joint costs are those
incurred prior to the point at which separately identifiable products issue from the same production process.
For purely technical reasons joint costs cannot be traced
directly and specifically to units produced. A separate
determination of costs before the point of separation is
impossible without the "reaching of an estimate resting
on theoretical assumptions of necessarily disputable
validity."[85] The arbitrary assignments of joint costs
by accountants are useless as far as cost determination
for pricing and decision making purposes is concerned.

The physical quantity basis is the most commonly used

for allocating joint costs. The costs of the joint
products are assumed to be equiproportionate to volume,
regardless of the type of product produced.[86] Products
are assumed to receive the same benefits from joint
costs incurred and, consequently, are charged proportionately with common costs, measured and apportioned in
terms of some common physical unit of measure.

For computation purposes technical indicators are
expressed as "equivalent units". For example, in the
manufacture of coke joint products emerge: coke measured
in tons, coal tar, and sulphate of ammonia measured in
cubic meters. In the case of coke costs are allocated
on the basis of theoretical yields extracted from a ton
of coal. The "equivalence coefficients" are based on
the simplified assumption that joint products emerge
in fixed proportions, which may or may not be true.
Each change in the structure of the composite units of
allocation (the weight of individual products in the
unit) results in distinct changes in respective unit
costs.

Notwithstanding the general objection to the advisability of allocating joint costs, the physical allocation basis distorts cost data. This method presupposes
from the start that production of each good is equally
remunerative. However, the use of physical indexes for
allocating common costs may have no bearing on the
revenue yielding ability of the various products
reduced to a common denominator by this method.

The second basis for allocating common costs, recognized in Polish literature, is the relative sales
value.[87] The contention here is that joint costs should
be allocated according to the relative sales revenue
generating ability of the respective products. But
prices should be based - according to the policy of
the state - on costs, and not costs on the final prices
of the product. The circular reasoning follows from
the inherent limitation of the labor theory of value.
Although this method is discussed as an alternative,
it is used only in exceptional cases, e.g.,the meat
industry. In this industry a lack of any objective
magnitude forces the use of prices as determining
coefficients for allocating costs.

In joint production processes some products result
incidentally from the manufacture of main products. By-
products generate only insignificant returns when com-

pared with those of main products. The costing problem
is how to treat the excess of revenue from by-products
less the expenses attributable to their processing after
separation from main products.   The excess of revenue
over cost is treated in practice as a reduction of common costs of joint production. This treatment does not
seem to be satisfactory. Joint production costs should
be reduced by an amount equal to the opportunity cost
of the by-product at the time of its separation from
the main product. Further processing of the by-product
has no bearing on joint costs.

It seems that no allocation technique of joint costs
should be used for the costing of products for pricing
and decision making purposes. Individual costs of
joint products (prior to the split-off point) cannot be
ascertained, since discontinuance of one product, by the
very nature of the technological processes, results in
forgoing the other joint product. The incremental costs
after the split-off point are the relevant ones. Joint
costs are common to all output and are not separately
traceable. Hence they cannot be logically allocated
to the quantities of individual products. By splitting
common costs between individual products the accountants
are introducing assumptions for which there are no
logical foundations and are reaching cost data of
questionable validity.

The problem of determining unit cost, to repeat, rests
on designating the total cost of the object of costing
and reducing the production volume to a common denominator. By following this procedure the accountant obtains
an average unit cost. In case of a heterogeneous volume
of production predetermined indexes are used to reduce
this figure to completed individual products. It follows
from the previous discussions that cost so determined is
not a definite, objective, dependable, and reliable
figure. Further details of the mechanics of accounting
may be spared without altering the major conclusions
drawn. The results cannot be better than the questionable validity of methods used in cost determination.

So far we have discussed the computation of "actual"
costs of production - or what might be more appropriately
termed as an attempt by the accountant to indicate what
it actually costs the firm to produce a unit of output.
Since planned cost is to a large extent a derivative of
actual cost and should be the basis for pricing, we shall

now examine briefly the methods presently used for the
determination of planned costs and whether the latter
perform their functions satisfactorily.

PLANNED COSTS

In Polish cost accounting practice planned costs
serve a dual purpose: they are the basis for price calculation and a tool of control over the firm or departmental activity measuring performance in terms of
variances. It seems that neither of the purposes are
served adequately. This deficiency stems from the manner
of determining both planned and actual costs, hence the
divergence cannot be a satisfactory measure of performance.[88]
Essentially the process of establishing planned costs
varies pending on whether they are established for
typical or non-typical production. Basically planned
costs of typical production are established by project-
ing actual costs of a preceding period, subject to
modification - the technical-economic plan of the firm
may require an over-all cost reduction by a given per
cent.[89] According to the Instruction Manual the following is the method for calculating the percentage index
of cost reduction W :

$$W = 100\%(P_1-P_2)/P_1$$

where P_1 refers to the preceding year's cost to output
ratio and P_2 the proposed cost to output ratio for the
current year. Cost P is calculated as follows:

$$P = 100\% \ K/C$$

where in a given period K and C refer respectively to
cost and value of output reckoned in factory prices.
The simple reduction of actual cost and its projection
in this state into the future as the planned cost, does
not necessarily indicate that the inherent error has
been eradicated. Given production cost as a basis for
pricing, planned costs cannot perform this function
satisfactorily due the inherent limitation of cost data
obtained.[90]
Non-typical production is priced on the basis of

planned unit cost. In such cases the usual procedure is
to find a typical product previously produced with a
degree of similarity to the non-typical one. This decision being left to the discretion of management is subject to considerable arbitrariness and manipulations.
It is apparent that management is prone to find the
higher cost products. Even in case of typical production with a high degree of similarity these costs may
be distorted. If in a previous period the product was
produced together with others the actual cost so obtained
is only an average one. Should the product mix have been
altered the average cost might have been different.

The next step is to modify the cost of the chosen
typical item according to the specifications for the
non-typical product received from the design offices.
The main problem here is that such specifications are
usually received too late to serve their purpose. The
departments responsible for the planned calculations
(accounting, design office, or planning office) are
unable to fulfil their duties because of a lack of
specifications. They hold up calculations to accumulate actual production data. As a rule planned
costs are calculated after the product has been assembled
and the actual calculation made. How can planned calculations so determined serve as a yardstick for
comparing performance?[91]

For control purposes planned cost does not fulfil
any useful function as far as the appraisal of performance is concerned. To evaluate performance one needs a
yardstick for comparing what costs "ought to be" with
what "they are". If the guidepost is not a meaningful
yardstick and the actually accumulated cost is an
arbitrarily determined figure, tracing the divergence
between those two becomes of little consequence. It
should be noted that Polish literature discusses the
use of standard costs, the so called normative costs,
and considerable research is conducted on their application. However, this method has not yet found widespread
acceptance in practice.[92]

Even if both planned and actual costs are calculated
properly the accounting concept of costs is limited by
lack of distinction between fixed and variable costs and
the assumption that average cost per unit is constant,
regardless of the volume of production. When planned
total cost has been obtained, it is then compared with

the total actual cost of production and conclusions are
drawn as to the variance between those two magnitudes.
Since costs are usually a function of production volume
and do depend on the shape of the cost curve, the
results obtained are based, it seems, on non-comparable
data.

A comparison of actual total costs of production with
planned total costs of production indicates whether the
planned cost reduction has been attained, but there is
no way of telling whether this is a result of real cost
reduction, accounting manipulation, or manifestation
of technological or economic forces. It cannot be distinguished whether the apparent cost reduction resulted
from a positive improvement in the production processes
and saving of resources (parameters of managerial action)
or from a movement along a "U" shaped curve (increasing
returns section). In the latter case management simply
reaps the fruits of the law of variable proportions.
If, on the other hand, the enterprise does not fulfil
the cost reduction plan it would be impossible to dis-
tinguish whether this was caused by inefficiency, poor
organization, waste, or the fact that production was
pushed along the rising section of the "U" shaped cost
curve. Management would then become the victim of the
manifestation of the law of diminishing returns applied
to industry - which is considered a fallacious dogma of
"bourgeois" economics.[93]

It seems that both from the point of view of control
and for decision making purposes classification of costs
into direct and indirect is not of fundamental importance.
If costs are to serve planners as indices of economic
choice and control of performance, they should be classified and measured according to their behavior in relation to the rate of change in the flow of production.[94]
The cost accountant's preoccupation with allocating
indirect costs obliterates the real issue, namely, that
some of the allocated indirect costs include elements of
cost which are functionally related and grow with the
volume of production, although they are not traceable
to particular cost segments. In the accountant's
language indirect costs mean both fixed and variable
expenditures. The emphasis is placed on the assignment
and allocation of costs incurred at a specific volume of
activity to various cost segments, whereas the variability
of costs with volume seems to be of primary importance

for decision making and control. The variable elements
of cost include both direct costs plus that portion of
indirect costs which changes with the rate of production.
The wisdom of allocating fixed costs to cost segments
is highly questionable.

From the point of view of output planning, the relevant
costs are those that must be incurred if additional output is to be produced. The alteration of cost, which
can be imputed in deciding whether or not to take a
certain action, is intended to reduce to quantitative
terms the relationship of cause and effect between the
changing volume of production and the variations in cost.
To decide which possible output volume to choose the
planners must know the different costs at which alternative volumes could be produced. The important element
is the calculation of costs at <u>various</u> levels of output.
The planners need a cost function at various output
levels which is really a schedule of different possible
choices. To concentrate on one single cost-output
relationship instead of a range of alternative ones
seems a fallacy from the analytical standpoint. The
planners need to know the rate of change of variable
costs (marginal costs), since rational economic decisions
can be made only at the margin. Professor Schultz,
evaluating the investigations into cost in a capitalist
economy, stated:

> These investigations, if they are to have theoretical
> as well as practical significance, should have for
> their object the determination of the production
> functions, the cost functions, and the supply
> functions of the important commodities and industries...
> the accountants who compile those records of cost and
> output and use them do not speak the language of the
> economists and do not, as a rule, recognize the import-
> ance for their work of such a tool as the marginal
> cost curve. They compute the average cost of produc-
> tion of an article to six or more decimals and then
> attempt to convince the entrepreneur - against his
> better judgement - that he ought not to sell it at a
> price which does not cover this average cost. The
> result of this practice has been not only uneconomical
> adjustment of output to cost and price but also the
> prevention of the establishment of such accounting
> and production records as would yield the economists'

marginal cost functions and production functions.
Without a knowledge of these functions, much of our
economic theory... must remain vague and indefinite.[95]

The objection raised by Schultz is very much to the
point in case of a centrally planned economy, where the
accountant not only works with obsolete tools but results
of his work are the guideposts for economic calculations.
Since in the Polish economy, according to the policy of
the state, prices are to be based on costs and the market
mechanism does not mitigate errors committed by the planners, it seems that if the advice given by Schultz was
heeded the danger of misallocation of resources would
be weakened.

4

FINANCE OF
THE STATE-OWNED
ENTERPRISE

Our previous discussion centered on prices of
producer goods, or, viewed from a financial angle, the
revenue accruing to the firm, and the mechanics
involved in calculating cost of production. The firm's
economic and financial activity is a function, _ceteris
paribus_, of both sales revenue and cost of production.
Hence our attention will focus on the excess of sales
revenue over the attributable costs, or what in Polish
practice is called financial accumulation. The main
constituents of accumulation are turnover tax and
profit. After the former has been exacted by the
state profit remains to be apportioned between its
main claimants: the state and the enterprise. Our
inquiry will then focus on the apportionment of the
firm's share of profit among the firm's various funds.

It is evident that the choice of material is dictated
by the need of a background for the discussion of the
role of profit as an economic incentive in the next
chapter.[1]

ACCUMULATION

The firm's monetary or financial accumulation is
defined as the excess of sales revenue over costs of
production in the given enterprise.[2] Accumulation is a
function of the value of products sold and their costs.
Its calculation does not take into account the value of
goods produced but not sold. One may speak of financial
accumulation only when a positive difference results
from sales revenue less costs. Negative accumulation
is a fallacious notion as no funds are accumulated
which could be apportioned between their various claim-

ants.[3]

Accumulation may pertain to the sale of a unit of product, total sales of a given product, total sales of the various assortments produced by a given enterprise, branch of industry, or the entire economy. The firm's total financial results may result in accumulation even when it suffers losses on some of its products. This may be so as long as the total of positive results of the difference between receipts and costs exceeds the total of negative results.[4]

An enterprise's accumulation is determined by the differences between transfer prices and costs of the various assortments produced multiplied by the volume of output of the particular assortments minus the losses incurred per unit of output on deficit assortments. Since the rate and absolute amount of accumulation usually vary on different assortments, total accumulation will be a function of the share of assortments producing the highest accumulation in total accumulation. To increase its accumulation the enterprise may choose either to reduce costs or produce more assortments rendering higher accumulation, since generally price variation is not its action parameter. Cost reduction is usually a difficult road towards improvement of financial results. Hence manipulation of assortments is the prevailing method chosen by enterprises for improving results.[5]

In Polish literature considerable space is devoted and much ink used to prove the divergence between the theoretical notion of surplus product and financial accumulation. This discussion does not seem to be overly relevant and for our purposes it may be disposed off briefly. Firstly financial accumulation, as previously mentioned, refers to products sold, whereas surplus product should encompass all products produced. Secondly according to the Marxist theory of value social security surcharges, interest on bank loans, penalties, etc. constitute distribution of the surplus product, whereas in financial practice they constitute costs. Hence theoretically they are part of accumulation although in practice they are reckoned as costs.[6] Notwithstanding other perplexing problems of the accounting definition of costs, there is the divergence between prices and "value". On a macro level the total prices are deemed to be equal to total value produced. But in a particular

branch of industry, on a micro level, financial accumulation may differ from surplus value if for policy reasons
prices are not set proportionately to costs.[7] Kierczynski
suggested that a distinction should be drawn between
financial accumulation and "accounting accumulation".
The former should represent accumulation strictly according to Marxist theory, the latter the accounting
result including the distortion brought about by accounting practices.[8] However, for reasons of financial
expediency, this suggestion was not implemented.
Financial accumulation has remained as previously defined
in this chapter, or what Kierczynski would call "accounting accumulation".

An issue of much greater importance seems to be
whether accumulation is realized on transfers of producer goods from one socialized enterprise to another, or
whether it has a purely formal character and is realized
exclusively on goods which reach the final consumer.[9]
It is questionable whether one may speak of accumulation realized on transfers between socialized firms
since such transfers are not evidence that the goods
will receive the consumers' seal of approval at the
postulated terms. Even when goods are produced according to plan, without manipulation of assortments, it
does not follow that the plan reflects the consumers'
needs and wants.[10] Indeed mounting stocks of unsold
goods seem to be prima-facie evidence of this statement.[11]

It seems also that essentially the division of
accumulation into profit and turnover tax is rather
arbitrary and does not indicate the relative performance and contribution of an enterprise or industry to
national income.[12] Turnover tax is usually calculated
as the difference between the transfer and factory
prices. Assuming sound calculation of costs, only the
difference between the transfer price and the planned
average cost of production, if, and only if, the former
is a derivative of the retail price that "balances"
supply and demand, indicates the contribution to output
of a given product. But profit is a purely calculatory
magnitude. In many cases the state regulates the rate
of profit by varying the turnover tax, hence, in a sense,
profit is the resultant of, ceteris paribus, the difference between accumulation and turnover tax. The
latter constitutes an expedient and convenient device

for extracting part of the accumulation produced and
simultaneously regulating the rate of profit. But the
resulting profit is not a <u>stricto sensu</u> economic category since neither its level, structure, nor relative
rate on different products are determined and verified
by economic mechanisms but are set arbitrarily at the
central level.

TURNOVER TAX

Since the state is reluctant to alter transfer prices,
turnover tax is used as a convenient method for syphon-
ing off a larger share of accumulation. In a sense
this reduces the price from the standpoint of the
producers' net receipts.[13] Theoretically turnover tax
should ensure equal profitability of all products with
the exception of those where transfer prices do not
cover factory prices and where the differential rate
of profit is intentional. When transfer prices are
lower than factory prices the firms receive subsidies
per unit of planned output. This subsidy and the turnover tax are means of regulating profitability.[14]
The reported rate of profit diverges greatly from
industry to industry as indicated in Table 19. Out of
total accumulation of 67,058.9 million zl. 55,400
million were collected by the state in the form of
turnover tax, 49,835.4 million of which were collected
from the sale of consumer goods, with the food industry
quantitatively the largest source of turnover tax. The
fuel industry shows a loss of 8,814 million zl. which
is mainly due to deficits in the coal industry amounting
to 8,889.5 million zl.[15] Notwithstanding the losses
incurred by the fuel industry, the compulsory turnover
tax on some items (especially products of the petroleum
industry) had to be paid.
From the standpoint of financial expediency and
control turnover tax is a most convenient device since
it is levied on sales revenue at source irrespective of
accumulation in the given enterprise. With the present
state of accounting records the state would have difficulties in collecting its revenue if turnover tax
were based on individually computed accumulation in
every enterprise.[16] It is expedient to collect revenue
in the form of turnover tax since usually the tax is

Table 19 - <u>Accumulation, Turnover Tax, and Profit in Industry in 1958</u>

Industries	Value of Production sold	Costs	Accumulation	Profit to Costs	Profit or Loss	Budget Differences	Turnover Tax
			In Millions of Zlotys (rounded)				
Socialized industry	379922	312864	67059	4	12902	-1243	55400
Producer goods	145468	137867	7601	1	1631	406	5565
Consumer goods	234454	174997	59457	6	11271	-1649	49835
Electric power	5348	4739	609	13	609	-	-
Fuels	19607	27239	-7632	-32	8814	93	1090
Ferrous metallurgy	22926	21853	1072	5	1070	-	2
Non-ferrous "	6044	6045	-1	-1	31	-	29
Metals and machine building	60432	51727	8706	13	6643	23	2039
Chemical	16426	14112	2313	9	1260	73	980
Rubber	3800	2773	1026	12	332	-5	700
Minerals and synthetics	431	399	33	8	32	-	1
Building materials	10453	8979	1474	6	530	221	723
Glass, china, pottery	2602	2141	461	15	317	2	143
Lumber	18355	16645	1709	8	1320	1	388
Paper	6439	5059	1381	8	402	-	978
Textile	48313	32160	16153	8	2639	45	13469
Clothing	14085	13046	1039	7	961	34	43
Leather, fur, shoes	14378	9729	4649	8	828	48	3772
Fats and cosmetics	3159	2018	1140	19	385	4	752
Food	121611	89728	31883	4	3968	-1785	29699
Others	5523	4470	1042	18	451	-	591

<u>Source</u> H. Krol, <u>Ekon.</u> No.4, 1960, p.893

deducted by the bank the moment payment of invoices is
made.[17]

From the standpoint of the state budget turnover tax
constitutes a regular and by far the most important
source of income which can be relatively easily forecast,
whereas accumulation is a rather   elusive magnitude.[18]
It is also claimed that leaving a substantial part of
accumulation at the temporary disposal of enterprises
would endanger the state revenue. The enterprises might
utilize those funds for financing unplanned ventures
that may prove undesirable from the standpoint of the
central planner. In addition the enterprises might
freeze the funds and deprive the state budget from its
revenue.[19] Once again the control function overshadows
any other uses that may be obtained from economic
instruments.

Not invoking the controversial issue whether indirect
or income taxes are more efficient,[20] it seems that the
Soviet-type economies have reverted mainly to the
former to extract purchasing power from consumers
because of expediency and also because the consumer
is not always aware of the burden he bears.

The share to turnover tax in total accumulation from
1956 to 1961 is illustrated in Table 20. It is evident

Table 20 - <u>1956-61 Accumulation and Turnover Tax</u>

Year	In billions of zlotys		Percentage of turnover tax in accu- mulation
	Accu- mulation	Turnover tax	
1956	78.4	48.5	61.5
1957	103.3	60.8	58.9
1958	89.8	58.3	64.9
1960	104.0	58.6	56.3
1961	116.1	57.5	49.5

Sources   RS 1959, p.376, RS 1962, p.431 and T. Kierczynski
          Istota akumulacji..., p.174

that this share is very high, ranging from 49.5 to 64.9
per cent. The fluctuations are mainly caused by increases in transfer prices of producer goods augmenting
the relative share of total profit in accumulation and

reducing the relative share of turnover tax.

But turnover tax is only the state's preliminary claim
to the substantial part of accumulation that it extracts.[21]
After extraction of turnover tax profit becomes a known
quantity, whereas the preliminary division of accumulation between turnover tax and profit is based on planned
quantities and is made irrespective of the actual size
of accumulation. Should the transfer prices remain unchanged, ceteris paribus, actual accumulation may differ
from planned depending on a) discrepancies between
actual individual costs and planned average costs, and
b) divergence between the actual and planned volume
and product mix. Hence actual accumulation differs
substantially from planned, and profit becomes another
important source of state revenue.

PROFIT AND SUBSIDIES

Whereas during the early 1950's enterprises were
financed largely from state grants and subsidies, it
is recognized at present that profit performs a significant role as a source of decentralized funds "whose
existence is an indispensable condition for real
financial independence of enterprises and their material
interest in the results of their activity... Profit
should be used first of all as an economic incentive
stimulating the enterprise to the most economical and
effective management of resources at its disposal."[22]

The notion that only a fraction of profit remains
at the disposal of the enterprise is still condoned.
Nevertheless the partial curtailment of free central
disposal of all funds is still somewhat deplored.[23]
The profit left with the enterprise is a function of,
ceteris paribus, transfer prices, costs, volume and
assortment of sales, and proportion of its division
among the claimants: the state budget, the association,
and the enterprise. For example, the 1961 division
of profit in the state-owned key industries is shown
in Table 21. In view of the enterprises' insignificant
share in profits, extraction of its substantial part
by the state becomes an important regulatory device
controlling the firms' activity.[24]

The general consensus is that the creation of decentralized funds from profit has an over-all beneficial

Table 21 - <u>1961 Division of Profit of Key Industry</u>

Ministries	In Millions of Zlotys		
	State	Associa-tion	Firm
Construction and Building Materials	1,327.8	29.0	618.0
Mining and Electric Power	2,813.7	67.3	1,643.5
Chemical Industry	3,381.2	139.0	656.7
Heavy Industry	16,210.7	212.6	1,719.4
Forestry and Lumber	1,252.2	2.9	218.0
Light Industry	4,067.3	146.4	709.8
Food Industry	3,640.7	51.0	433.6

<u>Source</u>   <u>RS 1962</u>, p. 432

effect, inducing attainment of higher accumulation resulting in an increase in production and cost reduction.[25] It is believed that the enterprise will use its own resources more effectively to improve financial results: the source of premiums and development funds.[26] Although the benefits of decentralized decisions are usually recognized their scope is restricted because of the mistrust that the central planner demonstrates towards such decisions.[27]

Availability of decentralized financial resources cannot be equated with freedom to allocate them unhampered by central directives and bank control over the specific destination of funds.[28] It seems that without such freedom of disposal decentralized funds could hardly be expected to perform their role.

After determining the part of profit remaining in the firm we should turn to its apportionment among the various decentralized funds. Due to the existence of deficit enterprises, subsidies serve partly to finance decentralized funds and a digression to examine the methods of subsidizing is in order.

The three prevailing methods for settling the losses of enterprises are: settlement prices, subsidies per unit of output, and subsidies covering planned losses.

Although the system of settlement prices cannot be equated with subsidies per se, it nevertheless assures

high cost enterprises recovery of costs plus a margin
of profit.   Since settlement prices were discussed in
Chapter II, here we shall be concerned only with their
financial aspect.

Settlement prices are based on the individual planned costs plus a margin of profit.   They are established
by the responsible ministers who may delegate their
authority in this respect to the directors of associations.   The introduction of settlement prices necessitates establishment of a price equalizing account in
associations.   The positive or negative differences
between settlement and factory prices are paid into or
received from this account.[29]   When this system is
used the associations are responsible for the financial
results of their firms.   Since the factory price is not
always a weighted arithmetical average the equalizing
account may often show accumulation of funds or shortages.   Although the association may cover shortages
from the ministry's reserve fund, it is interested in
assigning production tasks so as to achieve a surplus
in its equalizing account to supplement decentralized
funds.

The problem of goods where factory exceed transfer
prices is solved in a different manner pending on the
conditions prevailing in a given branch of industry.
The tendency is, however, to pay subsidies per unit
of output.   Such subsidies are allotted to the firm
by the association from funds provided by the budget.[30]
In a sense such subsidies increase the sales revenue
per unit of output.   The total amount of subsidy
depends on the absolute amount granted per unit of
output times the volume of sales irrespective of the
individual cost of production.   Until 1961 the subsidy
was restricted to the planned volume of output.   Since
then the rule was relaxed only for priority goods and
raw materials.   The intent of the system is not to
hamper cost reduction.[31]   As the subsidy per unit of
output remains unaltered it allows the enterprise to
benefit from cost reduction and bear the burden of
cost increase.   It is nothing but a device for augmenting the deficit transfer price to the level of the
factory price.

The third method presently in use refers to subsidizing planned losses of enterprises rather than
units of output.   This method is used when the plan-

ned flow of deficit output exceeds the profitable one.
A firm's planned losses are covered by the association
from profits of its other enterprises. When planned
losses exceed profits on the association's level a
subsidy may be obtained from the ministry's reserve
fund.[32] With this system the state expects to stimulate
improvement in financial results and restrict subsidies
to the planned level. The rigidity of the budget in
this respect is superimposed on the association, requiring it to meet above plan subsidies from its reserve
fund. This should prompt the association to exercise
control so as to keep losses to a minimum. However,
it seems that the associations in concert with firms
have an added incentive to overstate losses at the time
of planning to allow for a safety margin.

In the past the state covered any actual losses. The
obvious shortcoming was a lack of stimulus for firms to
manage their affairs economically. Later this method
was revised where the subsidy was to cover planned
losses only. Since it was immediately discovered by
firms that the easiest way to improve their financial
position was to reduce the volume of output the manner
of subsidizing has been changed. At present the
subsidy is increased with overfulfilment and decreased
with underfulfilment of the production plan.[33]

However, in firms where various assortments of different degrees of profitability or deficit are produced
a simple solution to decrease losses is to expand production of the profitable assortments, contracting that
of deficit ones.[34] Reduction of planned losses being
treated as an improvement of results further prods
manipulation of assortments within the bounds of possibility. This type of management's response would
be beneficial if profit would be an economic category
transmitting signals from the market with prices and
costs reflecting current economic scarcities. It is
in this connection that the fallacy of the pricing
system is once again apparent. The state sets prices
allowing the lowest rate of profit, and often deficit
prices, on necessities. Hence quantity demanded is
increased as a result of relatively low prices and
supply decreased by the producers.

Since enterprises avoid deficit production whenever possible this type of subsidy is not widely applied
at present.[35] It is used in enterprises where all assort-

ments produced are deficit ones and no opportunity to
manipulate assortments exists. In iron and copper
mining this subsidy is used since both of the above conditions are met. For the sake of expediency this system
is also used where many assortments are produced and
it may be difficult to administer subsidies per unit of
output.[36]

We may now return to the part of profit distributed
among the firm's decentralized funds. However, before
such distribution may be made profit is subject to
verification conducted by the "verification commission."
The commission audits the financial statements and
pronounces its opinion on the determination and division
of profit.[37]

The commission is charged with eliminating from
profit amounts which are deemed "unearned" by the firm.
The eliminated part of profit is exacted from the firm.[38]
The two types of results to be eliminated are those
independent of the enterprise's activity, unforseen
by the plan, resulting from changes in prices, tariffs,
wage, tax, interest, and depreciation rates, etc., and
the unwarranted results obtained through production of
inferior quality output, failure to comply with maintenance requirements and safety measures, underestimation of depreciation charges, and violation of regulations regarding prices, cost calculations, and the
assortment plan.[39]

The aim of the correction is that only profits
"earned by the enterprise" should constitute the source
and basis for decentralized funds. In practice, however, such an elimination, although quantitatively quite
sizable,[40] is of questionable validity especially in
case of manipulations in the product mix. The effect
of such manipulations on "the determination of financial
results is complex and difficult to detect and consequently the results of the verification undertaken are
largely problematic."[41] Moreover, should the verification be effective it would cause an artificial equaliza-
tion of profitability on all assortments. This may
prove to be an unfortunate solution nullifying the
influence of prices on the product mix. For example,
an increase in prices of export goods may not induce
the enterprises to produce them, although the increase
might have been designed to promote production of this
assortment.[42]

The verification of profit and ensuing reduction of
the contribution to the enterprise fund weakens the
influence of the enterprise fund, since the employees
comprehend neither the reasons for this verification nor
its mechanics.[43]

THE ENTERPRISE FUND

A part of the adjusted profit is contributed to the
enterprise fund.[44] "The institution of the enterprise
fund was called into being with the aim of creating a
financial inducement for employees of socialist enterprises to increase profits through increased production and reduced costs."[45] This fund is designated for
employee's premiums, construction of housing, and
social and cultural activities. For example, in
1962 74.2 per cent of the enterprise fund went for
premiums, 22.3 per cent for housing, and 3.5 per cent
for social and cultural benefits.[46] Not more than
75 per cent of this fund may be paid out as premiums
to employees. The sum of premiums is limited to 8.5
per cent of the planned annual wage fund, placing a
ceiling on wage payments.[47]

The postulate of relating the employee's material
benefits to the improvement of the enterprise's
financial results necessitated finding a satisfactory
basis for such a relation. Overfulfilment of the
profit plan, used as a basis for a number of years,
did not withstand the test. It prompted enterprises
to lower the targets of the financial plan to overfulfil
them by a larger margin.[48]

In 1957 Brus and Kalecki advanced rather similar
proposals. In their view additional compensation should
be correlated not to the difference between reported
and planned profits for the same period but rather
to the increase of reported profit of the current
year over the previous year or years. In this manner,
the employees would be interested in improving production methods and reducing costs without exerting pressure to have their financial plans lowered since the
formation of the enterprise fund would not hinge on
overfulfilment of the financial plan. Kalecki proposed
that the basis for the computation should be the average rate of increase of profit for the last three years.[49]

Brus suggested that it would be advisable to set two
rates. The basic contribution should be made as long
as the enterprise realized during the current year a
profit equal to last year's. An additional contribution should be made if the current year's actual profit
exceeds profit realized during the past year.[50]

Broadly speaking the proposal advanced by Brus was
adopted. The new law differentiated the computation of
the basic and additional contributions to the enterprise
fund. The condition for earning the basic contribution,
amounting to 2 per cent of the planned yearly regular
wage fund, is to plan and fulfil in a given year a
profit at least equal to the profit attained last year.
In order to afford comparable basis last year's results
and assortments are recomputed in the current year's
prices and assortments. This affords a comparison of
results brought up to some sort of common denominator.[51]
Thus the contributions to the enterprise fund depend
not only on profit but also on the production plan.

If the enterprise plans and fulfils a profit
exceeding last year's profit, then for every per cent
of improvement in profit it is entitled to an additional
contribution to its enterprise fund equal to a given
percentage of the wage fund. This is based on a table
showing on one side the percentage increases in profits
and on the other side the percentages of the wage fund
which may be added to the basic contribution to the
enterprise fund.[52] However, if the enterprise earns a
higher actual profit than planned, it is not entitled to
benefit from a higher rate. In such cases it is entitled
only to a higher absolute amount of the contribution and
the rate is applied to a larger amount of profit. An enterprise that does not fulfil its profit plan, but whose
profit attained exceeds last year's , is entitled to the
basic contribution to the fund as well as to an additional one according to the prescribed table. But a
penalty is imposed requiring it to use a lower rate
than it otherwise would had the actual profit attained
been incorporated in the plan instead of the larger
amount. If the actual profit falls below last year's
the basic contribution to the fund is decreased. Should
profit deteriorate by over 20 per cent the enterprise
is deprived of the enterprise fund.[53]

In many branches of industry (machine building, clothing, textile, etc.) due to the variability in output

composition, comparison of profits from year to year
cannot be employed in determining the contributions to
the enterprise fund. Firms of such industries are
entitled to the basic contribution from 2 to 4 per cent
of the wage fund if they have fulfilled during the
current year their profit plan and to additional
contributions if they have overfulfilled this plan.[54]

In subsidized enterprises the contributions to the
enterprise fund - drawn from subsidies - increase in
accordance with a reduction of the planned losses to
create material incentives for improvement of performance.[55]

The formation of the enterprise fund in light industry is a particular case and as such merits more detailed
examination. In 1956 the contributions to the enterprise
fund in this industry -- as in others -- were based on
the fulfilment of the profit plan. But turnover tax is
mainly levied on the products of this industry. In
many cases the profit earned on a given good is not
proportional to the turnover tax levied on it. During
1956 the enterprises of light industry tended to
produce goods of a high rate of profit at the expense
of those of a lower rate of profit but perhaps higher
rate of accumulation. This was immediately felt in
the form of diminishing income to the state budget.
As a result in 1957 the enterprise fund in light industry was made dependent on the accumulation instead of
the profit plan.[56] At the present time the conditions
for contributions to this fund in light industry are
similar to those in other industries with the exception
that in this case profit is replaced by accumulation.
This is one of the reasons why it is often stated
that the enterprise fund is related to accumulation
rather than profit, since in all other industries
profit and accumulation are almost equivalent.[57]

One of the greatest disadvantages of relating the
enterprise fund to the fulfilment of the accumulation
plan is that there exist much more potent stimuli for
the firm to manipulate assortments. The rate of accumulation being generally larger and differing to a
greater extent than the rate of profit, any manipulation of the assortment plan becomes more advantageous
to the enterprise. It was visualized that the enterprise fund based on accumulation would induce firms
to adapt their production structure to that of demand.[58]

It seems, however, that such a stand is unjustified.
As it has been pointed out previously, higher accumulation on a good is usually intended to discourage consumption. But producers will react by expanding production. Thus the interests of the producer and the planner are driven in opposite directions.

To give weight to specific conditions of a particular
industry or firm the indices and adjustments on which
the contributions to the enterprise fund are based have
become more and more numerous. This complicates the
formation of this fund, rendering its computation un-
intelligible to most workers and to many managers. It
reduces the stimulating effects which the premiums
may have had on the employees since the latter cannot
visualize clearly to what extent their individual performance has contributed to the allotment of a premium.
At the present time the working force regards the
enterprise fund as a distribution of a given sum allotted by superiors and not as a direct result of
performance.[59]

The functioning of the enterprise fund is in many
respects similar to that of the premium system for
management and to spare a needless repetition it might
be best to refer the reader to the appraisal of the
premium system in the next chapter.

It seems that the deficiencies and contradictions
in the enterprise fund system are not by all means the
only factors which have caused it to lose its hold as
a real and active economic incentive. Since 1958 the
enterprise fund has been on the decline both as an
absolute amount and in relation to the regular wage
fund.[60] Undoubtedly its meaning and significance as
an economic incentive declined in proportion to its
size.[61] Because contributions to the enterprise fund
become increasingly difficult to attain due to contradictions in the system, the enterprise fund declines.
But because it declines it ceases to be a potent
incentive.[62] Not only do statistics substantiate the
diminution of this fund but statements such as the
following are common:

> Several weeks ago I witnessed a passionate out-
> burst made by a director of one of the most
> prominent enterprises in the machine building
> industry at a Party meeting - "Tell me clearly

what is the future of the enterprise fund, because
with us, and as I gather in other related enterprises,
the enterprise fund diminishes from year to year and
becomes more difficult to attain."[63]

The concept of the enterprise fund as a powerful incentive stimulating the firm to attain the best possible
financial results hinges on prices concurring with the
incentive system to identify the interests of the firm
with those of the central planner. Since these conditions are not met, profit as the only yardstick to
measure performance has faltered. To ensure the firms'
conformity to the central planner's will other performance indices had to be added. Surely this does not
reflect negatively on profit as a measure of performance
- as some Polish economists would like to think[64]-
but rather on the price system in existence.
     After contribution from profit to the enterprise
fund has been made another enterprise's claim to the
balance of profit is the contribution to the development fund.

                    THE DEVELOPMENT FUND

     The development fund is intended to supplement
working capital and partly finance the firm's decentralized investments.[65] It was created to perform a dual
function: a) to enhance the firm's role and self-
interest in financing its development, and b) to induce
management to strive for a more rational employment of
funds.[66] But the incentive function of this fund does
not seem to be as effective as intended since generally
employees are more interested in immediate benefits
rather than those that may materialize in the future.[67]
     Contributions from profit to this fund are made
during the year on the basis of periodic financial
statements. The final contribution is determined on
the verified profit decreased by the contribution to
the enterprise fund.[68] A declining scale for the
contributions to the development fund has been imposed
in case of profit plan overfulfilment to counteract the
practice of concealing capacity and potential cost
reduction at the planning stage.[69] As in the case of
the enterprise fund, the regressive rates used have

little influence on the planning of a taut profit plan
since the penalty for underfulfilling the plan is of
greater consequence.

The development fund was instituted in 1958 and its
size and apportionment during the consecutive years are
illustrated in Table 22. Although the contributions to

Table 22 - The Development Fund from 1958 to 1961

Years	Total	In millions of zlotys		
		Applications for		
		Invest ments	Working capital	Other purposes
1958	3759.5	1881.6	1828.2	49.7
1959	6063.7	2688.8	3358.9	16.0
1960	7677.9	2938.1	4524.1	215.7
1961	9097.1	4642.3	4203.4	251.4

Source   RS 1962, p.433

the fund show an increasing trend until 1960 the share
of decentralized investment funds was declining in
favor of financing working capital. The data for 1961
indicate an increase in the share of decentralized
investment funds. There seem to be two reasons for
this change: As a result of the 1960 price reform costs
of investments increased considerably. Although the
disbursements for investments augmented from 1960 to
1961 by about 58 per cent, the actual increase of
decentralized investments amounted only to 16 per cent.
The primary reason for the relative increase of the
part allotted to investments is the state's desire to
curtail accumulation of inventories of materials by
applying funds to investments rather than working
capital.

The deficiencies of prices and costs complicate
the relation of the development fund to profit. It
is generally recognized in Polish literature and
practice that the contributions to the development fund
must depend both on profit and on the enterprise's
"needs" judged by the association. Should the development fund be based exclusively on profit the highly
profitable enterprises would apply their excessive
funds to less productive ventures. On the other hand,

deficit or less profitable firms would be deprived of
the opportunity to supplement their working capital and
undertake investments which may render relatively higher results.[70]

The size of the development fund is set annually
leaving the firm in the dark as to its future magnitude.
Management is induced to exhaust the fund every year
so as not to have the amount allotted curtailed in the
future and not to have the current year's fund reduced
by the balance left over from last year.[71] Under the
system presently in operation the associations have
essentially complete freedom in allotting the development funds to enterprises. This jeopardizes the fund's
incentive function. In practice the size of the fund
does not depend primarily on the size of profit.[72]
It has been transformed into a fund granted by the
association and not one obtained by the enterprise
through better performance. Summarizing his findings
on the role of the development fund Szyrocki concluded:

> For purposes of self-financing, exploitation of the
> development fund may be defined by the following
> adjectives: small, non-uniform, diminishing, with
> the amount left at the disposal of enterprises
> centrally determined, often accidental, and stripped
> of an incentive function to promote development of
> the enterprise.[73]

After contributions from profit have been made to
the firm's two decentralized funds the remainder is
apportioned between the association and the state budget.

FURTHER CLAIMS ON PROFIT

Another deduction from profit, before the residue
is finally confiscated by the state budget, is the
firm's contribution to the association's reserve fund.
This is conducted according to predetermined rates at
the beginning of the year.

In principle the reserve fund is a common fund for
all enterprises under the jurisdiction of the given
association. The main sources of the fund are profits
contributed by the enterprises, budget subsidies, part
of the excess of working capital confiscated by the

association from the firms at the beginning of the
fiscal year, excess of financial resources in the
association after settlement with the budget, etc.[74]
Generally the size of the reserve fund amounts to 10
per cent of the sum of contributions by enterprises to
their development funds.[75]

The reserve fund is used to supplement the firms'
working capital, settlements with the budget, financing
above plan production, and repayment of bank loans incurred by the enterprises but guaranteed by the association if the former are unable to meet payments.[76]

The state budget confiscates any residue of profit
after the foregoing contributions have been made.
Strictly speaking the state extracts all profits but
those that it considers advisable to leave at the enterprises' disposal. Generally from 1958 to 1962
profits increased considerably. However, the sums
allowed for decentralized funds were not augmented
proportionately but the state claimed a larger share.[77]
The enterprises must be financially restrained so that
they should not undertake ventures which may undermine
the central plan. In principle the state allows the
firms just enough financial resources to permit them
to fulfil faithfully the will of the planner. Should
their financial resources exceed the minimum required
the enterprises may be tempted to deviate from the
line of conduct mapped out for them. The central
planner faces the constant danger that the enterprises
may frustrate his will if allowed a greater financial
freedom. At the same time bitter experience has taught
him that performance must be tied with economic
incentives. The monetary incentive must be of sufficient
quantitative effect to exert a perceptible influence on
managerial behavior. But since prices are fallaciously
determined, directives reinforce the incentives to
ensure the desired effect. Experience indicated that
if enterprises are not allowed a certain freedom in
disposing with some investment funds and working
capital they become mere **automatons executing commands**
from above. Any initiative which is not suppressed
is channeled to circumvent the central planner's will.

WORKING CAPITAL

Working capital consists of factors engaged in all
phases of the enterprise's activity performing a complete cycle in a given period. According to Marxist
terminology working capital is usually understood to
constitute the sum of the "liquid means of production"
(fluessiges Kapital) and circulating capital. Consequently in the literature of Soviet-type economies,
working capital is classified as liquid production
capital and means in the process of circulation. Raw
materials, goods in process, and prepaid expenses are
elements of liquid production capital. The means in
the process of circulation consist of finished goods,
semi-fabricates intended for sale, means of payment,
receivables, etc. Regardless of the controversy
surrounding the classification in literature,[78] the
Polish financial system adopted the following classi-
ification of the enterprise's working capital:
1) inventory of materials: direct materials and
supplies, fuel, packaging, spare parts, tools, and
dies, 2) production inventories: goods in process,
semi-fabricates, finished goods, 3) inventories of
contracted production in industrial enterprises or
merchandise in trade centrals, 4) means of payment,
5) receivables, and 6) prepaid expenses.[79]

Of course, the percentage share of elements of
working capital differs among industries and their
firms.[80] Similarly the velocity of turnover of working
capital varies. The velocity is generally measured
in terms of a ratio between the value of goods sold
in a given period to the average stock of working
capital. Ratios are computed for the various elements
of working capital taking the relevant variables as
a basis.[81]

The problem of financing an enterprise's needs
for working capital may be equated with allowing the
enterprise sufficient funds tô cover requirements but
not to exceed them so as to prevent accumulation of
stocks and possible deviations from the prescribed
line of conduct.[82] Computations of turnover of working
capital and its components are required mainly for
establishing a firm's planned requirements for working
capital. The purpose of planning these indispensable

requirements during a given period is to impel the firm
to speed up the turnover employing a minimum of working
capital per unit of product and to enable the planner to
exercise financial control over the enterprise through
the banking system. An enterprise's requirements for
working capital vary from period to period pending
mainly on the size, composition, and operating conditions of production. There is a certain minimum, no
doubt difficult to quantify, indispensable for carrying
out operations efficiently. Such a minimum, below
which the level of available working capital cannot
fall, is the permanent requirement for working capital
per time period and the notion behind the normative of
working capital.[83]

During any period under consideration usually a
larger amount than the normative of working capital will
be necessary. However, in Poland it is officially conceived that only the normative should be financed from
the firm's own funds consisting of the original grant
of the state and supplemented with profits realized by
the enterprise during the course of its activity.[84]
Working capital requirements exceeding the normative
should be financed from other sources.[85] To classify
a component of working capital in the normative two
conditions must be satisfied: the enterprise must
indicate a permanent planned requirement for that
particular component per time period and it must be
deemed advisable to finance it from the enterprise's
own funds. In most cases enterprises' receivables are
not elements of the normative. Their collection is
usually accomplished through bank transfers with the
time of settlement usually determined by the buyer.[86]
Receivables are usually financed through bank loans.
Since enterprises are not required to keep reserves
on their bank accounts,[87] in most cases bank balances
are excluded from the normative and the enterprise's
original endowment.[88]

Current activity may be financed from other funds
than working capital. We refer to the so-called
permanent liabilities: the enterprise's commitments to
its employees in the form of wages paid bi-monthly,
accrued liabilities to suppliers and the state for turnover tax, and others arising at the time of sale but
paid at certain regulated intervals. When considering
the outside funds which always remain at the firm's

disposal, permanent liabilites are calculated at their
minimum level, individually for each liability incurred,
and their sum total is the permanent liability of the
enterprise.[89] Due to the existence of permanent liabilities, the enterprises' requirements for working capital
are lower than the normatives. The actual amount of the
working capital fund is equal to the normative of working
capital less the amount of permanent liabilities.

Prior to 1958 the regulations guaranteed every state-
owned enterprise _in toto_ coverage of requirements through
the enterprise's own working capital fund. At the end
of the fiscal year each enterprise was required to account
for its working capital. When it exceeded the assigned
normative the excess was automatically confiscated by
the state.[90] Conversely, when capital fell below the
granted normative the enterprise had to demand formally
a subsidy from its superiors. The only obstacle in
the way of getting an additional grant was the necessity
of justifying the request, and perhaps offering suggestior
for improving the financial position. Generally, the
supervisors did not control whether the suggested improvements were implemented. The central boards established normatives for the individual components of working
capital in a purely mechanical and bureaucratic fashion
without due weight given to a firm's particular conditions and requirements.[91] Requests and establishment
of exceedingly high normatives were common.[92] The excess
of financial funds promoted accumulation of materials
in short supply, aggravating the difficult situation in
the producers' "market".

The state covered every misuse of working capital,
in a sense, contributing to waste. Hence criticisms
were voiced against the automatism of the system. The
general premises of Fiszel's contention regarding
interest charges inspired suggestions proposing that
enterprises be deprived of their own working capital,
replacing it entirely by bank loans. The argument was
advanced that in such a manner the enterprises would
employ working capital economically applying the
commercial principle.[93]

Fedorowicz's criticism of this solution is that
it would curtail the firms' prerogatives due to bank
intrusion as the financing unit. But as was rightly
pointed out by Jaskiewicz the enterprises' financial
autonomy does not depend on the source of the funds

but the latitude allowed in disposing of them.   Therefore, such a solution would be quite in line with decentralization if, and only if, bank loans could be
obtained without the bank designating the purposes to
which the loans are to be applied.   This would call for
revamping the banking system which is still founded on
extending credits for specific expenditures, in a sense
empowering the bank to take production decisions for the
enterprise.[94]

The discussions prompted the setting up of a number
of experimental enterprises to evaluate practically the
feasibility and efficiency of the proposals.   Unfortunately due to the reversal of the decentralization trend,
and because of the short time allowed for experimenting,
the experiments died of a natural death.

Nevertheless the present Polish financial system
has benefited from some of the reforms.   The enterprise
is now allowed to establish its own normatives of working capital within the limit of the total working
capital normative imposed by the authorities.   In computing the normatives the firm must adhere to the
regulations issued by the Minister of Finance.   All
socialized enterprises must establish normatives of
working capital but not all identical components are
included in the normatives.   The scope of normatives
is the widest in the construction industry covering all
elements of working capital including receivables and
deposits in the enterprise's bank account.   In trade
enterprises normatives cover means of payment in transfer but not receivables or deposits in the firm's bank
account.   But in all cases normatives must be set for
inventories and prepaid expenses.[95]

Although the enterprise's own funds should cover the
normative, in most cases they are supplemented by
"normative bank loans".[96]   On March 12, 1963 the Minister
of Finance decreed that 25 to 30 per cent of the normative will henceforth be covered by bank loans in almost all industrial enterprises.[97] The bank exercises
considerable control over the normatives established
by enterprises. "Theoretically the magnitude of the
normatives is established by the enterprise.   Actually
this requires coming to terms with the bank which, in
turn, leads to 'haggling' where the advantages are
doubtless on the side of the financial institution."[98]
Should the bank find fault with the normatives, it may

either refuse or reduce the loan.[99] It seems that this
interference has both positive and negative aspects.
Since enterprises must supplement their working capital
with bank loans subject to interest charges it stands to
reason that they will be more careful in disposing with
these funds. But this amounts only to a half measure
in view of the low interest rates, usually 4 per cent,[100]
and the part of the normative subject to loans. Moreover the bank's constant intrusion into the establishment of normatives is hardly conducive to responsible
management and seems to be a substitution of one form of
intrusion from central organs by another.

Oftentimes the value of inventories will exceed the
normative and additional funds will be required for
financing operations. The enterprises may then seek
above normative loans and loans for components not
covered by the normative.[101] Before credit is extended
the bank must be assured of repayment and that the
credit sought meets with plan requirements. By exercising strict control and sanctions the bank is empowered to counteract or mitigate irregular activities. But:

> In practice these instruments are used very reluctant-
> ly and mostly only towards small enterprises... On
> the scale of the national economy refusal of credits
> during the first half of 1964 amounted only to .002
> per cent of the value of working capital in all
> enterprises.[102]

The central planner encounters many difficulties in
his efforts at controlling working capital. In particular "enterprises often exploit irrationally their
own funds by investing them in economically unsound
inventories from the point of view of the national
economy."[103] Hoarding of materials persists with
several methods of financing used by enterprises.[104]
Firstly pressure is exerted on the association for the
largest possible total normative and then the highest
possible normative is set for inventories of materials.
Although this situation has been mitigated by empowering the bank to control normatives, the latter is not
especially effective mainly because of its lack of
knowledge of an enterprise's internal requirements.
The delay of payments to suppliers, acquiring additional working capital to finance above normative require-

ments, is a "strongly developed and universal process."[105]
Thus the bank loses control over the firm's activity.
It finances indirectly what it refuses to finance
directly since the activity is then financed by suppliers who, in turn seek credit from the bank.

To gain wider control over the firms' above normative working capital the bank's rigid policy has been
relaxed allowing it to extend credit for excessive accumulation of materials provided that steps are taken to
mitigate the situation. Until very recently the bank
was very stringent in crediting overdue receivables.
At present it has become more lenient when the firms
cannot successfully collect from their debtors.[106]
But when extending credits for such "irregular activities" the bank imposes a higher interest rate
gravitating from 8 to 10 per cent. The bank branch in
Lodz reports that although the higher interest rates
are a deterrent against hoarding, some enterprises
would agree to any interest rate as long as their
stocks of materials are not questioned.[107] The failure
of the authorities to control working capital adequately
is perhaps best indicated by the growing inventories
of materials.[108]

Central control of working capital is further
complicated when enterprises have excesses of working
capital and may choose to apply funds towards decentralized investments, increasing their size beyond
the central planner's intent. To counteract such
action the bank, in agreement with the association,
is empowered to block part of the development fund
in the investment-repair account if it deems that too
large an amount is intended for these purposes.[109]
But in practice this blocking does not play an important role. For example, as of June 30, 1962 the blocked
funds amounted only to 4 per cent of all funds accumulated on these accounts. The reason for the in-
significance of this tool is twofold: the desire to
accumulate inventories of materials is never satiated
and stringent controls are imposed on decentralized
investments.

FINANCING OF INVESTMENTS

During the SYP period about 97 per cent of invest-

ments were decided at the central level.[110] As a result
of the relative decentralization of the 1957-58 period
some scope in performing the investment function was
left up to enterprises, followed in 1960 by restrictions
due to loss of control by the central planner. The
system in operation today does not offer a clear-cut
line of demarcation between centralized and decentralized investment decisions.[111] At present virtually all
investments undertaken in the state-owned industrial
sector may be divided into three categories: centralized, association, and enterprise investments.

    Although delimitation is difficult, investment
decisions made at the central level and financed from
budget subsidies pertain to new capital formation of
particular importance to the economy or industries.
They are what the Marxists call "expanded reproduction"
in contradistinction with "simple reproduction" which
is merely renovation and reinvestment of the capital
equipment without major alterations or improvements.
Investments affecting the basic proportions of the NEP
are decided by the PC or by the responsible minister.
In the latter case the investments must remain within
the financial limits imposed on the branch of industry
in the FYP and the annual limits imposed in the NEP.
Such investments pertain in particular to construction
of new industrial establishments or substantial
expansion of existing ones; general modernization and
reconstruction of larger plants; factory housing; construction and expansion of the communications network;
procurement of ships, airplanes, rolling stock, and
other important investment goods. Furthermore, the
central planner decides on investments resulting from
international agreements and those pertaining to
national defence.

    The investments undertaken and financed from the
associations' investment funds must be coordinated
within the given branch of industry and by the process
of elimination must be outside the category on which
the central planner decides directly.[112] Such investments usually pertain to the formation of new or
substantially expanded capacity of existing concerns.
These decisions are made by the association subject
to the minister's approval. They must remain within
the financial limits prescribed for the particular
association. Presumably the associations' closer

knowledge of their enterprises enhances the efficiency
of their investment decisions.

The enterprise decides on investments which it
finances from its own funds and bank loans. Such investments pertain to reproduction of existing equipment,
some modernization of technological processes, and
improvement in safety and working conditions.[113] In
principle the investment decisions made by the firm
must not materially alter its production capacity. A
substantial alteration may cause difficulties in coordination and proportions of the NEP, unbalancing the
material balances and intensifying bottlenecks.

Centralized investments are financed from state
funds. The state's financial outlays for investments
are non-reimbursable, granted without interest charges,[114]
as budget subsidies and subsidies from the central
amortization fund. The latter is composed of the part
of enterprises' depreciation which is not left at the
disposal of the enterprises or associations. The
associations' investments are financed from their funds
derived partly from their share in enterprises' depreciation and from budget subsidies.[115] Should the investment prove to be more expensive than the estimate -
which is almost always the case - the association may
cover the excess from its reserve fund or from inactive
funds of the direct beneficiary's investment-repair
account.

The sources for financing enterprises' decentralized
investments are the funds accumulated on the firm's
investment-repair account and bank credits.[116] As we
know, the financial system rests on separating the operation and investment activity of the enterprise with
strictly delimited investment and working capital funds.
Nevertheless the enterprise may borrow part of its
working capital for investment purposes as long as
this amount is reimbursed within a short lapse of
time.[117] The main sources of the investment-repair
account are the part of depreciation ramaining in the
firm,[118] the investment share of the development fund,
allowances from the reserve fund,[119] redistribution of
the association's amortization fund, disposal of fixed
assets and scrap materials, prepayments of future
users, special grants, and compensations paid from in-
surance on capital goods.[120]

Additional sources for financing decentralized invest-

ments are available in the form of bank credits. Two
types of credits are designed for investment purposes:
limited and non-limited credits. The limitation of
investment credits in the annual credit plan of the bank
is a constraint on decentralized investments.[121] The
limit may be augmented if enterprises unduly accumulate
funds on their investment-repair accounts and decreased
if the rate of expenditures on investments is too high.
Limited credits are extended for a period not exceeding
five years from the time of completion of the investment
project, but in any event not longer than eight years
from the time credit was granted. The credits are
reimbursable from the firm's investment-repair account.
If the enterprise does not possess sufficient funds at
the time reimbursement is due, payment may be made from
working capital or the association's reserve fund if it
has guaranteed the credit. Non-limited credit is
granted for financing short term investments of high
returns inducing technical progress, production for
export, or goods substituting imported ones. Non-
limited credit cannot exceed one million zlotys, the
project must be completed within a year, and reimbursement must be made within three years.[122]

The enterprise's investment activity is rigorously
controlled by the ministry, association, and the bank.
Not only are the financial aspects of the investment
project scrutinized, but also the adherence to the
investment limits prescribed by the plan, the kinds and
types of investments, and their conformity to regulations. Lately, due to the persisting excess of
actual investment costs over the estimates, great stress
has been laid on the control of investment costs by
the bank.[123]

The bank's control of the investment project begins
by verification of the plans to ascertain the effectiveness of the investment, the readiness of the enterprise for the particular type of investment, when the
investment can be started, and when it is to be completed. The banks are empowered to appraise the efficiency of investments undertaken by firms and have
the right to take action which will withhold such
investments, should they consider them to be undesirable. Secondly, the contracts entered into by the
investor and the construction firm are submitted to
the bank. This is called the registration of contracts.

The execution of unregistered contracts is followed by
financial restrictions against the contractors. The
control of contracts aims at balancing the potential of
the contractors with the needs of investors and at
specifying a given priority of needs. If the bank
refuses to register a contract, it will withhold any
payment for this purpose regardless of the source of
financing.[124] During the course of the investment
project the bank must verify that the payments are in
accordance with the estimate. It seems, however, that
this bank control is neither effective in preventing
underestimation of costs at the planning stage nor the
excess of actual costs over the estimate. The estimates
are usually crude approximations and the bank encounters
many obstacles in their verification.[125]
     When the enterprises were first allowed to make
investment decisions the latitude granted them was
much wider than at present. The curtailment of the
scope of decentralized investments was substantiated
during an inquiry conducted in 1961 among 450 major
enterprises of key industry. Doberski, who reported the
results, stated:

     Regardless of the prevalent opinion 67 per cent of
     enterprises report that in the past period (1956-60)
     they had the opportunity to dispose autonomously
     of funds designated for decentralized investments.
     However, the enterprises do not conceal the fact
     that in 1960 restrictions on these prerogatives
     were distinctly felt.[126]

The diminishing role of enterprises' investments has
continued since 1960. The MF has been called upon to
apply means limiting decentralized investments. In
1961 centralized investments amounted to 62.9 per cent,
association's 19.1, and enterprise's 18.0 per cent.
The respective figures planned for 1964 were 68.8,
21.6, and 9.6 per cent.[127] The firm's accumulation of
financial means for investments is not synonymous with
carrying out investments. The realistic premises for
implementing investments is their inclusion in the
physical investment plan. "The struggle for investments is above all apparent in physical planning."[128]

PRESENT SHORTCOMINGS AND IMPENDING CHANGES

In a recent survey of the developments of the firms'
financial system in postwar Poland, Professor Blass,
Vice-President of the NPB, maintains that the most
distinct decentralization undertakings in recent years
are in the sphere of enterprise finance: the division
of profit among the development and enterprise funds.[129]
Whereas before investments were essentially the prerogative of the central organs, financed by budget
subsidies, a scope of decentralized investments has
been allowed to enterprises. Limits were centrally
imposed on working capital, excesses confiscated, and
shortages subsidized by the state. But at present the
enterprise is generally allowed to set its own normatives
and in principle the excesses are not confiscated. Whereas before the state issued directives on the division of
profit for central purposes, for additional working
capital, capital repairs, and the enterprise fund, at
present the division has been reduced from a four-way
to a three-way division. But the enterprise cannot
alter centrally predetermined shares of profit for the
development fund, enterprise fund, and the state budget
(and association).
    The enterprise can allocate part of the development
fund for investments (within the limits allowed) and
increases of working capital as it sees fit. In other
words, it is claimed that at present the firm can choose
between allocation of funds for decentralized investments
or working capital. This alternative is open to it, and
in a sense the opportunity cost of added investments is
the forgoing of benefits derived from additional working
capital. Since working capital, or at least its increments, are usually applied for inventories, the initiators of the reform hoped that the enterprises will apply
additional funds for decentralized investments limiting
the undesirable accumulation of stocks of inventories.
However, the curtailment of undesirable investments in
materials could be accomplished only by making investments in capital assets available to enterprises. But
the investment policy of the last few years was geared
towards long range development projects. Conflicts
between central and decentralized investments arose.
They were solved in favor of the former, frustrating

enterprises faced with the availability of funds and
impossibility of disbursements. The final step was
confiscation of these funds by the state.[130]

The difficulties created for the central planner by
sizable decentralized investments have been discussed
before and do not need reiteration here. But when the
firms were first permitted to make decentralized investments, apart from losing control over the development
of the economy, the central planner had to compete for
increasingly scarce resources for investment purposes.
Difficulties and bottlenecks in the investment "market"
arose and the share of investments (accumulation) in
national income exceeded the planned level. But with
the curtailment of decentralized investment activity
the incentive for the enterprise to limit expansion in
inventory and carry out investments became rather
impotent.

Notwithstanding the stress on multi-year planning
in enterprises to broaden management's economic horizon,
the postulated establishment of indexes of development
fund formation, increase of normatives, and apportionment of depreciation for a period of four years (1962-
65) were not realized. Enterprises and associations
were left with a short run viewpoint discouraging
decentralized investments.[131]

Moreover the financial restrictions inflicted on
firms by blocking extra funds accumulated on their
investment repair accounts and limits on bank credits
for investment purposes are additional built-in constraints to keep the enterprises' investments within
the boundries prescribed by the central planner.[132]
Thus the planner keeps his finger on the pulse of decentralized investment activity. But by channeling
decentralized investments into the direction considered
advisable, the central planner has largely deprived them
of the beneficial influence they might have had on
enterprises.

Notwithstanding the limitations imposed on decentralized investments, the financial system is also responsible
for facilitating accumulation in inventories. In many
cases enterprises plan their normatives so as to
exceed the part of profit remaining at their disposal
for that purpose. They then demand budget or reserve
fund subsidies which they transfer to investment
purposes. In other cases the excessive normative is

lowered during plan fulfilment and the "freed funds"
transferred to investment purposes.[133]
   The right to set normatives for the elements of working capital and to decide autonomously on the repartition of the development fund among the investment-
repair account and working capital were limited indirectly by imposing the controls which we have mentioned. It bears repetition, however, that the controls
over working capital were further intensified by
restricting the financing of working capital normatives
from own resources and forcing the firms to supplement
them by bank loans. Thus the bank was enabled to
exercise constant control over enterprises, even
those that would have the means to finance working
capital from their own funds. The claims that firms
in Poland may exercise autonomously their prerogatives
in allocating funds among operation and investment
activities are not fully justified. Constraints are
imposed on the firm's financial activities and indeed
a need for such controls seems to follow from the logic
of the centralized system. The financial system per
se depends on the prevailing degree of decentralization and its changes are contingent on overhauling
the administrative and planning systems. In view of
the pronouncements at the IV Congress of the PUWP
impending but not fundamental alterations of the
financial system may be expected and are indeed
augured by the work conducted at the MF, reported
recently by the Vice-Minister.[134] Indications are
present that the future financial system (1966-70) will
be shaped along these lines.
   As a result of revitalizing the role of associations
and enhancing their performance of the investment function in expanding existing firms, the funds for financing such investments should not be as heretofore drawn
from budget subsidies but from a larger participation
in enterprises' profits and depreciation.[135] The
possibility of charging interest on the enterprises'
fixed assets is seriously contemplated, although the
variants of solutions, repercussions on cost determination, determination of the objects (base) of interest
levy, level and uniformity or differentiation of rates,
and methods of computation, are still unsettled.[136]
Enterprises should be allowed a wider latitude in
replacing and modernizing existing equipment. Their

investment-repair fund should be discontinued. A special fund should be set up for repairs and the firm's
investments should be financed largely from the development fund.

The development fund should be formed as heretofore
from profit and be the source for financing investments
and working capital. The enterprise should be allowed
to benefit from larger investment funds when it reduces
its working capital needs and vice versa. It is suggested to set up two bank accounts for this fund. In
account A funds from profit would be accumulated in a
given year and the following year transferred to
account B from which funds for working capital needs
would be drawn first and the remainder allotted to
investments. This procedure would afford the central
planner and the firm a clear picture of the availability
of funds for any given year. To induce economical
expenditures from account B its funds must be subject to
an interest charge lower than that levied on bank loans.
Bank loans will be available to supplement investment
funds but the bank will have to be satisfied with the
efficiency of the proposed investments.

It is suggested to do away with financial normatives
of working capital. The required working capital should
be financed in about 50 per cent by the enterprise's own
funds and the remainder by bank loans. When, as a
result of better performance or curtailment of investment expenditures, the enterprise augments its own
working capital it could then repay the loans reducing
the interest charges. When, as a result of deterioration in performance or hoarding of materials, the
enterprise will be short of funds to cover its own
working capital, it will have to supplement it with
investment funds or seek additional loans with a
higher interest rate, reimbursable immediately from
the following year's working capital.

Such a system hinges on the bank's ability to evaluate the situation and perform the control function
over financial activity at the lower echelons. It is
doubtful whether with the tools at its disposal, the
efficacy of economic parameters, and the quality of
its personnel, the bank can apply economic criteria
(which in themselves are of questionable validity)
in evaluating efficiency. Another dilemma facing the
initiators of the reform is that if the bank's

control is effective it cramps and stifles managerial action, and if it is not, it does not serve the central planner faithfully.

The proposed changes seem to rely heavily on the interest rate as an incentive and constraint. Without detracting from the usefulness of such a tool when used consistently, coherently, and concordantly with other methods, the present limited and discordant experiences with it are not a good omen. It seems that change of the producers' market from sellers' to buyers', revitalization of other economic parameters, transformation of profit into an economic category, and strengthening its hold over management would be necessary conditions to assure the success of the financial scheme. Indeed:

> Our past experience indicates that narrowly conceived changes may be almost completely unavailaing unless accompanied by other changes strictly connected with the former.[137]

5

MANAGEMENT
OF THE ENTERPRISE -
OBJECTIVES AND
PERFORMANCE

It is the purpose of this concluding chapter to scrutinize the economy's basic cell in action to furnish further insight into the efficiency, modus operandi, and performance of the system. In the process we shall describe the forces motivating managerial behavior, the rationale of performance criteria, the underlying incentive system, and how management plays the game.

MANAGEMENT AND ITS MOTIVATION

Organization of the Enterprise

The director of a state-owned industrial enterprise is appointed by the ministry. He is a custodian and manager of state property, but the state remains the ever powerful owner. He is responsible to his superiors for the firm's activities. He is to be obeyed by his subordinates in accordance with the principle of one man management and responsibility formulated by the decree of October 26, 1950 and reiterated in the latest decree regarding the firm's management.[1] The director is severely constrained in his activity by central commands and regulations as well as the control and supervision exercised by the association, the bank, and other state agencies.

Within the enterprise the Party cell and the various organs of the conference of workers' self-management are designed to control and curb management's activity. The firm's Party organization promotes current policies and slogans of the day. While allowing management

greater freedom, the PUWP uses the firm's Party cell as
a countervailing force to control management.[2]   The
role and duties of this Party cell and its activists
were clearly prescribed in article 50 of the PUWP
statutes:

> The Party organizations in enterprises are respon-
> sible to the Party for the economic conditions and
> effective activity of their enterprises. The
> essential duty of these Party organizations is
> political control and influence on the enterprise's
> management in matters pertaining to important
> production and economic problems, personnel
> policy, work and living conditions of the staff.
> The Party organizations in enterprises perform
> their role mainly by an active participation in
> the activity of the workers' self-management
> ensuring an appropriate conformity of the staff's
> interests and the national interests.[3]

The prerogatives of the workers' self-management
have been curtailed with the institution of the
conference of workers' self-management in November,
1958.   The conference and its organs meet four times
a year to deliberate and take decisions incumbent on
them.   The conference's activity is limited to approval
of production and development plans, evaluation and
analysis of the firm's activity, decisions on the
apportionment of the enterprise fund, and internal
work regulations.[4]   Lately a marked tendency has been
manifested by management in taking all current decisions
devolving on the workers' self-management. Groups of
three to four people, calling themselves "presidiums
of the conference of workers' self-management" or
"managerial collective", composed of the director of
the firm, the Party secretary, the chairmen of the
workers' council and factory council, make the actual
current decisions for the workers' self-management.[5]
Due to management's intrusion in the prerogatives of the
workers' self-management, the latter is not an effective
check on managerial activity. The control imposed
through the Party cell is weak as the personal interests
of the director and Party secretary often coincide.
   The firm's organizational structure and delegation
of authority by the director to his subordinates is

Chart IV - <u>Organizational Structure of the Enterprise</u>

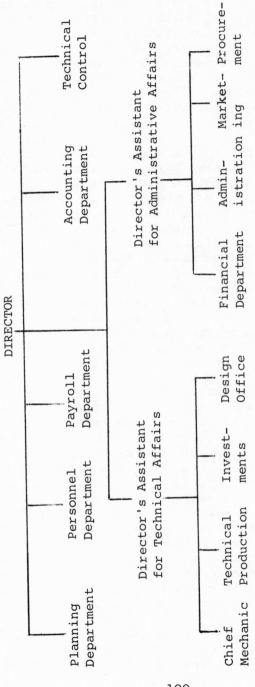

<u>Source</u> Skrzywan and Fedak, <u>Op. Cit.</u>, p.11

illustrated in Chart IV. The planning, accounting, personnel, payroll, and technical control departments are the immediate responsibility of the director to whom they are directly accountable. The planning department is charged mainly with gathering and summarizing statistical data and information as a basis for plan construction, drafting plans according to directives received, and with controlling and reporting the execution of plans.[6] The personnel department is responsible for the hiring, discharging advancement, and rewarding of the firm's employees with the exception of the director appointed by the ministry and his two assistants appointed by the association. The chief accountant is responsible to the director for the firm's financial and accounting records, reports, and control.[7] The payroll department prepares the employment plans, establishes wage tariffs on the basis of centrally prepared tables, and submits to the director reports concerning possible improvements of internal organization. The technical control department - employing quality control inspectors, sorters, and laboratory technicians - verifies the quality of incoming materials and inspects outgoing finished goods.

As a rule the director has two assistants directly responsible to him for several departments. The director's assistant for technical affairs is generally the chief engineer. His assistant for administrative and financial affairs is the chief accountant.[8] The following departments are the responsibility of the chief engineer and directly accountable to him: the technical production department which prepares the operative production plans, controls their execution, prepares the technical data, etc.; the design department which drafts and designs new products and improves existing ones; the department of the chief mechanic whose task is to maintain equipment in production readiness, draft repair plans execute them and control the procurement of electricity, steam, and water for the producing departments; the investment department which drafts the investment plans, controls their execution, and should analyze investment efficiency. The director's second assistant, his representative for administrative and financial affairs, is responsible for the following departments: the financial department which plans and

conducts all affairs connected with financing the firm;
the procurement department which plans and is responsible
for the purchasing and scheduling of the supply of
necessary materials and the existing stocks; the marketing department which markets and is responsible for
delivery of finished goods in accordance with the plan
it prepares and the contracts entered into with
purchasers; the office administration department
responsible for upkeep and procurement of office inventory, supplies, etc.; this department is generally
also concerned with the staff's social and cultural
affairs and employs a legal adviser.

In exercising its functions management largely
depends on its relations with the association.[9]   As
we have seen in Chapter I, since 1957 the number of
directives has grown markedly amounting at present to
19 legally prescribed directives: 1) value of marketable
output in transfer prices, including value of output
designated for the consumer market, 2) quantity of
production of the most important assortments decided
by the association and supported by receipt of centrally
distributed materials, 3) quantity of specific output
designated for export, 4) total wage fund, 5) wage
fund for white collar workers, 6) number of industrial
workers, 7) number of manual workers, 8) number of
technical and engineering employees and skilled
workers, 9) size of the administrative and office
staff, 10) profit or loss, 11) development fund, 12)
contribution to the reserve fund, 13) share of profit
to be paid into the state budget or subsidy to be
received, 14) budget subsidies for centralized investments, 15) budget subsidies for factory housing, 16)
import of equipment and limit of foreign currency for
these purchases prescribed by the ministry, 17) financial
limit for capital repairs, 18) apportionment of the
amortization fund among the firm and the state budget,
and 19) the aggregate normative of working capital.[10]

In practice the number of directive indexes transmitted from the association is even higher. As an example
we may cite the Association of Rolling Stock Industry
which in 1959 transmitted to the Cegielski enterprise
in Poznan the following additional directives: 1) value
of total output in comparable prices, 2) wage fund for
outside labor, 3) separation of the wage fund into the
part for the engineering and technical personnel and

the part for administrative and office personnel, 4) the
part of the amortization fund for financing capital
repairs, and 5) the part of the amortization fund for
financing decentralized investments.[11]

The association's infringement on the firm's prerogatives is not the only grievance that management may
have against its association. Even though management
has been empowered to question certain directives,
seldom does it get a chance to do so due to a lack of
synchronization between plan directives. Whereas the
production indexes are received early in the course of
the current annual plan, the financial directives are
sometimes transmitted in May or June, thus at a time
when the enterprise is half-way through the current
plan and counterproposals are of little effect. Plan
directives are frequently tabu and although some are
questioned answers are often delayed indefinitely with
hardly a chance of obtaining a reduction of targets.[12]
A director of a large enterprise spoke out bitterly
against his supervisory unit:

> The association has most effectively broken our
> habit of independent thought and action. The
> association deems that it possesses a much better
> evaluation of the production capacity of the
> enterprises.   Productivity, wages, and labor
> intensity are established for us, leaving us only
> the execution of the plan. In such a state of
> affairs the director does not feel any responsibility
> for the enterprise, he is only concerned with the
> fulfilment of the plan.[13]

When preparing data for submission to the association the enterprises attempt to conceal capacity
aiming at lower plan indexes.[14] But since the association must distribute the targets it received from the
ministry, the directives it transmits to the firm
include higher targets than warranted by the firm's
reports. Hence a mutual distrust prevails, "the
association thinks that the enterprise wants to
bamboozle it, and the firm thinks that the association
passes this judgment."[15]

Management distrusts the association in view of its
frequent upward revisions of targets during the year.
For example, in some enterprises of the machine building

industry directive indexes (of production, wage fund,
and accumulation) are changed three or even four times
during the year.[16] In the glass factory in Wolomin the
1961 directive indexes were still being changed at the
end of the year. In the women's apparel factory
"Glazewski" in Lodz the 1960 plan directives were
changed three times: early in 1960, June 1960, and
September 1960. In 1961 this happened twice: in
February and December. In the rubber factory in
Debnica the final directives for 1961 were received
in August of that year.[17] An enterprise which has
experienced such changes naturally expects their recurrence and reckons with the phenomenon when submit-
ting reports.

Notwithstanding the director's attempt at influencing
favorably his superiors' decisions, when these are transformed into commands, he is bound to implement them as
indeed failure to do so may result in his dismissal.[18]
In the light of directives received and attempts to
curtail the firm's prerogatives, it may seem that
the decisions made by the director are insignificant
and his position as executor of assigned tasks is a
subservient one. Although the most important materials
are centrally allotted, manpower and the wage fund
strictly controlled, and finished goods must be
marketed at prices fixed centrally, the director is
continually faced with a number of alternatives from
which he selects the ones best suited for achieving
his goals.

Contrary to the general belief these alternative
decisions are many and varied, covering almost all
fields of the firm's activity. Granted that some are
not of paramount importance, their cumulative effect
strongly influences the firm's success. The choice he
makes enables the director to fulfil his tasks and in
the process earn rewards and praise for himself and his
subordinates. Consequently some of the more important
decisions confronting the director should be recapitulated.

He takes an active part in drafting the technical-
economic plan. Since at present directive indexes cover
the annual plan, this has to be redistributed among the
quarterly, monthly, weekly, and daily plans.[19] With
the cooperation of his two assistants, and in conjunction with the chiefs of the planning and technical
production departments, he scrutinizes the capacity of

the plant, distributes, and assigns tasks to each respective department.

As previously discussed, only part of the planned output is broken up into assortments. For example, the returns of the 1959 investigation of the Economic Council, based on 10 per cent of nationalized industrial firms, revealed that on the average in 1959 55.4 per cent of assortments were centrally determined. In light industry 89.7 per cent of assortments were centrally set, in heavy industry 45.5, and in chemical industry 39.4 per cent.[20] Hence a good part of the responsibility for planning and executing the product mix, models, sizes, types, quality, etc. rests with the director and his subordinates.

Production norms and standards are fixed centrally and are usually antiquated as they are infrequently revised. In many cases the association transmits directives stipulating over-all cost reduction. But actual cost reduction and production with minimum inputs rests with the people on the spot.

Even though the major production materials are allotted to the enterprise centrally, the manager exercises a wide control over procurement and marketing. In most cases he seeks out suppliers entering into contract with them and buyers of his products.[21] He may also use his personal influence with suppliers to ensure prompt delivery of materials. In certain cases he may decide that it might be either more economical or expedient to produce certain necessary supplies on premises.

Development of new production methods, techniques, or designs depends mainly on the director's initiative and his willingness to utilize that of his subordinates. The director plans the investment projects financed from the firm's decentralized investment funds. Even though he cannot decide on investments financed centrally, his opinions and requests may have a definite bearing on these investments.

Although it has been asserted many times that the firm must sell its products according to prices fixed centrally by the SPC, there is no doubt that our director indirectly influences price formation. It is the cost of production, calculated by the accounting department and approved by the chief accountant and the director, that constitutes the basis for price setting. In addition,

as pointed out earlier, the state is not able to fix
prices centrally for all goods produced. Certain goods
perforce fall into the category of non-typical products,
priced within the firm in conformity with the regulations prescribed by law. But as we have seen, cost
manipulations are common. By approving cost manipulations, and what is more, deliberately demanding them
from his chief accountant, the director definitely
influences pricing.

There are multifarious rules, regulations, laws, and
decrees strictly governing management's activity. The
complaint voiced by the director and the technical
director of the Cegielski firm at the X Plenum of the
Central Committee of the Party is illustrative of this
fact:

It may be worth while to take cognizance of the growing wave of new normative acts which only too
often regulate in an overly detailed manner the
manifestations in our economic life. We do not know
whether and when the last managerial leader will
cease to exist, transforming himself into an office
worker. The fear that directors of enterprises
should cause perturbations in the financial economy
and break basic economic laws through their activity
has led to this state of affairs... It is our
opinion that if there are bad directors they should
be dismissed but that the prerogatives of all
enterprises should not be limited. We do not
believe that industry can be administrated centrally
in a minute and punctilious manner.[22]

The ever increasing regulations are often contradictory.
The director, although formally not empowered to do so
and may be very strictly dealt with if he is uncovered,
must select the regulations to be followed and those to
be disregarded or circumvented. It has been remarked
that "the time of the captains of industry is thought-
lessly squandered, their energy consumed in looking for
subterfuge and loopholes so that the enterprise should
come out safe and sound from under the deluge of
contradictory orders."[23] The director will at times
call his advisers to discuss the best possible manner
for circumventing the regulations with little risk.[24]

Of course, the risk involved is enormous. Aside

from the fact that the director accused of breaking a
regulation can be dismissed, the law states that he may
be imprisoned anywhere from one to five years. No differentiation as to which acts are punishable and which
are not is made.[25] Generally harsh sentences are not
very frequent. They are imposed not so much to punish
the guilty as to make a public showcase and warn the
others.

In view of a multitude of rewards accorded by the
state to recompense the execution of particular tasks
and because the execution of some often precludes the
execution of others,[26] the director chooses to execute
tasks bringing higher rewards at the expense of others
for which rewards are smaller. Hence on the grounds of
his "private" economic calculation the director will
execute one task at the detriment of another acting
in accordance with his goals.

The Goals of Management

The problem of goals in a socialist economy is a
controversial one. Some writers claim that due to the
"non-contradictory" nature of a socialist economy,
since the state's goal reflected in the NEP is supreme
and the role of the firm as plan executant subservient,
there can be no conflict between the goals of the
state, the firm, and its management, and the latter
are determined by the former.[27] At present we are witnessing a shift towards recognition that the central
planner's interests may diverge from those of the
firm and its management, forming a more complex means-
end structure where divergent, or even opposing, goals
clash.[28] At the pinnacle of the hierarchy of goals are
the central planner's goals, rather vaguely defined as
"maximization of national income".[29] To synchronize
management's goals with those of the state, or to
induce management to fulfil the "supreme goal of the
plan",[30] while fulfilling its own, the central planner must recognize what management's goals are and
adapt and integrate his network of directives, parameters, performance criteria, rewards, and punishments
so that the "formula" (prices - methods of computation -
incentives) constitutes an integrated whole with
compatible elements all steering the firm and its management in one direction.[31]

In search of the primary mover and explanation of management's economic behavior, the maximization function is assumed, and indeed this principle is accepted in Polish economic circles:

If there exist any possibilities of choice, the enterprise will choose the magnitude easiest to attain which forms the basis for evaluating its performance in the eyes of the superior authorities, or the one which brings highest material rewards. One of these magnitudes will be valued highest, will assume the prominent position in the hierarchy of goals and will become the object of maximization.[32]

As far as it is possible to determine, the maximization of personal rewards in the form of income is the primary goal motivating management's economic behavior.[33] The basic reward for the work that a manager performs is the salary that he receives. However, to stimulate the desired performance it is the state's policy to reward management with premiums in accordance with their performance measured by centrally established criteria.[34] Premiums, as the particularly variable part of management's income, are especially susceptible to augmentation and maximization. This is well illustrated in Table 23 contrasting the basic salary with the actual take-home pay of directors and foremen.

Table 23 - Relation Between Foreman's and Director's Salary and Take-Home Pay

Industries	Basic Salary		Take-Home Pay	
	Foreman	Director	Foreman	Director
Ferrous metallurgy	100	236	100	278
Electric power	100	216	100	323
Machine building	100	196	100	240

Source B. Fick, ZG, No.14, 1964

Hence premium maximization seems to be the primary goal motivating economic behavior of management of a socialist state-owned enterprise in the present Polish institutional setting.[35]

Generally speaking management will attempt to maximize premiums over a period exceeding the current by reckoning with repercussions resulting from "short run" or single period maximization endeavors. Actual performance should not set too high standards in order not to induce great increases in targets for the following periods.[36] Simultaneously the results reported should not exceed the maximum limits warranting receipt of premiums. Indeed they should be slightly lower to avoid suspicion from controlling organs. In firms where current results neither warrant receipt of premiums nor can be manipulate to qualify for premiums, the reported results will be even further decreased to build up reserves for the next period.[37] However, management would be unwilling to forgo current premiums for future benefits, particularly so if the lapse of time until future premiums are realized is an extensive one.[38] It seems that the behavior of Polish managers may lead one to assume their adherence to Keynes' dictum: "in the long run we are all dead".

The question arises - why are premiums such potent inducements towards fulfilment of targets? The answer is simple: they constitute a substantial part of take-home pay. Prior to the 1957-58 reforms the wage structure was greatly undifferentiated and management's salaries depressed.[39] However, these were largely sup-plemented with premiums. For example, in 1954 the enterprise "Paris Commune" in Warsaw, a producer of telecommunication equipment, paid out premiums amounting to 110.6 per cent of the basic salary of the director and chief engineer, 101.43 per cent to the managers of the production departments and director's assistant, and 82.98 per cent to the medium and lower engineering and technical personnel as well as the part of the administra tive personnel having an influence on production.[40] In the wool industry the premiums for managerial personnel reached the exorbitant amount of 400 per cent of basic salaries in 1955.[41]

During the discussion on the model it was stressed that due to the size of premiums indexes not connected with premiums were neglected so that premium conditions be fulfilled. It was recognized that premiums were necessary to ensure satisfactory performance by manage-ment. But it was suggested that it might be more

advisable to differentiate to a greater extent the wage
structure and reduce the quantitative amount of the
premiums.[42] In the course of reforms the wage structure
- although still far from satisfactory - was differentiated somewhat. At present the average premiums for
managerial personnel constitute about 35 per cent of
their take-home pay.[43] Hence premiums still constitute
a very substantial part of income.

Premiums are an integral part of the supply price of
labor and managers regard them as "permanent and stable
income". If a premium is not received as expected, it
might entail personal financial difficulties for the
manager. Consequently the drive to maximize premiums
is reinforced by the sheer necessity to obtain the
expected premium.

Premiums will also be maximized because of the power
and prestige factors. Undoubtedly it is the successful
and good manager who obtains high premiums since according to the official performance criteria he has executed
his duties in an exemplary manner. His enterprise will
expand and grow, benefiting from centralized investment
funds which he will have little difficulty in securing.
A successful manager will wield more power with the
authorities. He will encounter fewer difficulties in
securing centrally distributed materials, and may put
stronger pressure on his suppliers. His opinions will
be reckoned with and in his squabbles with the association he may have the upper hand. Hence through the
process of premium maximization the director will not
only gain financially but also largely enhance his
authority. He will contribute to the expansion of the
enterprise he manages. This will result in increased
personal financial gains because of added responsibility.
The additional financial rewards will mean a larger
salary and, if his success continues, higher premiums.

Besides the premium drive and the power and prestige
aims, another goal of management is advancement to
higher rank.[44] However, these goals are complementary
rather than contradictory. Since premiums reward achievements they serve as indicators for the state to recompense the man for the excellence of his performance.
Hence premium acquisition is a success criterion.[45]
Premiums and advancement complement each other, and the
manager who earns more premiums will be more likely to
be promoted. Consequently all four main goals motivat-

ing managerial activity, the direct one - financial rewards - and the indirect ones - power, prestige, and
advancement - could be easily brought to a common
denominator - the maximization of premiums.[46]

But the premium maximization process and by and
large the firm's activity depend on the performance
criteria set by the state for evaluating enterprises.[47]
Hence before examining the actual means management uses
to attain their goals, we must concentrate on the
performance criteria employed for evaluating the firm
and its management.

PERFORMANCE CRITERIA AND PREMIUM SYSTEM

To appraise the performance criteria and the premium
system emanating from them and judge the progress made
in the last few years, the main currents in the evolution of the premium system in postwar Poland should be
followed.

The Inception of the System

An incentive system in the form of premiums over and
above basic salary as the variable part of income was
introduced to increase the employees' efforts and tie
in their performance with their income.[48] By 1945 the
labor contracts included premiums for the fulfilment
and overfulfilment of the production plan. In metallurgy premiums from a special fund amounting at the
beginning to 10 per cent of the wage fund were introduced
for labor productivity and for zealous work. The
effectiveness of these first attempts to reward good
performance was slight. Nevertheless total expenses
for premiums grew. At the beginning of 1946 individual
premiums amounted already to 100 per cent of basic
salaries.[49]

In 1946 new uniform principles for payment of premiums were introduced. The conditions for obtaining
premiums were fulfilment of the production plan in
value terms and increase in labor productivity in relation to the preceding period.[50] The system broke down
very rapidly as a result of the newly introduced policy
of rigid basic wages which ignored the simultaneous
increase in the cost of living. The danger of a de-

crease in real wages brought about pressure on wages.
Since the rigid basic wage rates could not be changed,
the premium system was overriden with a substantial increase in premiums which lost their incentive role.   It
was decided to counteract the spontaneous increase in
premiums by introducing a ceiling on individual premiums.
But this measure was ineffective as premiums soon
reached the allowed limits transforming themselves into
stable salary additions.[51]

By 1947 the system was somewhat revised by excluding
the employees who had no direct influence on production
results from participating in these premiums.   Simultaneously the concept of distributing premiums on a uniform basis in all firms was abandoned.   The number of
performance criteria was broadened and differentiated
for particular branches of industry.   Specialized
premiums, stimulating attention to particular phases of
the firm's activity, were introduced.   A characteristic
of this system was that it did not apply two or more
titles to a premium but always fulfilment of one specific task entitling the individual employee to a premium.[52]
The specialized premiums were not effective.   Stimulating the employees' interest into particular directions,
they induced the attainment of specific tasks at the
expense of others.   The common feeling was that the
premium is an addition to salary independent of the
results attained by the individual employee.   By the
end of 1948 the system was practically inoperative.
The premiums were distributed mechanically as increases
in salary.[53]

During the 1946 to 1948 period there was yet another
type of premium in operation.   By 1946 a collective
premium for all employees was introduced as a share in
profit realized by the enterprise.[54] This fund amounted
from 5 to 15 per cent of the firm's profit and was
intended to satisfy the "collective needs" of all
employees.[55]   During the years 1947 to 1948 this system
was transformed so that the collective premium amounted
to 10 per cent of planned and 20 per cent of above plan
profits.[56]   The system failed due to the application of
uniform rates of contribution resulting in great
divergencies of premiums in individual enterprises.[57]
By the end of 1948 the first system of incentives based
on synthetic results was completely compromised causing
the state to forgo this type of performance criterion.

The Six-Year Plan Period

Under these conditions preparations for a general reform of the premium system were initiated in 1949 in conjunction with a substantial wage reform.[58] The reformed premium system was to depart completely from the narrowly conceived specialized premiums. The foundations of the new system were the production plan, labor productivity, the assortment plan, and quality indexes. This was deemed to be one of the essential cornerstones of the wage policy at the threshold of the SYP.

The single most important drawback of this reform was the neglect and omission of the problem of costs and savings. The central target of the plan was to be increase of output with the premium system built exclusively around it. Premium distribution depended on: the degree of fulfilment of the production plan and fulfilment of the labor productivity target. But the former remained at the forefront as the performance criterion.[59] Although similar solutions were proven inadequate in the past,[60] it was hoped that the unlimited increase in individual premiums would improve the system. This largely enhanced the attractiveness of premiums transforming them into powerful incentives, whereas heretofore they had been regarded as automatic salary increases. The 1950 basis for the premium system remained unchallenged until 1954, and with insignificant modifications continued its existence until 1957. Consequently this was a more stabilized system and its mechanics merit closer and more detailed examination.

Premiums paid out according to production plan fulfilment were to apply almost exclusively to top management and higher rank personnel whose work directly influenced the firm's output. In practice these premiums were received by the director, the chiefs of departments, their assistants, shop superintendents, foremen, and other technical and office personnel. The differentiation in premium rates may be illustrated by reverting to the 1953 regulations of the Ministry of Machine Building Industry. This industry's firms were divided into three categories and the following table illustrates the premium rates in the second category as an average for that industry.

Table 24 - <u>1953 Premium Rates in Machine Building</u>

Groups of employees	Percentage rates of basic wages		
	At 100% fulfilment of output plan	For each percentage of over-fulfilment	Paid in 1954 in "Paris Commune" enterprise
Director and chief engineer	60	6	110.60
Chiefs of production, director's assistants	55	5.5	101.43
Average and lower engineering, technical, and office personnel	45	4.5	82.98

<u>Source</u>   Brus, <u>ND</u>, No.12, 1955, pp.68-9

   The premium rates for fulfilment and overfulfilment of the plan varied greatly. Employees of high priority industries and enterprises were entitled to higher premium rates inducing more considerable overfulfilment in those areas than in the lower priority ones. The 1954 regulation in light industry stipulated only a 5 per cent increase for each percentage of plan overfulfilment. Overfulfilment was limited to 102 per cent with no additional premiums applicable for exceeding the limit.[61] But in certain branches of heavy industry the premium rates were much higher. For example, in ferrous metallurgy each percentage of plan overfulfilment warranted additional premium amounting to 12 per cent of basic salary and no ceiling was imposed for overfulfilment.[62]
   As mentioned, in some industries, for example the wool industry, premiums for output plan fulfilment depended also on fulfilment of the quality and assortment plans. This was accomplished by deducting from the premium 0.25 or 0.5 per cent for each per cent of second or third class merchandise produced over the specified quantity, and 5 per cent for each per cent

of shortages or scrap material.[63] Similarly for each
percentage of shortage in the assortment plan 6 to 8
per cent of the premium was deducted. But each percentage of production plan underfulfilment reduced the
premium by 20 per cent, whereas fulfilment of the production plan below 90 per cent deprived the employees of
premiums altogether.[64] Decreases of premiums due to
production plan underfulfilment were incommensurate
with deductions for neglect of quality and assortment
plans. The interest of management was first and foremost concentrated on fulfilling the quantitative output
targets. Consequently the incentives to comply with the
assortment and quality plans were ineffective and did
not perceptively improve quality or adherence to the
assortment plan.[65]

It was realized that this premium system neglected
costs as management strove for output flagrantly disregarding costs. By 1954 a cost reduction premium was
instituted. For example, in light industry this premium was calculated uniformly in relation to the current quarterly plans. For each 0.1 per cent of above
plan cost reduction management was entitled to a premium amounting to 3 per cent of basic salary. Underfulfilment of the cost reduction plan did not entail
any sanctions, and its 100 per cent fulfilment did not
produce any premiums.[66]

In relation to the premiums for output those for
cost reduction were rather insignificant. The manager
faced with a decision whether to increase output or
reduce costs would undoubtedly follow the former course.
As it has been pointed out, whenever contradictory incentives, stimulating in different directions, are
simultaneously directed at the same employees it is
unavoidable that conflicts between such incentives
must arise, where the preponderant incentives are those
affording more immediate and higher financial benefits.[67]

The managers of many firms were not even confronted
with conflicts between increase of output and cost
reduction, as concealment of cost reduction possibilities
is one of the relatively easiest manipulations. None of
the firm's plan indexes are as difficult for supervisors
to prepare as the projected cost reduction.[68] The firms
received from the central boards cost reduction tasks
based on data submitted by them, results and conditions
of the preceding plan period, and the remaining plan

elements, especially assortment and procurement possibilities. Very often cost reduction premiums rewarded
planning error. In a majority of enterprises the errors
in planning did not stem from erroneous judgment or in-
advertence but from a conscious underestimation of possibilities since premiums were received for above plan
reduction of costs. For example, the cost reduction
target for the "Struga" enterprise of the wool industry
was set by the central board at 1,800 thousand zl. for
1955. But the plan did not reflect the changes in the
processing of scarves. Whereas in 1954 they had been
printed at a cost of 4 zl. each, in 1955 their printing
was to be subcontracted at a cost of 1.20 zl. each.
The resulting savings would be 2.80 zl. a piece. The
1955 production plan stipulated 780 thousand pieces of
this assortment, and cost reduction only on the printing of scarves would amount to 2,184 thousand zl.[69]

The cost reduction plan was a product of broad approximations and estimates without calculations of
planned unit costs. For example, the wool industry's
results for individual quarterly plans diverged
greatly from plan assumptions as illustrated in Table

Table 25 - <u>1955 Cost Reduction Targets in Selected Firms</u>

Enterprises of wool industry	In percentages					
	First Quarter		Second Quarter		Third Quarter	
	P	F	P	F	P	F
Pietrusinski	1.6	2.1	2.0	0.2	1.5	4.7
Tomaszow	1.8	3.9	1.2	6.9	2.3	10.3
Nowotki	2.8	5.5	2.1	5.5	3.1	8.7
Zlocieniec	1.8	4.4	6.1	0.9	3.4	12.9

P = plan, F = fulfilment

Source W. Moscicka, et al., op.cit., p.25

25. In all four enterprises listed above the cost reduction plan was greatly exceeded in the first quarter. In
the Tomaszow and Nowotki enterprises, notwithstanding
overfulfilment of the target in the first quarter, the
central board lowered the cost reduction index for the

second quarter considering the possibilities exhausted.
Nevertheless the second quarter's results indicated
once again considerable cost reduction. In view of
the substantial reductions reported for the first
quarter by Pietrusinski and Zlocieniec the central board
increased the second quarter's targets which remained
unfulfilled. These enterprises shifted their cost
reduction reports to the third quarter, realizing that
the third quarter's targets will be substantially
lowered, enabling them to report exorbitant overfulfilment of cost reduction indexes. This would provide
management with a much higher premium than if the second
quarter's indexes had been only slightly overfulfilled.

Hence no matter what side conditions were imposed
on the distribution of premiums for the production plan,
neither the sanctions nor the stimuli were successful
in mitigating the nefarious consequences brought about
by rewarding increase of output. It was evident that
the state did not reckon the benefits ensuing from
increased production against additional costs incurred.

Since production plan fulfilment was the criterion
for judging and rewarding managerial performance, and
since it is easier to fulfil a lower plan than a higher
one, the firm's management endeavored to minimize the
output target. A lower target would allow a wider
safety margin for overfulfilling it.[70] To accomplish
this management reduced reported capacity to the
central boards. Undoubtedly the setting of the production plan for the enterprise and the appraisal of its
capacity rested finally with the central board but it
drew heavily on data submitted by the firm. Concealment of capacity was a rather simple operation. For
example, as a basis for all 1955 quarterly plans the
cotton mill in Ozorkow reported the spindles on hand
reduced by 509 which had to undergo repairs. Actually
these spindles were gradually returned to production
in the following order: on February 27, 1955, 114
spindles were returned; on May 16,88; on June 25,137;
on July 14,53; on July 30,90, so that from August on
only 27 spindles remained to be repaired. The 1955
production plan for the enterprise Nowotki was based
on the capacity of 38 looms as reported by the firm,
but fulfilled on 41 looms. During the first half of
the year the output of the 3 additional looms amounted
to 7,790 meters of wool valued at 2,058,000 zl., con-

stituting 4.69 per cent of total value of production.[71]

The wise and successful manager did not strive for excessive plan overfulfilment surmising that the plan for the following period would automatically be raised. Such increases endangered plan fulfilment and robbed him of the safety margin necessary for overfulfilment. When the production plan was excessively overfulfilled the excess would be excluded from the report to the central board. The director acted in this manner "in order not to uncover his cards and let sleeping dogs lie."[72] But this concealment was also prompted by the need to accumulate reserves for the following period. The unreported output assured the manager of production plan fulfilment in spite of unforeseen future perturbations. For example, Nowotki fulfilled its production plan in June of 1955 by 107.9 per cent. A part of the fabric produced amounting to 270,000 zl. was unreported and withdrawn from the stocks of finished goods. It was then returned in July and reported as produced that month. Safety measures taken to ensure premiums were also noted in the Bularz enterprise. In January,1955 total output amounted to 85,400,000 spindles there. Only 83,864,000 were reported. Whereas production in February amounted actually to 81,257,000 spindles, it was reported as 83,016,000. In April the production plan was fulfilled by 104.7 per cent with only 101.9 per cent reported. In May production was fulfilled by 99.7 per cent with 101.9 per cent reported.[73]

When the firm was faced with flagrant underfulfilment of the output plan and no reserves were available from the previous months, management would augment the total amount of reported production by other devious methods.[74] Such increases were obtained through a difficult to detect cost manipulation. Due to arbitrariness in determining the degree of readiness of unfinished production, management reported semi-finished production as processed to a higher degree than it actually was.[75] Consequently production plan fulfilment hinged partly on the valuation of work in process by the cost accountant.

It should be stressed that the enterprise's wage fund and number of employees were limited and strictly controlled in relation to output. The road to higher value of output led naturally to preference of material intensive production.[76] The higher the cost of material inputs, the higher, <u>ceteris paribus</u>, the value of gross production.[77] Although high costs did not deprive management from premiums earned for production, given the limited wage fund, labor costs could not be expanded. But waste of materials was largely condoned. The almost exclusive use of piece rate wages for production workers aggravated waste of materials at the level of direct production. In their efforts to obtain the highest possible wages the workers were concerned uniquely with increasing output. If material waste resulted in the process it was of no consequence.   In many industries output was measured in weight. This induced management to produce the heaviest possible goods wasting in the process an incredible amount of materials. Thus it was revealed that the control of 2,400 metal sheets at the ZISPO plant indicated that only 80 sheets were sized and weighed according to standards. The balance exceeded standards by about 4.2 per cent.[78]

Management's effort to produce goods of high material costs led to a development beyond conceivable boundaries of subcontracted production, or what is termed in Soviet-type economies as cooperation. No wages or production time would have to be expanded on the semi-fabricate and its value, calculated at transfer prices, would be included in the value of the finished good, augmenting the total value of output. Without any additional productive effort and time the firm increased its total value of output.[79]

To obtain the premium for output fulfilment management was bound to adhere to the labor productivity index. The index resulted from total value of production divided by the number of workers employed. This again steered management towards preference of material intensive production.[80] The easiest way to increase labor productivity is to produce goods of higher material costs.

All factors prompting management to produce material intensive goods also incited it to replace materials for labor without paying due heed to the costs of one or the other solution. Increased costs of replacing materials for labor would not deter management from shifting materials for labor. Increased costs were of little consequence, but increased labor costs might cause severely sanctioned overexpenditures of the wage fund or underfulfilment of the labor productivity index endangering management's personal financial gains.

The 1957 Reform of the Premium System

As we know, in November, 1956, the firms became officially more independent and their economic role was enhanced.
This necessitated a simultaneous revision of the premium
system. But the revision was delayed by a year, resulting in individual premiums skyrocketting to enormous
proportions. Unjustified wage disproportions between
branches of industry and enterprises developed. The
first half of 1957 was a period of growing confusion and
spontaneously arising disproportions.[81]

In 1957 a reform of the premium system was undertaken.
It was introduced progressively beginning with the third
quarter of 1957. In view of premiums acting in divergence
with commands it was postulated and then implemented to
weaken the incentives' intensity by decreasing the share
of premiums in total remuneration of managerial personnel
and augmenting basic salaries. In metallurgy, for
example, salaries were increased and the maximum premium was limited to 30 per cent of salary.[82] However,
since the reform was introduced progressively the firms
embraced later endeavored in the meantime to increase
their employees' salaries and augment premiums.[83]

The 1957 reform made an effort at departing from
premiums for output. But the existing premium system
was not replaced by one based on synthetic results.
Detailed criteria and conditions for premiums were not
specified. They were to be elaborated by the firms
themselves on the basis of regulations issued by the
responsible ministries.[84] Instead of the heretofore
progressively increasing premiums the institution of
the premium fund was introduced.[85] The premium fund
amounted from 10 to 12 per cent of the basic wage fund.
Premiums could not exceed 30 to 35 per cent of an
employee's basic salary.[86] The introduction of a
ceiling for the premium fund was deemed to be one of
the greatest achievements of the reform. The attempt
to constrain the spontaneous growth of premiums was
successful.

A special premium amounting to 1 per cent of basic
salary for each percentage of output exceeding the base,
which could not be lower than the output produced last
year, or planned for the current year, was introduced
in priority industries to reward managerial personnel
in technical departments. This was a revamped type of

progressive premium for overfulfilment of the production
plan. It was a concession to the advocates of premiums
for overfulfilment of the production plan.[87]

Although the reform was a step forward in improving
the premium system, it did so only superficially. The
ministerial regulations continued using production plan
fulfilment as the basis for distributing premiums.[88]
In general the enterprises did not elaborate any new
criteria. The associations also fell short of expectations, forgoing the possibilities offered to them by
the system.[89]

The system introduced in 1957 functioned until the
end of 1959. In time payment of premiums depended
entirely on fulfilment of the production plan with a
renewed concentration of the most important incentives
on production. The interests of managerial personnel
were still narrowed down exclusively to the fulfilment
of the output plan.[90]

The 1960 Reform of the Premium System

The turning point in the evolution of economic incentives in Poland was the year 1960 described as:

> In 1960 a serious step forward was made towards
> the synchronization of the activity of the entire
> system of material incentives for employees. This
> was accomplished by making the basis for the cal-
> culation of the enterprise fund and the premium fund
> uniform. The acceptance, in principle, of uniform
> methods and solutions for these basic systems
> awakening the interest of the employees in an
> improvement of economic and financial results was
> a positive and constructive element in the entire
> system of economic incentives.[91]

The reform aimed at applying a synthetic criterion focusing on all economic tasks of the enterprise. Such a
criterion could be profit (or accumulation),[92] a variable
of both the value of production reckoned in transfer
prices and cost reduction.[93] The principle of basing
incentives on profit engendered many controversies. It
was conceived that if the magnitude of premiums would
be tied in with the improvement of profitability
actually attained, this would create far-reaching dis-

parities in the material situation of individual firms.
Other reservations resulted from the fact that reserves
for increases in profitability are limited within firms
and it is impossible to count on any substantial improvement in financial results from year to year.[94]

The principle of basing premiums on profits and the
improvement of profits with respect to the preceding
year aspired at creating stimuli, on the one hand, for
a complete exploitation of production capacity in enterprises, and, on the other hand, to live up to the
principle of economic calculation and sound management.
It was contemplated that the system would depart from
production plan fulfilment as a basis for the attainment of premiums and at the same time would afford a
possibility to reinstate to the firm a positive role
in the construction of plans.[95]

The reform of the premium system initiated in January 1960 embraced the bulk of centrally planned industry with profit or accumulation becoming the performance
criteria.[96] Improvement in profit was expressed in a
percentage ratio (i.e., the result of the current year
decreased by the result of the preceding year) to the
production costs of goods sold during the current year.[97]
As in the computation of the enterprise fund the basis
of comparison (last year's profit) was to be recalculated
to provide a consistent frame of reference. Even though
the principal assumption of the new premium system was
the use of last year's results as a frame of reference,
it could not be applied when the plan directives
stipulated a deterioration of results, or when a substantial change of product mix precluded comparisons.
In such cases planned results for the current year
constitute the frame of reference. This procedure was
to be an exception rather than the rule.

The premium fund consists of three separate parts:
the basic, additional, and guarantee funds.

As a condition for the formation of the basic premium
fund the enterprises must plan and fulfil a financial
result equal to last year's result. The basic premium
fund's size is set at 10 to 25 per cent of the basic
wage fund of white collar workers.[98] The ceiling for
individual premiums is 35 per cent of basic salary. If
the firm's financial result deteriorates in relation to
last year's the basic premium fund will be subject to a
proportionate decrease and should the deterioration

exceed 4 per cent the premium fund will not be formed.[99]

It was stipulated that white collar workers receive "regulation premiums" and "premiums as tokens of appreciation". Regulation premiums are received exclusively by employees in managerial positions "whose work has a direct bearing on the results of the enterprise's economic activity." The remaining white collar workers may receive premiums as tokens of appreciation for high attainments in their individual work.[100]

Premiums are calculated quarterly and payments constitute advancements only. If the yearly financial result proves to be lower than last year's the basic premium fund formed and distributed in the first quarters is charged against the premium fund of the following year. This is a "two-way street" permitting enterprises to make up for shortcomings during the previous quarters at the end of the year, enabling them to form premium funds for the quarters when the funds could not be formed because of a deterioration in results.

The 1960 percentage ratio of the basic premium fund to the basic wage fund of white collar workers was much lower than expected. The average for the entire industry was below 9 per cent of the basic wage fund.[101] Similarly the individual premiums were much lower than the allowed limits. The average quarterly premium from the basic premium fund and the corresponding percentage to average quarterly salary was 672 zl. and 9.3 for administrative personnel, 846 zl. and 10.0 for engineering and technical personnel including the director and his assitants, and 410 zl. and 8.0 for office workers.[102] But these figures cover only distribution of premiums from the basic premium fund for 1960. Substantial distribution of premiums from the basic premium fund for the fourth quarter was conducted during January, 1961, distorting somewhat the statistical data reported. In 1961 the premium fund was still below the allowed percentage of the basic wage fund. The average payment per recipient amounted to below 800 zl. per quarter, indicating an increase of about 130 zl. in relation to 1960.[103] As for the division among regulation and token of appreciation premiums in the leading chemical combine in Oswiecim the proportions of regulation premiums to basic salary were 13.8 in 1960 and 13.5 in 1961, whereas the respective figures for token of appreciation premiums were 4.2 and 4.5.[104]

The essential incentives were incorporated in the additional premium fund to be formed at the <u>end</u> of each financial year. Its formation was subjected to planning and fulfilling a financial result higher than that of the preceding year. The additional fund was to vary and its magnitude made, in principle, fully dependent on improvement of profit. Only managerial personnel is entitled to premiums from the additional premium fund. Although the size of the fund is unlimited, a ceiling is imposed on individual premiums amounting from 15 to 20 per cent of basic annual salary.

The mechanism of the additional premium fund is built in such a manner that it should induce the firm to high but down to earth planning of financial results.[105] The magnitude of this fund hinges on whether the improvement of financial results has been actually planned by the firm. When establishing the planned improvement in profit for the given year the firm indicates on the basis of a progressive table the additional premium fund which it will receive if it fulfils the improvement assumed in the plan. The problem of the formation of this fund in case of over or underfulfilment of the planned improvement in profit was solved by applying preferential rates. The rate of this fund is the percentage ratio between the planned amount of improvement of profit and the amount of the additional premium fund according to the table received from the association.[106]

There are three possible relations between the planned and actual magnitudes of improvement of profit. 1) In case of fulfilment of the planned improvement the enterprise is entitled to an additional premium fund as planned, i.e., corresponding to the amount resulting from the table. Due to the progressive rates this situation is the most attractive for management. 2) If the enterprise exceeds its planned improvement, it receives the additional premium fund based on the rate of the fund resulting from the plan applying it not to the planned but to the actual amount of improvement of profit. In this case the firm does not take advantage of the progressive rates. It loses the advantages it could have obtained had it planned the result attained. 3) If the enterprise does not realize the planned improvement, it forms the fund at three

positions lower on the table than the position allowed
for the improvement in profit actually attained. In
this case the enterprise loses the advantages it could
have gained if the plan had not been set too high.
Consequently it would be most advantageous for the firm
to plan a high but realistic improvement in profit.

The mechanism of these incentives was tied in
directly with the apportionment of plan targets down
the chain of command from the PC until they reach the
firm. The directives include the amount of profit (accumulation), the absolute amount of the additional premium
fund, and its relation to the planned wage fund. On
this basis the enterprise prepares its plan "not lower
than the directive indexes set for it, but it may pro-
pose higher targets" to obtain a higher additional
fund.[107]

If such an incentive is to be operative, directive
indexes regarding the accumulation plan and the premium fund must be transmitted from the association to
the enterprise simultaneously with the other plan
indexes. If the plan directives are not complete it is
impossible to correlate the financial and production
parts of the plan. Financial planning is then reduced
to futile monetary recalculations of elements previously set in the technical production plan. Increase in
profit must be closely tied in with increase in
production targets and solution of technical, technological, and organizational problems affecting costs.[108]
Nevertheless procrastinations in the distribution of
financial plan indexes were such that in July,1961,many
enterprises had not yet received the 1961 financial
plan indexes. The same was true of 1962 and the plan
for 1963 showed only a slight improvement.[109] The steel
mill Lenin in Nowa Huta, the pride of Polish heavy
industry, had its financial plan indexes for 1962
finally approved by December of that year.[110] Those
delays are of particular importance since delays of
even lesser magnitude make it impossible to increase
the tasks incorporated in the plan.

The delays are caused by shortcomings in profit planning featuring lengthy controversies and discussions on
the subject of the magnitude of the plan indexes.[111]
Although firms may be induced, ceteris paribus, to raise
the assigned profit target in drafting their financial
plan, they are simultaneously interested in obtaining

the lowest possible initial target since "the lower the
tasks stipulated in directives, the easier it is for the
enterprise to increase them in the technical-economic
plan, and the easier it is to fulfil and overfulfil this
plan."[112] In their controversy with enterprises the
associations suffer from a lack of knowledge of the
firms' internal conditions, and are "lacking objective,
scientific criteria for the determination of plans.
They are lacking the methodology to ascertain the
actual production capacity and the criteria for the
evaluation of efficiency of investments and technical
progress."[113]

The association is under pressure from above to
distribute among its enterprises the total index of
profit assigned to it by the ministry. The association distributes directives mechanically resulting in
some incorporating a wide safety margin whereas others
are almost impossible to fulfil.[114] The inequitable
intensity of plans in different firms is a product of
the enterprises' pressures for low targets versus
the association's "working knowledge of the theory of
the game". But the part of accumulation that the
association is unable to allocate among its enterprises
brings about the phenomenon of "undistributed accumulation". This may be mitigated if enterprises overfulfil
their plans. But it immensely complicates the situation
when firms do come forward to have their directive
indexes increased. The association must then notify
the MF of an increase in its planned accumulation.
It is impossible for it to do so if it was unable to
allocate the undistributed accumulation among its
firms. This results in serious confusion and attempts
by the association to foist the undistributed accumulation on the enterprises which have unveiled their
capacity by coming forth with a proposal to raise the
plan index. The enterprises are then not entitled to
benefit from the counterplan they proposed as the
additional tasks are in the form of directive plan
indexes.

As we know, the association often changes directive
plan indexes. The firms cannot treat the financial
indexes obtained as final. Under such circumstances to
come out with proposals to increase the plan is treated
by management with particular distrust. Hence the
incentives to increase the plan are largely eliminated.[115]

The incentives directed towards increase of the plan by the enterprises have in practice met with yet another impediment. We refer to the essential disparities between the firms' premium system and that of associations. Premiums for the associations' employees amount from 5 to 15 per cent of the wage fund and are paid out for meeting the production plan and cost plans by the associations' enterprises.[116] The firms' strife for the lowest possible accumulation targets is reinforced by the associations' interest that the enterprises should obtain low directives to ensure the fulfilment of their production and cost plans, hence the associations' personnel's premiums.[117] However, this accord ceases to exist if the enterprise should attempt to increase its tasks, as in such action the association can only see a threat to its own premiums. Hence the association's and enterprise's interests are in accord when they should diverge, and diverge when they should be in accord, defeating the incentives incorporated in the additional premium fund.[118]

It is most difficult to approximate the average premium per employee from the additional premium fund, since only managerial personnel is entitled to these premiums and there are no adequate records of this personnel. From estimates it has been gathered that these premiums are received by 30 to 40 per cent of white collar workers in industry. This high percentage results from inclusion of foremen in managerial personnel. The average payments could be estimated at approximately 1,700 zl. per year. In the group of enterprises investigated by the MF the individual premiums varied greatly in size, and their recipients fluctuated from 10 to 45 per cent of white collar workers. Monthly premiums received by managerial personnel in this group are illustrated in Table 26. In these enterprises the payments fluctuated from 918 zl. to 5,150 zl. per year. The highest payments were observed where only a scant number of employees participated in them. Whereas the average payment of premiums amounted to about 5 per cent of a manager's salary, it amounted to 8.1 per cent in the enterprises investigated.[119] In the Oswiecim chemical combine the 1960 average premiums from the additional premium fund amounted only to 5.7 per cent of basic salary. They were reported as hardly incentives for their recipients.[120]

Table 26 - <u>1960 Monthly Premium From the Additional</u>
            <u>Premium Fund</u>

Position	In Zlotys		
	Minimum	Maximum	Average
Director	160	862	481
Technical director	145	783	450
Chief accountant	115	663	346
Chief mechanic	114	700	302
Technical department heads	80	600	230
Foremen	23	329	144

<u>Source</u> B. Fick, <u>Fin</u>., No.11, 1961, p.22

Hence the premium is far below the allowed limit of 15
to 20 per cent of salary. Moreover formation of an
additional fund is not universal. In 1960 10 per cent
of enterprises did not form any premium funds. Twenty-
nine per cent formed only the basic premium fund, being
unable to attain a basis for the formation of the additional premium fund.[121]
    When the additional premium fund is not entirely
distributed its excesses are transferred into a guarantee
fund remaining at the firm's disposal and cumulated over
the years. The guarantee fund was to be an automatic
yardstick measuring economic results for a number of
years. However, this function of the guarantee fund
was considerably weakened by imposing on it a ceiling
of 10 per cent of the basic salaries of white collar
workers. When the ceiling is reached excess funds
are reckoned as the firm's profits. Should the
guarantee fund reach the ceiling the limits on individual premiums from the additional premium fund
would be raised from 15 to 20 per cent of salary.
    Direct distributions of premiums from the guarantee
fund are to mitigate risks involved in the introduction of technical progress causing a temporary decrease
in profit endangering the basic premium fund. Under
such circumstances instead of the usual premiums from
the basic premium fund, premiums may be paid out
directly from the guarantee fund. This fund is an

adroit and clever construction incorporating, however,
in its very foundations serious weaknesses. One of them
is the unnecessarily rigid limitation of the amount of
the guarantee fund. The other is the needless narrowing
down of premium distribution only to cases where technical progress is introduced. It seems that there
should have been no risk in allowing the guarantee
fund to be used in all cases where there would be no
possibility of obtaining a basic premium fund. This
might have enhanced its role and increased managerial
personnel's concern with it.

Only scant data were reported on the guarantee fund
and it is impossible to judge adequately its magnitude
in industry. Estimates indicate that in 1960 only 10
per cent of enterprises were entitled to form this
fund. From these estimates it was deduced that approximately 13 per cent of the additional premium fund was
incorporated into the guarantee fund, constituting
about 0.5 per cent of the wage fund of white collar
workers.[122]

But the premium system was not based exclusively
on incentives tied in directly with the formation of
the premium fund. It was conceived that the attainment
of a given profit would not be sufficient as a condition
for distributing premiums. Hence a number of other
conditions were superimposed. The decision whether
the premium funds should be distributed was vested in
the association. It became a tool serving the association to influence the firms. The conditions for the
activation of the premium funds were differentiated into
"constant", binding on all enterprises, and "variable"
ones.[123]

Neither the basic nor the additional premium funds
can be activated if the constant conditions are not
fulfilled. These conditions are: 1) fulfilment of the
production plan and 2) adherence to the wage fund
limits. In 1961 these conditions were supplemented
with: 3) adherence to the cost plan limits and 4)
fulfilment of the planned delivery of export orders.[124]
In practice the most important constant condition is
the fulfilment of the production plan and secondly
adherence to the wage fund. As for the remaining two
they appear rather on paper.[125] It is the general
consensus that actually the only constant condition
that management is prone to observe is fulfilment of

the production plan:

> The distribution of legally established types of
> premiums takes place when the enterprise has ful-
> filled its planned tasks and, strictly speaking,
> when it fulfilled 100 per cent of the production
> plan. Then very little attention is paid to other
> technical and economic indicators. From time to
> time sporadic events occur which symbolically lower
> the premiums distributed because of such "trifles"
> as underfulfilment of the assortment plan, excess
> of planned production costs, excess of the wage
> fund, underfulfilment of the planned cooperation
> tasks, etc. However, this "penalty" is unpropor-
> tionately low in comparison with the penalty for
> underfulfilling the production plan.[126]

The introduction of some of these conditions prompts
very serious reservations. This is especially true of
production plan fulfilment. The fact that this condition actually numbs the incentives of the system was
either overlooked or not sufficiently considered.
Another serious misconception was the introduction of
the condition of adhering to the cost plan. In conjunction with the condition of production plan fulfilment it renders management's concern with raising the
plan indexes highly questionable. An increase in
profit is closely tied in with cost reduction and/or
increase of output. An enterprise aspiring at increasing its planned profit target must, ceteris paribus,
either increase its output or decrease its cost targets,
or both. But should it be unable to realize fully the
increased profit plan it is still entitled to an additional premium fund even though lower than the one
originally planned. But if it is unable to fulfil
the augmented production and cost targets it forgoes
premiums from the additional and basic premium funds.
The sanctions for underfulfilling the raised counter-
plans are too severe to warrant counterproposals by
the enterprise.[127] Consequently the firm may be interested in increasing its profit targets resulting in
increased additional premium fund, but it is simultaneously interested in setting the lowest possible
output and cost reduction targets as underfulfilment
of these indexes will deprive management of premiums

emanating from the basic and additional premium funds.
Hence it is inconceivable to expect enterprises to
accept the risks involved in an increase of profit
plans as they would be most unwilling to hazard the
relatively attractive premiums from the basic premium
fund. It is evident that the imposition of conditions
for activating the premium fund was a great impediment
on the operation of the incentive system, creating contradictions which management certainly cannot surmount.[128]

In .addition the associations were empowered to
operate at will with a wide gamut of variable conditions for activating the premium funds in their firms.
In practice, however, the associations have not taken
advantage of the possibilities offered by such a tool
for influencing their firms. The only conditions management has had to reckon with are the constant ones,
uniformly applied.[129]

The "Branch Principles for the Granting and Payment
of Individual Premiums From the Premium Fund" were
intended as a basis for every enterprise to elaborate
its own internal system of distributing premiums. The
firms were to avoid mechanical distribution and ensure
the effectiveness of incentives for channeling the
interests of particular departments and positions towards specific accomplishments. But in practice the
majority of firms employ the standardized "Branch
Principles" received from their ministries. They do
not elaborate them according to their specific
conditions.[130] The system suffers from negligence in
assigning specific instructions for the firm's
individual departments indicating the influence of the
execution of those tasks on the improvement of profit
and the amount of the premium fund.

There is a definite tendency to extend the payments
of regulation premiums beyond the ranks of managerial
personnel, decreasing the size and importance of such
premiums. The token of appreciation premiums perform
only the function of a simple adjustment in salaries
calculated as a percentage of salary regardless of
performance. In the chemical industry they constitute
approximately 4 per cent of basic salary.[131]

From the evidence available, the premium system
inducing the firms to take profit as a variable in
their maximization of premium calculation certainly
seems like a step forward in the entire system of

evaluating performance and economic incentives. Apart
from its basic weakness of gearing the incentive system
to the fulfilment of the production plan, no remedy
was found nor forces generated against minimization of
plans by enterprises. Failure in this respect seems
to be complete. Another shortcoming of the 1960 reform
of the premium system, which to a large extent has
nullified its successes, is the existence of specialized
premiums with which the reform did not cope successfully.

Specialized Premiums

Prior to the 1960 reform of the premium system
numerous specialized premiums were accorded for the
execution of specific tasks. With the introduction of
the new premium system an attempt was made to rid the
scene of specialized premiums.[132] These premiums had
lost their meaning as the indices on which they were
based were incorporated in the newly created premium
system. They also created the danger of conflict with
the premiums from the basic and additional premium funds.
However, unsurmountable resistance was encountered
against abolition of specialized premiums:

It must be realized how colossal the practical
difficulties are. The existing premiums had become a somewhat social reality. The attempt to
liquidate or diminish them encountered protests...
The inclusion of the abolished specialized premiums into the basic remuneration is not a simple
matter. Usually they pertain to a particular group
of employees and the inclusion of premiums in basic
pay would disturb the proportions in the wage structure or the common premiums.[133]

The 1960 attempts to put some order in the specialized
premiums were not successful. From the 40 types of premiums uncovered only two were successfully discarded:
premiums for cooperative delivery and savings of lumber
in the lumber industry. Sporadic attempts were made by
individual branches of industry to liquidate some of the
specialized premiums in their particular branch.[134]
Little was done to limit the amounts set aside for these
premiums, especially for economic progress (improvement
of financial results), the collection of scrap, and

economical use of fuels and electricity. At least an
attempt was made to tie in specialized incentives with
the reformed premium system. The distribution of these
premiums was made dependent on whether the firm was
entitled to a basic premium fund in the given period
forestalling a situation where premiums could be obtained for executing segmentary tasks with the firm's main
targets remaining unfulfilled.

But even premiums which strikingly duplicated the
activity of the reformed premium system, as for instance
premiums for economic progress, were not discontinued.
Similarly export premiums paid for the fulfilment of
the export plan remained in existence, although one of
the conditions for distributing premiums from the premium fund is the delivery of export orders. Premiums
paid out for input savings were not altered although
such savings are reflected in cost reduction, therefore,
in the increase of profit.

A ceiling of 200 per cent of basic monthly salary
was imposed on the annual sum of individual specialized
premiums, excluding those for technical progress. It
was expected that the ceiling would weaken the quantitative concentration of premiums on managerial positions.

Some of the specialized premiums are applied locally
and others throughout state-owned industry. The
economic progress fund, technical progress fund, export
activation fund, and special premiums for economical use
of inputs and other savings are among the most important
ones in general application.

The premiums from the economic progress fund are
paid in practice for recognition of individual performance. No concrete regulations or criteria are applied.
Generally those premiums are concentrated on the highest
managerial positions, duplicating payments from the
additional premium fund.[135] The sum of premiums paid out
from this fund in 1961 amounted to 90,343.3 thousand
zl.[136]

The technical progress fund could play a substantial
role but the regulations for premium distribution are
imprecise. Distribution of premiums varies considerably.
Premiums are often allotted to employees who contribute
little to technical progress.[137]In many cases if an
inventor wants to construct a prototype and have his
invention approved he has to go through his superiors
and promise to pay them a percentage of his premiums in

an underhanded manner. In some cases his superiors are
written in as cooperators on the project and the percentage paid out legally.[138] The technical progress fund is
one of the more plentiful among the firm's premium
funds.[139] Some of the inventions submitted are not
strictly controlled. Thus "in the sugar industry
people were rewarded for designing machines which in
all respects resembled the machines that eighteen years
ago the sugar plants received from the UNRRA."[140]

The lack of long range planning is a serious blow
against technical progress. Since management is unable
to forecast prospective premiums accruing from future
performance, all efforts are concentrated on current
plan fulfilment. This situation is aggravated by a
turnover of employees affecting on the average one
third of a firm's staff annually.[141] It is frequently
remarked that management is interested in benefits
which it can reap for current performance and will pay
little heed to future benefits flowing from technical
progress. Since the introduction of new or modified
technological processes may cause a temporary deterioration of profit technical progress is "unprofitable"
for the firm's management.[142]

A case in point is the predicament of the steel mill
Labedy ordered in 1962 by its association to use mazut
for its six 100-ton open hearth furnaces. The introduction of the new fuel caused many difficulties in
the production processes, and costs during 1962 rose
considerably entailing underfulfilment of the profit
plan. The steel mill had to forgo the premium fund
for the fourth quarter. The employees were threatened
with reimbursement of premiums advanced during the
first three quarters of the year. The right to form
an enterprise fund was completely denied. Management's
dissatisfaction was aggravated when 120,000 zl. were
accorded by the association for distribution among
the employees who participated in the introduction of
the new fuel. The director withheld payment of those
premiums fearing deteriorating employee relations as
some blame the people to be rewarded for the "injustice"
suffered by the others.[143]

But the size of premiums from the technical progress
fund does little to promote inventions in the firm.[144]
The value of individual premiums depends essentially on
the savings which the invention will bring in to the

enterprise and whether it will be classified as an
invention, technical reform, or improvement. The
discrimination of the size of premiums is illustrated
in Table 27. Even though the amounts seem considerable

Table 27 - Premiums for Inventions

Amount of savings in zlotys	Amount of premiums in zlotys		
	Invention	Technical reform	Improvement
10,000	2,290	1,300	740
50,000	6,900	3,650	2,000
100,000	10,800	5,700	3,100
200,000	17,200	9,200	4,800
500,000	32,200	17,000	9,000
1,000,000	52,200	27,000	14,000
5,000,000	157,000	94,000	40,000
10,000,000 and up	247,000	189,000	62,500

Source   Z. Madej, W poszukiwaniu miliardow, (Warsaw:
         1962), p.78

it should be remembered that they are usually distributed
among a wide circle of employees who are deemed to have
participated either in the preparation or implementation
of the invention. This considerably reduces the magnitude
of the individual premium. Premiums exceeding 3,000 zl.
are paid by instalments and complaints are raised in
the press that this further reduces the attractiveness
of those premiums.[145]
     Although the export activation fund was originally
intended to reward initiation of incremental exportable
output, in practice its premiums are also paid for export
production incorporated in the plan. As a rule these
premiums are paid out to employees who do not contribute
to the activation of export. A concentration of those
premiums has been observed among top management.[146]
The size of premiums often exceeds the total amount of
premiums obtained by management from the basic and
additional premium and enterprise funds.[147]
     Among the premiums for savings of inputs, those for
economical use of fuels and electric power are the most
prominent.[148] Sizable sums are paid but their induce-

ment activity is inadequate mainly because savings are
calculated on obsolete norms of material usage seldom
updated.[149] These premiums are again paid out to a
wide circle of employees who do not contribute to the
savings. The failure of these incentives is indicated
by their sporadic reinforcement with commands. As
pointed out by Bobrowski, if the incentives are effective the commands are unnecessary.[150]

The premium paid for collection of scrap is in direct
conflict with the economical use of materials. Considerable quantities of materials are simply transformed
into shavings and scrap as delivery of an adequate
quantity of scrap will ensure premiums.[151]

Failure to cope with specialized premiums was not
only demonstrated in leaving the existing titles to
premiums almost untouched but also by allowing additional ones to be introduced,intensifying the confusion and
chaos in the field of incentives.[152] One of the newly
introduced specialized premiums is the one for savings
of the wage fund in the machine building industry. Since
the standard of comparison in calculating this saving is
the production plan, this mechanism creates enormously
strong stimuli for overstating the initial wage fund
required and understating the production plan to attain
the highest possible corrections of the wage fund.[153]
This type of premium disorganizes the process of planning, induces confusion in the administration of the
wage fund, and flagrantly contradicts the premium system.

Although bonuses paid by buyers to their suppliers
for above plan orders are not strictly special premiums,
they are nevertheless quite frequent. In view of their
quantitative importance they may detract management from
tasks rewarded by premiums of lesser financial attrac-
tion. A case in point was recently accorded publicity
in the press:

The Establishment $Ł$-2 received an order for the
production of three television transmitters for large
cities. The order was difficult, above plan, and
could be fulfilled only with overtime. Since
the overtime limit was exhausted and the authorities
- the Association of Radio and Television Stations -
did not allow the enterprise an additional wage fund,
the customers agreed to cover labor costs and premiums allowing nearly 900,000 zl. for this purpose.

But when the time for distribution came the workers
were paid for the time worked, whereas the premiums
were apportioned between the people who decided on
the apportionment. With the exception of designers
who undoubtedly earned the financial rewards, the
largest part of premiums was grabbed by a small
group of managers and representatives of the workers' self-management. The entire process was conducted in the greatest of secrecies on the basis
of "you play my game and I'll play yours."
The "big four" sat at the conference table and
awarded 30,000 zl. to management, which, in turn,
awarded 28,500 zl. to the four representatives of
the social and political organizations. To each
according to his functions and the authority
wielded from 3,500 zl. to 9,500 zl. per person.
The list of premiums was not published but the list
of workers who had been paid for overtime was
ceremoniously exhibited.[154]

Undoubtedly an enterprise's director who receives
9,500 zl. in premiums for this type of production, or
about 12 per cent of his annual salary in comparison
with the limit of 15 per cent from the additional premium fund - which incidentally at present is almost
never attained - will be more than willing to sacrifice
the premium derived from the fund based on the profit
index for the attainment of this type of premium.
At the end of 1963 there were over 50 types of
specialized premiums in socialized industry. ·The total
amount of annual payments from these premiums exceeded
1.3 billion zl., surpassing the basic premium fund in
state-owned industry.[155] But the magnitude of these
premiums would not be decisive if they would not be
concentrated on top managerial ranks. Individual
payments from the special premium funds are illustrated
in Table 28.
Directors' premiums from the additional premium fund
reached 8,000 zl. per year, constituting a rather small
share of the total premiums. About 67 per cent of all
directors received specialized premiums totaling about
10,000 zl. per year and 22.5 per cent of the directors
received such premiums reaching about 20,000 zl. a year.[156]
Hence incentives incorporated in the additional premium
fund cannot be decisive. The incentive system lacks unity

Table 28 - Some Special Premiums Paid in 1961

Funds	Total Payments	Average Annual Premium	Annual Premiums	
			From	To
Economic Progress	90,364,300	926	23	18,000
Technical Progress	66,539,500	1,700	23	49,000
Export Activation	73,829,608	1,385	31	17,600

Source   M. Misiak (ed.), op.cit., pp.76 and 565

of purpose. Instead of being the crucial premium, payments from the basic and additional premium funds have
become one of a number of incentives. Their force
depends on the relation between the advantages management can derive from the different specialized premiums and those that the reformed premium system can
offer. It is hard to disagree that:

> The new premium system constitutes at present only
> one of the elements of the complicated system of
> incentives which at times duplicate each other or
> contradict one another... An improvement of the
> system of premiums should be in the direction of
> enforcing the role and weight of the premium system
> based on synthetic measures of economic progress
> (financial results). This may be realized by
> abrogating special premiums and shifting those
> funds towards the principal premium system.[157]

The inherent conflicts between profit as a performance criterion, the reintroduction of production plan
fulfilment through the back door as the criterion sine
qua non, and the existence of a multitude of specialized premiums must be reconciled by management.

HOW TO PLAY THE GAME

The decisive number of economic incentives regulating
the activity of management still incite a desire for
lower plans and understatement of capacity. The distribution of premiums from the basic and additional
premium funds depends on the fulfilment of the planned
value of output. The increase of the planned wage fund
rests on the degree of overfulfilment of the production
plan, and successful operation hinges on fulfilment and
overfulfilment of the plan. The premiums for the
association's employees depend on the fulfilment of the
production plans by its subordinate enterprises. Finally appraisals by units of authority, Party, and social
organizations are based mainly - and at times exclusively - on the index of production plan fulfilment.[158]

As we know, there exists an interdependence between
data emanating from enterprises and directives received.
The directives depend on data emanating from the firms,
but due to their very nature of directives and incentives linked with them, they influence the formation of
data. This influence distorts data, leads to uninformed
and disorganized planning by the supervisory units of
authority. When planning the supervisory units correct
the data received. Corrections made are unsubstantiated
by analysis of existing conditions in firms, resulting
in an abstraction of corrected plan indexes transmitted
by the association to the enterprises from the ones the
enterprises estimated. Searching for a means of defence
from this correction enterprises vie with each other in
distorting information. Faced with the necessity of
making heavier and heavier corrections the supervisory
units of authority face the danger of greater and greater approximations, underestimates, and irrational
allocation of tasks. In their relation with the ministry
the associations demonstrate the same tendency. In their
reports they aim at minimizing the capacity of their
branch of industry.[159] The cumulative effect of the
underestimates and corrections has enormous repercussions
on the validity of the entire NEP. It generates confusion and an enormous waste of resources.

The production plan fulfilment condition induces
management to underestimate existing capacity. However,
there are limited opportunities to expand the rate of

output and increase profitability over the years without increasing capital intensity and modernization.
Although management is most reluctant to disrupt current operations, it is interested in expansion
accomplished basically by new additions to existing
capacity. Such expansion should not upset present
operations and should enable management to reap future
benefits with minimum loss of current ones. While
flagrant underutilization and unwillingness to renovate
the existing facilities prevail, expenditures for new
productive capacity are plaguing the Polish economy.

How to Secure Centralized Investments

    In his endeavors to expand the productive capacity
of the enterprise the director must resort to the
centralized allotment of subsidies for centralized
investments. He will submit to the association or
ministry proposals for the purchase of equipment and/or
expansion of plant together with a rough estimate of
the cost and efficiency of the proposed investment.
If the central authorities concur the investment
project will be approved, investment subsidies
allotted, and the green light to proceed given to
the enterprise.
    One of the reasons for the stupendous minimization
of planned investment costs is that "the cheaper the
investment, the easier it will be to 'shove' it into
the plan. The principle of underestimating costs is
applied with the purpose that its chances of entering
into the plan will be greater."[160]
    The limits imposed on the associations' and ministries'
centralized funds seriously constrain the investment
funds which may be expanded on a given enterprise.
However, depending on the prestige of a director **and the**
power he may wield with the association and ministry,
or the fact that centralized investment funds have been overlooked for a given enterprise, regardless of its needs,
the association may resort to manipulations similar to
those that took place in Nowy Targ during the construction of a shoe manufacturing combine. The shoe industry
was buying new machines for other factories for which
there were no investment funds, charging them to the
Nowy Targ construction.[161]
    But it is not always difficult to obtain centralized

investment funds, especially if a given enterprise
enjoys a high priority position. Although a certain
industry may be on the top priority list and all types
of centralized investments open to it at a given time,
the state's future policy may change.[162] Hence as a
precautionary measure, management will grab centralized
investment funds when available. The insecurity factor
governs the policy which the director adopts towards
centralized investments. There is little constraint
on the enterprise to minimize centralized investments
as management will be evaluated favorably albeit costs
are reduced through additional application of (free)
capital.

Only too often uninstalled equipment lies in stock
or under open skies. At the end of 1958 the value of
this equipment amounted to 3.2 billion zlotys, at the
end of 1960 4.5 billion, whereas at the end of 1963
the figure climbed to 8 billion zl.[163] An investigation
conducted at the beginning of 1963 revealed that in the
majority of cases uninstalled equipment amounts to 30
per cent of all acquisitions of capital goods. The
actual average interval between acquisition and transmission for installation exceeds 22 months.[164]

Concrete examples illustrate even better the almost
unbelievable delays. In 1955 the steel mill Kosciuszko
acquired a driving gear for 28.5 million zl. It was
reported that it may be installed in 1964. The nitrogen
plant Kiedzierzyn acquired in 1956 a gas compressor for
26 million and in 1957 and 1959 three boilers and turbines at the expense of 95.5 million zl. The estimated
installation deadline was 1963. This was also the
estimated deadline for the installation of equipment
acquired in 1956 by the chemical plant Rokita. Similarly a wire mill acquired for 55.5 million zl. by the
Lenin mills in 1957 remained uninstalled till 1963.[165]
The chemical combine in Oswiecim possesses equipment
valued at 95 million zl. to be installed in the current
FYP. According to the plans the bulk of the equipment
should have been exploited in the production processes
for some time now.[166]

Undoubtedly management will secure centralized investments whenever subsidies to this purpose are made available whether or not the capital asset can be presently
exploited. But this does not seem to be the only reason
for these unusual delays. As we have previously seen,

the installation of new equipment may endanger the
production plan, current profits, cost plan fulfilment,
and result in excesses of the wage fund. The director
is then faced with the alternative to forgo, or reduce,
premiums during the current period and in view of technological improvements expect future benefits or delay
installation and reap current premiums. If, and when,
pressure is exerted by the supervisors for installation
arguments and justifications for delays are found.

Recently a regulation has been introduced to counteract these delays. However, it pertains only to equipment exceeding 400 thousand zl. It stipulates an 8 per
cent interest levy on domestic and 12 per cent on
imported capital assets which have not been installed
promptly.[167] This seems like one of those half measures
so popular in recent times, but unlikely to succeed
unless integrated into a coherent system.

Estimates indicate that a huge stock of uninstalled
equipment valued at 200 million zl. will never be used
because of its obsolete design, low productivity, and
partial or total unadaptability to present production
processes, abstracting from the deterioration to which
it has succumbed as a result of lengthy storage in
inadequate conditons. It has been predicted that this
equipment will have to be written off by the state as
a total loss.[168]

But in conjunction with central allotment of investment and basic materials, the state attempts to control
strictly the size of the wage fund allowed to the firm.

How to Obtain an Adequate Wage Fund

It is generally recognized that in the maze of
directives that the enterprise receives from its association the indexes of employment and wage fund are among
the most strictly enforced.[169] The annual index of a
firm's wage fund is related to its planned output.
About 50 per cent of total output is reckoned in comparable prices (e.g., electrical machines, automotive equipment, agricultural implements, majority of chemicals,
etc.), 27 per cent of marketable output in transfer
prices (e.g., majority of light industry, building materials, ferrous and non-ferrous metallurgy, and machine
tools), 9 per cent (e.g., clothing industry) in terms of
labor costs, 7 per cent (e.g., coal mining) in physical

units, 2 per cent in standard labor costs, and the
remaining 5 per cent in terms of total "corrected output", excluding e.g. material inputs. The percentage
of enterprises employing various yardsticks is:
comparable prices 31, transfer prices 50.8, labor
costs 6.6, physical units 1.6, standard labor costs
7.6, and others 2.4 per cent.[170] Comparable prices are
used to measure output where there is a large volume
of work in process at the end of the plan period.
Where there is none marketable output is reckoned in
transfer prices.[171]

The index of labor productivity, the total number
of employees divided into categories, and each category's average wage must be reckoned in wage fund
computation. The association's computations of labor
intensity of products and average wages are hindered
by diverging capital intensity, costing deficiencies, etc.
Hence the wage fund is, as a rule,related to output
only.

The state regards the total wage fund as a variable
having an income effect rather than a cost effect
albeit it is a significant element of total production
costs in the economy. Since production of consumer
goods is planned in relation to the aggregate wage fund,
it is mandatory that the latter remain within the prescribed limits. Overexpenditures on wages result in
enormous pressures on the consumer market and with
rigidity of supply market "equilibrium" is undermined.
Notwithstanding the economic effects the state fears
inflationary pressures because of the social and politica
repercussions which may ensue. In his aim at output
maximization and desire to keep the wage fund within
the limit prescribed by the NEP, the planner faces a
fundamental dilemma solved in favor of output maximization. Hence a form of bank correction of the wage fund
has been instituted.

Only the part of the wage fund for workers directly
engaged in production is subject to correction by the
bank in accordance with the degree of fulfilment of the
firm's production plan. Whenever the plan is fulfilled
by 100 per cent the wage fund is not subject to correction. The problem of wage fund correction causes the
planner considerable difficulties as it is not easy to
depict a simple correlation between an increase in the
size of production and the wage fund. Particularly in

the case of heterogeneous production aggregated in value
terms the ratio of labor to output is a variable one
pending on the type and assortment of production, the
application of various methods of rewarding labor, changes
in work norms and labor productivity, changes in the
internal wage structure, etc.[172] Since output is still
considered as the important target, changes in the wage
fund are correlated to the movements in output, however
imperfect the measure may be.

The wage fund is corrected by the bank according to
centrally predetermined coefficients. Assuming the
correction coefficient is 0.5 per cent, if an enterprise
fulfilled its production plan by 103 per cent it would
be entitled to a 1.5 per cent increase of the wage fund
for production workers and if the plan was executed by
98 per cent, it would be decreased by 1 per cent.[173]
However, as a rule the coefficient for underfulfilment
is higher than the one for overfulfilment to penalize
the firms for not meeting the output targets. The
average coefficient for overfulfilment by 1 per cent
is 0.6 per cent, whereas the corresponding coefficient
for underfulfilment is 1 per cent.[174] The planner
varies the coefficients to stimulate overfulfilment of
output in particular branches of industry. For example,
the coefficient is 0.5 for steel mill repair firms
and as high as 1.1 for mine construction firms. In
coal mining the average coefficient is 0.9, and in some
mines it reaches 1.1. The average coefficient in
ferrous metallurgy is 0.8, non-ferrous metallurgy
0.7, chemical industry 0.4 to 0.6, light industry 0.6
to 0.75, and machine building 0.5 per cent.[175]

The bank is also authorized to penalize firms that
exceeded the corrected wage fund in a given period by
withholding up to 50 per cent of the premium fund,
discouraging management from indulging in these overexpenditures.[176] When no premium fund has been formed,
the bank may withhold the wage fund for white collar
workers in the amount of the excess, but no more than
10 per cent of the wage fund. The blocked funds are
held in abeyance by the bank until the enterprise has
liquidated the excesses.[177]

However, these sanctions are not overly effective.
Given that at the present time the average premium from
the basic premium fund approximates 7 per cent of
salary, it has been computed that the average engineer

earning 3000 zl. per month would be entitled to a 200
zl. monthly premium. Since he usually benefits from
much higher specialized premiums it may be safely
assumed that the sanction of 100 zl. per month would
be of little consequence.[178] Further retributions
have been imposed by resolution **No. 39 of** the CM
stipulating that "the employees responsible for the
administration of the wage fund and those who have
broken wage discipline are to be deprived of the total
amount of premiums due to them on the basis of premium
regulations."[179] However, this sanction instead of
applying to top management usually befalls the payroll
department's officers and the expression "deprive of
premiums" is interpreted as "withhold until such time
as the excesses have been liquidated." [180] Breakage of
rules and seeking loopholes in wage regulations is
particularly common. The wage fund is planned allowing
a wide safety margin, its reserves are concealed, and
indexes are manipulated so that the wage fund should
not be substantially exceeded.[181]

But how would management benefit from a wage fund
allowing a larger safety margin? Firstly, it is easier
to fulfil the plan with a larger wage fund. Secondly,
the enterprise can then successfully cope with the
employee's pressures for higher wages and attract a
higher caliber working force.[182] Even though a larger
wage fund will probably decrease profit, wages will
be maximized at the detriment of uncertain future
benefits.[183] Perturbations in materials supply constant-
ly threaten the firm with work stoppages, while the
idle working force receives its remunerations. But
the production plan has to be fulfilled no matter
whether the interruptions are due to circumstances
beyond management's control or negligence.[184]
Consequently overtime will be required to make up for
lost time.[185] Since work stoppages cannot be forecast,
management aims at obtaining the largest possible wage
fund to ensure availability of funds for overtime.
Moreover wage fund savings cannot be cumulated. The
firm is induced to use up its wage fund as any savings
in one period may cause reduction of the wage fund
allowed for the following period.[186] Hence the wage
fund is depleted during the given period.

Management's primary concern with acquiring a large
wage fund has led it to devise means for achieving this

end.   The strategy evolved consists of minimizing the
output target, maximizing the wage fund index, manipulating assortments and the work in process to inflate the
value of output.   The two former steps are taken at the
time of planning, and the latter pursued during plan
execution.   The applicability of this strategy depends
on management's ability to influence the directives
received, the range of goods produced the extent and
enforcement of central regulation of the product mix,
the degree of preponderance of the seller over the
buyer, and, of course, the premium system.

Since the wage fund is a function of production plan
fulfilment, to obtain the highest possible wage fund
the enterprise will be prompted to maximize the value
of output.   But this is only advantageous when labor
intensity is relatively low since otherwise labor
costs would exceed the increment of the wage fund
obtained through correction.   Consequently concentration on production of material intensive assortments
is common.[187]

For example, in firm X the output target for the
first three quarters of 1962 was 212.4 million zl.
and fulfilment reported at 221.2 million zl. or 104.1
per cent.   Whereas the majority of assortments remained underfulfilled, the annual output of one
particular assortment, where an expensive raw material
is used, was fulfilled by over 200 per cent during the
first three quarters.   The degree of overfulfilment of
this particular assortment enabled the firm to exceed
its total output target.   An average of 3,110 workers
were employed, and only 20 of them were directly
engaged in the production of the material intensive
assortment.   But the wage fund was corrected in
relation to the degree of overfulfilment of the output
plan.   Even though 3,090 workers did not fulfil their
production plan, the firm's wage fund was increased by
1,771,900 zl.[188]

In some industries attempts to adopt substitute
inputs which are cheaper, lighter, of higher quality,
etc. meet with unsurmountable difficulties.   Although
the use of cheaper materials will reduce costs and
thereby improve financial results, it will also reduce
output.[189] For example, in 1960 the price of aluminum,
a domestic product, was established below that of copper
to induce replacement of copper by aluminum.   In response

to an extensive inquiry conducted by the SPC with reference to the results of the price reform, the enterprise
Buczek in Ozarow, one of the largest cable producers in
Poland, indicated that the reasons restraining the use
of aluminum and inducing that of copper in the production of conduits are the indexes of productivity, and
the limits of the wage fund foisted on them. Hence
production of the more expensive conduits from copper
is more advantageous since the labor intensity is
lower than that of aluminum conduits and they are
worth more in the total output plan.[190]

     Buczek's attitude is not unique. The predicament
is vividly apparent on the association's level. In
1960 the cable industry produced 58,000 km. of copper
wire and 59,000 km. of aluminum wire conduits. To
reduce material costs the first version of the 1962
plan estimated that 19,500 km. of copper and 94,000
km. of aluminum wire conduits were going to be produced.
Use of copper would be reduced by 62 per cent and the
decrease in material costs would amount to over 40 per
cent. However, the prices of aluminum wire conduits
are lower than those of copper wire conduits by an
average of 14 per cent and labor input for aluminum is
15 per cent higher than that for copper wire conduits.
Consequently with a large predominance of aluminum
wire conduits the value of total output would fall,
decreasing the labor productivity index. Since the
production of aluminum wire conduits is more labor
intensive, the labor productivity index would deteriorate even further. A lower wage fund would be received
and a smaller number of employees allowed. The attempts
to reduce material costs collided with the method of
calculating labor productivity and the wage fund. To
obtain an adequate wage fund and employment index for
the cable industry, a compromise was reached and the
final plan set at 47,970 km. of copper and 67,200 km.
of aluminum wire conduits.[191]

     In conjunction with manipulation of assortments,
management uses cooperation as a modus operandi to
ensure a higher wage fund.[192] The value of the finished
product incorporates the cost of all its components.
When the firm produces the components on premises,
instead of subcontracting them, it does not enhance the
value of its output but decreases the productivity
index as extra labor is expanded. To obtain a better

labor productivity index, higher fulfilment of the output plan with less labor expanded, and the accompanying
higher wage fund, the enterprise will naturally prefer
to subcontract the greatest possible number of components
of finished goods.[193]

At times the cost of subcontracting exceeds the cost
at which these parts could be manufactured on premises.
For example, the Kielce metal producer uses a special
screw in the assembly of the SHL motorcycle. These
screws are purchased at a cost of 7 zl. per unit. The
enterprise could produce them at a cost below 2 zl. per
unit, but only with increased wage expenditures which
would be disregarded by the bank when correcting the
wage fund.[194] From the wage fund standpoint it does not
pay the firm to produce the screws on premises. But
such action would result in substantial cost reduction,
increasing profit. Such an improvement in profit,
increasing the premium fund, would not be advantageous
as it may result in excesses of the corrected wage
fund and the bank will withhold part of the premium
fund.

Paradoxical as it seems, management might be prompted
to subcontract a product because it would augment costs.
This would be true, for instance, in case of non-typical
products. Here the individual costs are the basis for
price formation, and the higher the cost, the higher the
transfer price, hence the higher the value of output, and
the profit calculated as a percentage of costs.

The strict control over the wage fund induces management to substitute materials for labor whenever possible.
Labor saving devices are welcome even when they entail
outright waste of materials.[195] The stress on labor
cost reduction and neglect of material costs is evident
from the following data: In 1960 the Ministry of Heavy
Industry paid out 18,590 million zl. in premiums for
cost reduction; **out** of this, 16,390 million or 88.16
per cent for reduction of labor costs, 2,146.9 million
or 11.54 per cent for over-all cost reduction, and
only 53.6 million or 0.3 per cent for savings of
material costs.[196] To allow less than half a per cent
for rewarding savings of materials seems to be a rather
strange policy in view of the intense shortages of materials and the perplexing problems with the balance of
payments.

Waste of materials is still one of the most difficult

issues facing the Polish economy. The pricing and premium systems have not created potent enough incentives
to counteract it.[197] Notwithstanding that no cogent
stimuli are offered for material cost reduction, waste
of materials in certain enterprises is encouraged by the
means used for measuring output. Whenever output is
measured in weight and multiplied by the value per unit
of weight, the producers will tend to turn out the
heaviest possible goods wasting a considerable amount
of raw materials in the process.[198] Since production of
castings and forgings is usually measured per unit of
weight, the foundries and forges supply products
which are so heavy that a considerable quantity of
steel is turned into scrap when the castings and forgings are processed in the machine shops of the final
producers. For example,25 per cent of cast steel and
iron is returned by the machine building industry to
foundries as scrap. In the machine shops turning out
large roller bearings 40 per cent of expensive bearing
steel results in scrap when machining the imprecise
forgings supplied by the forges.[199]

    Moreover production workers are prompted to waste
materials due to the piece rate wage system. Essentially the piece rate consists of setting norms for particular jobs and inducing workers, through increased
rates, to overfulfil them. Although the piece rate
system definitely incites increase of output, it
certainly does not stimulate material savings.
Contrariwise the worker, interested in obtaining the
highest possible pay will most likely increase the
rate of his output through uneconomical use of materials and tools and above all disregard of material
input norms.[200]

                    How to Procure Materials

    To understand the procurement problems facing the
firm, perhaps we should pose for a moment and examine
the sellers' market prevailing in Poland. This is a
phenomenon where the seller, having no difficulty in
disposing of his products, will control economic exchange and where only buyers compete to acquire the
desired products. The buyer, requiring materials to
fulfil his production plan, plays a subservient role
and must cater to the will of the seller.[201] This is

a situation where no particular efforts are required to
dispose of a product, whereas a constant and painstaking
struggle must be exercised to procure materials. Hence
the seller can deteriorate quality without repercussions on his position. As Adam Wang, the late Vice-
Chairman of the PC, pointed out:

> Such a situation places the seller in an especially
> privileged position. The buyer, on the other hand,
> must either stop the production process or is forced
> to accept the goods and work with worse initial raw
> materials. In such a case the buyer chooses, as a
> rule, the second alternative.[202]

Consequently the buyer is forced to accept lower grade
materials in many cases at the price which he would have
to pay for the higher qualities. This situation assures
the seller of a constant demand for his products. It
places the buyer in an insecure position where he is
never sure that the supply of materials will cover his
requirements, forcing him to hoard materials contributing to waste on a large scale.

Some factors contributing to a seller's market were
already discussed; they are: the inherent deficiencies
of material balances,[203] absence of a mechanism for
rectifying the errors committed within the four walls of
the PC, irrationality and inflexibility of prices, lack
of adjustment of supply to changes in demand, unrealistic
tautness of plans, poor raw material base and undeveloped
foreign trade, erroneous performance criteria and output yardsticks, and an incentive system resulting in
breakage of assortment plans to satisfy the producer but
not the user.

As previously mentioned, only the most important
producer goods are presently subject to central allocation. They are: coal, briquettes, coke, rolled steel
products, steel pipes, cement, pine boards, lumber,
aluminum, tin, copper, machine tools, machines for the
production of synthetics, wood working machines, bull-
dozers, construction and road building machines,
cranes and conveyors, means of transportation and shipbuilding. In addition central distribution encompasses
materials in periodic short supply. Distribution is
conducted on the basis of material balances prepared
by the PC. After output targets have been specified

for particular ministries, the ministries-suppliers prepare their distribution lists and advise the ministries-
users of the quantity of materials allotted them. These,
in turn, distribute those materials among their associations. The associations proceed similarly towards their
enterprises, and simultaneously inform the branch marketing offices. Central allotments, backed by orders
placed by the users or other contracts, may then be
honored by the suppliers.[204]

The method of preparing procurement plans in individual enterprises in itself causes severe difficulties in
the procurement system.[205] The firm's procurement plan
must be set prior to the receipt of directive plan
indexes from the association. Orders have to be placed
with the supplier before he receives his final output
targets so that he may elaborate his production plan
on orders received and adhere to his output targets.
Hence the procurement plan is based on wide approximations of requirements. Directives are often changed
during the year contributing further to an abstraction
of the procurement plan and the orders placed from the
specific requirements.[206]

Because the procurement plan is perforce a wide
approximation of actual needs and because of chronic
shortages and considerable delays in delivery the
safety **factor** plays an important role in the preparation of the procurement plan and the placement of
orders with suppliers.[207] In view of the pressures on
output plan fulfilment, work stoppages due to inadequate
supply of materials must be avoided.[208] Management's
remarkably nervous reaction to all, even momentary,
procurement shortages leads it to place excessively
high and rash orders.[209] A certain bargaining ritual
has become the order of the day. The buyer, as a
matter of course, orders more than he needs and the
supplier cuts down the order. Anticipating that cut
the wise manager inflates the order.[210] As a result
the buyer in need is often left empty handed, whereas
the shrewd operator becomes overstocked and only when
cornered by the bank is he forced to unload part of
his stock. For instance, the harvester factory in
Plock was forced in 1961 by the bank to unload 11.5
per cent of its annual supply of rolled steel.[211]
However, bank control over the firm's administration
of materials is, in practice, most ineffective. Inter-

ferences by the bank withholding credit for further
working capital are not too frequent.[212]

Hoarding of materials is further favored by the
suppliers' conditional acceptance of orders stipulating
"if we receive the required raw materials". Consequently the purchaser places several orders for the same
materials. But a failure in supply usually affects
all producers and the orders remain unfulfilled. However, when raw materials are available all suppliers
deliver and materials accumulate.[213] Because the
procurement plan is based on the material usage norms,
management opposes their periodic revision. Whenever
norms are revised pressures are exerted to have them
set up as loosely as possible. Loose norms will allow
the firm a wider safety margin and ensure receipt of
an adequate supply of materials, even if the orders
placed should remain partially undelivered, or should
the association intervene and cut down the procurement
plan.[214] Hoarding is furthered by the unsatisfactory
quality of materials forcing management to order more
than required.[215]

Due to a considerable shortage of distributing out-
lets where small quantities could be procured, materials
are hoarded by enterprises in excessive amounts.[216]

Management is prompted to hoard materials in view of
chronic shortages of certain goods throughout industry.
The products in short supply are mainly those which are
disfavored by the producers as their production is
excessively labor intensive and their cumulative value
does not greatly enhance total output. A case in point
may be the spare parts' shortages which have plagued
the Polish economy throughout the postwar years.[217]
It is still more beneficial to produce a complete machine
than its parts. Spare parts shortages are so intense
that when excavators come in for repairs they are robbed
of their good parts the moment they are unloaded so
that repairs of excavators in progress may be continued.[218]
Another case in point is the production of screws.
Although the total 1963 output plan did not cover even
the rudimentary requirements for screws, it was underfulfilled by 7 per cent. The small and precision
screws assortments were fulfilled by 55 to 70 per cent
only.[219] Since output of screws is reckoned in weight
"one enormous screw" could satisfactorily replace a
host of the little ones; "not in real life - in the

plan."[220]   Consequently an enterprise that could purchase a sufficient number of screws and spare parts to
last a number of years will be eager to do so. Management will also be prompted to hoard materials as it
would then have a stock in trade to barter with other
firms.

   At this point a question may arise: How can profit,
as a variable in premium calculation, be reconciled
with excessive hoarding of materials decreasing the
turnover of working capital and, ceteris paribus,
profit? But should the production plan remain unfulfilled even though a premium fund has been obtained,
premiums will not be forthcoming. Undoubtedly attainment of a smaller premium fund with guaranteed distribution is vastly more attractive to management than
formation of a large premium fund from which distribution is withheld.

   Paradoxically hoarding may mean more economical use
of materials. Because of shortages of steel products
more expensive and qualitatively higher grades are often
used whenever the lower grades are in short supply.[221]
The enterprise with a large and varied stock of steel
may counteract such waste and in the process increase
its profit.

   To impede hoarding sanctions were imposed on the
procurement department's personnel by depriving it of
premiums.[222] But this type of penalty does not seem
to substantially ameliorate the situation. Firstly,
the procurement personnel's influence on the level of
materials in stock is imperceptible. This sanction is
as unjust as the one imposed on the employees of the
payroll department for wage fund excesses as the
responsibility devolves primarily on top management.
The little influence that the procurement personnel
has on the administration of materials cannot be
successfully directed to counteract the excessive
accumulation of materials. This is so since their
premiums emanate from the premium fund and, therefore,
hinge on output plan fulfilment. The procurement
personnel faces a dilemma: If the authorities discover
that materials are hoarded their premiums are cut off.
If materials are not hoarded and the production plan
underfulfilled, they will be deprived of premiums. No
doubt it is easier to search for ways and means to
conceal hoarding of materials than to oppose hoarding

and face the untractable reality of production plan
underfulfilment.

The following table may indicate the extent to which
materials are actually hoarded:[223]

Table 29 - 1955-61 Increase of Inventories of Materials

| Year | In transfer prices - billions zl. | | |
	Plan	Fulfilment	Excess
1955	4.9	16.0	11.1
1956	3.7	15.0	11.3
1957	9.3	25.7	16.4
1958	11.2	23.7	12.5
1959	15.6	21.6	6.0
1960	18.4	25.5	7.1
1961	17.0	31.3	14.3

Source   J. Wierzbicki, WNBP, No. 1,1963   p.17

For example, in the Ministry of Heavy Industry the
increase of stocks of materials in 1961 in relation to
1960 amounted to 15.3 per cent, whereas the increase in
production amounted to 13.9 per cent. The increase in
production of the Ministry of Construction and Building
Materials in 1961 was 10.5 per cent, whereas increase
in stocks of materials was 11.8 per cent. In 1960 the
respective figures were 13.3 and 20.0 per cent.[224]
Generally increases of stocks of materials exceed
increases warranted by an increased output. The tendency
to hoard materials has not subsided and demonstrates an
upward trend.

To facilitate disposal of materials, when the firms
are prepared to dispose of them the state has instituted
exchanges of producer goods. The first such exchange
took place in Wroclaw in December,1962. It was followed
by similar ones in Bielsko, Katowice, Poznan, Cracow,
Lodz, and Warsaw. In the latter exchange over 300 enterprises participated offering for sale goods valued
at over half a billion zlotys.[225] Since enterprises are
unwilling to dispose of materials and bank control is
rather ineffective, this is further indication of the
extent to which materials are hoarded.

The results of a local exchange of producer goods
initiated for firms in the Praga district of Warsaw indicate how hoarding intensifies waste. This exchange,
held at the beginning of 1963, offered 100 million zl.
worth of materials, sold for a little over 10 million
zl.[226] Consequently 90 million zl. were lost at this
exchange alone. Only 10 per cent of the initial value
of these materials was recuperated. The direct and
indirect waste of materials brought about by hoarding
is far-reaching. Records of inventories are inaccurate
and garbled. Nobody really knows what stocks are on
hand. One of the participants at the conference of
economists in Wisla in 1963 remarked:

> I would like to have as many zlotys as many thousands
> of them are involved in all sorts of materials in
> several departments in our enterprise. The value of
> these materials has been written off as costs of
> production a long time ago. Consequently we have an
> imprecise and falsified record of inventories.[227]

Waste of materials due to hoarding is a direct
result of serious shortages in stocking facilities.
Direct production facilities have always been at the
forefront of investment plans with construction of
warehouses relegated to a later date.[228] For example,
it has been estimated that the pharmaceutical establishment in Tarchominsk requires 18 warehouses to stock its
basic inventories of materials, whereas it has only 4.
Similar situations are encountered in over one third
of all enterprises in the chemical industry.[229]
Even firms that possess adequate stocking facilities
for basic inventories - and such cases are rare enough -
must stock their excess materials in inadequate facilities
usually factory yards.[230] This is most vividly described
by Madej in his account of a visit to a firm in Lower
Silesia:

> On the territory of the Establishment M-13 producing
> electric motors a construction firm stocks its mat-
> erials in a place accessible to all. Whoever wants
> to accommodates himself in building materials from
> this free source. To make matters worse sacks of
> cement, torn and abandoned, lie about the entire
> construction project. In this same Piechowice, but

already on account of the firm M-13, housewives
hang up their laundry on wires which serve for
wiring electric motors.[231]

Storage of materials under open skies results not
only in considerable losses due to theft, but also
causes deterioration of materials followed by scrapping,
an almost universal phenomenon.[232] The bank is even
suspected of favoring scrapping as a radical solution
decreasing the value of inventories and improving the
index of turnover of working capital. Scrapping may
also result from a house cleaning action to make space
for additional incoming supplies.

I value the magnitude of losses in our country
resulting from scrapping to several hundred million
zlotys a year. During twelve years as an employee
I have participated in this type of scrapping
amounting to at least 200 million zlotys. Since
such large losses took place in only two enterprises
there are sufficient grounds to assume that at
least similar... losses have certainly occurred in
other enterprises in our country.[233]

The very existence of a sellers' market has engendered
a situation where the buyer is "treated as a necessary
evil disturbing the realization of plans."[234] The
necessity of getting supplies has perforce transformed
procurement personnel into travelling purchasing agents.
They roam the country in search of possible suppliers
of goods, or visit suppliers to supervise personally the
shipping of materials as "nothing will be settled if it
is not done personally."[235] The activity in a typical
procurement department is most vividly depicted in the
following excerpt:

Please look into a procurement department of any
enterprise and it will be clear to you that ten to
fifteen people live here with a timetable in hand.
In the morning the office boy puts a pile of letters,
telegrams, and memos on the desk. If it has been
announced that an order has been turned down the
procurement agent packs his shaving kit into his
brief case and journeys to the supplier. Maybe
he will get there before other buyers, perhaps he
will be able to extract for himself some rolled

steel, lacquer, or tools. Between the reading of
one and another letter telephones ring. Chiefs of
production departments inform that the assembly
line is stopping because they are short of some
parts. Another procurement agent gets ready for
a trip. Half of the department is always on the
go. The remaining employees write admonishments
and reminders to the suppliers with copies to the
association and ministry. Throughout the entire
year, one day is similar to another, one month to
another, the procurement agents travel...[236]

But a personal visit to the supplier may be worth-
less if it is not supported by a token of appreciation
for the supplier's marketing agent or stockkeeper. As
the story goes:

It happened that an inexperienced director sent an
inexperienced procurement agent to another city for
some steel parts and spare parts. The stockkeeper
declared that he will not give out the goods
because there is a shortage. Furthermore they
were intended for enterprises in his own district.
The procurement agent came back empty handed. But
the same day a procurement agent of a neighboring
enterprise received the goods from the same supplier. He had bought dinner for the stockkeeper.[237]

In the course of criticism voiced against rationing and
central distribution of producer goods during the SYP
it was often remarked that rationing demoralized and
warped socialist trade. It led to the apparition of
"socialist graft" paid by socialist enterprises for
the possibility of obtaining producer goods from other
socialist enterprises.[238] It seems, however, that
the phenomenon of socialist graft was not only due to
strict rationing of producer goods but is also a consequence of a sellers' market. The procurement conditions force the director to adopt the widespread
custom of arranging affairs at the dinner table or
for bribes.
    It is an accepted fact that the director sends out
his procurement agent with money covering two missions:
one of them the cost of the trip, the other the socialist
graft. Needless to say, this is all highly illegal, but

to continue operations successfully the director must
continually "stick his neck out". The breakage of laws
and regulations is nowhere more apparent than in the
field of procurement:

> There are hundreds of such directors in Poland.
> They are all criminals, they realize this very well.
> They should be sat on the prisoners' bench. Themis
> would certainly deal with them very severely. But
> who then would manage our enterprises?[239]

At this point it might be instructive to examine
briefly the adverse circumstances which may befall
management when, for example, its supply of screws is
short of requirements. Borrowing an example from
Wroblewski, let us look into the enterprise in Torun,
a producer of low voltage equipment. Just as anywhere
else a mass of screws is required there. Screws are
ordered on a quarterly basis. At the beginning of the
quarter the firm **receives** a memorandum from its supplier
indicating that, due to circumstances beyond their
control, the screws will not be produced in all assortments required. The average coverage of requirements
will amount to 40 per cent. The enterprise is faced
with a shortage of over half the necessary amount of
screws. At first the procurement agent prepares a long
list of the types and sizes of required screws. It is
mimeographed and mailed to all seventeen wholesalers
and some thirty enterprises which, he suspects, might
have an excess of these screws in stock. Of course,
a few days later he receives from these same enterprises,
in analogous predicaments, similar lists covering their
own requirements. But sometimes this procedure may help.
Let us assume that he may be able to procure another 10
per cent of the required screws, leaving him with a 50
per cent shortage.
    At this time the procurement agent boards the train
and roams the countryside. He may go to Silesia because
there are many wholesalers and enterprises there, or to
Bialystok because there are not many users of screws there,
or to Kielce because he has an uncle who works in a
wholesale enterprise there. Let us assume that during
the course of these trips, and thanks to the approach
used, where the recurring arguments are that some **time**
ago his firm has rendered a service to the other en-

terprise or promises of tokens of appreciation, he may
accumulate another 10 per cent of the required screws.
But such a trip must come to an end when all avenues
of procurement have been investigated.

Now some of the required screws will have to be
produced on premises. It has been calculated that a
screw produced on premises costs approximately three
times as much as when it is procured from specialized
enterprises. In this manner the enterprise secures
70 per cent of its requirements. There are no more
free machines available and an order has to be placed
somewhere else. But since the state-owned firms all
have "taut" plans, the order will go to a cooperative.
Of course, the price paid to the cooperative is much
higher than the one listed in the official price
catalog. The cooperative calculates its price on its
own production costs. But the price charged by the
cooperative is not the most important problem facing
the director. The cooperative is willing to accept
the order, but it has no steel. Steel is not a
product easily available to a cooperative. The customer will have to furnish the material. But since the
steel available in the enterprise has been used in the
production of screws on premises, another obstacle
confronts the director. But he is resourceful. He
telephones a director of another firm. He has never
met him but is on the friendliest possible terms with
him since they have often saved one another in dire
need. Thus the director has secured the steel he needs
which incidentally he has promised to return within a
week although he does not yet know where he will take
it.[240]

Faced with chronic shortages of producer goods,
fearing that roaming throughout the countryside and
the underhanded manners of procurement may not produce
the required goods, it is not at all surprising that
customers often demonstrate an incredible liberality
in accepting materials of poor quality and hardly in
accordance with technical standards.[241]

During an investigation conducted by the SPC in
June,1960,it was revealed that although goods produced
were often qualitatively inferior and did not adhere
to standards, this does not deter producers from
charging the uniform transfer prices.[242] Suppliers
often endeavor to sell inferior grade products at the

prices received for the highest quality materials.   To
achieve this end, lower grades are marked as grade one
and shipped out to the customer.   This was the case of
the brick factory Lubna which shipped out 9,000 bricks
class 100, grade I.   After an examination of the shipment, the engineer in charge of the construction project called a commission of representatives from the
procurement department and the supplier.   After a
detailed examination and extensive "haggling" the representatives from the brick factory agreed that the
bricks were not exactly as specified.   It was resolved
that there were no bricks of grade I in the shipment.
From these 9,000 pieces, 2,700 or 30 per cent were not
acceptable since they were mere rubble.   From the remaining 6,300 pieces, half were only class 75.[243]

But in the majority of cases suppliers meet with
quite a different treatment, which incidentally is one
of the reasons why they can apply these methods.   The
regulation, dating back a number of years, stipulates
that the customer may deduct 5 per cent from the invoice
of the supplier if it has been established that the
quality of materials received is unsatisfactory.[244]
However, the customer faced with the danger of losing
a supplier is reluctant to exact penalties.   In the
majority of cases customers do not take advantage of
their prerogatives to penalize the suppliers.[245]
Naturally the acceptance of low quality goods by the
users prompts the producers to use this method
extensively in their drive to increase output.

How to Produce at the Greatest Speed

As we have seen, in the prevailing sellers' market the
producer is all powerful.   Since little, or no, attempt
will be made by his customers to penalize him for his
deterioration of quality, he will do so to speed up
production and in the process reduce costs reflecting
favorably on his fulfilment of the profit plan.   It has
been remarked that "the methods used by crooked peddlers
are very backward in comparison to the ones used by state-
owned enterprises.   Only here are the masters of the
trade."[246]

Assuming that some customers may exact the penalty,
it is still more attractive to produce low quality goods
and lose the 5 per cent then to adhere to quality

standards. Furthermore the producer may always interpret
deterioration in the quality of his products as resulting from the low quality of inputs. In most cases he
has proof to substantiate this claim.[247]

As we know, the firms employ quality control inspectors. Why then are the defective products not rejected?
It has been remarked that these inspectors are all
"local patriots".[248] Surely there are more potent
reasons inciting the quality control inspectors to
overlook the shortcomings of materials shipped out from
the enterprise than just "local patriotism". Prior to
1960 the quality control inspector was paid a premium
based on the fulfilment of the production plan. Hence
quality control was slack as the inspector personally
benefited from output augmentation. But changes in the
premium system have not improved the situation much.[249]

Even if sanctions in the form of cutting off premiums would be applied against the quality control
inspector for neglect of his duties, they might not be
powerful enough to counteract the tendency to overlook
quality deterioration. The quality control inspector
depends on the firm's director for his salary classification, promotion, and allotment of premiums.[250]
He may be most unwilling to upset his superior by a
constant, vigilant, and strict output control,
especially if he knows that his activity may bring about
the underfulfilment of the production plan. Recently
Kalecki stressed the necessity of rendering the quality
control department independent of the firm's director,
to improve this department's performance.[251]

There are few obstacles facing the director in his
endeavors to increase output at the expense of quality
of production.[252]

Another device successfully used for speeding up
output is to neglect repairs of capital assets.[253]
As we know, labor productivity is measured by dividing
the value of production by the number of employees. The
more workers are employed in the repair shops, the lower
is the general labor productivity. No self-respecting
director can approve of this. On the other hand, deterioration of capital assets in the long run decreases
labor productivity in general. Hence the director
often faces a dilemma: to discharge repairmen and
report immediate results or think of the future.
Because of the prevailing short run philosophy repair

shops are understaffed and repairs neglected.[254]
Machines are exploited without pity. Replacements are
often acquired when the existing equipment could still
be repaired.

     Whenever strict restrictions on the wage fund occur,
forcing enterprises to reduce the number of workers,
the first victims are the repairmen. For example,
during the third quarter of 1963 the machine building
plant in Elblag was forced to reduce its staff by 24
workers, 23 of them were employed in the repair shop.
The Cieplice paper machines producer discharged 15
employees, 12 of them employed in the repair shop.[255]
When the production plan is threatened with underfulfilment repairs are immediately stopped and the
repairmen shifted to the production departments.[256]
In this manner the labor force engaged directly in
production is illegally increased.

     It was remarked that during the SYP period, because
of miscalculations at the central level, detailed
central distribution of materials, shortages and
delays, and the drive to fulfil the production plan
at all costs gave rise to a fluctuating volume of
production, or what is often referred to as the
process of storming:

     An observation of daily production graphs indicates
     with surprising regularity that the results attained
     in the last ten days of the month greatly exceed the
     results of the first and second ten days of this
     month, and in turn the fulfilment of the first ten
     days of the next month is much lower than the ful-
     filment of the last ten days of the preceding month.
     The situation is analogous when observing longer,
     say quarterly periods. The production of the third
     month of the quarter is as a rule the highest and
     the production of the first month of the following
     quarter greatly lower. Furthermore, it is no
     exception that during the fourth quarter of the
     year the best production results are observed and
     they fall violently during the first quarter of the
     following year.[257]

Analyzing the index of fluctuation of production in the
machine building industry during the SYP period
Kuzinski remarked that "during the first ten days of

the month only a small fraction of the monthly production was executed. In the next ten days 10 to 30 per
cent, but during the last ten days of the month up to
50 or 70 per cent. It is not necessary to argue what
waste is behind these indexes."[258]

However, due to the predominance of the sellers'
market and pressures on production plan fulfilment
storming is still a deeply engrained and recurring
phenomenon in Polish industry.[259] The conditions under
which management labors force it to continue operations
in this manner. A director of an association pointed
to one of his enterprises that had a 30,000 hours work
stoppage during a short period of time due to circumstances beyond the firm's or association's control.
The director of the enterprise, supported by the
association applied to the ministry for a correction of
the plan indexes to permit premium distribution. But
no one was found to take such a momentous decision.
Consequently the enterprise had to make up for time
lost by a devastating and exhaustive drive of production during the last part of the planned period. But
the production and accumulation plans were fulfilled.[260]

Once the process of storming has been deeply entrenched even if the supply of materials during a
certain period should be regular, storming cannot be
totally eradicated. After the exertion of the last
ten days of the preceding month, it is quite natural
for the workers to slow down and machines to be oiled
or. repaired. As a matter of course production will
only pick up during the next ten days. By the time
the last ten days of the month are reached reports
will indicate serious shortcomings, and during the
last ten days of the month the plan must be saved by
once again reverting to storming.

The fulfilment of the plan at all costs during the
last ten days of the month, during the last month of
the quarter, and during the last quarter of the year
is an accepted evil throughout industry. The fluctuations in production and the phenomenon of storming are
best described in the words of a grinder employed by
an enterprise of the machine building industry:

In the second half of May a pressing export order
arrived. The foreman said that we will have to
work a few evenings. But for three evenings I

sat idle at the machine, the work was not yet ready.
From the fourth evening on an unspeakably horrid
grind began. For one week the machine and I were
on the go for fourteen to sixteen hours a day.
The order was fulfilled.

The first ten days of June arrived, and the first
ten days of almost every month are days of grace
after the drudgery of the last ten days of the
preceding month. And not because I cannot stand it,
no, the grinder gives out, it is indispensable to
have some time for repairs. Even though the
grinder is new, imported two years ago, it is
already deteriorated by the murderous technology
which was worked out for it to save the plan.
Besides, no question about it, during the last
ten days of the month I increase the parameters
of the feed. Therefore, during the first ten
days of June I fulfilled hardly 8 per cent of the
monthly plan. During the following ten days work
began to get lively and I fulfilled 30 per cent of
the plan. I was left with 62 per cent of the plan
to be fulfilled during the last ten days of the
month. This means that during the last ten days
of June I will have to work fifteen hours per day
and if a pressing order comes in, even more. I
will overwork myself, it is true, but I will also
earn quite a bit.[261]

How to Fulfil Output and Accumulation Plans

In connection with our inquiry how to secure an
adequate wage fund we have observed the methods used to
augment the value of output with the least possible labor
input. But due to the construction of the premium system
management is interested in increasing the size of accumulation (profit) as well. Generally speaking, the
higher the accumulation (profit) per unit of output, the
larger the value of output. But since the rate of accumulation (profit) varies greatly, and the amount of
accumulation (profit) depends on output composition (the
degree of material intensity) management does not face
a simple choice where all variables move in the same
direction. In an attempt to maximize premiums, the fulfilment (overfulfilment) of the accumulation (profit)

plan must be reckoned by management, since the maximization of the joint value of both production and accumulation (profit) plans is the most favorable solution under
the prevailing conditions.

As we know, the directive plan indexes stipulate output targets for the most important assortments. However,
the assortment plan indexes are the least observed on an
industry wide basis.[262] In addition the firms have a
wider field of manipulation in assortments which are
not centrally established. Manipulation of assortments
is especially pronounced in the process of plan overfulfilment. The percentage of overfulfilment will never
be spread out evenly on all assortments but will be
concentrated exclusively on the products that are most
advantageous to produce.

Disregard of customers' orders and production to ac-
comodate the plan, at the detriment of the market, is
most flagrant in the consumer goods industries. Because
of the existence of turnover tax the rate of accumulation
realized is much higher and more differentiated than
profit. This creates a more potent incentive to manipulate assortments so as to produce goods of the highest
rate of accumulation often equivalent to production
of the most expensive commodities and the neglect of
the cheaper ones. Such possibilities are offered in
many enterprises. For example, in the wool industry,
the 1963 average rate of accumulation was 118 per cent,
but the rate was highly differentiated among the many
assortments produced ranging from a few per cent deficit
to nearly 200 per cent accumulation. The same was true
of the cotton industry where the average rate of
accumulation was 18 per cent ranging on particular
assortments from 5 to 100 per cent. The rate of accumulation on leather shoes averaged 20 per cent ranging
from 10 to 80 per cent on different assortments.[263]

Although the entire apparel and hosiery industry
boasts that the 1961 plan of delivery of commodities
to the consumer market was overfulfilled by 350 million
zlotys the enterprises of this industry did not, as
a rule, deliver the assortment of commodities in accordance with the orders placed. The industry did not,
for instance, deliver over 2 million pieces of children's
underwear, simultaneously exceeding the planned delivery
of ladies' lingerie and men's underwear by over one
million pieces. The enterprise Sira in Sieradzk ful-

filled the over-all plan by 102 per cent including a
delivery of goods ordered amounting only to 87 per cent.
In the enterprise Olympia in Lodz the respective indexes
were 98 and 85. In the fourth quarter Olympia fulfilled the production plan of ladies jackets by 196 per
cent and girl's jackets by 75.7 per cent as the process
and materials for both assortments are identical but
accumulation greatly varied. In the fourth quarter of
1961 for 170 articles ordered by 14 wholesalers the
enterprise Finder did not deliver one article in
accordance with the percentage of sizes ordered. Without the approval of customers Sira changed the plan for
the third quarter of 1961 as follows: It reduced the
production of baby's overalls and men's shorts by 150
thousand pieces (where the return in transfer prices
for 1 kg of raw materials used is 140 zl. and the accumulation rate 8 and 27 per cent) and increased by 135
thousand pieces the production of unordered sweaters
and ladies' blouses (for which the return is 637 and
201 zl. per kilogram of raw materials, and the accumulation rate 63 per cent).[264]

The breakage of the assortment plan is not confined
to light industry. For example, in heavy industry
several television models are produced ranging from the
"Neptun" at an average cost of 3,490 zl. and retail
price of 6,000 zl. to the "Klejnot" costed at 4 700 zl.
and sold at 11,500 zl. Whereas the calculated costs
of the different assortments do not vary greatly,
there is a wide discrepancy between prices and, therefore, accumulation. As Struminski so judiciously
points out "it is clear that within its possibilities
each firm aims at producing the articles most beneficial
for itself."[265]

The ubiquitous breakage of the assortment plan is
not a response to buyers' needs but producers' preferences. It is equivalent to turning out output that
lacks the final test of realization. It forces the
consumers to buy not what they want but what the
producers will make available. If the wholesaler wants
assurance that he will receive at least part of the
goods ordered he must yield to the producer's pressure
and accept goods the producer wants to foist on him,
even knowing that they will be difficult to sell to
the consumer. Thus in the second quarter of 1963
the Arged wholesaler accepted 180 thousand enameled

bowls instead of the 108 thousand ordered, 31 thousand
large saucepans instead of 15 thousand, and 102 thousand deep saucepans instead of 80 thousand. Simultaneously their order for teaspoons was fulfilled by
69 per cent and that for small saucepan lids by 60 per
cent.[266]

It is significant that the conventional financial
penalties that may be exacted from the supplier for
not living up to his contract are not sufficiently
powerful to counteract these manipulations. The
perspective of production and accumulation (profit) plan
overfulfilment and benefits flowing thereof transcends
the possibility of incurring penalties that are not
strictly exacted by customers.[267]

It would be possible to fill volumes with examples
and excerpts describing the malpractices and deficiencies
generated by the present system. As we have endeavored
to point out these malpractices are not isolated cases
but are the rule rather than the exception. They are
engendered by the performance criteria, the pricing
system, cost computation, the financial system, and
other aspects of the institutional framework. The
pitfalls of the performance criteria are often
deplored in the press, at Party meetings professional
conferences, etc. Recently concrete steps were taken
to ameliorate the system and in the light of past
errors we may now gauge what changes, if any, may
be expected, and how successful they are likely to be.

LASTING PREDICAMENTS AND LATEST REMEDIES

Enhancing the role of economic incentives, adoption
of performance criteria steering enterprises in the
desired direction, and furnishing firms with meaningful
value parameters are among the foremost conditions for
decentralizing economic activity. But such action can
be successful only if the internal strife between incentives, performance criteria, and prices is eliminated
and these components integrated to function consistently.
However, the present system is not a coherent whole.
Jedrychowski recently said:

I cannot agree with those comrades who do not perceive that there is a central concept in our economic

incentive policy. Such a fundamental concept
exists and aims at making these incentives
dependent on synthetic performance criteria.[268]

Unfortunately I will have to classify myself in the
ranks of those "non-perceptive comrades". It seems to
me that a fundamental distinction must be drawn between
the source or basis for the formation of premium funds
and the conditions for the distribution of premiums
from these funds. The receipt of premiums hinges on
production plan fulfilment. Consequently management
does not face the problem of maximizing a single variable
(profit) but joint value of two or more variables (output and conditions for special premiums) which may
drive management's efforts into opposite directions.
Since the size of the wage fund is geared to the
value of output, the crucial significance of the latter
is further enhanced. It is reinforced by the political
pressures for production plan overfulfilment due to a
deeply rooted belief that this is the most important
target.[269] The history of the Polish incentive system
indicates that in practice one magnitude assumes the
predominant role as the basic target, with the other
targets playing second fiddle. Until very recently
such a magnitude was gross value of output.
But increase of production is not by itself a sufficient test of rational allocation of resources. It
is a fundamental proposition of the theory of the firm
that optimum allocation of production factors requires
that, ceteris paribus, in every case the value of the
marginal product should equal the marginal (opportunity)
cost of each factor in all its alternative uses.
Quantitative increase of production as the main target
motivates an augmentation of output at almost any
cost as long as the increase is a positive magnitude.[270]
Within the capacity and resources at its disposal, management will strive to expand production even should
the cost of the increase diminish the profit attained
reducing the premium fund. It will do so because it
is more advantageous to form a smaller premium fund
which will be activated than a larger one from which
premiums will not be distributed. The increase of
production is often attained by deteriorating quality,
manipulating assortments, inflating value of goods in
process, undue development of subcontracting (not

dictated by the benefits flowing from a division of
labor and specialization), negligence in maintenance of
capital equipment, storming, waste of materials and
unwillingness to introduce technical progress and new
product lines if they unduly disrupt the current production flow.

As we know, the present system of price formation
rests on the computation of average costs of production
for a given branch of industry plus a small percentage
of profit computed on cost. Since any element of cost
is deemed "price determining", it will enhance the cost
and "value" of production and with a given rate of
profit will increase the amount of "profit". Theoretically the value of output and the size of the wage fund
will increase if the enterprise would produce the most
material intensive products, given a uniform rate of
profit on all products, or would produce goods where
a minimum of value should be added on premises.
Under these circumstances maximization of output will
produce higher profit even without real cost reduction.
Needless to say, in its pursuance of this course the
enterprise is constrained by the availability of materials, possibilites of subcontracting, directives as to
the assortment plan, and its technological processes.
We can conceive, as indeed the information at our disposal
suggests, that as a rule the enterprise will first
produce the most material intensive commodities, and
then by force of necessity, reconcile itself to
production of less material intensive goods in a
descending order on its scale of possibilities.

But since the rate of profit differs on particular
goods, another variable enters the calculation. Should
the rate of profit be relatively low on a material
intensive product and high on a labor intensive one a
balance must be struck. In case of a uniform rate of
profit the higher the cost the higher the absolute
profit and the higher the value of output. However,
with a differentiated rate of profit the value of
output may rise whereas profits may fall as a result of
changes in the assortment plan. It is not important for
management to increase profit alone but to augment profit
in conjunction with fulfilling the production plan, in
other words, to maximize the premiums ensuing from a
maximization of the joint value of profit and output
plan. Generally the highest possible value of produc-

tion is best achieved with material intensive output
and extensive subcontracting, whereas the improvement
of profitability is most easily accomplished by manipulating the assortment so as to produce a profitable
product mix which may or may not be most material
intensive. Since the benefits derived from overfulfilment of the production plan generally outweigh those
flowing from high profits, should a conflict arise
between the two, the assortment will be juggled in
favor of the former.

By retaining output maximization as a most important
parameter of managerial action the state did not eradicate from management the desire for minimal plans. The
weak incentive prompting increase of plan indexes by
firms must fail, as it does since its benefits are
incommensurate with the penalties for underfulfilling
the plan. That our conclusions are not farfetched is
substantiated by Vice-Premier Woniolka's bitter comment:

> The following situation is still universal: During
> the year enterprise A increased production by 20
> per cent reduced costs, reduced labor inputs but
> fulfilled the yearly plan by only 98 per cent.
> Enterprise B increased production by only 2 per
> cent, exceeded the wage fund, cost plan, but ful-
> filled the plan by 102 per cent. Common sense
> tells us that better results were achieved by
> factory A. Yet all splendor will descend on
> factory B. Because - it fulfilled the plan...[271]

The desire for lower targets which may be easily met
brings about understatement of production capacity by
firms, creating a situation where the central planner
does not possess the necessary information for plan construction. Investments are pursued for expansion of
capacity, while existing plants are underutilized.
Uneven overfulfilment of plans, often caused by some
enterprises being less successful in concealing capacity
than others, creates perturbing bottlenecks in material
supply, hoarding of materials, work stoppages, loss of
potential output, irregular flow of production, overtime,
and great waste in the process of procurement and
distribution of goods. Overfulfilment of the plan has
become a fetish. It is not generally grasped that
premiums are actually paid for deficient planning rather

than efficient performance as only a slack plan can be greatly overfulfilled. One cannot help but agree with Jedrychowski that "from the point of view of the national economy and individual enterprises it would be much better to have realistic but high plans and overfulfil them to a smaller degree than to greatly overfulfil slack plans."[272]

The performance criteria used are hardly correct for evaluating enterprises. Gross value of output may indicate spurious results, as we have already pointed out, since it does not disclose the contribution of a firm to the national product (value added) and could be augmented simply by juggling assortments and subcontracting. Moreover, reckoning unsold output contributes to an abstraction of the producer from the needs of the market as goods are not produced to satisfy buyers' requirements but for the plan. Production is disrupted since the industrial buyers receive unsuitable or low quality materials. The buyer cannot oppose the seller's deterioration of quality and nonadherence to the order since the producer dominates the market and only buyers compete to seize the limited supplies. Given the general scarcity of materials and the desire to fulfil the plan at almost any cost, the producer accumulates whatever supplies he can. In some firms stocks of materials mount, whereas total depletion and unavailability cause others to cease operations temporarily. Procurement difficulties bring about socialist graft. Barter of materials is common. The procurement market unduly absorbs and wastes resources.

Mindful of pressures on the consumer market, the state has placed observance of the wage fund limits on a pedestal as a performance criterion. Due to the pressures within the enterprise to expand the size of the wage fund, its magnitude has become of paramount importance. The significance attached by the state to the wage fund necessitated finding adequate means for controlling its size and a relatively simple method of computation. Due to unremitting preoccupation with the repercussions on the consumer market, it resulted in complete disregard for administration of resources in the enterprise. As we know, the wage fund is simply related to the value of output, which is one of the crudest methods available. Without repeating the various methods of enhancing the value of output and

enumerating the shift parameters of the production function, even in the simple case of a single product of one
assortment, quality and specifications, a direct correlation between the size of the wage fund and the
magnitudes of output could exist only if the labor intensity would not be subject to change, the structure and
composition of the labor force would remain unaltered,
and the remuneration of employees would be proportionate
to labor productivity and would depend on nothing else.
It is hardly necessary to add that these conditions are
almost never satisfied. The oversimplified computation
of the wage fund is higly inequitable and contributes
to serious difficulties in some enterprises whereas
others reap unwarranted benefits.

It seems that the use of gross value has yet another
pitfall. At the present stage of its economic development Poland has a relative shortage of basic raw materials and in many instances depends on their import.
To alleviate the balance of payments it could save on
the use of imported materials and contract their import
and by parsimony of domestic raw materials perhaps increase their export. With the present relatively
abundant supply of labor it would generally be preferable to save materials and substitute labor for materials whenever economically justified. It goes without
saying, that long run factors of growth and many other
variables must be considered. Labor and materials
could not be taken as homogeneous aggregates but the
benefits accruing from substitution in every particular
case would have to be analyzed. However, the system is
directed mainly towards savings on labor costs. Waste
of materials is largely condoned. The computation of
the value of production and the wage fund related to
it are de facto incentives for increasing the consumption of materials. The prevailing method of wage
payments to production workers, the piece rate system,
is uniformly directed towards augmenting output offering,
in a sense, an incentive to the individual worker to
substitute materials for labor.

There seems to be a contradiction between the price
and incentive policies. As we know, the state lowers
or increases prices of substitutable products to promote
or restrain their use due to their relative abundance
or scarcity. From the standpoint of profit maximization,
the firm, subject to constraints, would endeavor to

minimize costs but only if the ensuing benefits would
be larger than those flowing from production plan
fulfilment. However, for this purpose it is in the
interests of the enterprise to use a more expensive
raw material that may be less labor intensive to
process. Indeed the larger the cost of materials the
more expensive the product and the larger the value of
output. In a sense, the firm's demand function for
materials is often upward sloping largely influenced
by performance criteria.

On January 1, 1964 the regulations governing the
wage fund were altered embracing enterprises producing
about half of the industrial output. The existing regulations were retained for extraction, metallurgy,
food, and some branches of the light industry. The
changes in the remaining industries were not far-
reaching extending only to the automatic correction
of the wage fund by the bank. Thus the initial wage
fund granted an enterprise is still computed in relation
to the planned gross value of output. But the firm
cannot expect an augmentation of the fund in relation
to overfulfilment of the output target. However,
reduction of the wage fund by the bank in case of
output plan underfulfilment has been retained.

The new system hinges on wage fund reserves formed
by the ministries and associations to be distributed
to enterprises that overfulfil the output targets of
assortments "in short supply" that the planner wishes
to promote (reserve B),[273] and production for export
(reserve A). When the firm exceeds its wage fund in any
one period, the excess is deducted from the association's reserve B. However, this excess cannot exceed
20 per cent of reserve B. If it does the balance will
be deducted from the ministry's reserve. Hence an
alarm system has been incorporated notifying the
superiors of wage fund excesses. It should be noted
that the ministry and association should specify in
which assortments overfulfilment will be honored for
wage fund adjustments to be calculated in relation to
the products' labor intensity. The reserve may also
be used by the superiors to supplement the wage fund
of firms that have been assigned above plan targets.[274]

Fick claims that the 1964 experience with the new
wage fund system showed that although the enterprises
subject to it remained within the limits of the planned

fund, they overfulfilled their production targets by
2.3 per cent, indicating that overfulfilment of the
production plan must not necessarily be accompanied by
an increase in wages.[275] However, the result hinges,
inter alia, on the composition of output and substitution of materials for labor. But the reform was not
mainly aimed at restricting the wage fund. Primarily
the idea was to curtail inutile above plan production,
secondly to enable overfulfilment of planned production
in needed assortments, and thirdly to shift the responsibility for the wage fund from banks to the firms'
supervisors. The 1964 experience in this sphere was
not particularly encouraging. Obtaining additional
funds from reserves was greatly bureaucratized. For
example, the Ministry of Heavy Industry did not
distribute reserves among its associations. The firms
had to demand funds from the association, and after
approval the request was forwarded to the ministry for
further processing.[276] Enterprises demanding additional
funds received replies to their requests with two to
three month delays , **hence** often too late to execute
the above plan targets.[277] The new system has not
fostered a swift process of adaptation to changing
requirements during plan realization. Associations
blamed the trade centrals for not supplying them with
lists of articles in short supply on the market.[278]
But the associations also fell short of expectations.
As a rule, they did not assign their firms above plan
targets for specific assortments. Wage fund reserves
were distributed generally upon specific requests
emanating from enterprises. Furthermore, although
complaints were voiced that the total 330 million zl.
reserve allowed to industry was a mere pittance,[279]
at the end of the third quarter there remained 155
million zl. undistributed.[280]

    Notwithstanding the above shortcomings the new
wage fund system suffers from its relation to gross
value, the difficulties of establishing and quantifying
this relation, etc. Hence a search is presently continuing for a more meaningful yardstick, concentrating
primarily on variants of value added.

    To eliminate material inputs and intra-industry flows
from influencing the size of the wage fund, it is proposed to depart from relating the wage fund to gross
value of output, replacing it by a yardstick approximat-

ing the value added (v + m) by the enterprise.[281] There
are considerable difficulties in arriving at a workable
definition of value added that could be applied for
computing the wage fund in various industries. In the
definition adopted by the CSO value added is reckoned
as gross value of output at current prices, or a)
direct materials, b) indirect materials, c) fuels,
d) electric power, e) services procured f) depreciation, g) direct labor, h) indirect labor, i) labor
surcharges, j) profit or loss, and k) turnover tax or
budget differences, less a,b,c,d,e, and f.[282]

The problem whether output should be reckoned in
transfer or factory prices must be faced when deciding
on the use of value added as well. The irrationality
of prices constrains the validity of this yardstick.
Total output embraces products sold, changes in
inventories of finished goods, work in process, and
production designated for the firm's internal uses.
Consequently no matter whether output has received
the buyers' seal of approval, and with the prevailing
difficult to detect juggling of work in process, output reported in value added can indicate a rate of
increase larger than when reckoned in gross value.[283]
If the transfer price falls below cost the calculated
value added may be negative and reported value added
would decrease as output would increase.

The limited experience with value added confirms
that to overfulfil the production plan material inputs
are inflated at the planning stage resulting in lower
value added targets, while at the executing stage value
of materials is deflated reporting a larger value
added.[284] This would be of foremost interest in
industries where bank correction of the wage fund is
still in force. Similarly to gross value the use
of value added induces assortment manipulations to
satisfy the producer aiming at producing the most
labor intensive output.[285] But in view of material
shortages this may be the lesser of the two evils.
Although generally it would be preferable to induce
replacement of labor for materials, whenever feasible,
it does not necessarily follow that it would be efficient
in all cases. Because of irrational prices computation
of the rate of substitution in particular cases will be
of little assistance in guiding decisions.[286] In view
of procurement difficulties firms have little control

over the size of material costs and value added will
fluctuate pending on the source and quality of materials
the firm was able to procure. Hence hoarding of materials will still prevail.

In favoring labor intensive production value added
may be an impediment for introducing technical progress.
But in view of the present unwillingness towards the
introduction of technical progress and the magnitude of
malpractices generated by the present system, it would
seem that the computation of output in terms of value
added has much to recommend it. Although not grossly
misled by material intensity, the correlation between
the wage fund and value added is also a spurious one
as it does not simply depend on labor input but, inter
alia, on changes of differential rate of accumulation,
prices, capital intensity, quality of material inputs,
wage differentials, etc.

So far, with the notable exception of the clothing
industry, application of value added is at the experimental stage. Two notable variants have been evolved to be
adopted for particular industries during the years
1966 to 1970: standard labor costs (machine building,
electrical, and transport equipment industries) and
standard processing costs (the clothing, chemical,
furniture, glass, sugar, food concentrates, fruit and
vegetable, brewing, china, leather and shoes, apparel,
fur, and insulating materials industries) with an
altered version for metallurgy and building materials
industries. The corresponding yardsticks in the
extraction and electric power industries will be
variants of physical units and those of the textile
and paper industries will still be gross value in
transfer prices.[287]

Standard labor costs are reckoned on the basis of
technological norms or past statistical data indicating
labor input per unit of output multiplied by the standard wage. Hence the sole component of value added in
this case is standard direct labor.[288] The standard
cost measure is impaired by the technocratic, as
distinct from economic, approach to the problem. It
disregards the substitution effect of the marginal
productivity theory and market valuation. The standards are subject to distortions due to setting and
verifying time norms for products, classifying and
shifting labor from direct to indirect and vice versa,

changing the product mix, converting work in process
into whole units, and altering the extent of subcontracting. Moreover, standards will vary depending on their
computation for all operations or identifiable cost
centers, groups or individual products, all producers
or individual firms. An additional problem is defining
the qualifications needed to perform operations and
wage differentials. Notwithstanding the foregoing,
standards will be inaccurate in view of management's
pressures to have them set at the highest possible
level and revised only sporadically.

The components of the standard processing cost are:
direct and indirect labor plus surcharges, indirect
materials,[289] fuel, electric power, depreciation, and
services procured. Hence this variant of value added
differs from gross value by excluding direct materials,
profit, and turnover tax.[290] The standard processing
cost is computed on the average standards in a branch
of industry. By its very nature standard processing
cost suffers from shortcomings similar to those
attributed to standard labor costs.

The report of a joint Party and government commission, headed by **F. Blinowski** of the Central Committee's
economic department, indicated that although the
results of the clothing industry are rather favorable,
standard processing cost is far from being an accurate
yardstick for wage fund computation. Since the standard processing cost does not cover particular operations
it is also vulnerable to subcontracting manipulations.
It offers no inducement for savings of materials, does
not encourage production of new goods and introduction
of new processes, and is unsuitable for industries
where preparation for production is labor consuming.[291]
Due to the differential rate of labor and other components in the standard processing costs in different
enterprises and for different assortments, the computation of the wage fund may be inequitable. In view of
the magnitude of indirect non-labor costs in some
industries muddled by the process of allocation, the
wage fund is related to elements that do not directly
influence its size. For example, in one branch of the
chemical industry the components of the experimental
standard processing cost are: direct labor 27 per cent,
overhead 26 per cent, and departmental costs 47 per
cent.[292] Furthermore the contemplated stability and

data used for computing the standard processing cost are
highly questionable. For example, the experiments in
the pharmaceutical industry were based on 1962 cost
computations. Hence the standard processing costs for
many products are obsolete at their very inception.
With the passage of time such a situation would be
intensified making the standard less and less representative.[293]

No matter what variants of value added will be applied within the next few years, according to the
present forecasts they will serve only to measure
output for calculating the wage fund and labor productivity. Gross value will still remain as the yardstick
for planning output at all levels. Notwithstanding the
optimistic pronouncements that the wage fund problem
will be solved during the next FYP (1966-70) through
a systematic adaptation of yardsticks approximating
value added,[294] the present experiments are meeting
with many difficulties in practice.[295] The planning
apparatus is not eager to abandon the routine entrenched
gross value methods. This reluctance is reflected,
inter alia, in the notorious non-execution and postponement of experimental adaptations of value added:[296]

The dominating role of gross value of production
index creates simply too favorable and too long
exploited possibilities to compensate for deficiencies in planning and administration of industry that everyone should be willing to give it
up so easily.[297]

In view of the prevailing juggling of assortments
by producers resulting in intense shortages of certain
products, the existing premium system in the heavy,
chemical, light, and building materials industries was
amended on January 1, 1964 by removing the condition
of production plan fulfilment, replacing it with
fulfilment of the output targets of specified assortments. A revised premium system was introduced in enterprises and associations effective July 1, 1964.
Simultaneously a number of specialized premiums were
discontinued and their funds directed towards the main
premium fund. However, it should be noted that
specialized premiums for technical progress, savings
of fuels and materials, export activation, etc. have

still been retained.[298]

The two main characteristics of the new premium
system are: 1) upper limit of the total premium fund
allowed for that year transmitted as a plan directive,
and 2) it is a mixed system employing both profit and
execution of special tasks with a pronounced shift of
importance to special tasks. The firm's total premium
fund is divided by the association's director into
three parts: 1) premium fund for managerial personnel
(with individual premiums limited to 80 per cent of
salary), 2) premium fund for engineering, technical,
financial, and administrative personnel (with individual premiums limited to 50 per cent of salary), and
3) premium fund for white collar workers (with individual premiums limited to 25 per cent of salary).
The parts so established are rigid and no funds can
be transferred from one part to another. Parts 2 and
3 are further subdivided by the firm's director into
funds for individual departments. The mainspring of
the system is the assignment of tasks and the corresponding amount of premium granted for execution
to particular organizational units within the firm.
To prevent the frittering away of premiums a maximum
of 5 tasks may be assigned to each unit. The execution
of each task entitles the unit to receive a previously
stipulated number of points. The total of all points
granted for the execution of all tasks should equal
100 corresponding to the total premium fund allotted
to that unit. The points for all tasks should be set
so as to allow 65 (and in special cases 75) for the
execution of planned tasks and the remainder for
execution of above plan or overfulfilment of the
planned ones.[299]

The general conditions for distributing premiums
to managerial personnel are fulfilment of the profit
plan or fulfilment of the planned share of costs in
sales revenue. The general task imposed on management
in all enterprises is fulfilment of the production plan
in stipulated assortments. A given number of points
should be assigned for this task. The remaining tasks
and corresponding points are assigned by the association's director. They may vary according to particular
needs, e.g., introduction of new technical processes,
decrease in stocks of materials, greater utilization
of production capacity, etc. The **premium** fund for

engineering and administrative personnel is subdivided
into two parts. Payments from the first part are
contingent on management's fulfilment of its tasks,
whereas those of the second part are solely subject
to fulfilment of those employee's individual tasks
assigned to them by the director of the enterprise.
Finally the premium fund for white collar workers is
entirely dependent on those employees' execution of
tasks assigned to them by the firm's director.[300]

To eradicate the existing contradiction the premium
system in associations has been constructed along
similar lines. The size of the premium fund is set
by the minister and differentiated according to planned improvement in the production of desired assortments, increase in export production, assimilation of
technical progress, use of capacity, increase in
labor productivity, and profitability. As in the
enterprises, the fund is divided into three parts
and payment made according to points granted for
execution of assigned tasks. The general tasks
imposed on management of all associations are: introduction of new products into production and fulfilment
of export orders. The minister assigns the remaining
tasks, e.g., execution of given assortment orders,
improvement of quality, improvement of profit, etc.

Although overshadowed, the profit criterion has
been introduced in two steps. Firstly underfulfilment of the planned financial result will decrease the
premium fund. When the planned financial result is
fulfilled by only 95 per cent the premium fund cannot
be activated. Secondly 30 per cent of management's
premium fund is intended for an annual premium paid
out in half for fulfilling the planned financial
result of the past year and the other half for taut
planning of those results for the following year,
improving them in comparison to the preceding year.[301]

This construction is intended to counteract the firms'
pressures for lower plans resulting from relating their
premiums to plan fulfilment. Nevertheless the effectiveness of this tool is highly doubtful as the part
of premium paid to a manager for taut planning amounts
to a maximum of 15 per cent of his annual premium.
Moreover, he is induced to be rather careful in profit
planning as payment of the other 85 per cent of his
premium is contingent on the fulfilment of the financial

plan. Hence a tendency to lower the financial plan may
be expected at the enterprise's level with little
oppostion at the association's level.

The construction of the system assumes that the firm's
director will assign his subordinates tasks which will
promote the execution of his own tasks assigned to him
by the association. It is doubtful whether with the
present quality of data at his disposal the director
can successfully allocate tasks in such a manner. Moreover the system relies on subjective appraisals of the
intensity of tasks. Should it prove in practice that
the assigned tasks are not taut enough, the entire
system will collapse and its premiums will be transformed into additions to salary.

The scant experience with the new premium system
indicates that the tasks are not sufficiently differentiated according to specific conditions. As a rule,
neither the ministries nor the associations have
assigned above plan improvement of profit as a task
to their subordinates, assuming that execution of the
other tasks will improve the financial result. But
practice indicates that execution of such tasks as
overfulfilment of the plan of stipulated assortments,
decrease in the use of certain materials, improvement in quality of output, etc. cannot always be
equated with improvement of profit.[302]

The elimination of profit as a performance
criterion from a wide range of premium recipients is
a move away from synthetic criteria. Essentially the
new premium system boils down to a replacement of
profit by several variable performance criteria directed
towards particular work segments. This will threaten
**neglect of all tasks other than those rewarded by
premiums.**

Profit, by the very nature of its computation,
embraces both revenue and costs and prima facie is a
superior measure than gross value, value added, any
specific tasks, or even cost reduction, as it reflects
both costs and benefits and their mutual relationship.
It is the only criterion that presents an over-all
picture of the enterprise's or association's performance. Banned in the past as incompatible with socialism, profit is now gaining respectability and is re-
currently advocated by economists as a superior performance criterion.[303] Nevertheless in practice a

distinct trend away from profit is observed. Indeed,the
revision of the premium system seems to bear out the
contention that the fallacy of the price system makes
profit an inadequate performance criterion.

   In fact profit is a purely accounting, as distinct
from economic, category since prices do not reflect
current economic scarcities. In view of the fundamental deficiency of the price system, the measure of
profitability may not be considered a sufficient guide
for the direction, expansion, or contraction of production. If production of low profitability or even
deficit goods, e.g.,children's shoes, is to be expanded
in view of great shortages on the market, with the
simultaneous abundance of highly profitable assortments,
e.g.,women's shoes, whether or not sold to the final
consumer, the producer will naturally endeavor to produce
the latter at the expense of the former, although it
would be deemed that production of children's shoes
is socially more desirable. Neither sales revenue nor
costs are meaningful categories as both output and
input prices are generally fallacious. Cost calculations are incomplete, methodologically deficient, and
tendenciously distorted. Hence the residual profit
cannot be more meaningful than the components that
went into its determination. Prices and profit cannot
guide enterprises in economic choice and it seems to
follow from the very logic of the system that directives must instruct firms to produce more of one product
and less of another, in our example children's and
women's shoes. If the use of raw materials in short
supply is to be curtailed, it must be conducted by
fiat since the price ratios in the obsolete catalogs,
even assuming that they were originally correct, no
longer constitute indexes of economic choice. The
fallacy of the price system nullifies any serious
attempts at decentralization of economic decisions.
If management cannot be guided by prices, maximization
of profit may not be in the state's interest. If
there is a serious chance that maximization of profit
will be arbitrary and not in the general interest,
profit cannot be used as a performance criterion.
In such a case there is a necessity for a multitude
of performance criteria which leads us right back
into the present highly unsatisfactory situation.

   Notwithstanding its shortcomings, the central plan-

ECONOMICS OF SOCIALIST ENTERPRISE

ner basically distrusts profit as a performance criterion because it is a resultant of many variables. The
direction and intensity of each variable may be different and their importance may not seem additive from
the standpoint of the central planner's scale of
preferences. The increase of profit that results from
a decrease in total production costs without an
unchanged. Furthermore it may be deemed that a reduction in material costs and equiproportional increase
in labor costs, although neutralized in the computation
of profit, may not be of the same order of magnitude.
This is related to the material balances where every
element enters into a separate central balance and
even though equivalent in monetary terms is not substitutable without the central planner's decision.
The guidance of the economy through material balances
precludes acceptance of profit as the only perform-

An awareness of the present shortcomings prevails
and is echoed in Party pronouncements, the press, and
economic literature. The continuing deliberations
of special commissions and conferences studying planning methods, prices, performance criteria, industrial
organization, and economic incentives indicate a prima
facie desire to revamp the system. Nevertheless,
perusal of the latest promulgations indicates that
remedies are sought for specific ills and there is a
lack of understanding of the interdependence of the
system's components. There is still a widespread
belief that the desired effects can be produced by
half measures, whereas for efficient functioning the
entire system must be integrated into a coherent whole.
Doubtless the direction, speed, and magnitude of future
changes will largely be determined by political forces
which I do not feel competent to judge.[304] However,
no matter what the political trend, it seems that
the leaders of the regime would be well advised to
keep in mind these words of a great Soviet economist:

...in our country where the centralized planned
economy of the proletariat has been established,
and the law of value has been limited or replaced
by the planning principle, foresight and knowledge

play an exceptional role as compared with the
capitalist economy. Errors in foresight committed by our central leadership may have much
heavier consequences than errors committed by
managers of private enterprises where mistakes
in one direction are often cancelled out by
mistakes in the opposite direction according to
the law of great numbers.[305]

To counteract false judgment, improve knowledge,
and enhance foresight leading to a better use of
resources, the central planner needs more precise
tools for plan construction and implementation. It
is perhaps in this respect that a closer tie between
economic theory and practice would be most desirable.
In Professor Brus' words:

For the last seven or eight years economics... is
offered far more favorable conditions for development than before. The results... are evident:
greater freedom in scientific research and confront-
ation of different views, strengthened Marxist
socialist economic thought, and in certain fields
and works serious creative enrichment of theory...
Economics belongs, however, to the fields of knowledge which should not be satisfied with purely
intellectual achievements. This is why it should
not be surprising that at least some theoretical
economists are convinced that their influence - in
the broad sense - on reality is minimal, and, at any
rate, incommensurate with the intellectual achievements and actual needs. It is possible that they
are wrong, that they overestimate the real value of
what they have to offer... However, if they are not
wrong, conclusions must be reached rapidly and
consistently for the point in question is not only,
and not primarily, of importance to economists.[306]

NOTES TO CHAPTER 1

1. During World War II Poland lost some six million
people or about 20 per cent of the prewar population.
The destruction of war amounted to 38 per cent of prewar national wealth. A. Karpinski, Poland and the World
Economy, (Warsaw: 1960), p.10. Losses in industry
reached 11.04 billion prewar (1938) zlotys corresponding to a destruction of the production potential amounting to 33 per cent. K. Secomski, Analiza wykonania planu
trzyletniego, (Warsaw: 1950), p.12. For a background
and analysis of the Polish economic scene between 1918
and 1939 see F. Zweig, Poland Between Two Wars, (London:
1944). A good interpretation of postwar political
changes may be found in M.K. Dziewanowski, The Communist Party of Poland, (Cambridge, Mass: 1959), pp.183-
207

2. It should be remembered that loss of oil deposits
intensifies the problem of balance of payments in postwar Poland. Whereas in 1938 Poland produced 500 thousand tons of crude oil, its 1962 production amounted
only to 203 thousand, with import exceeding 1.1 million
tons. S. Hatt, et al., System planowania w Polsce,
(Warsaw: 1964), p.6

3. C. Bobrowski in Polityka gospodarcza Polski
Ludowej, I, (Warsaw: 1962), pp.16-7

4. W. Piotrowski, Ekonomika przemyslu, (Lodz: 1962),
p.50

5. B. Minc, Planowanie i polityka gospodarcza,
(Lodz: 1961), p.337

6. O. Lange, The Political Economy of Socialism,
(The Hague: 1958), pp.16-7

7. DU, no.3, 1946, item 17

For abbreviations used in the NOTES, see BIBLIOGRAPHICAL
ABBREVIATIONS, Page 382.

8. In 1946 the state-owned and cooperative sectors
accounted for 79 per cent of total industrial output in
1937 prices. B. Minc, op.cit., p.341. The respective
shares in output of state-owned, cooperative, and private
industry for 1949 were 87.7, 6.2 and 6.1 per cent; for
1955, 89.8, 9.6 and 0.6 per cent; for 1958, 85.9, 13.2,
and 0.9 per cent; and for 1961, 89.1, 10.0, and 0.6 per
cent. RS 1959, p.76 and RS 1962, p.83. Announcing the
new policy of the Polish government in 1957, the chairman of the Planning Commission said: "It is a known
fact that large and medium private establishments were
nationalized on the basis of the law on nationalization
while small private enterprises came under compulsory
state administration.... The Party takes the position
that these enterprises should remain in the hands of
the state. The odd establishment which stands idle or
is definitely unprofitable may be handed over to private
individuals, but this can apply only to establishments
which the state has been unable to run until now and
will not be in a position to do so in the future.
Private initiative should put into operation establishments that are standing idle or open up new ones."
S. Jedrychowski, The Fundamental Principles of
Economic Policy in Industry, (Warsaw: 1957), p.7

9. Z. Pirozynski and E. Winter, Budzet panstwowy
Polski Ludowej, (Warsaw: 1961), p.29

10. B. Minc, op.cit., pp.338-9

11. Ibid., p.340 and S. Hatt et al., op.cit., p.100

12. Bobrowski, op.cit., p.18

13. The term "index" is a translation of the Polish
term wskaznik and implies a plan target in quantitative
terms usually transmitted as a directive from above.
B. Minc, op.cit., p.341

14. M. Lesz. GP, no.7, 1964, p.14

15. Cf. T. Dietrich, GP, no. 7-8, 1948, p.230. As
Dr. A. Zauberman points out "there was more than a grain
of truth in the saying that Poland's economy looked
toward Marx with one eye and towards Keynes with the

other." Industrial Progress in Poland, Czechoslovakia, and East Germany, 1937-1962, (London: 1964), p.2

16. B. Minc in Zarys rozwoju metodologii planowania w Polsce Ludowej 1944-1954, (Warsaw: 1956), p.4

17. H. Minc, ND, no.3, 1948, pp.34-6. Unfortunately this is the only published material on the Polish "industrialization debate". As far as can be determined the opposing views were not given any coverage in the press at that time. Cf. Bobrowski, Ekon., no.5, 1964, p.976

18. B. Minc, GP, no. 1, 1950, p.9

19. B. Minc, Zagadnienia dochodu narodowego, (Warsaw: 1951)

20. An excellent exposition of the Soviet debate may be found in the brilliant study by A. Erlich, The Soviet Industrialization Debate 1924-1928, (Cambridge, Mass: 1960), Cf. N. Spulber, Soviet Strategy for Economic Growth, (Bloomington: 1964), pp.101-11 and passim

21. W. Brus, Ogolne problemy funkcjonowania gospodarki socjalistycznej, (Warsaw: 1961), p.150

22. Lange, op.cit., p.17. It is interesting to note that in this connection Brus writes: "I do not share the opinion that forced industrialization requires an unlimited centralization of decisions.... None the less violent changes in the economic structure bring about tensions of such a type and magnitude that operation by economic means proves completely impossible in some cases and in others not efficient enough." Brus, op.cit., p.331

23. GP, no.7-8, 1948, p.270

24. Administrative units directly responsible for supervision of enterprises

25. J. Sekotowski, GP, no.11, 1948, pp.389-93

26. S. Rog in Zarys rozwoju..., p.16. There was,

however, a distinct lack of coordination between the
technical and financial plans. B. Blass, GP, no.3,
1949, p.148

27. A. Wang, GP, no.1, 1949, pp.4-5

28. A table illustrating the targets drafted in
1948 and the 1950 revisions may be found in the useful
study by T.P. Alton, Polish Postwar Economy, (New York:
1955), p.117, cf. Erlich, AER, no.2, 1959, pp.94-101
and J. Marczewski, Planification et croissance des
democracies populaires, I, (Paris: 1956), pp.187-92

29. Lange, Some Problems Relating to the Polish
Road to Socialism, (Warsaw: 1957), p.11

30. B. Ruminski, ND, no.10, 1956, p.70

31. Erlich, AER, no.2, 1959, p.100

32. According to official statistics the share of
accumulation in national income increased from 16 per
cent in 1949 to 28 per cent in 1953 calculated in
1956 prices. Calculated in 1950 prices the respective
figures are 22.7 and 38 per cent. S. Kuzinski, O
czynnikach wzrostu gospodarczego Polski Ludowej,
(Warsaw: 1962), p.10. According to Zauberman's
recalculation of gross capital formation as a percentage of GNP (Western method) the figure for the
early 1950's is 48 per cent. Zauberman, op.cit., p.40.
According to Marczewski, who does not offer a basis
for his estimate, the investment limit that the
Polish economy could have sustained was 20 per cent
of national income. ZG, no.1, 1957

33. "The raising of the standard of living was
treated as a product of a number of factors and not
as one of the main tasks to which other factors should
be subjected during the course of the plan." H. Minc,
ND, no.10, 1956, p.122

34. Kuzinski, Glowne proporcje rozwoju gospodarczego
Polski Ludowej, (Warsaw: 1960), p.38. Cf. Kuzinzki,
O czynnikach..., p.14 and Jedrychowski, op.cit.,
p.18

35. A. Karpinski, op.cit., pp.20-1. According to
estimates the cost of completing investments started
during the SYP period would be approximately 50 billion
zlotys (in 1956 prices). This sum exceeds the average
investment expenditures incorporated in an annual
investment plan. A. Szerwentke, GP, no.1, 1957 p.16

36. H. Minc in his self-criticism referred to
investments in the defense industry as follows:
"Development of the armaments industry skimmed the
cream off production, high grade steels, roller bearings,
pipes, precision machines, etc. It also took away the
best technicians and engineers making it impossible to
fulfil the investment plans in many branches of industry. ND, no. 10, 1956, p.123

37. B. Ruminski, op.cit, p.70, A. Szerwentke, op.
cit., p.18, and Kuzinski, O czynnikach..., p.10. The
increase of industrial output during the SYP was
facilitated by shifting a considerable share of labor
from agriculture to heavy industry. In addition
throughout the entire postwar period Poland has had an
exceptionally high rate of natural increase of population, amounting to 18 per 1000 annually, resulting
in an annual increase of about half a million. Karpinski, op.cit., p.11. It should be noted that the
growth of industrial output during the SYP period was
accomplished largely by an increase in the labor
participation rate rather than by an increase in labor
productivity. W. Krencik and Z. Twardowski, GP, no.1,
1957, p.31

38. Kuzinski, Glowne proporcje..., p.60

39. For example, considerable delays in the construction of steel mills in Warsaw resulted in drastic
shortages of high grade steels. Consequently many
machine building plants were producing only at 30 to
50 per cent capacity. Kuzinski, ND, no.9, 1956, p.13

40. "...by labelling them as disproportions Polish
economists meant not merely to emphasize that some areas
of the economy had been growing faster than others, and
that the fulfilment of plans had been uneven. Their
point was that these divergencies when pushed as far

as they actually had been were bound to cause loss of
potential gains as well as actual waste in the advancing
areas." A. Erlich, AER, no.2, 1959, p.96 and **ibid.**,
pp.96-8

41. For example, whereas output of the construction industry increased by 400 per cent during the
SYP, the increase in output of basic raw materials
was in the range of 63 to a little over 100 per cent.
T. Gradowski and A. Kiernozycki, GP, no.9, 1956, p.7

42. Lange in Dyskusja o polskim modelu gospodarczym,
(Warsaw: 1957), p.15

43. S.J. Kurowski, ZG, no.7, 1957

44. Professor Grossman attributes the term "command economy" to Halm. G. Grossman, AER, no.2, 1959,
p.52. On the theory of a command economy see Grossman,
Sov. Stud., no.2, 1963, pp.104ff. Cf. P. Wiles, The
Political Economy of Communism, (Oxford: 1962), pp.
67-205 and W. Eucken, Economica, May,1948, pp.79-100
and August,1948, pp.173-93, A. Nove, The Soviet
Economy, (New York: 1961), and A. Bergson, The
Economics of Soviet Planning, (New Haven: 1964),
passim

45. For a full discussion of central planning and
its effects on the economy see the valuable study by
Professor J.M. Montias, Central Planning in Poland,
(New Haven: 1962)

46. Cf. B. Minc, Zmiany w metodologii planowania
na rok 1952, (Warsaw: 1951), p.12. The first cost
reduction tasks were incorporated in 1951. Z. Augustowski, GP, no.3, 1951, p.8, S. Rog, op.cit., p.33

47. B. Minc, Zmiany w metodologii..., pp.10-3.
For a good discussion of short-term planning in the
U.S.S.R. see H. Levine in F.D. Holzman (ed.), Readings
on the Soviet Economy, (Chicago: 1962), pp.329-59 and
Bergson, op.cit., Chapter 7

48. It goes without saying that our description of
planning procedures refers to an idealized scheme rather

than its practical application.

49.   Goods whose production has been fairly standardized

50.   S. Rog, op.cit., pp.36-40

51.   The use of the term "model" differs from its
use in Western economics and econometrics. For the
Western interpretation see E.F. Beach, Economic Models,
An Exposition, (New York: 1957), Chapters 1 and 2.
According to Professor Bobrowski: "In Poland we mean
by model a certain variant of the socialist economic
structure. In other words, the whole complex of management and planning methods or the economic policy applied
in a certain concrete country or in a certain concrete
period." in Lange (ed.), Zagadnienia ekonomii politycznej
socjalizmu, (Warsaw: 1960), p.238. Cf. Brus, op.cit.,
pp.7-10; J.G. Zielinski, Rachunek ekonomiczny w socjalizmie, (Warsaw: 1961), pp.33-4; S. Kruszczynski,
Polityka ekonomiczna i planowanie gospodarki narodowej,
(Poznan: 1964), pp.72-3; and P. Wiles, op.cit., p.2

52.   Although the consumer can only choose among the
goods the planner decides to produce and skilled workers
and technicians are often assigned to high priority
industries and enterprises

53.   Our exposition in this section draws heavily
on Brus, op.cit., pp.116-47. Cf. C. Bettelheim, Studies
in the Theory of Planning, (New York: 1959), Chapter 1

54.   Z. Madej, Zysk w gospodarce socjalistycznej,
(Warsaw: 1963) p.27

55.   Lange, Niektore zagadnienia centralizacji i
decentralizacji w zarzadzaniu, (Warsaw: 1962), pp.2-3,
Zielinski, ZG, no.10, 1963

56.   Cf. Drewnowski's argument on the dual preference
system in a socialist economy. He maintains that there
are two interacting systems of valuation: the single
state preference function, expressed in economic plans
and policies, and the multiple system of individual
preference functions, and that the former emanates in

a very general way from the latter. JPE, August,1961,
pp.341-54; cf. Zielinski, Rachunek ekonomiczny...,
pp.134-75

57.   In Polish economic literature the term "accumulation" usually refers to the non-consumed share of
national product (value added in material production
only). "Accumulation" is defined in the Statistical
Yearbook as "the value of net investments and increase
in inventories and reserves". RS 1962, p.55. It should
be noted, however, that in Polish financial literature
"accumulation" is also used to denote the positive
difference between sales revenue and the attributable
production costs.

58.   A. Wakar and J.G. Zielinski, Ekon., no.1, 1961,
pp.21-2; cf. B. Csikos-Nagy, Polityka cen w gospodarce
okresu przejsciowego, (translated from Hungarian),
(Warsaw: 1961), pp.70-85

59.   Cf. L. Robbins, The Great Depression, (London:
1934), p.155

60.   Grossman, Sov. Stud., no.2, 1963, p.108

61.   Cf. Montias, AER, no.5, 1959, pp.963-85 and
Central Planning..., passim

62.   "The 'Method of Balances', to which the Soviet
writers themselves invariably refer, hardly deserves its
high-sounding name. It simply requires that the over-
all national economic plan be constructed in such a way
that the total output of each kind of goods be equal to
the quantity which all its users are supposed to receive.
The method does not, however, say what information and
what computational procedures can be used to achieve
the simultaneous balancing of many thousands of different
goods and services covered by a comprehensive blueprint
of a national economy." W. Leontief, Foreign Affairs,
January,1960, p.263

63.   On the limiting assumptions of constant tech-
nological coefficients in input-output analysis see
R. Dorfman et al., Linear Programming and Economic
Analysis, (New York: 1958), pp.209, 230-1, and 247-52

64. Cf. E. Czerwinska, Samodzielnosc finansowa przedsiebiorstwa przemyslowego, (Poznan: 1963), pp.69-70

65. Cf. Grossman, Sov. Stud., no.2, 1963, p.116 and P. Wiles, op.cit., p.68

66. Cf. Madej, op.cit., p.104 and D. Granick, JPE, April,1959, pp.115-23

67. Bobrowski, GP, no.6, 1957, p.2, cf. R. Bicanic in M.I. Goldman (ed.), Comparative Economic Systems, (New York: 1964), p.275

68. Lange, The Political Economy..., pp.17-8

69. Brus, Oxf. Econ. Papers, June,1957, p.207. Professor Lange opened the congress with a mild praise for the SYP. Brus' impassioned speech came as a great surprise and purified the air from obsolete ideas. It is ironical that he used the ideas expressed in Lange's prewar model of market socialism as an inspiration. At the end of the congress Lange in accord with the prevailing spirit admitted the existing shortcomings. A report on the congress may be found in J. Glowczyk and J. Niegowski, ND, no.6, 1956, pp.92-101

70. Lange, The Political Economy..., pp.20-1

71. J. Pajestka, Oxf. Econ. Papers, June,1957, p.223

72. Kurowski, op.cit.; cf. Brus, Ogolne problemy..., pp.147-53

73. J. Mieszczankowski, ZG, no.11, 1957; cf. Bobrowski, ZG, no.19, 1957 and Secomski, GP, no.1, 1957, pp.2-3

74. Brus, Oxf. Econ. Papers, June,1957, p.213

75. In this connection Dr. Zauberman's comment regarding the Soviet economy is worthy of notice since the same seems to be true of Poland: "Paradoxical as it may appear, developments in Soviet economic thought and attitudes seem to bear out, to a point, the contention that concern with scarcity relations (even if in-

articulate as in the Soviet Union) deepens as an economy
gets richer." in Grossman (ed.), Value and Plan,
(Berkeley: 1960), p.17. This "Zauberman Law" - to
borrow Professor Nove's expression - was, in my opinion
inappropriately questioned by Wiles.

76. Brus, Oxf. Econ. Papers, June,1957, p.210

77. Ibid.

78. Lange, Pol., no.22, 1964

79. We are only referring briefly here to the
problem of prices since this issue cannot be ignored
completely in an account of the model discussion. The
price controversy in connection with this discussion
will be examined in greater detail in Chapter 2.

80. Kurowski, TL, February 6, 1957. Criticizing
Kurowski's stand Jedrychowski stated: "Large and
medium industrial establishments do not lend themselves to conversion into cooperatives. They constitute the property of the whole of society; the
whole of society provided the means for their construction and therefore cannot be treated as the group
property of the people who work there.... Ideas about
turning large industrial enterprises into cooperative
establishments have nothing in common with building
socialism." op.cit.,p.9

81. Kurowski, ZG, no.7, 1957. Jedrychowski unequivocally expressed the official stand, shared by
a substantial number of economists, when he said:
"We take the stand that central planning should be
maintained as an indispensable instrument of the
planned socialist economy and we oppose all theories
and views which would aim at undermining the planned
character of our economy or reduce the plan merely
to a sum of forecasts... Although Kurowski grants the
central planner the role of coordinator whose main
instrument should be monetary policy, it is essentially
reduced to a scope not exceeding economic intervention
by the capitalist state." TL, May 31, 1957

82. Kurowski, TL, February 6, 1957

83.   Theoretically we can conceive many variations
of a decentralized model; the limiting case would be
the classical model of perfect competition. Cf. J.
Tinbergen, Centralization and Decentralization in
Economic Policy, (Amsterdam: 1954), p.18, Wiles, op.
cit., and L. Hurwicz, in Grossman (ed.) op.cit., pp.
166-75

84.   Zielinski, ZG, no.10, 1963. As the Wakar-
Zielinski contribution is intimately connected with
types of economic calculation its discussion is relegated
to the next chapter.   Lange, Niektore zagadnienia..., p.4

85.   Brus, Ogolne problemy..., pp.245-6. For a
similar view see the recent contribution by Madej, op.
cit., pp.142-3. In an analogous presentation Lange
specifies the major assortments as steel, coal,
cotton textiles, wheat, lumber, etc. in Dyskusja...,
p.12. According to E. Lipinski, domestic production
of such goods as train engines must be centrally
planned, whereas the planning of assortments in the
light and food industries may be subject to a wide
decentralization. in Dyskusja..., p.20. We have
refrained from comparing this model with the Yugoslav
reality as the material was relegated to a special
study.

86.   Pajestka in Dyskusja..., p.128

87.   Brus, Ogolne problemy..., pp.246-7 and ZG, no.12,
1957. According to Professor E. Lipinski, the creation
of new enterprises must be centralized. Op.cit., p.19

88.   Brus, Ogolne problemy..., pp.258-9. E. Lipinski considered price formation the prerogative of central authorities particularly for major products. Op.
cit., pp.19-20

89.   Brus, Ogolne problemy..., pp.247-8; cf. Madej,
op.cit., p.145. According to E. Lipinski, a socialist
enterprise must be "an autonomous unit, decentralized,
 endowed with a great scope of decisions, freedom of
making adjustments, and the right to take risks."
Op.cit., p.30

90.   Lange, Ekonomia polityczna, (Warsaw: 1963),
pp.75-6

91.   Brus, Ogolne problemy..., pp.249-51; cf.
Lange in Dyskusja..., pp.8-9 and Madej, op.cit., pp.
145-6

92.   M. Kalecki, in Dyskusja..., pp.35-6

93.   Jedrychowski, Fundamental Principles..., p.11

94.   Ibid., p.3

95.   Jedrychowski, TL, May 31, 1957

96.   ZG, no.22, 1957

97.   See the recent "obituary" of the Economic
Council by Brus, ZG, no.6, 1964

98.   Madej in Polityka gospodarcza..., I, p.50

99.   Piotrowski, op.cit., p.101, United Nations,
Economic Survey of Europe, (Geneva: 1957), Chapter 1,
p.39, and B. Glinski, Teorie i praktyka zarzadzania
przedsiebiorstwami przemyslowymi, (Warsaw: 1964), pp.
260 ff.

100.   DU, no.53, 1956, item 238

101.   L. Zabkowicz and W. Doberski, Eksperymenty
ekonomiczne, ich wyniki i przyszlosc, (Warsaw: 1958)

102.   Secomski, Polityka gospodarcza Polski na
tle wynikow lat 1956-1958, (Warsaw: 1959), pp.16-7

103.   W. Gomulka in III Zjazd PZPR, (Warsaw: 1959),
p.99

104.   The Economist, November 5, 1960, p.576.   For
years absenteeism has plagued the Polish economy.
M. Ziomek estimated that annual losses approximate one
billion working hours equal to employment of half a
million workers a year.   For the causes see Absencja
w pracy, (Warsaw: 1964)

105. Kuzinski, Glowne proporcje..., pp.64-6; cf.
Krencik, Badania polityki zatrudnienia i plac w gospodarce socjalistycznej, (Warsaw: 1962), pp.194ff.,
and Lange, Ekon. no.5, 1964, pp.974-5, L. Zienkowski,
Ekon. no.5, 1964, pp.1010-11

106. Pajestka, ZG, no.32, 1964

107. Gradowski and Kiernozycki, GP, no.10, 1959,
p.13 and Madej, in Polityka gospodarcza..., I, p.51

108. DU, no.77, 1958, item 397

109. The respective rates of growth of total industrial production, producer, and consumer goods in
1956 were 8.9, 10.6, and 7.2 per cent; in 1957, 9.9,
7.8, and 12.3 per cent; in 1958, 9.9, 9.1, and 10.8 per
cent; in 1959, 9.2, 13.2, and 7.4 per cent; and in
1960, 10.9, 11.5, and 10.3 per cent. C. Niewadzi,
SE, no.7, 1962, p.132. During the first three years
of the 1961-65 FYP production of producer goods was
to increase by 28 per cent and consumer goods by 23
per cent. The actual fulfilment was 31 and 17 per
cent respectively. A. Paszynski, Pol., no.3, 1964.
The official fulfilment statistics of the present
FYP (until mid-1964) can be found in GP, no.7, 1964,
pp.32-5, cf. Lange, Ekon. no.5, 1964, p.974

110. Karpinski, The Polish Economy 1961-1965,
(Warsaw: 1962), pp.10-1 and A. Paszynski, Pol., no.5,
1964

111. Cf. E. Szyr, ND, no.6, 1964, p.120

112. Pajestka, ND, no.11, 1964, p.83

113. Piotrowski, op.cit., p.104, S.Hatt, et al.,
op.cit. p.13, Madej in Polityka gospodarcza..., I, p.34,
and B. Minc, Planowanie..., p.33

114. Madej in Polityka gospodarcza..., I, p.36,
Gomulka in IV Zjazd Polskiej Zjednoczonej Partji
Robotniczej, (Warsaw: 1964), p.120, and J. Rozmus,
ND, no.6, 1964, p.106

115. J. Walewski, ND, no.6, 1964, p.74

116. Firms serving essentially local needs are as a rule under the jurisdiction of local people's councils.

117. A. Plocica, ZG, no.21, 1959 and Madej in Polityka gospodarcza..., I, pp.38-9

118. J. Lutoslawski, GP no.10, 1958, p.8 and Madej in Polityka gospodarcza..., I, p.41

119. Jerzy Zielinski, ZG, no.21, 1964, cf. Szyr, op.cit., pp.65 and 71

120. Madej, in Polityka gospodarcza..., I, p.42

121. Pol., no.9, 1963. Vice-Premier Szyr remarked that "where there is no choice there is no problem of autonomy". Op.cit., p.71

122. Gomulka in IV Zjazd PZPR, pp.117-8 and resolutions pp.325-6

123. Walewski, op.cit. p.74 and Pajestka, ZG, no.32, 1964, ND, no.11, 1964, pp.85-6; cf. Szyr, op.cit., pp.69 and 124, Pajestka, Funkcje ekonomiczne przed-siebiorstw i zjednoczen, (Warsaw: 1965), and S. Michal-ski, Instrumenty finansowe w mechanizmie funkcjonowania przedsiebiorstw i zjednoczen, (Warsaw: 1965)

124. J. Nowak, ND, no.6, 1964, pp.76-7 and Walewski, op.cit., p.74

125. A more detailed analysis of the proposals will be found in a study now in progress.

126. Referring to administration of the economy as an industry a Soviet economist stated that "the raw material processed by this industry is information; ... the product that it turns out is decisions; and ... its technological process is reduced to obtaining, conveying, and processing information." I. Czerniak, Econ. of Plan., April,1963, p.23

127.   This may be contrasted with Professor Hurwicz's ingenious decentralized structure where under the rule of operationalism the central planner is prevented from exacting internal information - a requirement which alone, as Professor Berliner correctly points out, would frustrate the planner's claim at decision making. Under the rule of **anonymity** Hurwicz's planner cannot issue detailed orders to individual firms but only general instructions without differentiating between recipients of the message.   L. Hurwicz, op.cit., p.169 and J.S. Berliner, in Grossman (ed.), op.cit., p.177

128.   Cf. Hurwicz, op.cit., p.174.   In this connection Lange sees the benefits flowing from the installation of electronic computers enabling a more rapid transmission of messages.   Niektore zagadnienia..., p.10

129.   Cf. Pajestka, Ekon., no.2, 1964, pp.252ff. and F.A. Hayek, AER, September,1945, p.524

130.   Lange, Niektore zagadnienia..., pp.2-9

131.   Secomski, in Polityka gospodarcza..., I, p.514; cf. Bobrowski, Ekon., no.5, 1964, pp.984-5

132.   Pajestka, in MEE, p.465

133.   On the conflicts and frictions during plan construction see Pajestka, Funkcje ekonomiczne..., p.9.   Our exposition of plan construction is based mainly on S. Hatt, et al., op.cit., pp.108-26, Pajestka, Ekon., no.2, 1964, M. Weralski, Rola budzetu w planowaniu gospodarczym, (Warsaw: 1963), passim, and M. Misiak (ed.), Bodzce ekonomiczne w przedsiebiorstwie przemyslowym, (Warsaw: 1963), pp.135-69

134.   The instructions for drafting the 1965 plan introduce two-year planning by including with the 1965 plan the basis for the 1966 plan.   The control figures issued for drafting the latter cover: quantity of industrial output, marketable and total output in value terms, goods for the domestic and foreign markets, reckoning of machine building production according to its destination, import, and other

elements essential for the preparation of material
balances, services in value terms, employment, wage
fund, etc. They do not cover procurement, distribution
of materials, machines, and equipment, cooperation, or
production costs. The necessary data for the latter
will be estimated by the PC when required. M. Wolski,
GP, no.8-9, 1964, p.52, cf. M. Krzak, ZG, no.47, 1964.
In the most recent proposals it is suggested that the
minimum span of time covered by the plan should be
three years. Michalski, op.cit. p.5

135. On the problem of balancing and resolution of
shortages see Montias, Central Planning..., particularly
pp.91-102 and Pajestka, Ekon no.2, 1964, p.254. Cf.
Levine's discussion pertaining to the Soviet Union on
the technology of balancing, op.cit., pp.341ff.

136. More direct weapons at the central planner's
disposal (NEP directives, wage and price setting, etc.)
restrict the role of the budget as a tool of economic
(fiscal) policy. J. Weralski, op.cit., p.39

137. IV Zjazd PZPR, p.321. For an extensive
bibliography on planometrics see K. Porwit, Zagadnienia
rachunku ekonomicznego w planie centralnym, (Warsaw:
1964), pp.264-71. On the practical experiments with
new planning techniques see Lesz, GP, no.4, 1963, pp.
21-6, Lange, Pol., no.11, 1963, and GUS, Przeplywy
miedzygaleziowe 1962, (Warsaw: 1964)

138. Rather than by the irksome process of sequential
trial and error series in quest of a suitable solution.
The iterative model to solve the consistency problem
is admirably pursued by Professor Montias, Central
Planning..., passim; for the efficiency problem see
also ibid., Appendix B. Professor Levine argues that
the iterative approach is not the basic method used
by Soviet planners to achieve consistency. According
to him they rely heavily on balancing methods which
avoid second round effects by tightening the input
norms. Op.cit., pp.343-5. Cf. Porwit's description
of the successive phases of drafting the balances
constituting the first stage of the iterative
procedure. Op.cit., Chapter 3

139. We can only scratch the surface of the subject here. The reader would gain immensely by referring to Zauberman, *Sov. Stud.*, July,1962, pp.62-73 for the evaluation of recent practice and prospects of mathematical methods and high speed computation in the Soviet Union. A brief statement of the problem in reference to Poland can be found in Zauberman, Industrial Progress..., pp.16-22. For an illuminating exposition of "perfect computation" see Wiles, op.cit., pp.197-203. Cf. the competent exposition of planometrics in Soviet planning by Levine, op.cit., pp. 348-52, B. Ward on Kantorovich in Holzman (ed.), op. cit. pp.393-404, and R.W. Campbell, *Slav. Rev.*, 1961, pp.402-18

140. As Wiles points out "input/output has an interesting relation to the curious Marxist habit of beginning the plan with intermediate products... and use this as determinants of their plans." Op.cit., p.201, cf. Zauberman, *Sov. Stud.* July,1962, p.67

141. On the importance of consistency and coordination in maintaining balance in Soviet planning see Grossman, *Sov. Stud.*, October,1963, p.108; cf. Bobrowski *Ekon*. no.5, 1964, pp.993-6

142. Wakar et al., *Materialy do studiowania ekonomii politycznej socjalizmu*, (Warsaw: 1963), pp.84ff. "In treating technical input coefficients as independent structural parameters this approach assumes them to be independent of the prices of the respective cost factors and thus eliminates from this particular general equilibrium model the 'substitution effect' of the marginal productivity theory. This can be considered to be its fundamental weakness." Leontief in H. Ellis (ed.), *A Survey of Contemporary Economics*, (Philadelphia: 1948), p.409

143. Wakar, et al., op.cit., pp.185ff.

144. Lesz, *GP*, no.5, 1963, p.11 and *GP*, no.7, 1964 p.14, cf. Lange, *Pol.*, no.11, 1963 and *Introduction to Econometrics*, (Warsaw: 1962), p.204

145. R. Dorfman, et al., op.cit., pp.28-30. The

objective function is defined simply as "whatever is to
be maximized. In an economic context the objective
function is usually the measure of social valuation
adopted by whatever social unit controls the values of
the choice variables. To invest the objective function
with meaning then involves locating the social unit
which has effective control (which is not always easy)
and ascertaining its objectives (which is almost never
easy)." Ibid., p.30

146.   Zauberman, Sov. Stud., July,1962, p.67

147.   Lesz, GP, no.7, 1964, p.15

148.   Wiles, op.cit., p.202, and passim, and Lange,
Introduction to Econometrics. On the Jasny-Levine
controversy see references in Levine, Sov. Stud.,
January,1964, p.24; cf. Lange, Ekonomia polityczna,
pp.204-8, R. Schlesinger, Sov. Stud., July,1964, p.24

149.   Cf. Lesz, GP, no.7, 1964, p.16 and Porwit,
GP, no.5, 1963, p.51

150.   In addition to other shortcomings the
quality of data must be improved by rendering the
divergent nomenclature and prices in industry, domestic,
and foreign trade uniform. Lesz, GP, no.7, 1964, p.17;
cf. Porwit, Zagadnienia rachunku..., pp.19-20 and
Bobrowski, Ekon. no.5, 1964, p.993. On the Hungarian
experience and difficulties see R. Horvath, Econ. of
Plan., December,1963, p.220

151.   A. Nove in J. Degras and A. Nove (eds.),
Soviet Planning, (Oxford: 1964), p.203; cf. Zauberman,
Sov. Stud., July,1962, p.73. The reader is also referred to the enlightening article by Smolinski and Wiles
who analyze the inherent contradictions in Soviet
planning and refer to the pronouncements of outstanding
Soviet scholars to testify that the present system is
a serious handicap to further economic growth and
technical progress. Prob. of Com. November-December,
1963, pp.21-34

NOTES TO CHAPTER 2

1. J.E. Meade, Economica, February,1948, p.34

2. Cf. Bergson, in H. Ellis (ed.), op.cit., p.448
and Nove, Econ. of Plan., December,1963, p.185

3. Berliner, op.cit., p.179,where the reader is
referred for illuminating comments

4. J. Schumpeter, Capitalism, Socialism, and
Democracy, (New York: 1947), p.83

5. Wiles, op.cit., p.216

6. For a definition of economic efficiency see
T. Koopmans, Uses of Prices, (Chicago: 1954), p.3
and Hurwicz, op.cit., p.163. On the distinction between
the economic and technical aspects of production see
L. Robbins, An Essay on the Nature and Significance of
Economic Science, (London: 1932), Chapter 2

7. Hayek, op.cit., p.525

8. Schumpeter, in Economic Reconstruction, (New
York: 1934), p.173; cf. P.H. Wicksteed, The Common
Sense of Political Economy, L. Robbins (ed.),
(London: 1933), p.28

9. Koopmans, op.cit., p.2

10. Wiles, op.cit., p.53; cf. Lange, in B.E.
Lippincott, (ed.), On the Economic Theory of Socialism,
(Minneapolis: 1938), pp.139-42 and M. Dobb, An Essay
on Economic Growth and Planning, (London: 1964), pp.
70-80

11. See note 56, Chapter I. See also Joan Robinson, "Consumer's Sovereignty in a Planned Economy" to be published in Political Economy and Econometrics, (Essays in honour of Oskar Lange), (Warsaw: 1965)

12. Lange, in Lippincott (ed.), op.cit., pp.60-1

13. For a good discussion of the Soviet price system see M. Bornstein, AER, March,1962, pp.64-103 and references therein, Grossman, AER, May,1958, pp.50-64, Nove, The Soviet Economy, pp.128-136 and 218-224, and Bergson, The Economics of Soviet Planning, pp.158-77

14. Wakar et al., op.cit., p.293; Robbins, The Great Depression, pp.152-3; cf. G. Halm, in Hayek (ed.), Collectivist Economic Planning, (London: 1935), pp.150-1. For a critical view cf. Dobb, Political Economy and Capitalism, (London: 1940), pp.300-2. For the German experience see Eucken, op.cit., pp.88-91

15. Robbins, The Great Depression, p.155

16. P. Sweezy, Socialism, (New York: 1949), p.221. For the background material see Hayek (ed.), op.cit., pp.1-40, T. Hoff, Economic Calculation in the Socialist Society, (London: 1949), pp.1-10, and C. Landauer, European Socialism, II, (Berkeley: 1959), Chapter 46

17. L. Mises, Socialism, (London: 1951), pp.385-6. It is indeed interesting to ponder on Stalin's often quoted statement: "Some time ago it was decided to adjust the prices of cotton and grain in the interest of cotton growing, to establish more accurate prices for grain sold to the cotton growers, and to raise the prices of cotton delivered to the state. Our business executives and planners submitted a proposal on this score which could not but astound the members of the Central Committee, since it suggested fixing the price of a ton of grain at practically the same level as a ton of cotton, and, moreover, the price of a ton of grain was taken as equivalent to that of a ton of baked bread. In reply to the remarks of members of the Central Committee that the price of a ton of bread must be higher than that of a ton of grain, because of the additional expense of milling

and baking, and that cotton was generally much dearer than grain, as was also borne out by their prices in the world market, the authors of the proposal could find nothing coherent to say." J. Stalin, Economic Problems of Socialism in the U.S.S.R., (New York: 1952), pp.19-20

18. E. Barone, in Hayek (ed.), op.cit., p.289

19. Robbins, The Great Depression, pp.148-56

20. Hayek in Hayek (ed.), op.cit., pp.207-8

21. The competitive solutions, which vary considerably, were presented, inter alia, by Lange, Lerner, Dickinson, Taylor, and Durbin. As Wiles points out, one cannot speak of the Lange-Lerner solution. In Lerner prices are set by the firms, whereas in Lange they are determined centrally. Op.cit., p.190. On the Lange-Lerner controversy see P. Beckwith, Marginal Cost-Price-Output Control, (New York: 1955), pp.66-76

22. Dobb, Political Economy and Capitalism, (London: 1937), p.273. See also Dobb's criticism of the competitive solution, ibid.

23. Freedom of choice of consumption and profession are maintained to maximize the position of households. Consumer preferences are revealed by their demand prices and influence output composition. There is a genuine market for final consumer goods and labor but only a quasi-market for producer goods. Lange, in Lippincott (ed.), op.cit., p.73

24. Ibid., pp.60-89

25. The managers of decreasing cost industries would increase production irrespective of the coverage of average cost until MC equals price. For criticisms see Hayek, Economica, May,1940, p.159 and Hurwicz, op.cit., pp.165 and 182

26. Lange, in Lippincott (ed.), op.cit., pp.75-8 and 84

27.   Ibid., pp.89-90

28.   Hayek, Economica, May,1940, pp.131-5

29.   Dobb, On Economic Theory and Socialism, (London: 1955), p.57.   Referring to the "market solution" Dobb, stressing the disequilibrating effects of uncertainty, argues: "What this view seems to overlook is the full significance of the difference between socialism and capitalism, and in particular to fail to appreciate the crucial significance of a planned economy as consisting in the unification of all the major decisions which rule investment and production, by contrast with their atomistic diffusion.   The difference is a difference of calculability of events in the one which are incalculable in the other, with a consequent difference in the shape which events tend to assume." Political Economy and Capitalism, pp.273-4

30.   Sweezy, op.cit., p.233, cf. Dobb, Political Economy and Capitalism, p.273

31.   Brus, Ogolne problemy..., pp.53-78 and 311-18, Zielinski, Rachunek ekonomiczny..., Wakar, ZG, no.9, 1960, and Porwit, Zagadnienia rachunku....   A notable contribution in this field is the outstanding work by a distinguished Soviet mathematician L.V. Kantorovich, Rachunek ekonomiczny optymalnego wykorzystania zasobow, (translated from Russian), (Warsaw: 1961), in particular pp.151-2 and 174-92.   In his latest work on the economic efficiency of Soviet planning Professor Bergson wrote: "The economic merit of a socialist system is not quite as controversial a topic in the West as it once was, and it is generally understood that positions taken on either side in the famous theoretic debate on this matter have often been untenably extreme.   But within these bounds the economic case regarding socialism remains an open issue." The Economics of Soviet Planning, p.4

32.   Brus, Oxf. Econ. Papers,   June,1957, p.210

33.   It is interesting to note that according to Dobb the Soviet discussion on price policy did not present any views on the possibility of price formation by the interplay of market forces.   Dobb

asks: "Should central planning of economic decisions
be replaced by a mechanism whereby economic decisions
are taken automatically by economically autonomous
units ('enterprises') on the basis of market prices?
In the Soviet discussion no proposal of this kind has
been canvassed...", Sov. Stud., October,1957, pp.131-2
cf. the illuminating paper by Dr. Zauberman and
Professor Bergson's comment in Grossman (ed.), op.cit.,
pp.17-45 and the valuable account of the Soviet price
discussion by Bornstein, QJE, February,1964, pp.15-48.
For a background of the Soviet debate see R.L. Meek,
Studies in the Labour Theory of Value, (London: 1956),
particularly pp.263-84

34.   Kurowski, TL, February 6, 1957

35.   A. Brzeski, ZG, no.3, 1957

36.   J. Popkiewicz, TL, January 7, 1957

37.   Although Kurowski, Brzeski, and Popkiewicz were
grouped together as value-men, it is instructive to note
that both Brzeski and Popkiewicz did perceive the mis-
allocations which could result from monopolistic price
fixing if not counteracted by indirect state intervention.   On the possibility of competition under socialism see Zielinski, Rachunek ekonomiczny..., pp.71-82

38.   Jedrychowski, The Fundamental Principles...,
p.13

39.   Wang, TL, December 17, 1956.   The German
experience is very instructive in this respect ; cf.
Eucken, op.cit., p.92

40.   Jedrychowski, The Fundamental Principles...,
p.11

41.   Lange, Some Problems Relating..., pp.22-3

42.   Brus, in Spor o ceny, (Warsaw: 1958), p.29

43.   Brus, Ogolne problemy..., p.258

44.   Cf. Wakar and Zielinski, op.cit., pp.19-22 and

Madej, Zysk..., pp.52-3

45.   Brus, Ogolne problemy..., pp.304-8

46.   Brus, Oxf. Econ. Papers, June,1957, p.211

47.   Fiszel pointed out that prices of basic consumer goods, such as foodstuffs, should be regulated
centrally; however, the majority of consumers' prices
should be determined by demand and supply. Especially
where a wide range of assortments occurs, flexibility
of the market is indispensable. Prices established
centrally for such goods stiffen the market. A wider
scope of interaction between demand and supply for
such articles as haberdashery, clothing, textiles,
etc. would be especially desirable. Zagadnienia cen
i rachunku ekonomicznego, (Warsaw: 1958), pp.146-8

48.   Brus, Ogolne problemy..., pp.260-2; cf. Madej,
Zysk..., pp.281-95

49.   Kalecki, op.cit., pp.37-8. Commenting on the
German experience Eucken said: "Competition can be used
to improve efficiency, but as a mechanism of direction
for an important section of the economy it cannot be
applied without the abdication of the central authority."
Op.cit., p.94; cf. Meade, Planning and the Price System,
(London: 1953), p.4

50.   Cf. A. Lerner, The Economics of Control, (New
York: 1944), p.64, Meade, Planning..., pp.5-9, and
W.A. Lewis, The Principles of Economic Planning,
(London: 1952), pp.14-20, and Joan Robinson, Collected
Economic Papers, II, (Oxford: 1960), pp.46-7

51.   Cf. Madej, Zysk..., p.67. The deficiency of
cost reduction as a criterion is stressed by Blass,
Zagadnienia systemu finansowego przedsiebiorstw przemyslowych w panstwach socjalistycznych, (Warsaw: 1964), p.
92

52.   See the recent pronouncements by Vice-Premier
Szyr on the associations' investments to mitigate
arising bottlenecks, ND, no.6, 1964, pp.66ff., and
J. Pajestka, Funkcje ekonomiczne..., pp.13-4

53. Cf. Hayek, AER, September,1945, p.524 and
Lewis, op.cit., pp.20-2

54. Brus, Ogolne problemy..., pp.260-78

55. Recently Porwit published a book on economic
calculation under central planning where the problem
of dual prices (shadow prices) as estimates of efficiency
measures is discussed at length. Unfortunately it was
published too late to take full cognizance of it.
Zagadnienia rachunku...

56. Brus, Ogolne problemy, pp.321-7

57. Rationing of goods is reverted to as a drastic
measure. But the rationing of living quarters is common. Freedom to choose an occupation and place of work
is often violated by assigning workers to particular
areas.

58. S. Turetski, Planovoe Khozyaystvo, no.10, 1929

59. Stalin, op.cit., p.42

60. There is no adequate English equivalent of the
Soviet term khozraschet (or the Polish rozrachunek
gospodarczy); cf. A. Baykov, The Development of the
Soviet Economic System, (Cambridge: 1947), p.116.
Following Professor Grossman we have adopted the term
"business calculation"as the closest equivalent. An
excellent discussion of the development of business
calculation in the U.S.S.R. may be found in Grossman,
AER, May,1958, p.52. For divergent interpretations of
khozraschet see Wiles, op.cit., p.33-5, Granick, op.cit.
p.123 and Bergson, Economics of Soviet Planning, passim

61. In Marxist parlance "value" embraces (c)
consumption of fixed capital and material inputs,
(v) wages of production workers, and (m) surplus
product. Should there be no deviation of price from
value, price would equal c + v + m. Cost is equal to
c + v. Surplus product is added at every stage of
production but (m) is realized only at the time of
sale of consumer goods. One of the most controversial
issues in Soviet economic theory is the determination

at which stage of production the surplus product or accumulation is realized. Cf. Dyskusja o prawie wartosci i cenach w ZSRR, (Warsaw: 1958)

62. Turetski (Turecki), Zarys planowanego ksztalt-owania cen w ZSRR, (translated from Russian), (Warsaw: 1962), pp.27-8

63. B. Minc, Zarys teorii kosztow produkcji i cen, (Warsaw: 1958), p.200. Handicrafts and small private industrial producers may buy producer goods at the much higher retail prices to the extent that such goods are made available to them.

64. H. Fiszel, Prawo wartosci a problematyka cen w przemysle socjalistycznym, (Warsaw: 1956), p.120, Augustowski, GP, no.1, 1953, pp.42-3

65. Use value is defined as a "conglomeration of objective attributes of the product determined by its physical, chemical, etc. features." So understood, use value has nothing to do with the subjective utility of goods. A. Plocica, GP, no.8-9, 1961, p.69. Many examples and expositions of deviations from average cost pricing may be found in J. Borysiewicz, System cen srod-kow produkcji w przemysle na przykladzie hutnictwa, (Warsaw: 1955). This question is discussed in greater detail in the works of the Soviet adherents to average cost pricing: L. Maizenberg, Ksztaltowanie cen w gospo-darce narodowej Zwiazku Radzieckiego, (translated from Russian), (Warsaw: 1955), Chapter 3 and Turetski, Zarys planowego..., Chapter 3

66. "By the very nature of its functioning the planned economy cannot endure permanent changes in prices which cause frequent confusions in planning." M. Kucharski, ZG, no.24, 1960

67. D.D. Kondrashev, Tsenoobrazovaniye v promyshlen-nosti SSSR, (Moscow: 1956), pp.116-9. According to Turetski "the constancy of wholesale prices in the years when costs were increasing would be unthinkable without subsidies from the state budget." Zarys planowanego..., p.61

68. For an extensive discussion of the problem and evaluation of different interpretations see J. Lipinski, Ekon., no.4, 1954, pp.52-79

69. B. Minc, Zarys teorii..., pp.206-10

70. W.B. Sztyber, Ekon., no.4, 1962, p.841. For an opposite view see E. Winter, Fin., no.1, 1960, p.16. For a searching criticism see J. Zajda, Zagadnienia przebudowy systemu finansowego gospodarki narodowej, (Poznan: 1960), pp.21-8

71. M. Pohorille claims that to stimulate development of agriculture, taking into account exchange between town and country, low prices of agricultural implements stimulate mechanization of farming and are better economic policy weapons than increase of the farmers' income. Wstep do teorii regulowania cen rolnych w okresie przejsciowym do socjalizmu, (Warsaw: 1960), p.444ff.

72. This is even admitted by the strongest supporters of a dual price system. Cf. B. Minc, Zarys teorii kosztow..., p.210

73. They admit the possibility of "mixed models" incorporating elements of each type of calculation. However, they consider them inferior to a pure solution as they would combine incompatible elements. Wakar and Zielinski, op.cit., p.38. A number of writers have challenged them on the grounds that in practice economic life is better described by mixed rather than pure models; W.B. Sztyber, Ekon. no.4, 1963, pp.722-37, Z. Bosiakowski, Ekon, no.6, 1963, pp.1209-10, and Madej, Zysk..., pp.22-30

74. Indirect calculation is not performed directly in physical units. The central planner is not concerned with multifarious details but calculates indirectly through firms and consumers promulgating strictly enforced rules of conduct for the administrative apparatus and firms. The rules are patterned on a purely competitive market and economic units make decisions on the basis of given value parameters. The central planner prepares plans which must satisfy

both the consistency and optimality tests. However,
the method of arriving at a balanced plan differs:
prices play an active allocative role. The system
overcomes Leontief's "fundamental weakness". Wakar,
et al., op.cit., pp.73-82

75. Zielinski, Rachunek ekonomiczny..., pp.52-70

76. Brus, in Lange (ed.) op.cit., p.284; cf. A.
Plocica, Podstawy cen srodkow produkcji, (Warsaw:
1964), p.3 and J. Drewnowski, op.cit. p.341

77. Dr. Zauberman, a keen observer of the Soviet
economic scene, views the Soviet discussion "as an
intellectual performance the debate has been one of
those familiar schoolmen's battles in Soviet economics
which amaze the outsider by their fervor and elan, and
the input of effort into subjects of hopeless sterility,"
in Grossman (ed.), op.cit., pp.18-9; cf. note 33 to
Chapter II, pp.306-7

78. "Regardless of what we mean by costs... we
face a category which is defined in literature as
'normal price' and in our country... has been called
lately the point of departure price." Brus, in Lange
(ed.), op.cit., p.316; cf. Plocica, Podstawy cen...,
pp.70-2 and Madej, Zysk..., pp.166-70

79. Marxist theory rejects marginal calculus as
the product of the subjective school. In the controversia
third volume of Capital Marx is interpreted as arguing
that "socially necessary" input is reflected in
average and not marginal costs. B. Minc quotes a
letter to Engels where Marx disagrees with Ricardo's
stand that under all conditions of the market the
product produced under most unfavorable conditions
determines its exchange value on the market. Zarys
teorii..., p.103. By production costs the Soviet
economists always meant average costs. The issue
whether weighted average or simply costs of the
prevalent producer consituted the "socially necessary"
costs was raised. But the principle of average cost
was not openly challenged before and marginal cost
was banned as a "bourgeois" tool. Kantorovich's book
appeared after the Polish discussion. Cf. Bergson,

The Economics of Soviet Planning, pp.329-31 and Wiles,
op.cit., Chapter 3

80. Another distinguishing feature of the Polish
discussion, not encountered in Soviet literature, is
the proposal to base relations of prices of basic raw
materials on price relations on the world market, which
we shall discuss later.

81. ZG, no.51-52, 1957. The production of a given
good, given the demand for it, may be divided into
several groups listed according to the ascending increase of costs, assuming that each group incorporates
an essential part of total output and that no substantial variations are taking place within each group.
Broadly speaking, production may be divided into three
groups: cheapest, average, and most expensive producers,
although further subdivisions may be conceded.

82. J. Lipinski, Ekon., no.4, 1958, p.783

83. ZG, no.51-52, 1957

84. The most ardent supporters of marginal costing
were Professors Brus, J. Lipinski, Wakar, and J. Mujzel.

85. Brus, Ekon., no.3, 1958, pp.559-60

86. J. Lipinski, Ekon, no.4, 1958, p.785

87. Both Brus and Lipinski, as well as the other
discutants, were vague as to the position of the
demand curve and as to the point of intersection of
the demand curve with the supply curve.

88. Brus, in Spor o ceny, p.57

89. J. Lipinski, Ekon, no.4, 1958, p.782; cf. Brus,
Ogolne problemy..., pp.303-7

90. B. Minc's attacks on marginal costing may be
found in J. Lisikiewicz, Ekon, no.3, 1958, pp.695-701,
and 722-3, B. Minc, Ekonomia polityczna socjalizmu,
(Warsaw: 1961), pp.334-6, Zarys teorii..., pp.266-80,
and Studia i polemiki ekonomiczne, (Warsaw: 1959), pp.

117-60. During the discussion Minc's voice was not
isolated. In particular he was supported by Z.J.
Wyrozembski, ZG, no.10-11, 1958 and J. Lisikiewicz,
op.cit., pp.708-10, J. Gordon, ZG, no.3, 1958 and
Lisikiewicz, op.cit., pp.715-7, and Fiszel, Zagadnienia
cen..., Chapter 2

    91. Lisikiewicz, op.cit., p.695. See the interesting
controversy between Professor Minc and K. Laski revolving
around the possible insufficiency of effective demand
due to a decreased share of wages and increase of
accumulation in high prices based on marginal costs.
ZG, nos. 18,21, and 33, 1958 and the enlightening
comments by Professor Erlich in Grossman (ed.), op.cit.,
p.66

    92. Brus, Ekon. no.3, 1958, pp.564-9

    93. Lisikiewicz, op.cit., pp.696-7 and 713.
Professor Joan Robinson maintains that the "pricing
system has only a very limited contribution to make to
investment planning. Nevertheless, subject to necessary
corrections, the revenue yield of different investments
(net of depreciation) may be a useful guide to the planners in trying to get the pattern of production into
line with the pattern of demand. In so far as they
follow this guide, one bottle-neck after another will
be broken as time goes by. Outputs of scarce commodities gradually expand and their demand prices
come down." Collected Economic Papers, II, p.45

    94. Lisikiewicz, op.cit., p.723 and J. Lipinski,
Ekon., no.4, 1958, p.785

    95. Lisikiewicz, op.cit. p.716

    96. Fiszel, Zagadnienia cen..., p.82. He was sup-
ported in his contention by Brus, Ekon. no.5, 1956,
Blass, Fin. no.3, 1957, Laski, ZG, no.33, 1957 and
Plocica, ZG, no.18, 1958

    97. For doctrinal reasons Fiszel protects himself
by quoting a letter to Engels where Marx gives a
practical computation of a factory where together with
other cost elements interest on fixed and working capital

is included. Fiszel adds that from a purely theoretical
viewpoint interest on capital does not constitute a
cost element, but rather a part of profit. The firms,
however, cannot, no matter what the computation may be,
disregard interest in their calculation. Zagadnienia
cen..., p.82. The controversial issue of Soviet-type
economies' allowance for interest on capital outlay
in the measurement of the return on invested capital
has a rich Western literature. Cf. Zauberman, RES,
no.39, 1948-49 and Economica, August,1962, pp.234-54;
H. Hunter, RESt., no.31, 1949, pp.54-62; N. Kaplan,
JPE, 1952, pp.133-44; Grossman, QJE, 1953, pp.311-43;
Z.M. Fallenbuchl, CJEPS, February,1963, pp.26-39; and
Bergson, The Economics of Soviet Planning, Chapter 11

98. Wakar and Zielinski contend that the reason
for disregarding interest and rent is not the ideologic-
al barrier but their superfluousness in direct calculation. Op.cit., p.20

99. Fiszel, Zagadnienia cen..., p.83

100. The magnitude of the deviation is indicated
in a comparison of the amount of fixed and working
capital required per one zloty of output during a
year. Ibid., p.84

101. Ibid., p.87

102. Ibid., p.104

103. Ibid., pp.105-8

104. B. Minc, ZG, no.27, 1957; cf. Z. Wilkosz, Fin.
no.6, 1957

105. Although the Polish theoretical discussion was
the forerunner of such discussion in other Soviet-type
economies, Hungary has implemented as of January,1964,an
interest rate (about 5 per cent) on the gross value of
capital assets and working capital to constitute a cost
element. A similar system is to be introduced shortly
in East Germany with a differentiated rate but charged
against profit. At the time of writing the Soviet
Union and Poland are still at the experimenting stages.

106.   Z. Fedak, Fin., no.6, 1964, p.17, Zajda, Fin., no.6, 1962, p.26, and Czerwinska, op.cit., p.132, Michalski, op.cit., pp.11-3

107.   P. Sulmicki, Fin., no.3, 1963, p.14, Zajda, Fin. no.6, 1962, pp.23-9, Z. Fedorowicz, WNBP, no.9,1964, pp.291-5, and Misiak, ZG, no.41, 1964

108.   Zajda, Zagadnienia przebudowy..., pp.61-6. In Polish financial literature objections against interest levy are usually raised on the grounds that such action would not produce desirable effects in view of limited mobility of capital assets, the firms' restricted possibility of influencing important investment decisions, divergent structure of capital assets due to dissimilar rate of investment in the past, etc.

109.   J. Gorynski, TL, April 30, 1964

110.   Fiszel, ZG, no.49, 1964

111.   Fiszel, Zagadnienia cen..., pp.115-8. Generally Fiszel was opposed to marginal cost pricing. Ibid., pp.22-76. He did, however, conceive the usefulness of marginal calculations in certain cases.

112.   Among the most outstanding contributors were: J. Zachariasz, Professor Kalecki, and S. Polaczek.

113.   Zachariasz, Fin., no.6, 1956, p.40

114.   For example, 600 zl. could purchase either 171 kg. of aluminum oxide, 4 tons of coal, 656 kg. of zinc concentrate, 3.3 tons of iron ore, or 2.3 tons of cement. However, in foreign trade the dollar equivalent of the same quantities of aluminum oxide is $19, coal $75, zinc concentrate $67, iron ore $42, and cement $23.

115.   Zachariasz supports this contention by a table illustrating the low prices of raw materials in comparison with the high prices of processed goods in Poland in relation to the world market. Op.cit., pp.42-3

116.   Kalecki and Polaczek, in Spor o ceny, pp.63-75

117.   Fiszel, Zagadnienia cen..., pp.125-41; cf.
I. Rzedowski, ZG, no.38, 1957

118.   Kalecki, Ekon, no.3, 1958, p.577

119.   Fiszel, Zagadnienia cen..., pp.123-4 and B.
Minc, Zarys teorii..., p.265

120.   Polaczek, ZG, no.15, 1958

121.   Kalecki, Ekon., no.3, 1958, p.578

122.   Zachariasz, op.cit., p.46

123.   Kalecki and Polaczek, op.cit., p.63

124.   Rzedowski, op.cit., and Fiszel, Zagadnienia
cen..., p.142

125.   Zachariasz, op.cit., p.46

126.   Winter, Rach., no.7, 1960, p.267

127.   Sztyber, Ekon., no.4, 1962, p.836

128.   For example, as a result of the reform the
factory prices of 3000 items produced by the Ministry
of Light Industry exceed their transfer prices. The
differences in this industry are covered by subsidies
only on shoes for children and adolescents. The
differences on the remaining products are covered by
profits realized on other products. W. Moscicka,
Fin., no.2, 1961, p.37

129.   In practice the rate of profit is generally
calculated on average total production costs with the
notable exception of the clothing industry where it
is computed on costs of processing. Gordon, Ekon.,
no.4, 1960, p.714, H. Stankiewicz, in Mierniki oceny
dzialalnosci przedsiebiorstwa przemyslowego, (Warsaw:
1964), p.100 and Ibid., pp.164-5. Some enterprises
experiment at present with the calculation of profit
in relation to the investment in fixed and working
capital on the line proposed by Liberman in the Soviet
Union. Michalski, op.cit., p.12

130.   On August 26, 1960 the Chairman of the PC stipulated the upper limit as being in the range of 6 to 8 per cent. Gordon, Ksztaltowanie cen wyrobow przemyslowych, (Warsaw: 1963), p.137

131.   MP, no.32, 1960, item 155

132.   MP, no.13, 1963, item 67

133.   Sztyber, Ekon., no.4, 1962, p.837. As late as 1961 Dudzinski omitted the economic incentive function, writing: "Factory prices serve as a basis for the calculation of turnover tax (difference between transfer price and factory price), for settlement with the budget (contributions from profit), and for settlements with the foreign trade centrals regarding export production." ZG, no.15, 1961

134.   Stankiewicz, ZG, no.7, 1960

135.   Kalecki in Mierniki oceny..., p.227 and Plocica, in Gordon (ed.), Ekonomika przedsiebiorstwa przemyslo- wego, (Warsaw: 1962), p.290

136.   Stankiewicz, ZG, no.7, 1960

137.   Gordon, Ekon., no.4, 1960, pp.747-8

138.   GP, no.5, 1964, p.15. "Although factory prices exist in a number of industries for a number of years, they perform a purely computational function and hardly influence the firms' activity." E. Matyja, Rola cen w mechanizmie funkcjonowania przedsiebiorstw i zjednoczen, (Warsaw: 1965), p.3

139.   Dudzinski, ZG, no.15, 1961

140.   M. Kucharski, ZG, no.24, 1960

141.   GP, no.5, 1964, p.15

142.   Gordon, GP, no.3, 1960, p.8

143.   Moscicka, op.cit., p.38 and Dudzinski, ZG, no.15, 1961

144.   Sztyber, Ekon., no.4, 1962, p.838

145.   Moscicka, op.cit., pp.37-8

146.   Dudzinski, ZG, no.15, 1961

147.   GP, no.5, 1964, p.15

148.   J. Struminski, GP, no.5, 1964, p.22

149.   Kalecki, in Mierniki oceny..., p.226

150.   Ibid., p.227

151.   GP, no.5, 1964, pp.15-7

152.   Fiszel, Prawo wartosci..., p.173

153.   B. Minc, GP, no.6-7, 1949, p.348

154.   Ibid., p.349

155.   Fiszel, Prawo wartosci..., p.179

156.   W. Budzinski, in Z zagadnien cen srodkow
produkcji, (Warsaw: 1956), p.243; cf. E. Torun,
loc.cit., p.238

157.   Fiszel, Prawo wartosci..., pp.200-1

158.   Fiszel, in Z zagadnien..., p.223

159.   "The main goal in applying comparable prices
is to measure the dynamics of total output, establish
proportions between specific branches of industry, and
measure the productivity of social labor.... Comparable
price relations are to correspond to relations of
labor inputs." W. Stacewicz, GP, no.9, 1959, p.34

160.   Gordon, Ksztaltowanie cen..., p.141

161.   MP, no.32, 1960, item 155

162.   Cf. J. Iszkowski and S. Rog, GP, no.4, 1963,
p.2

163. R. Cierpial, in Z zagadnien..., p.236

164. Cost data computed according to the accepted precepts may be illustrated by data cited in two studies by S. Felbur, SE, no.2, 1959 pp.17-29 and no.7, 1962, pp.11-20

165. Plocica, in Gordon (ed.), op.cit., p.295

166. MP, no.32, 1960, item 155

167. The financial expert Kierczynski defines settlement prices as "such a price which the seller receives as a result of the sale of the product if the price differs from that paid by the buyer." Fin. no.2, 1961, p.26. The definition does not differentiate between factory and settlement prices since in case of a divergence between transfer and factory price (turnover tax or subsidy) the factory price may be viewed as a settlement price in his definition. However, it seems that a distinction is necessary here.

168. J. Czarnek, in Z zagadnien..., p.121

169. MP, no.A-94, 1953, item 1304

170. B. Rotsztajn, in Z zagadnien..., p.113

171. MP, no.17, 1963, item 96

172. In the past whenever firms were faced with non-typical production they accepted it most readily since such production was one of the sources of additional profits. To what extent enterprises exploited this situation may be witnessed by the following example: "In 1954 the steel mill Zabrze executed a special construction for the Bierut Foundry. Based on the calculation of the enterprise, Mostostal confirmed a price of 2,550 zl. per ton. The actual production costs amounted to 1,952 zl. per ton. Instead of the planned profit amounting to 5 per cent of costs, the profit obtained amounted to 30 per cent." Rotsztajn, op.cit., p.114

173.   Cf. Csikos-Nagy, op.cit., p.82

174.   Pirozynski and Winter, op.cit., p.29

175.   Ibid., p.103

176.   Ibid., pp.31-2; cf. Blass, Fin., no.9, 1961, p.21

177.   B. Minc, Planowanie..., p.112

178.   Fedak, ZG, no.5, 1949, p.204

179.   Augustowski, GP, no.9, 1948, pp.310-1

180.   Blass, Fin., no.9, 1961, p.25; cf. Minc, Planowanie..., p.113

181.   Referring to the German (1940) experience Eucken writes: "The costs of production of the individual firms were calculated and prices fixed accordingly for each individual firm on the basis of its costs. Consequently, the firms had no interest in working economically for profits were a percentage of costs, and were greater if costs were high than if they were low." Economica, May, 1948, p.90

182.   U. Wojciechowska and W. Szczegielniak, in Zarys rozwoju..., p.317

183.   Blass, Fin., no.9, 1961, p.26

184.   Augustowski, GP, no.1, 1951, p.14

185.   Blass, Fin., no.9, 1961, p.26

186.   Pirozynski and Winter, op.cit., p.46

187.   MP, no.A-55, 1950, item 630

188.   Glinski et al., GP, no.4, 1956, p.39

189.   The use of the term "reform" might be farfetched in this connection as essentially it refers to price changes rather than a basic reform of the methods of

calculating prices. However, the term "reform" is used
in the former context in Polish literature on the
subject and, therefore, has been adopted here in the
same sense.

190.   Augustowski, GP, no.1, 1951, p.13

191.   Ibid., p.14

192.   R. Fidelski, GP, no.5, 1951, pp.16-7 and
E. Szymanski, GP, no.10, 1951, pp.20-4

193.   Augustwoski, GP, no.1, 1953, p.45

194.   Pirozynski and Winter, op.cit., p.40; cf.
A. Chlebowczyk et al., Materialy do badania relacji
cen, (Warsaw: 1958), pp.362-3

195.   Cf. L. Nowicki, in Z zagadnien..., p.56

196.   Data on the rate of deficit as a percentage
of individual costs of production can be found in
Fiszel, Prawo wartosci..., p.141

197.   Ibid., p.116 and Nowicki, op.cit., p.56

198.   Zachariasz, GP, no.6, 1960, p.3

199.   Augustowski, GP, no. 11, 1955, p.7 where a
detailed list of the reform's aims can be found.

200.   Nowicki, op.cit., p.57. Prices of consumer
goods remained at the same level, and only turnover
tax collected on these goods was proportionately
reduced. The reduced budget receipts from turnover
tax were counterbalanced by the decrease of
expenditures for subsidizing industries manufacturing
producer goods. Fiszel, Prawo wartosci..., p.131

201.   Augustowski, in Z zagadnien..., p.71

202.   Zachariasz, GP, no.6, 1960, p.3

203.   Fiszel, Prawo wartosci..., p.148

204. Borysiewicz, op.cit., p.79

205. Fiszel, in Z zagadnien..., p.37

206. The rate of price increases and their relations
are illustrated in Fiszel, Prawo wartosci..., pp.144-6

207. Kurowski, GP, no.11, 1955, p.12

208. The relative shares of material and labor costs
in the machine building industry can be found in
Piotrowski, op.cit., p.396. For similar data on
metallurgy, electric power, and chemical industry see
Fiszel, Prawo wartosci..., p.128

209. The results of the study were reported by
Madej, GP, no.12, 1957, pp.1-5

210. The rate of profit is defined as net profit
(excluding turnover tax) to cost of production, and
the rate of deficit as the negative difference between
price and cost to cost. Total profits in 1956 were
12.35 billion zl., whereas losses amounted to 9.75
billion zl., resulting in a profit of 2.60 billion zl.
compared to a loss of 2.28 billion zl. in 1955. In
1956 the greatest deficits were incurred by the
coal industry amounting to 3.35 billion zl.

211. Fedorowicz, Kierunki przebudowy systemu
finansowego przedsiebiorstw przemyslowych, (Warsaw:
1958), p.15

212. Madej, GP, no.12, 1957, p.3

213. A. Cournot, Researches Into the Mathematical
Principles of the Theory of Wealth, (New York: 1927),
p.127; cf. Porwit, Zagadnienia rachunku..., p.5

214. Cf. Nowicki, op.cit., p.57

215. Gomulka, TL, October 18, 1959

216. MRS 1960, pp. 59-61 and 153

217. Zachariasz, GP, no.6, 1960, p.3 and RS 1961,

pp.101-2

218.   The 1959 index of price changes in the lumber
industry was 194.6, paper 203.5 and building materials
154.1 (1956 = 100). Plocica, Podstawy cen..., p.97

219.   T. Kierczynski, Przedsiebiorstwa deficytowe
w gospodarce socjalistycznej, (Warsaw: 1962), p.112

220.   RS 1962, p.122. In 1938 pit coal extracted
per worker per day was 1718 kg.; in 1951, 1378 kg.; in
1953, 1308 kg.; in 1955, 1267 kg.; and in 1957, 1247 kg.
RS 1960, p.143. From 1952 to 1957 use of lumber
increased by 18 per cent and that of explosive
materials by 40 per cent. Dietrich, Przemowienie
Ministra Finansow, (Warsaw: March 9, 1957), p.9

221.   The situation was indeed critical. It led
Gomulka to state: "I know of cases where material
norms are established at 30 per cent over the
indispensable level. In many establishments unused
machines run for hours using electricity unnecessarily.
In the construction industry waste of materials is
enormous. Such culpable facts are encountered there
as breaking glass to avoid cleaning it..."
Przemowienia wrzesien 1957 - grudzien 1958, (Warsaw:
1959), p.215

222.   ZG, no.21, 1960

223.   Struminski, Polityka cen w Polsce Ludowej,
(Warsaw: 1958), p.60

224.   Ibid., pp.61-2

225.   L. Siemiatkowski, ZG, no.21, 1960

226.   S. Stopinski, Rach., no.8, 1960, p.315

227.   Zachariasz, GP, no.6, 1960, p.1. These
difficulties are also described by Siemiatkowski,
ZG, no.21, 1960. A systematic exposition of preparations for a price reform in a Soviet-type economy may
be found in the study by B. Csikos-Nagy, op.cit., pp.
256-82

228. M. Krol, GP, no.1, 1961, pp.36-40 and
Siemiatkowski, ZG, no.21, 1960

229. Gordon, GP, no.3, 1960, Ksztaltowanie cen...,
p.160, and Struminski, GP, no.1, 1962, p.8

230, Struminski, in Polityka gospodarcza..., II, p.252;
cf. GM, no.7, 1960, pp.244-6. A comprehensive analysis
of costs in the new and old steel mills may be found in
J. Gwiazdzinski, GP, no.1, 1960, p.1; cf. Z. Sprycha,
Koszty wlasne w nowych zakladach przemyslowych,
(Warsaw: 1961), passim

231. Sprycha, op.cit., pp.23 and 33 and Struminski,
GP, no.1, 1962, p.8

232. Stopinski, op.cit., p.316

233. Struminski, in Polityka gospodarcza..., II,
p.253

234. Kierczynski, Przedsiebiorstwa deficytowe...,
p.137

235. Gordon, Ksztaltowanie cen..., p.74

236. In 1957 the cost of the most expensive mine
of pit coal was 401.60 zl. per ton, whereas the average cost of the industry was 211.07 zl. per ton.
Felbur, SE, no.2, 1959, p.25, J. Kowalski, GP, no.1,
1962, p.13

237. Gordon, Ksztaltowanie cen..., p.161

238. For example, in 1957 the average share of
transportation costs in total production costs of coal
was 8.2 per cent, coke 4.4 per cent, bricks 5.4 per
cent, and lumber 1.2 per cent. S. Pozniak, GP, no.8-9,
1960, p.28

239. Zachariasz, GP, no.6, 1960, p.4 and Struminski,
in Polityka gospodarcza..., II, p.252. Freight costs
as elements of total production costs of Portland
cement increased from 5.7 per cent in 1959 to 13 per
cent in 1960. For detailed data see Plocica,

<u>Podstawy cen</u>..., pp.201-4

240. Struminski, in <u>Polityka gospodarcza</u>..., II,
p.248

241. Zachariasz, <u>GP</u>, no.6, 1960, pp.2-3. The 1960
price increases of cement are itemized in Plocica,
<u>Podstawy cen</u>..., p.168

242. Stopinski, <u>op.cit.</u>, p.317

243. Zachariasz, <u>GP</u>, no.6, 1960, p.2 and Stopinski,
<u>op.cit</u>., p.316

244. Struminski, <u>GP</u>, no.1, 1962, p.8

245. Struminski admits that one of the primary
accomplishments of the reform was the liquidation of
huge deficits. <u>GP</u>, no.7, 1964, p.25

246. Struminski, <u>GP</u>, no.1, 1962, p.9

247. Matyja, <u>op.cit</u>., p.19. The same seems to be
true of the Soviet Union, cf. K. Ostrovitianov,
<u>Budownictwo komunizmu a stosunki towarowo pieniezne</u>,
(translated from Russian), (Warsaw: 1963), p.158

248. Plocica, <u>Podstawy cen</u>..., pp.97-102

249. Kierczynski, <u>Przedsiebiorstwa deficytowe</u>...,
p.122. Actually the deficit incurred on the negative
budget differences amounted to 30.8 billion zl.
Pirozynski and Winter, <u>op.cit</u>., p.150. The great
discrepancy results from the inclusion of export
negative budget differences which are subsidies paid
to the foreign trade centrals to make up for the
differential between the domestic and export price
when the latter is lower.

250. Gordon, <u>GP</u>, no.10, 1960, p.19

251. Gomulka, <u>TL</u>, Aptil 18, 1963

252. Struminski, <u>GP</u>, no.7, 1964, p.25

253.   Pirozynski and Winter, op.cit., p.149

254.   Kierczynski, Przedsiebiorstwa deficytowe...,
p.125

255.   RS 1962, pp.93 and 289

256.   Gomulka, TL, May 29, 1960

257.   S. Majewski, Fin., no.9, 1960, p.2

258.   Cf. R. Wilczewski, GP, no.6, 1960, p.13

259.   It is also explained in quite a different
light by Struminski: "In this case we based ourselves
on the anticipated production costs in the forthcoming
years when the factories will be producing many thousands of tractors." In Polityka gospodarcza..., II,
p.254

260.   Kierczynski, Przedsiebiorstwa deficytowe...,
p.139

261.   Struminski, in Polityka gospodarcza..., II,
pp.253-4

262.   Ministry of Chemical Industry, Price Catalog,
no.109/z60, p.42, as quoted by Kierczynski, Przedsiebiorstwa deficytowe..., p.136

263.   Majewski, op.cit., p.3

264.   Ibid.

265.   Kierczynski, Przedsiebiorstwa deficytowe...,
pp.141-2 and Plocica, Podstawy cen..., pp.166-8

266.   Gordon, GP, no.10, 1960, p.20

267.   Actually the accumulation is smaller than
indicated because the textile industry received domestic
wool at prices below the procurement prices paid by the
state to the producers. The subsidy amounted to
approximately 1 billion zl. in 1962. Struminski,
GP, no.2, 1963, p.16

268.   Gordon, Ksztaltowanie cen..., pp.52-3

269.   Struminski, in Polityka gospodarcza..., II,
p.265

270.   Pirozynski and Winter, op.cit., p.145

271.   Practically speaking, prices of pharmaceuticals
have not been altered for 18 years hampering adaptability
of output to needs. H. Tarchalska, ND, no.6, 1964, p.92.
There are indications of a tendency to replace over-all
reforms by annual price adjustments on some goods.
Struminski, GP, no.7, 1964, p.25

272.   Szyr, ND, no.6, 1964, p.121

273.   This was stressed by a Party-government
commission under Vice-Premier Szyr and reported by
Pajestka, ND, no.11, 1964, p.93. Arguments in favor of
a dual price system at the present stage of development
are stressed by Matyja, op.cit., pp.10-3

274.   IV Zjazd PZPR, p.324. When a stable price
for the buyer and variable one for the producer are
desired, the difference between the two must be
siphoned off or added by the budget. Hence introduction of turnover tax becomes necessary. Matyja, op.cit.,
p.19

275.   Unadaptability and lack of flexibility in
adjustments of supply to demand were admitted by
Struminski, GP, no.2, 1963, p.15; cf. Matyja, op.cit.,
pp.6-8

276.   Schumpeter, History of Economic Analysis,
(New York: 1954), pp.869-70

NOTES TO CHAPTER 3

1. Cf. G.R. Feiwel, Cost: The Various Meanings of the Concept, (Edmonton: 1964), pp.3ff.

2. S. Skrzywan and Z. Fedak, Rachunkowosc w przedsiebiorstwie przemyslowym, (Warsaw: 1960), p.13. In a theoretical study Fedak raises the question whether different manifestations of economic calcul- ation such as investment efficiency calculations, profitability of exports, optimal product mix, etc. should be included in cost accounting. However, he rejects their inclusion on the grounds that "account- ing registers only actual conditions." Rachunek kosztow produkcji przemyslowej, (Warsaw: 1962), p.9

3. In Polish state-owned firms "land, forests, water resources, ore deposits, and mines are not counted as fixed assets... except for the cost of investments executed on this land." W. Bien in MER, p.471

4. As Professor Schumpeter put it: "Discussion of the marginal utilities of means of production in the theory of imputation easily leads to the recognition of the relevance to these marginal utilities of the elements of complementarity and substitutability... of factors and of their alternative uses. By this route the Austrian arrived at what has been called the alternative - use or opportunity theory of cost... - the philosophy of the cost phenomenon that may be expressed by the adage: What a thing really costs us is the sacrifice of the utility of those other things which we could have had from the resources that went into the one we did produce." History of Economic Analysis, p.917

5. The term "cost" has no single meaning. J.M. Clark
rightly said that "a graduate class in economic theory
would be a success if the students gained from it a
real understanding of the meaning of "cost" in all its
many aspects." Studies in the Economics of Overhead
Costs, (Chicago: 1923), p.ix

6. Mises, Human Action, (New Haven: 1949), pp.346-7

7. A good discussion of the deficiencies of Soviet
accounting can be found in R. Campbell, in Grossman (ed.),
op.cit., pp.76-94

8. V.I. Lenin, State and Revolution (New York: 1929),
p.204. Referring to the objectives of accounting in
socialist Poland Blass stated that accounting had three
functions to perform: planning, reporting, and control.
Blass (ed.), Komentarz do jednolitego planu kont dla
panstwowych przedsiebiorstw przemyslowych, (Warsaw:
1950), p.8

9. Z. Paryzinski, Rach., no.7, 1964, p.194

10. S. Skrzywan and A. Kmiotek, GP, no.2, 1950, pp.
77-9; J. Mosczynski, Rach. no.1, 1952, p.23; U. Wojciechowska and W. Sczegielniak, in Zarys rozwoju..., pp.
315ff; and J. Doraczynski, in MER, pp.487-93. The
last article contains a comprehensive classification of
accounts.

11. Wytyczne w sprawie zasad rachunku kosztow produkcji przemyslowej przedsiebiorstw, (Warsaw: 1960),
pp.3-4

12. Cf. J. Jaworski and M. Kubala, Rach., no.7, 1963,
pp.217-21

13. MP, no.58, 1958, item 278; cf. L. Parusinski,
Fin., no.4, 1964, p.57

14. DU, no.50, 1954, item 255 and DU, no.47, 1957,
item 224; cf. K. Sztajer, in MER, pp.195-7

15. The reader might find that many accounting precepts in Poland are similar to their Western counterparts.

However, neither their similarities nor divergencies
will be noted here since a comparison of Soviet-type
and Western accounting is outside the scope of this
study. Our main concern here is with the conceptual
framework of Polish accounting and its procedures to
shed some light on the validity of the cost data
generated by the enterprise.

16. MP, no.11, 1961, item 62. The following items,
although they satisfy the above definition, are not
treated as fixed assets: products designated for sale
by the firm (e.g., automobiles in an automobile factory),
investments in progress, or machinery in the firm's
possession still requiring assembly and installation.
A comprehensive discussion of the accounting aspects
may be found in Bien, Ewidencja srodkow trwalych i
amortyzacji, (Warsaw: 1962)

17. Biuletyn PKPG, no.47, 1952, item 219

18. The exception to this rule occurs when the
firm disposes of idle equipment or when obsolete
equipment is replaced.

19. MP, no.95, 1959, item 503

20. But in Polish practice no estimate of the
salvage value is made, hence no value is imputed. Cf.
Fedak, Rachunek kosztow produkcji..., p.56

21. The following criticism of Mises, although
made in connection with accounting in a market economy,
is applicable to Poland: "The task incumbent upon the
businessman is always to use the supply of capital goods
now available in the best possible way for the satis-
faction of future needs. In the pursuit of this aim he
must not be misled by past errors and failures the consequences of which cannot be brushed away. A plant
may have been constructed in the past which would not
have been built if one had better forecast the present
situation. It is vain to lament this historical fact.
The main thing is to find out whether or not the plant
can still render any service, and if this question is
answered in the affirmative, how it can be best
utilized. It is certainly sad for the individual

entrepreneur that he did not avoid errors. The losses
incurred impair his financial situation. They do not
affect the costs to be taken into account in planning
further action." Human Action, p.344

22. Cf. Bien, in MER, p.472, Fedak, Rachunek
kosztow produkcji..., p.53, and Fedorowicz, Finanse
w gospodarce socjalistycznej, (Warsaw: 1962), p.265

23. Fedak, Rachunek kosztow produkcji..., p.54

24. For example, the steel mill Nowotki calculated
a price of 287,750 zl. for an undercarriage and vat
construction, whereas the 1go Maja steel mill calculated a price of 137,700 zl. for identical equipment.
J. Matuszewicz, Rachunek kosztow w przedsiebiorstwach
o produkcji jednostkowej i maloseryjnej, (Warsaw:
1962), p.60

25. Bien, in MER, p.472; cf. Zabkowicz and Doberski,
op.cit., p.21

26. I. Haendel, in Z zagadnien..., p.66

27. Rog, GP, no.10, 1960, p.9

28. Gordon, Ksztaltowanie cen..., p.163 and Fedak, Fin.
no.12, 1961, p.34

29. Cf. Campbell, in Grossman (ed.), op.cit., pp.
78-82

30. B. Minc, Ekonomia polityczna socjalizmu, p.464

31. Fiszel, Zagadnienia cen..., p.93. On the shift
of Soviet views on obsolescence see Campbell, Accounting
in Soviet Planning and Management (Cambridge, Mass: 1963),
pp.152ff. and Nove, The Soviet Economy, pp.151-2.
Professor Nove quotes Academician Strumilin who attributes
the new interest in the Soviet Union in obsolescence to
the marked changes in the relative scarcities of
capital and labor.

32. W. Holtzman, Problemy amortyzacji w przemysle,
(Warsaw: 1961), p.203. The old and new rates are

respectively for factory buildings 3 and 1.8 per cent,
machinery and equipment 10 and 8.2 per cent, and transportation equipment 20 and 17 per cent. Fedak, _Fin_.,
no.12, 1961, p.37

33. _Ibid_., p.34

34. _Ibid_.

35. The 1962 catalog of depreciation rates contains
560 rates uniform for all state-owned enterprises.
Fedak admits that the classification of assets into
groups is somewhat arbitrary and that there is no
sufficient relationship between the rates assigned to
particular groups. _Ibid_., p.37

36. An investigation conducted by the ECCM during
1957-59 revealed that 73.2 per cent of industrial
firms used machinery from 40 to 100 per cent over
thirty years old. Plocica, _Podstawy cen_..., p.108.
An anecdote by Professor Paton is most instructive
in this case although his irony was directed at
Western accounting practices: "A young lady in the
accounting department of a certain business was moving
a bookkeeping machine from one room to another. As
she came alongside an open stairway, she carelessly
slipped and let the machine get away from her. It
went careening down the stairs with a great racket
and wound up at the bottom in some thousands of pieces,
completely wrecked. Hearing the crash, the office manager came rushing out, and turned rather white when he
saw what had happened. 'Someone tell me quickly', he
yelled, 'if this is one of our fully amortized units.'
A check of the equipment cards showed that the smashed
machine was, indeed, one of those which had been
written off. 'Thank God!' said the manager."
W.A. Paton, _Accounting Review_, April,1947, p.200

37. Cf. Fedak, _Fin_., no.1, 1958, pp.1-13, where a
good summary of the controversy may be found and
Fin., no.1, 1959, pp.14-9

38. Fedak, _Rachunek kosztow produkcji_..., p.40
and Bien, in _MER_, p.15

39. MP, no.77, 1957, item 471, Bien, in MER, p.265;
cf. also the critical comments by Czerwinska, op.cit.,
pp.92ff.

40. Fedak, Fin., no.12, 1961, p.34

41. Fiszel, Zagadnienia cen..., p.100

42. J. Trendota, ZG, no.50, 1964; cf. C. Kulik,
TL, April 15, 1964

43. The amount of the adjustment is usually sizable.
Cf. P. Tendora and Z. Messner, Rachunkowosc w przedsiebiorstwie przemyslowym, (Katowice: 1959), p.87

44. MP, no.97, 1961, item 408; cf. Dudzinski,
ZG, no.23, 1963

45. Fedak, Rachunek kosztow produkcji..., p.39 and
Chapter 5

46. Biuletyn PKPG, no.48, 1952, item 220; cf.
Wytyczne..., pp.14-5

47. Matuszewicz, in MER, p.509; cf. S. Gorniak and
B. Siwon, Zarys rachunkowosci przedsiebiorstw, (Lodz:
1962), p.113

48. Matuszewicz, Rachunek kosztow..., p.133 and
Fedak, Rachunek kosztow produkcji..., pp.92-3

49. Wytyczne..., pp.25-6

50. Investigations of industrial fraud indicated
this type of manipulation to be quite common in Poland.
K. Krupa, ZG, no.47, 1964

51. Matuszewicz, Rachunek kosztow..., p.59.
Speaking of the financial results reported by firms
Gomulka stated that in part they are a "result of all
kinds of accounting manipulations, as for example,...
the non-inclusion of all production costs actually
incurred by the enterprises." Przemowienia..., p.74;
cf. W. Jachniak, in Mierniki oceny..., pp.259-66

52. MP, no.37, 1959, item 167

53. J. Bolesta, Zasady prawne ustalania cen, II,
(Warsaw: 1963), p.22

54. Fedak, Ewidencja i kalkulacja kosztow w
przemysle, Part I, (Warsaw: 1957), pp.17-44

55. Moszczynski, in MER, p.343

56. Skrzywan and Fedak, op.cit., p.218

57. Cf. Ibid., pp.230-2 and Tendera and Messner,
op.cit., pp.95-6

58. Wytyczne..., pp.12-5 and Fedak, Ewidencja i
kalkulacja..., pp.67-106

59. Bolesta, op.cit., pp.13-4 and Fedak, Rachunek
kosztow produkcji..., pp.39,54, and 59

60. Wytyczne..., p.12

61. T. Troszczynski and A. Hutorowicz, in MER, pp.
211-3 and Fedak, Rachunek kosztow produkcji., pp.57-8

62. TL, August 25, 1964

63. Matuszewicz, Rachunek kosztow..., p.85

64. B. Fick, ND, no.1, 1962, p.179

65. A comprehensive study of labor productivity,
evaluating the changes in Poland from 1949 to 1959
may be found in Z. Fiejka, Wydajnosc pracy w przemysle
polskim, (Warsaw: 1962). A study of real wages in the
Polish machine building industry appears in S. Boracki,
Place realne pracownikow przemyslu maszynowego Polskiej
Republiki Ludowej w latach 1948-58, (Cracow: 1961). A
survey of the wage policy in Poland may be found in
H. Diamand, in Polityka gospodarcza..., II, pp.353-430

66. Matuszewicz, Rachunek kosztow..., p.104

67. Wytyczne..., p.14; cf. Matuszewicz, Rachunek

kosztow..., p.82

68. Wytyczne..., p.14

69. Moszczynski, in MER, pp.209-10

70. Ibid., p.209

71. Wytyczne..., pp.21-2

72. Cf. Matuszewicz, Rachunek kosztow..., p.134, and Z. Keh, ZG, no.17, 1963

73. Occasionally the assumption is modified by supposing that auxiliary departments do render services to others but do not benefit from services of other auxiliary departments. Skrzywan and Fedak, op.cit., pp.271-8

74. The auxiliary departments do not bear their share of enterprise overhead. The exception to this rule is when a service is rendered by an auxiliary department to an outside firm, then a proportional share of enterprise overhead is added to costs. Wytyczne..., p.40

75. Cf. M. Majchrzak, Rach., no.11, 1962, p.455

76. It should be noted that a single basis for allocating enterprise overhead is used. Ibid., and Matuszewicz, Rachunek kosztow..., p.115

77. The Poles understand enterprise overhead to be equivalent to fixed costs in the economic sense of the term. One should recognize, however, that there are many semivariable costs included in the enterprise overhead account which for the sake of convenience are treated as fixed. Skrzywan and Fedak, op.cit., p.233

78. Majchrzak, op.cit., p.455; cf. J. Anderko, Rach. no.11, 1962, p.451

79. This fact is often pointed out in literature. Cf. Skrzywan and Fedak, op.cit., pp.308-12,where the

authors present extensive numerical computations to prove their point.

80. Skrzywan and Fedak, op.cit., p.309 and Gorniak and Siwon, op.cit., pp.152-3

81. Skrzywan and Fedak, op.cit., pp.250-4

82. Ibid., p.281 and Gorniak and Siwon, op.cit., p. 162

83. Cf. Z. Paryzinski (ed.), Vademeccum bieglego ksiegowego, (Warsaw: 1962), pp.81-91

84. Skrzywan and Fedak, op.cit., pp.299-305

85. J. Viner, Dumping - A Problem in International Trade, (Chicago: 1923), p.243

86. Fedak, in MER, p.167, where the author illustrates this method comprehensively

87. Skrzywan and Fedak, op.cit., p.322

88. Cf. Z. Sprycha, op.cit., p.18, Misiak, ZG, no.50, 1964, and Jachniak, op.cit., p.264

89. It should be noted that the planning of over-all cost reduction for enterprises is done on the level of the association. However, generally speaking, the planning department of the enterprise indicates the distribution of the assigned cost reduction by the superior unit of authority to individual products. Thus it is left up to management to decide the apportionment of the cost reduction index to individual products. It is self evident that manipulations will occur, which will enable the enterprise to fulfil the assigned over-all cost reduction target in the easiest manner. A common manipulation is the following procedure of Polish cost accountants: An attempt is made to classify as typical production products whose unit costs tend to rise and as non-typical those products whose unit costs tend to decline as the flow of production increases. At the same time every attempt is made to allocate the largest possible share of indirect costs to the non-

typical production at the expense of typical production.
In such a manner not only a substantial cost reduction
for comparable production is "accomplished" for the
current accounting period, but simultaneously reserves
for future cost reduction are "created". What usually
is considered as non-typical production in the current
period becomes the comparable (typical) production in
the next accounting periods. Since the initial costs
are artificially augmented,cost reductions in the
following periods are easily attainable. Misiak, in
Misiak (ed.), op.cit., pp.143-4

90. At present research is conducted on improving
methods of calculating planned and precomputed costs.
Examples of this type of research are: J. Marzec and
I. Haendel, Kalkulacja wstepna w przemysle maszynowym,
(Warsaw: 1962), and Z. Kurpinski, Kalkulacja wstepna
w przemysle spozywczym, (Warsaw: 1962). See also the
recent contributions by Fedak, Rach., nos. 5,6, and 7,
1964

91. Matuszewicz, Rachunek kosztow..., pp.63-4

92. Sprycha, op.cit., p.19

93. Professor B. Minc has made a career out of
negating the manifestation of the law of diminishing
returns in industry. Cf. Zarys teorii..., pp.17-85,
Studia i polemiki ekonomiczne, pp.117-58, and Ekonomia
polityczna socjalizmu, pp.279-86. See also the
critical remarks by Lange, Ekon., no.4, 1964, pp.698-9,
and the more sympathetic treatment by Wakar et al.,
op.cit., Appendix A and Madej, Zysk..., p.111. In
all fairness it must be admitted that the shape of the
cost curve is of considerable controversy among Western
economists as well. Cf., inter alia, J. Johnston,
Statistical Cost Analysis, (New York: 1960), particularly
pp.136-94 and Committee on Price Determination, Cost
Behavior and Price Policy, (New York: 1943)

94. Although in practice there is no separation
between fixed and variable costs, accounting literature
raises the problem in Poland. However, the accountants'
concepts of fixed and variable costs are most confused
and muddled. They tend to identify overhead with

fixed costs, abstracting from the fact that overhead
consists of both fixed and variable elements. Cf.
Skrzywan and Fedak, op.cit., pp.230-4

95. H. Schultz, The Theory and Measurement of
Demand, (Chicago: 1938), p.665

NOTES TO CHAPTER 4

1. A more complete study of theoretical issues
and the evaluation of the firm's finances in Soviet-type
economies and Yugoslavia was relegated to a separate
work to be completed shortly.

2. Fedorowicz, Kierunki przebudowy.., p.71 and
J. Wierzbicki, Zagadnienia akumulacji pienieznej w
gospodarce socjalistycznej, (Warsaw: 1964), pp.85-6

3. Blass, Fin., no.9, 1962, p.10

4. Total accumulation in a branch of industry is a
sum of the accumulation produced by the various firms
constituting the branch of industry less the losses
incurred by the deficit enterprises. Total accumulation in the economy is the sum of accumulation
produced by the various branches of industry less the
losses incurred by deficit branches.

5. B. Minc, ND, no.2, 1962, p.180; cf. Struminski,
GP, no.2, 1963, p.16

6. Kierczynski, Istota akumulacji pienieznej przedsiebiorstw socjalistycznych, (Warsaw: 1960), p.182 and
Wierzbicki, op.cit., pp.84-5

7. Blass, Fin., no.9, 1962, pp.11-2; cf. Fedorowicz,
Finanse..., pp.120-1

8. Kierzynski, Istota akumulacji..., pp.175-92

9. The issue was raised by Brus, Prawo wartosci
a problematyka bodzcow ekonomicznych, (Warsaw: 1956),
pp.28-9

10. This was recently admitted by Szyr, ND, no.6, 1964, p.68

11. S. Bolland, Fin., no.2, 1963, pp.1-8; cf. K. Przywara, Fin., no.5, 1961, p.20

12. For convenience purposes we have adopted the division of accumulation into turnover tax and profit, however, strictly speaking, accumulation may be divided into profit, turnover tax, and budget differences, the latter pertaining mostly to trade enterprises. In some enterprises, mainly engaged in domestic and foreign trade, accumulation may be remitted to the budget in the form of positive budget differences. In the trade positive budget differences constitute the excess of the sale price over the purchase price increased by a trade margin. The positive budget difference replaces here turnover tax. In industry budget differences may occur also in cases where turnover tax is levied. This may occur in cases where the enterprise sells its products at various prices pending on the identity of the buyer. If the firm sells goods at retail prices a difference between the factory price and transfer price would constitute turnover tax, whereas the difference between transfer price and retail price would be a budget difference. Contrary to turnover tax which is always a positive magnitude the budget difference may also be a negative magnitude, in which case subsidies are received to cover the difference. Cf. S. Chudzinski and W. Sidor, in Rozliczenia z budzetem, (Warsaw: 1960), pp.74-120

13. A background of the development of turnover tax in Poland may be found in Pirozynski and Winter, op.cit., pp.102-4. For a good account of the development of turnover tax in the U.S.S.R. see Holzman, Soviet Taxation, (Cambridge, Mass: 1955), particularly Chapter 6 and R.W. Davies, The Development of the Soviet Budgetary System, (Cambridge: 1958), pp.213-20

14. Cf. O. Niedzialkowski, Fin., no.11, 1963, pp. 24-5, Czerwinska, op.cit., p.49, Zajda, Zagadnienia przebudowy..., pp.47-57, and Weralski, Kierunki reformy polskiego systemu podatkowego, (Warsaw: 1960), pp.211-23 where the deficiencies of turnover tax as a tool for

regulating the profitability of enterprises are pointed out.

15. H. Krol, Ekon., no.4, 1960, p.892

16. Fedorowicz, Finanse..., pp.124-31

17. When the bank does not deduct the turnover tax the firm must prepare a statement every ten days and remit turnover tax within fifteen days after the statement has been submitted. In any event a detailed statement must be submitted every month and differences settled. Niedzialkowski, in Rozliczenia z budzetem, pp.121-76

18. Cf. Pirozynski, Fin., no.9, 1961, p.13

19. Fedorowicz, Fin., p.139; cf. Czerwinska, op.cit., pp.69-70

20. Cf. M. Friedman, Price Theory, (Chicago: 1962), pp.56-67

21. The problem of extracting profit at all from the enterprises was questioned by L. Kurowski who suggested that the state should extract its income by wider application of turnover tax. Fedorowicz, Kierunki przebudowy..., pp.105-6

22. Fedorowicz, Finanse..., p.148. For statistical evidence of the growing quantitative importance of decentralized profits left at the firm's disposal see Pirozynski and Winter, op.cit., p.89

23. Kierczynski, Istota akumulacji..., p.165

24. Cf. Blass, Fin., no.9, 1961, p.32

25. Blass, Fin., no.11, 1962, p.3

26. Brus, ZG, no.25, 1957

27. Cf. J. Boguszewski, GP, no.9, 1959, pp.2-13

28. Czerwinska, op.cit., p.73; cf. Wierzbicki,

WNBP, no.5, 1960, p.209, and Zajda, <u>Zagadnienia prze-budowy</u>..., p.134

29. <u>MP</u>, no.32, 1960, item 155

30. Blass, <u>Fin</u>., no.9, 1961, p.31. In Poland the list of products subject to subsidy and the subsidies per unit of output are established annually by the CM. For example, subsidies per unit of output in 1961 in the shoe industry were 25 zl. for boys' leather boots, 35.59 zl. for boys' and girls' shoes, and 11.19 zl. for children's canvas shoes. Kierczynski, <u>Przedsiebiorstwa deficytowe</u>..., p.243

31. Pirozynski and Winter, <u>op.cit</u>., pp.145-7

32. Z. Rostowski, in <u>Rozliczenia z budzetem</u>, pp. 31-2

33. Kierczynski, <u>Przedsiebiorstwa deficytowe</u>..., p.203 and Pirozynski and Winter, <u>op.cit</u>., p.145

34. Cf. Madej, <u>Zysk</u>..., p.108

35. Blass, <u>Fin</u>., no.9, 1961, p.31

36. Kierczynski, <u>Przedsiebiorstwa deficytowe</u>..., pp.207-8, Wierzbicki, <u>Zagadnienia akumulacji</u>..., p. 313

37. Skrzywan, in <u>MER</u>, p.181

38. The state takes 75 per cent with the balance going to the association's reserve fund. When the preliminary division of planned profit is computed at a higher rate, say 90 per cent, the latter rate is applied for the division of unearned profit between the state and the reserve fund of the association. T. Okulicz, <u>Fin</u>., no.2, 1962, p.30

39. <u>MP</u>, no.13, 1960, item 61

40. In 1958 2.5 billion zl. were eliminated from profit. Wojciechowska, <u>Problemy tworzenia funduszu zakladowego</u>, (Warsaw: 1961), p.44. Madej reports

elimination in the pharmaceutical industry as 19 per
cent of reported profit in 1957, 20 per cent in 1958,
and 15.3 per cent in 1959. In some enterprises the
eliminations reached from 48 to 142 per cent. Zysk...,
p.98. As a result of verification of profits contributions to the enterprise fund were decreased by
430 million zl. in 1959, constituting 8.1 per cent of
contributions computed by enterprises. H. Druska,
Fin., no.12, 1960, p.20. In 1960 the contributions
to the enterprise fund were decreased by 250 million
zl. constituting 5 per cent of the contributions
computed by enterprises. Fin., no.1, 1962, p.65

   41. Wojciechowska, Problemy tworzenia..., p.44
and Blass, Zagadnienia systemu finansowego przedsiebiorstw przemyslowych w panstwach socjalistycznych,
(Warsaw: 1964), pp.99-100

   42. Misiak, ND, no.1, 1962, p.182; cf. Jedrychowski,
ND, no.4, 1962, pp.9-10, and Wakar et al., op.cit.,
p.236

   43. This view was upheld in a study conducted by
the economic analysis section of the Metallurgists
Trade Union and reported by J. Hellman, Fin., no.12,
1961, p.47

   44. Since the enterprise fund is primarily based
on distribution of profit among all employees of the
firm, its formation and source are strictly connected
with the profit realized by the enterprise. Contrariwise, premiums for management, which essentially
affect the behavior of managerial personnel, do not
constitute in Poland a distribution of profit and will
be examined in the following chapter.

   45. Wojciechowska, Problemy tworzenia..., p.3;
cf., Blass in Druska (ed.), Fundusz zakladowy, fundusz
za osiagniecia ekonomiczne, fundusz premiowy,
(Warsaw: 1961), pp.3-17. For the pre-1956 experience
see Madej, Fin., no.8, 1960, pp.13ff.

   46. ZG, no.32, 1963

   47. B. Miszewski, Mierniki oceny dzialalnosci przed-

siebiorstw przemyslowych, (Warsaw: 1963), p.46.
Although the conference of workers' self-management
apportions premiums from the enterprise fund according
to its judgment of an employee's performance, the
annual premium paid to the employee may not exceed one
month's salary. This is the so-called thirteenth wage.

48. Madej, Fin., no.8, 1960, p.18

49. Kalecki, ZG, no.29, 1957

50. Brus, ZG, no.25 and 26, 1957

51. DU, no.4 and 13, 1960, items 24 and 78; cf.
Blass, Zagadnienia systemu..., p.116

52. The table was reproduced in Druska (ed.),
op.cit., pp.40-2 and numerical computations may be
found in Ibid., pp.46-57

53. Z. Krzyzkiewicz, in Gordon (ed.), op.cit.,
p.356

54. Blass, Fin., no.5, 1963, p.2

55. Kierczynski, Fin., no.4, 1962, pp.10-11

56. Wojciechowska, Problemy tworzenia..., p.59

57. Sztyber, Ekon., no.4, 1962, p.839

58. Misiak, ZG, no.30, 1958

59. L. Drozdz, ND, no.3, 1962, p.101 and H. Sobon,
ND, no.1, 1962, p.185

60. RS 1962, pp.392 and 433

61. Blass, Fin., no.9, 1961, p.30

62. The Polish experience with the enterprise fund
prior to 1956 has shown that the fund performed only a
minor and insignificant role as its size and that of the
premiums paid out per worker were small and of little
significance in relation to other premiums. Madej,

Fin., no.8, 1960, pp.13-5

    63. S. Jakubowicz, ND, no.2, 1962, p.167

    64. "Taking profit as the main or one of the criteria
for material incentives leads very often in a socialist
economy to such negative results as the production of
'convenient' assortment because it brings in a high
rate of profit but may also be unnecessary and uneconomica
use of materials and delays in the introduction of new
techniques. Experience proved that premiums based on
profit do not stimulate the reduction of costs of
production because a high profit may be reconciled with
high costs and an increase in profit is easier to
attain in any other manner than through the arduous
road of cost reduction. It must be added that profit
is difficult to calculate adequately and even with
good will it is subject to 'dressing up' as the
accountants very well know." Minc, ND, no.2, 1962,
p.180

    65. MP, no.91, 1960, item 411; cf. Kucharski,
ZG, no.38, 1959, Winter, EiOP, no.3, 1960, Misiak,
ZG, no.51-52, 1960, and Wojciechowska, Fin., no.8, 1961

    66. Wojciechowska, Fin., no.8, 1961, p.23

    67. Cf. S. Gora, Bodzce ekonomiczne w gospodarce
socjalistycznej, (Warsaw: 1961), pp.160-1

    68. The firm may add to its development fund the
excess at the beginning of the year resulting from
the following calculation: fixed assets plus normative
of working capital, minus permanent liabilities, if,
and only if, the Minister of Finance, in agreement
with the responsible industrial minister, does not
order this excess transferred to the budget.

    69. The table is reproduced in Fedorowicz,
Finanse..., p.183 and the computation illustrated
in Rostkowski, op.cit., pp.20 and 24

    70. Wojciechowska, Fin., no.8, 1961, p.24

    71. K. Czyzniewski, Fin., no.9, 1964, p.35

72. In 20 firms of key industry analyzed by J. Szyrocki the share of profit in the development fund was 69.1 per cent in 1958, 40.7 per cent in 1961, and 53.9 per cent in 1962. Fin., no.12, 1963, p.27. Cf. Wierzbicki, Zagadnienia akumulacji..., p.356

73. Szyrocki, op.cit., p.28

74. MP, no.91, 1960, item 411

75. Krzyzkiewicz, op.cit., p.359

76. Fedorowicz, Finanse..., p.184

77. In the 20 firms analyzed by Szyrocki the state extracted 72 per cent of profit in 1958, 80.7 per cent in 1961, and 84.0 per cent in 1962. Op.cit., p.26

78. Fedorowicz, Finanse..., pp.114-9

79. Krzyzkiewicz, op.cit., pp.321-2

80. The Institute of Economics of the Polish Academy of Science conducted an analysis of the structure and rate of turnover of working capital and basic components classified as inventories of materials, goods in process, finished goods, and pre-paid expenses for 1957 to 1960. The respective shares were 54.3 per cent, 21.4 per cent, 20 per cent, and 4.3 per cent. The study was based on the financial reports of the state-owned industrial enterprises aggregated in 112 organizational units. The frequency distribution of the above mentioned elements was sum-marized and reported. However, no analysis of the distribution of enterprises among industries was report-ed, hence it is difficult to infer the causes of the deviations from the reported average. Chlebowczyk, Ekon., no.4, 1962, pp.803-23

81. The average velocity of turnover of inventories was 4.23 during 1959; the average stock of inventories to the flow of production designated for sale (valued at cost) was during that time 23.7, indicating that on the average for every 100 zl. of flow of production 24 zl. were tied up in inventory. Ibid., p.818

82. Czerwinska, op.cit., pp.69 and 157, cf. Blass, Zagadnienia systemu..., Chapter 5 and Wierzbicki, Zagadnienia akumulacji..., Chapter 4

83. Fedorowicz, Finanse..., p.199. This notion was questioned by Sulmicki. On this controversy see Fedorowicz, Kierunki przebudowy..., pp.129-31 and my forthcoming publication on finance in socialist economies. Cf. Michalski, op.cit., p.7

84. For a dissenting view see, inter alia, S. Ficowski, WNBP, no.11, 1956, p.562 and Michalski's comments on the failure of normatives in practice. Op.cit., p.7

85. Fedorowicz, Finanse..., p.201; cf. Wierzbicki, Zagadnienia akumulacji..., pp.302-10 and WNBP, no.4-5, 1960; Blass, Zagadnienia systemu..., pp.169-77, Kucharski, WNBP, no.5, 1960; Zajda, in Roczniki ekonomiczne, XVI, (Poznan: 1963-64); and Michalski, op.cit., pp.8-9

86. It should be noted that transactions conducted between socialized firms are not transfers of currency but are effected through bookkeeping transfers at the various branches of the NPB. The most common type of transfer is the bank collection of invoices. Skrzywan and Fedak, op.cit., pp.28-31

87. The share of currency in total working capital usually does not exceed 1 to 2 per cent. Piotrowski, op.cit., p.306

88. Fedorowicz, Finanse..., p.205

89. The difficulties encountered in quantifying permanent liabilities are discussed by M. Kacprzak, WNBP, no.11, 1964, pp.403-4

90. Cf. Blass, Fin, no.9, 1961, p.28. For a retrospective examination of the methods of financing working capital see Pirozynski and Winter, op.cit., pp.115-8

91. Ficowski, op.cit., p.562

92. Zabkowicz and Doberski, _op.cit._, pp. 33-4

93. Z. Jaskiewicz, _Mysl Gospodarcza_, no.1, 1957, p.43 and Ficowski, _op.cit._, p.563

94. Fedorowicz, _Finanse_..., p.203, Jaskiewicz, _op. cit._, p.43, and Czerwinska, _op.cit._, pp.76-7 and 158

95. _MP_, no.10, 1959, item 36

96. Own working capital covers only 80 per cent of the normative in coal mines, 70 per cent in light industry, 70 per cent in firms of the Ministry of Forestry and Lumber, 85 per cent in the firms of the Ministry of Communications, and 30 per cent in retail and 50 per cent in wholesale trade. _MP_, no.24, 1961, item 115

97. _ZG_, no.8, 1964

98. Szyr, _ND_, no.6, 1964, pp.66-7

99. After analysis of the 1964 firms' plans the bank reduced the sum of normatives by over 4 billion zlotys. Misiak, _ZG_, no.38, 1964

100. _Ibid._,

101. The interest rate for above normative loans is also 4 per cent for almost all firms. _Ibid._

102. _Ibid._

103. Winter, _Fin._, no.1, 1960, pp.14-5

104. A recent issue of _WNBP_ was devoted to this serious problem. _WNBP_, no.1, 1963. See in particular Wierzbicki's article devoted to inventories in the Polish economy in recent years, pp.16-24; M. Nitecki and W. Prus discuss inventories in the socialized sector of the economy in 1962 and 1963, pp. 24-9; and Siemiatkowski concentrates on the current problems of the administration of inventories in heavy industry, pp.29-35. The reasons behind the drive to hoard materials will be discussed in Chapter 5.

105.   Szyrocki, op.cit., p.21 and W. Jaworski, Fin.
no.8, 1961, pp.40-1; cf. Wierzbicki, Zagadnienia
akumulacji..., p.355 and Michalski, op.cit., pp.15-7

106.   Jaworski, op.cit., p.50. However, on all
overdue accounts the supplier is empowered to add a
12 per cent interest charge. This induces him generally
to tolerate overdue accounts since they may contribute
to his profit. In 1962 the Building Materials Central
in Opole earned 429 thousand zlotys from this source.
W. Slipko, ZG, no.15, 1963

107.   B. Stepien, WNBP, no.9, 1964, p.325

108.   Wierzbicki, WNBP, no.1, 1963, p.17

109.   MP, no.27, 1961, item 131

110.   Madej, Zysk..., p.262; cf. W. Lissowski, GP,
no.4, 1959, p.24, and Z. Szymczak, Zeszyty Naukowe
Wyzszej Szkoly Ekonomicznej Poznan, no.4, 1957

111.   L. Pasieczny, in Gordon (ed.), op.cit., p.88.
According to the MF the respective shares of centralized
and decentralized investments in state-owned industry
were approximately as follows in 1962: centralized 69
per cent, associations 19, and enterprises 12 per cent.
Due to a change in classification of investments these
data are not comparable with those on centralized and
decentralized investments published in the RS 1959,
1960 and 1961. For previous years see Pirozynski and
Winter, op.cit., pp.156 and 161

112.   The priority of the central planner's investments over those of the associations is enforced not
only by financial measures but also by forbidding
the implementation of associations' investments at the
expense of the central planner's investments. However the planner may curtail the associations' investments in favor of centralized investments. W. Witakowski, Fin., no.3, 1961, p.14

113.   H. Swidzinski, GP, no.8-9, 1961, pp.29-30

114.   Witakowski, op.cit., p.14. The statistics on

the share of central investments from 1951 to 1960
were reported by Pirozynski, op.cit., p.13. W. Karpinski questioned the advisability of financing central
investments by state grants and suggested financing
by reimbursable interest bearing bank loans. GP,
no.5, 1957, p.39, Wierzbicki, Zagadnienia akumulacji...,
pp.314-9

115. In 1961 the associations financed 92.6 per
cent of their investments from their investment funds
and the balance from other sources. For the first
six months of 1962 all of the investments were
financed from the investment funds. If the required
investment expenditures and replenishment of the funds
are not synchronized in time, the association may seek
loans to cover the necessary outlays. Cf. Wierzbicki,
Zagadnienia akumulacji..., p.353

116. In 1961 93.6 per cent of decentralized investments were financed from the investment-repair funds
and 6.8 per cent from bank credits. During the first
half of 1962 the respective figures were 93.2 and 7.5
per cent. The overexpenditures are mainly due to pre-
payment for materials and payments covering accrued
liabilities.

117. Skrzywan and Fedak, op.cit., pp.404-34. In
practice the distinction between working capital and
investment funds is not always clearly made. Cf.
B. Borys, Fin., no.11, 1961, pp.38-41

118. The part of depreciation left at the disposal
of firms amounted to 36 per cent in 1961 and 26 per cent
in the first half of 1962. In the 20 firms analyzed
by Szyrocki this part was 31.9 per cent in 1958, 47.6
per cent in 1961, and 28.2 per cent in 1962. Op.cit.,
p.27. The reason for the decreased share of firms in
depreciation seems to be the increase in depreciation
charges due to the 1962 revaluation of fixed assets.

119. In 1961 the main sources of the investment-
repair fund were: depreciation 56.1 per cent, development fund 22.7 per cent, reserve fund 3.2 per cent, and
others 18 per cent. The respective shares for the first
six months of 1962 were: 67.4, 17.4, 8.7, and 6.5 per

cent. In the 20 enterprises analyzed by Szyrocki the
respective shares of depreciation and the development
fund were 51.4 and 19.4 per cent in 1958, 52.2 and 24.2
per cent in 1961, and 66.8 and 17.8 per cent in 1962.
Op. cit., p.27

120. MP, no.31, 1961, item 150; Cf. Czyzniewski,
Fin., no.3, 1961, p.1

121. Szyr, ND, no.6, 1964, p.69

122. MP, no.11, 1961, item 61

123. W. Uhlenberg, Fin., no.7, 1961, pp.54-5 and
A. Wolowczyk, Fin., no.9, 1961, p.86

124. M. Jaslar, Fin., no.6, 1961, pp.19-21

125. Polityka, no.51, 1962

126. Doberski, GP, no.10, 1961, p.24; cf. Tarchalska,
ND, no.6, 1964, p.93 and Trendota, ND, no.6, 1964, p.116

127. Trendota, ND, no.6, 1964, p.116

128. Misiak, ZG, no.38, 1964; cf. Szyr, ND, no.6,
1964, p.69

129. Blass, Fin., no.9, 1961, pp.32-3

130. Trendota, ZG, no.50, 1964

131. Ibid. It has been suggested that development
indexes should be established for a minimum period of
three years. Michalski, op.cit., p.5

132. Blass, Zagadnienia systemu..., p.157

133. Trendota, ZG, no.50, 1964

134. Ibid.

135. Cf. Szyr, ND, no.6, 1964, who stresses, inter
alia, the importance of bank credits in financing
associations' investments.

136. IV Zjazd PZPR, p.118; cf. Pajestka, ND, no.11, 1964, p.90, Fedak, Fin., no.6, 1964, pp.13-21, and Fedorowicz, WNBP, no.9, 1964, pp.291-5

137. Pajestka, ND, no.11, 1964, p.82

NOTES TO CHAPTER 5

1. <u>DU</u>, no.49, 1950, item 439 and <u>MP</u>, no.18, 1960, item 111; cf. Gomulka, <u>Przemowienia</u>..., p.220

2. Cf. Madej, <u>ND</u>, no.6, 1964, p.113

3. J. Balcerek and L. Gilejko, in <u>Polityka gospodar-cza</u>..., II, p.116

4. <u>DU</u>, no.77, 1958 and <u>DU</u>, no.18, 1960, item 111

5. Gilejko, <u>TL</u>, April 23, 1964 and J. Waclawek, <u>TL</u>, October 20, 1964

6. "A good planner in the understanding of the enterprise is a person who can balance individual directive indexes so that the enterprise fund should not suffer. But the good planner in the ministry is, in turn, a specialist who knows of the manipulations used by his colleagues in the enterprises and is able to counteract them." A. Paszynski, <u>Pol</u>., no.52, 1962

7. "To their professional know-how the accountants have had to add a knowledge of the principles of diplomacy and tactics to reconcile the 'enterprise's interests' with the manifold regulations. The results of such tactics are financial reports purposely distorting results to report them in a more favorable light. The outcome of these distortions are numerous and time consuming external controls." Gutowski, <u>Pol</u>., no.43, 1963

8. The familiar and interesting conflict between the technocratic and economic approach to management prevails with constant friction between engineers,

economists, and accountants. Ibid.

9. The proposals for enhancing the association's role are vague as to its future relations with its firms.

10. Gradowski and Kiernorzycki, op.cit., pp.13-4; cf. Szymanski, GP, no.3, 1961, p.51

11. Gradowski and Kiernorzycki, op.cit., p.15; cf. A. Bober, ZG, no.27, 1964

12. B. Lewicki, TL, May 21, 1963; cf. A. Dominirski, in Misiak (ed.), op.cit., pp.119-22

13. Pol., no.44, 1962

14. H. Mienicki, GP, no.11, 1962, p.24

15. Pol., no.44, 1962

16. Hellman, op.cit., p.46

17. Mienicki, op.cit., p.25

18. Misiak, ZG, no.36, 1963 and W. Szyndler-Glowacki, ZG, no.36, 1963

19. We have purposely omitted here the firm's multi-year plan since it is a fairly recent development which, according to our information, has not gained great significance in practice.

20. Glinski, Teorie i praktyka zarzadzania przed-siebiorstwami przemyslowymi, (Warsaw: 1964), p.265

21. Szymanski, GP, no.3, 1961, p.51

22. W. Kostuj and Z. Lukomski, ND, no.7, 1962, p.35

23. Pol., no.13, 1963

24. Pol., no.7, 1962

25. Pol., no.10, 1962

26. "The director often unfolds his hands and says:
We cannot do everything at once. Either we ensure cost
reduction, or execute the new constructions and proto-
types. Either we will produce the maximum output
required by the market, as judged by the association,
or we will adhere to the wage fund and employment limits,
etc." M. Doroszewicz, ND, no.6, 1964, p.90

27. Cf. J. Gajda, Ekon, no.1, 1958, p.116 and
E. Lukawer, ZG, no.24, 1958. The economic contradictions under socialism are discussed by Brus, Ogolne
problemy..., pp.14-26

28. Madej, Zysk..., Chapter 2 and Wakar, Morfologia
bodzcow ekonomicznych, (Warsaw: 1963)

29. Madej, Zysk..., pp.41-53. Professor Lange
expressed the hierarchic structure of ends as a
feature of socialist planning in these words: "The
integration of the aims of the activity of socialist
enterprises by a common end established in the social
economic plans leads to a hierarchic structure of ends.
At the top of this structure stands the main end, i.e.
the end of the social economic plans which we shall
call the first order end. The means serving directly
to implement that end are second order ends. The
means serving directly to the realization of aims of
the second order are third order ends, and so on. The
aims of the activity of various enterprises occupy
different levels in this hierarchy of ends." Political
Economy, (New York: 1963), (translated from Polish by
A.H. Walker), pp.179-80

30. Lange, Ekonomia polityczna, p.201. "...social
rationality of economic activity demands that the aims
of individual enterprises be subordinated to an end
which embraces the whole of the social process of
production and distribution; in other words, it requires
the coordination of the activities of individual enterprises, the integration of their aims by a common end
directing the economic activity of society. This coordination is called the planning of the social economy....
Maximization of profit is no longer the ultimate end.

The activity of a socialist enterprise is subordinated
to the general social end, expressed in the plan for
the social economy." Political Economy, pp.177-8

31. Cf. Wakar, Morfologia..., pp.70-152

32. Madej, Zysk..., p.57

33. Management is usually composed of the director,
his assistants, chiefs of departments and sections,
technical, and engineering personnel which often
includes the plant foremen. Cf. Pasieczny, Kierownik
a bodzce materialnego zainteresowania, (Warsaw: 1963),
Appendix 15. Since inclusion in the ranks of management depends on premium classification and due to
pressures exerted by employees to obtain as high
premiums as possible the term "management" is very
loose. Its connotation in this chapter is related to
people who receive premiums and are subjected to
economic stimuli affecting their behavior. Cf.
Lange, Ekonomia polityczna, p.59

34. Gora, op.cit., p.8, Gajda, Ekon. no.1, 1958, p.
159, and Fick, Bodzce zainteresowania materialnego
pracownikow przedsiebiorstw i zjednoczen a funkcje
ekonomiczne tych jednostek gospodarczych, (Warsaw: 1965),
p.1

35. Madej, Zysk..., pp.57 and 77, Miszewski, op.cit.,
p.18, B. Haus and P. Kotlarek, GP, no.12, 196Q, p.26.
Rather similar conclusions on the importance of premiums
for management were reached by Professor Berliner in
his significant contribution to the literature on the
enterprise in the U.S.S.R., Factory and Manager in the
U.S.S.R., (Cambridge, Mass: 1957), pp.26-43. The
relative importance of premiums to a Soviet manager
was also emphasized by another distinguished authority
in this field, Professor David Granick, Management of
the Industrial Firm in the U.S.S.R. (New York: 1954),
pp.192-5 and The Red Executive, (Garden City: 1960),
pp.130-4. Vide the formularized contribution by
Professor B. Ward in Grossman (ed.), op.cit., pp.143ff.
The importance of substantial premiums for the director
and his senior staff in the Soviet Union is stressed
by Professor Nove, Economica, January,1958, pp.1ff.

and <u>Soviet Economy</u>, pp.31 and 155-63. The significance
of premiums as economic stimuli in Hungary is emphasized
by Professor B. Balassa, <u>The Hungarian Experience in</u>
<u>Economic Planning</u>, (New Haven: 1959) and in Dr. J.
Kornai's study of the Hungarian light industry, <u>Over-</u>
<u>centralization in Economic Administration</u>, (translated
by J. Knapp), (London: 1959). See also the newest
addition to the literature on the Soviet Union by the
eminent scholar Professor Bergson, <u>The Economics of</u>
<u>Soviet Planning</u>, p.75

36. Management's short run premium maximization
and the ensuing detrimental effects on implementation
of technical progress were particularly stressed at
the April,1965,conference on the economic functions of
enterprises and associations organized by the
Polish Economic Association in Warsaw. Matyja, <u>op.cit</u>.,
pp.5 and 7 and Pajestka, <u>Funkcje ekonomiczne</u>..., p.10;
cf. Wakar et al., <u>op.cit</u>., p.238

37. "Lately our mine has had very good production
results. It belonged to the best. We exceeded the
plan by 3 to 5 per cent. Presently our reserves are
rather depleted and <u>disclosed</u>. At best we can exceed
the plan by 1½ to 2 per cent. Consequently our
technical and production personnel earns less than
in the past, notwithstanding the general increase in
production and labor productivity. These are really
difficult times." <u>Pol</u>., no.24, 1962

38. Cf. Blass, <u>Zagadnienia systemu</u>..., p.101

39. The basic salaries of engineering and
technical personnel were often lower than those of
qualified manual workers. Spotan, <u>GP</u>, no.4, 1957,
pp.39-40

40. Brus, <u>ND</u>, no.12, 1955, pp.68-9

41. Moscicka et al., <u>Fin</u>., no.2, 1956, p.19

42. J. Toronczyk, <u>TL</u>, January 20, 1956; cf. Brus,
<u>Prawo wartosci a problematyka</u>..., p.120 and Kalecki,
<u>Szkice Ekonomiczne</u>, (Warsaw: 1958), p.43

43. Computed on the basis of data for 1960 reported by Pasieczny, Kierownik..., Appendix 11

44. Cf. J. Kordaszewski, Place wedlug pracy, (Warsaw: 1962), pp.63-4

45. Cf. Madej, Zysk..., p.77

46. It should be noted that exhortations and appeals by Party leaders are often made for the execution of particular tasks. It seems that they are not of paramount importance in motivating managerial activity, but it is indeed difficult to determine their influence with any certainty.

47. E. Lipinski, in Misiak (ed.), op.cit., p.19

48. W. Krencik, ND, no.2, 1962, pp.174-5

49. Fick, GP, no.6, 1962, p.34

50. DU, no.35, 1946, item 216

51. Fick, GP, no.6, 1962, p.34

52. Krencik, ND, no.2, 1962, p.176

53. Fick, GP, no.6, 1962, p.34

54. Madej, Fin., no.8, 1960, p.13

55. The law stipulated 2.5 to 7.5 per cent as an original contribution with the possibility to double it if the cost and quality plans were fulfilled. DU, no.35, 1946, item 216

56. DU, no.120, 1947, item 762

57. Cf. Miszewski, op.cit., p.39. The increase of premiums was made dependent and proportionate to increase in profitability, making further improvements less rewarding. With the chaotic and irrational prices the profitability results were of spurious validity resulting in cases where "for similar efforts employees of different enterprises received different

amounts of premiums or for dissimilar efforts the same
amount of premiums." Madej, Fin., no.8, 1960, p.13

58. Cf. J. Janiak, GP, no.2, 1949, pp.85-6

59. Brus, ND, no.12, 1955, p.68; cf. B. Minc, GP,
no.3, 1956, p.20

60. Fedak, GP, no.2, 1949, p.118

61. Moscicka et al., op.cit., p.18

62. Brus, ND, no.12, 1955, p.69

63. Moscicka et al., op.cit., p.18

64. Gora, op.cit., p.19

65. Fick, GP, no.6, 1962, p.36

66. Moscicka et al., op.cit., p.25

67. K. Jerzewski, Mysl Gospodarcza, no.6, 1957, p.
21

68. Cf. J. Toeplitz, ZG, no.47, 1960. "The method
of comparing costs of comparative output applied before
1956 has failed completely. The present state of cost
records and verification in enterprises does not
warrant to base economic incentives on this basis."
Jedrychowski, ND, no.4, 1962, p.6

69. Moscicka et al., op.cit., p.26

70. "The system of paying premiums to management
pending on the fulfilment of the production plan
inevitably generates tendencies towards lowering the
plans of production, labor productivity, and cost
reduction." B. Minc, Aktualne zagadnienia ekonomii
politycznej socjalizmu, (Warsaw: 1956), p.382

71. Moscicka et al., op.cit., p.22

72. Brus, ND, no.12, 1955, p.69 . "The fact that
premiums paid to managing personnel... in the enterprises

were connected with the extent in which the plan is overfulfilled, has caused with the regularity of an economic law two consequences: first, that plans are too low, because there is an incentive to have a low plan which can be easily exceeded, second, that plans are only slightly overfulfilled in order not to have the plan raised too much next year." Lange, _The Political Economy_..., p.11

73. Moscicka, et al., _op.cit._, p.23

74. Brus, _ND_, no.12, 1955, p.69

75. "To increase total production it is sufficient to transfer materials from the stockroom to the producing departments (resulting in an increase of work in process augmented by the cost of materials)." W. Bogusz, _Fin._, no.3, 1961, p.46

76. By material intensive production in this context we mean the production of goods where the share of material costs to the unit price (cost) of the product is relatively high and the share of labor cost to the unit price (cost) of the product relatively low. The attempt here is to produce goods with the least labor expenditure that "bring in high value". Such products are generally material intensive in a physical sense, but to satisfy attainment of management's goal materials also have to constitute a substantial share of the cost of the product. It is in this sense that we use the term "material intensive".

77. "In order to achieve high value of total output the enterprises developed above all the most advantageous production, i.e., bringing in the highest value with a relatively minimum effort." B. Minc, _GP_, no.6, 1960, p.8

78. Kuzinski, _Glowne proporcje_..., p.55. Cf. data on comparison of weight of heavy machinery in Poland and several other countries. Matuszewicz, _Rachunek kosztow_..., p.65

79. The phenomenon of cooperation will be examined at length later in this chapter in connection with the

calculation of the wage fund.

80.   "Labor productivity in aggregate industry as well as in individual firms is determined on the basis of a comparison of aggregate output (completed and un-completed) in comparable prices with the number of employees (either with total employees or those employed in material production only)." Fiejka, op.cit., p.69

81.   Fick, GP, no.6, 1962, p.37

82.   Uklad zbiorowy pracy dla przemyslu metalowego, (Warsaw: 1958), p.65

83.   Fick, GP, no.6, 1962, p.38

84.   Cf. Miszewski, op.cit., pp.46-7 and Zabkowicz and Doberski, op.cit., pp.147-63

85.   Fick, in Druska (ed.), op.cit., p.367

86.   Blass, Pol., no.3, 1959

87.   Fick, GP, no.6, 1962, p.38

88.   Miszewski, op.cit., p.47

89.   Jedrychowski, GP, no.2, 1960, p.2

90.   The Economic Council of the Council of Ministers, Sytuacja ekonomiczna kraju, (Warsaw: 1960), p.40

91.   M. Cielecki, Fin., no.9, 1961, p.75

92.   As discussed in the last chapter, accumulation and not profit is the synthetic performance criterion used.

93.   Blass, GP, no.9-10, 1962, p.1

94.   Cf. Wojciechowska, Problemy tworzenia..., Chapter 4 and Sobon, op.cit., p.185

95.   Fick, Fin, no.11, 1961, p.14

96. <u>MP</u>, no.9, 1960, item 43. The exceptions were the coal and ore mining industries. The bases for the formation of the premium fund in the coal industry was to be fulfilment and overfulfilment of the extraction plan in conjunction with the attainment and excess of a unit settlement price reflecting the quality of coal extracted. Cf. Miszewski, <u>op.cit.</u>, pp.119-29.

97. It bears repetition that this measure is deficient not only due to the methods of pricing inputs but also due to the exclusion of rewards for capital and land.

98. Relation of the premium fund to the wage fund is usually explained as a measure "equalizing the objective conditions" among firms. For example, **consider two** enterprises, one highly mechanized with a relatively smaller labor force, the other backward with a larger one, and both reporting equal profit. If the premium fund was related to profit only, it would be the same in both firms. The employees of the former would be favored as premiums would be distributed among a smaller number. But the equalizing effect is impaired by differentiating the wage fund among firms and industries according to central preferences. Blass, <u>Zagadnienia systemu</u>..., p.101. Of course, if a charge for capital was made there would be no need to equalize the "objective conditions", <u>ceteris paribus.</u>

99. <u>MP</u>, no.9, 1960, item 43

100. Kordaszewki in Gordon (ed.), <u>op.cit.</u>, pp.228-9

101. Fick, <u>GP</u>, no.9-10, 1962, p.43; cf. Dominirski, <u>op.cit.</u>, p.124 and J. Olszewski, <u>ND</u>, no.2, 1962, p.82

102. Fick, <u>GP</u>, no.9-10, 1962, p.43

103. <u>Ibid.</u>, p.45

104. Dominirski, <u>op.cit.</u>, p.121

105. Miszewski, <u>op.cit.</u>, p.49

106. The table was prepared centrally, <u>MP</u>, no.14,

1961, item 73. It was reproduced by Fick, in Druska (ed.), op.cit., pp.410-11

107. Szymanski, GP, no.3, 1961, p.52

108. Dominirski, op.cit., pp.119-21; cf. Cielecki, op.cit., pp.76-7

109. Misiak, ND, no.1, 1962, p.182, Lewicki, TL, May 11, 1963

110. ZG, no.21, 1963. At the Fourth Party Congress Gomulka stressed that all directive indexes must reach the firm at least one month prior to the new plan period. IV Zjazd PZPR, p.117

111. Misiak, in Misiak (ed.), op.cit., pp.153-65

112. S. Wilczynski, Fin., no.3, 1961, p.35

113. Toeplitz, ZG, no.47, 1960

114. The inaccuracy of directives assigned by associations is vividly illustrated in the case of the Lenin Steel Mill. For 1962 the Association of Ferrous Metallurgy set an index of cost reduction at 900 million zl. That was in April,1962. By June it already decreased the index to 450 million. The firm suggested that the index would be closer to reality at 150 million. Finally the plan was fulfilled at 118 million zl. cost reduction. ZG, no.21, 1963. Cf. Szyr, ND, no.6, 1964, p.65

115. As a rule, the firms come up with proposals to lower the plans rather than to increase them. ZG, no. 21, 1963

116. Fick, GP, no.9-10, 1962, p.47, J. Obodowski, ND, no.6, 1964, p.162

117. Fick, ND, no.1, 1962, p.179; cf. Misiak, Fin., no.6, 1961, p.6, and Brus, ND, no.1, 1962, p.177

118. Fick, Fin., no.11, 1961, p.19; cf. Spotan, GP, no.7, 1964, p.43. On July 1, 1964 the association's

premium system has been reformed and based on similar
principles as in enterprises to eradicate the contradiction between the two. Cf. Fick, ZG, no.31, 1964
and Bodzce zainteresowania..., pp.8-21

119.   Fick, GP, no.9-10, 1962, p.45

120.   Dominirski, op.cit., p.128

121.   Fick, GP, no.9-10, 1962, p.45

122.   Ibid., p.46

123.   Cf. Kordaszewski, in Gordon (ed.), op.cit.,
pp.226-7, Fick, in Druska (ed.), op.cit., pp.390-7,
and Blass, Zagadnienia systemu..., p.120

124.   MP, no.14, 1961, item 73

125.   Basing his conclusions on empirical data of
the MF, Fick wrote: "Among all conditions for the
activation of the premium fund, generally only two
constant conditions operate without reservation,
namely, the fulfilment of the production plan and
adherence to the wage fund limits. The two additional
conditions are not always adhered to. For instance,
in the enterprises Boleslaw Chrobry, Bialy Kamien, and
Mieszko the premium fund was activated regardless of
the transgressions on the cost plans." Fin., no.11,
1961, p.16; cf. Obodowski, ND, no.6, 1964, p.160

126.   Sobon, op.cit., p.184

127.   Wilczynski, Fin., no.3, 1961, p.41

128.   In practice the firms augmenting their plans
are the exception rather than the rule. Gutowski,
Pol., no.15, 1963

129.   Fick, Fin., no.11, 1961, pp.16-17

130.   Fick, ZG, no.19, 1964

131.   Dominirski, op.cit., pp.123-6

132. Madej, _Fin_., no.8, 1960, p.5

133. Jedrychowski, _ND_, no.4, 1962, p.5

134. Fick, _ZG_, no.14, 1964 and Madej, _Fin_., no.8, 1960, p.6

135. Z. Krawczynski, in Misiak (ed.), _op.cit_., p.284

136. Misiak (ed.), _op.cit_., p.565. Fick reports that amounts paid out in 1961 from the economic progress fund approximated 40 million zl. _GP_, no.9-10, 1962, p.42. There seems to be a misprint in Fick's article.

137. Jedrychowski, _ND_, no.4, 1962, p.12 and Krawczynski, _op.cit_., pp.280-1

138. For example, the assistant accountant in the mine Milowice recommended that a premium should be paid out to him for calculating the economic efficiency of an invention submitted, even though the finance department of an enterprise should conduct this type of work within the scope of its duties. J. Urban, _Pol_., no.36, 1962

139. Premiums paid out in 1961 from the technical progress fund amounted to 140 million zl. and the plan for 1962 stipulated 170 million. J. Kopinski, in _Polityka gospodarcza_..., I, p.485

140. Urban, _op.cit_.

141. J. Walclawek, _TL_, September 26, 1964; _cf_. Matyja, _op.cit_., p.5, Pajestka, _Funkcje ekonomiczne_..., pp.12-4, Cielecki, _ZG_, no.48, 1960, and Wojciechowska, _Fin_., no.9, 1961, pp.71-4. The advantages that Poland may gain from the Czechoslovakian experience in multi-year planning for the enterprise are particularly stressed by Blass, _Fin_., no.7, 1962, pp.59-60 and _Zagadnienia systemu_..., pp.108-11, _vide_ Michalski, _op.cit_., pp.10-1 and Fick, _Bodzce zainteresowania_..., p.2

142. Szyndler-Glowacki, _ZG_, no.36, 1963; _cf_.

Z. Gotesman, in Misiak (ed.), op.cit., p.403. In his
paper for the April,1965,conference Matyja pointed to
a specific feature of the present Polish economy
manifested in "the lack of economic stimuli for technical progress, from the standpoint of narrowly conceived group or personal interests, due to short run
calculation and existing impediments on technical
progress, unwillingness to take risks (often linked,
inter alia, with threats to plan fulfilment) and
exertion of effort and costs without assurance of
material rewards or due to the lapse of time involved
in their realization, fear of revision of norms, the
automatic increases of tasks in the future, discharging
staff, etc. This gives rise to contradictions between
the interests of the state and society in the long
run all-encompassing development of the enterprise and
the short run interests of the staff. The lack of
technical progress does not threaten the enterprise
with any repercussions, unless technical progress has
been specified by higher units and the non-execution
of tasks is punished." Op.cit., p.5

143. A. Zmuda, TL, May 31, 1963

144. Cf. J. Kaleta, in Misiak, (ed.),op.cit.,
pp.476-8, TL, June 1, 1963 and TL, June 16, 1964

145. B. Stachura, ND, no.3, 1962, p.114

146. J. Niegowski and W. Rydygier, in Polityka
gospodarcza..., I, pp.649-50 and Krawczynski, op.cit.,
p.282

147. A study conducted by the Metallurgists Trade
Union has disclosed that in 35 enterprises in the
Warsaw area the average export premium approximated
1,253 zl. in 1960. The average export premiums for
manual workers were 868 zl. (lowest 100 zl. and
highest 5,680 zl.), the average for office and
administrative personnel were 1,146 zl. (lowest 200
zl. and highest 18,500 zl.), and the average for the
engineering and technical personnel were 1,629 zl.
(lowest 200 zl. and highest 18,500 zl.). Krawczynski,
op.cit., p.283. The 1962 and later investigations
conducted by the Work and Wages Committee support these

findings.   Obodowski, ND, no.6, 1964, p.164 and Spotan, GP, no.7, 1964, p.43

148.   Krawczynski, op.cit., pp.284-8

149.   In the machine building industry material usage norms have not been revised from 1955 to 1961. Approximately 80 per cent of norms are still outdated. The main reasons for this state of affairs are the oppositions within the enterprises against tight material norms.   The piece-rate worker is interested in a loose norm since the tighther the norm, the more difficult it is to observe it.   Management is interested in loose norms because the procurement plan is based on material usage norms.   K. Witkowski, in Polityka gospodarcza..., I, pp.290-1.   In light industry the norms for the usage of fibers in textile mills have not been brought up to date since 1950 and all of them should be verified.   Madej, W poszukiwaniu miliardow, (Warsaw: 1962), p.52

150.   Because of serious shortages of fuels it was decided to limit the use of electricity in industry during February, March, and April, 1963, by command. It was estimated that in relation to the plan for those three months over 200 million kw-hr of electricity were saved.   It was reported that the savings were mostly realized on a more intensive exploitation of machines, discontinuation of such often occurring incidents as machines running without being used, etc. During those three months it was boasted that 147,000 tons of coal were saved.   TL, May 8, 1963; cf. Bobrowski, ZG, no.19, 1957

151.   Sobon, op.cit., p.184

152.   W. Paszonka, in Misiak (ed.), op.cit., pp.384-5; cf.   Spotan, GP, no.7, 1964, p.43

153.   The mechanics of wage fund correction will be found later in this chapter, Infra, pp.242-3

154.   J. Adamowski, TL, May 31, 1963

155.   Fick, ZG, no.14, 1964

156. Fick, GP, no.9-10, 1962, p.43

157. Fick, ND, no.1, 1962, pp.178-9

158. Misiak, ND, no.1, 1962, pp.180-1; cf. Adamowski, TL, June 15, 1963 and Matyja, op.cit., p.1

159. Moscicka, ZG, no.23, 1964, cf. Pajestka,
Funkcje ekonomiczne..., pp.8-9

160. J. Budaszewski, ZG, no.28, 1963. Experts
estimate conservatively that the current FYP's investments are underestimated by 12 to 17 per cent.
Paszynski, Pol., no.43, 1962. As a rule the actual
investment costs of individual projects exceed the
planned amounts from 30 to 100 per cent. Budaszewski,
op.cit.; cf. W. Iwanicki, TL, July 8, 1964

161. Paszynski, Pol., no.43, 1962

162. Paszynski, Pol., no.45, 1962

163. Z. Szeliga, Pol. no.45, 1962, Dudzinski, ZG,
no.31, 1963, and Z. Slomkowski, TL, June 2, 1964

164. W. Pellowska-Wisniewska, ZG, no.23, 1963

165. Szeliga, op.cit.

166. Dudzinski, ZG, no.23, 1963

167. Slomkowski, TL, June 2, 1964. "Of course we
can always foist technical progress tasks on the enterprise from outside. But this does not promote technical progress initiative which should appear in every
producing establishment. A situation, where the technical progress initiative emanates from outside, from
the central authorities, associations, or ministries,
is not healthy. This initiative should emanate from
the producing establishment itself, and this is lacking
in Poland at present." Biuletyn Naukowy WSNS - Wydzial
Ekonomiczny, (Warsaw: 1962), as quoted by Matyja, op.cit.,
p.5

168. Szeliga, op.cit.

169. Bober, ZG, no.27, 1964. Strictly speaking,
the directive index of the wage fund is not absolutely
binding on the enterprise in all cases. It may be
changed when the enterprise proposes a counterplan
increasing the total production plan. When the counterplan is approved by the association the wage fund is
raised accordingly. MP, no.29, 1961, items 123, 124,
and 125

170. M. Borun, Fin., no.2, 1963, p.12, Iszkowski
and Rog, op.cit., p.1, and Mierniki oceny..., pp.133,
135, and 150

171. Blass, GP, no.2, 1964, p.17

172. Krencik and Spotan, GP, no.5, 1960, pp.21-5;
cf. Krencik, Ekon., no.6, 1960, pp.1366-78, R. Korwan-
ski, Fin., no.7, 1961, p.47, and Krencik, in Misiak, (ed.)
op.cit., pp.184-8

173. The computation of a corrected wage fund
based on actual data of a cement plant is illustrated
in H. Walica, GP, no.2, 1963, p.51

174. Fedorowicz, Fin., no.10, 1960, p.10

175. M. Holdys, Fin., no.1, 1961, Borun, op.cit.,
pp.15-6, and A. Zwass, GP, no.6, 1961, p.49

176. The banks have on many occasions exercised
this prerogative; cf. E. Bilski, in Misiak (ed.),
op.cit.,p.179. For example, according to Fick, the
sum of premiums blocked by the bank as of September
30, 1961 constituted 26 per cent of premiums paid for
the first three quarters of that year. GP, no.9-10,
1962, p.44

177. Borun, op.cit., pp.10-1

178. F. Zamojski, ZG, no.20, 1963. The Polish
experience testifies that the banks do control and
limit excess of wage payments; however, they are not
successful in eliminating excesses altogether. Vide
Gomulka, TL, April 18, 1963 and M. Markiewicz, ZG,
no.36, 1963. Excess payments of the wage fund in

industry over and above the increase "warranted by the increase of production" were 768 million zl. in 1961, 606 million zl. in 1962, and 316 million zl. in 1963. Blass, Fundusze plac w mechanizmie zarzadzania przedsiebiorstwem uspolecznionym, (Warsaw: 1965), p.9. Actual and planned wage payments statistics for 1961 to 1963 and adjustments made due to the increase in wage rates are reported by Blass, in Mierniki oceny..., pp.52-3

179. DU, no.9, 1961, item 49

180. Zamojski, op.cit. In addition the payroll personnel is dispossessed of premiums from the enterprise fund.

181. "The wage fund is a magnitude determined by central authorities in relation to the total production plan. The enterprise has no direct influence on the final magnitude of the tasks and means, but during the period of preparation of the plan it makes use of all factual and fictitious difficulties in order to obtain the lowest possible tasks and the highest possible means (wage fund and number of employees) since only such a formation will enable it to fulfil and overfulfil the production plan without a greater effort and obtain the additional means to which it is entitled for the overfulfilment of the production plan (correction of the wage fund). The pressures for an increase of the labor force and the wage fund are transmitted from enterprises to associations... and from there to ministries, and it is only the central planning organ that must restrain these tendencies." Madej, Fin., no.8, 1960, p.3. Cf. Krencik, in Misiak, (ed.), op.cit., p.183

182. Although the wage structure and norms are predetermined centrally and datum for the enterprise, the latter has a wide possibility of increasing the wages of particular employees by promotion and reclassification into a higher wage bracket. Consequently the wage and salary increases depend on the size of the wage fund. Cf. Miszewski, op.cit., p.37

183. Matyja, op.cit., pp.2 and 5, Haus and Kotlarek,

op.cit., p.27, and Blass, Zagadnienia systemu..., p.93

184. Although the regulations state that the initial
plan may be reduced if circumstances beyond the firm's
control engender work stoppages, the associations and
ministries are most reluctant to do so. Cf. A.K.
Wroblewski, Pol., no.13, 1963

185. This point may be illustrated by the findings
of an investigation conducted in 11 enterprises in
Lodz. It was found that during a short period of time
a total of 568,000 hours of overtime were worked.
During that same period about 1 million zl. were paid
out for idle hours during work stoppages. TL, May 21,
1963; cf. Madej, W poszukiwaniu miliardow, pp.23-4

186. Madej, Fin, no.8, 1960, p.3

187. Krencik in Madej (ed.), op.cit., p.183,
W. Borochowski, loc.cit., pp.439-42, and Bilski, op.cit.,
p.178. For example, the factory of metal products in
Myszkow fulfilled its 1962 orders for kitchen utensils
as follows:

Products	Value of out- put per 1 hour of labor input %	Fulfil- ment of orders %
8 cm. ladles	52.6	69.0
10 cm. ladles	57.4	56.7
12 cm. covers	45.3	60.5
28 cm. covers	97.3	95.4
40 cm. bowls	107.8	173.9
45 cm. bowls	177.6	179.8
50 cm. bowls	189.2	270.2
24 cm. saucepans	205.2	157.1

Source Blass, Fin., no.3, 1964, p.7

188. A. Melich, ZG, no.18, 1963

189. Z. Szretter, ZG, no.18, 1963; cf. Szyndler-
Glowacki, ZG, no.36, 1963

190.   Struminski, GP, no.1, 1962, p.10

191.   Madej, W poszukiwaniu miliardow, pp.55-7, cf.
Borochowski, op.cit., pp.442-3 and Sztyber in Misiak
(ed.), op.cit., pp.422;3

192.   Iszkowski, GP, no.10, 1960, p.13, Madej,
Zysk..., p.62, and Blass, Zagadnienia systemu..., p.91

193.   Sobon. op.cit., p.184

194.   A. Malachowski, Pol., no.3, 1963

195.   Cf. Madej, W poszukiwaniu miliardow, p.12.
A direct consequence of this system of wage fund regulation is not only inefficient combination of inputs
but   undesirable composition of output.   In an article
on the labor productivity index and savings of materials Moskalewski writes: "The introduction - at the
demand of buyers - of new products of small or normal
material intensity and large labor intensity would
cause losses for the enterprises producing these
products since it would increase the required wage
fund and decrease the labor productivity index.   It
is purposely that we have used here the conditional
tense, for in practice these products are either not
introduced into production or produced in minimal
quantities.   The enterprise does not suffer losses
and that the national economy does not receive the
products it needs - is a completely different
problem."   GP, no.6, 1961, p.21

196.   Madej, Fin., no.8, 1960, p.2

197.   Cf. Blass, ND, no.12, 1964, pp.120ff.

198.   K. Draganski, TL, no.145, May 27, 1964 and
J. Gwiazdzinski, GP, no.10, 1960, p.7

199.   Moskalewski, TL, April 22, 1964.   For example,
Dr. Madej points out that in the production of the TUC
lathe which weighs 3400 kg the weight of steel scrap
and shavings is about 1200 kg or 35 per cent of the
weight of the finished machine.   W poszukiwaniu
miliardow, p.47

200. Fick, _Fin_., no.10, 1962, p.15. Fifty to
sixty per cent of industrial workers are remunerated
according to the piece rate system, H. Feder, _GP_, no.2,
1961, p.30

201. M. Sobolewski, _TL_, May 27, 1964. Cf. Matyja,
op.cit., pp.6-7

202. Wang, _GP_, no.7, 1961, p.10

203. At the 1963 Wisla conference devoted to the
serious difficulties of procurement of materials and
large scale waste, Szyr stressed the need for improving
material balances. He forecast that by 1970 there would
be 600 electronic machine stations at the service of
planners. _TL_, May 3, 1963

204. Hatt, et al., op.cit., pp.65-7

205. Madej, W poszukiwaniu miliardow, p.25; cf.
Adamowski, _TL_, July 7, 1964

206. G. Pisarski, _ZG_, no.12, 1963; cf. Szyr, _ND_,
no.6, 1964, p.68

207. Delays in the delivery of materials are sometimes of astounding proportions. Deliveries from
steel mills and metal fabricating plants range from
four to seven months from receipt of orders incorporated
in the plans of the producers. Above plan orders are
only delivered one year from receipt of order. B.
Pryzynski, _GP_, no. 11, 1960, p.32

208. Examples of losses incurred due to work
stoppages resulting from failures in material supply
are presented by Madej, W poszukiwaniu miliardow, pp.
23-4

209. Pisarski, _ZG_, no.12, 1963

210. B. Garlinski, _EiOP_, no.7, 1964, p.300. For
data on discrepancies between orders and use of materials see K. Witkowski, op.cit., p.307

211. W. Wasilewski, _TL_, May 10, 1963

212. F. Bozyczko, ZG, no.15, 1963

213. ZG, no.42, 1962

214. K. Witkowski, op.cit., p.291

215. Adamowski, TL, July 7, 1964; cf. J. Smietanski, Pol., no.29, 1963

216. S. Frankel, ZG, no.44, 1962

217. B. Malinowski, TL, May 13, 1964; cf. Adamowski, TL, May 22, 1963

218. B. Wisniewska, ZG, no.22, 1963

219. Lewicki, TL, November 2, 1964

220. Wroblewski, Pol., no.7, 1962

221. Sobon, op.cit., p.183

222. J. Piwowar and W. Pietkiewicz, GM, no.23, 1962, p.22

223. For example, in 1961 the zinc establishment in Szopienice exceeded the above normative stocks by 119 per cent, the forge Ustron by 94 per cent, the metal establishment in Zakrzew by 89 per cent, and the machine building industry as a whole by 121.7 per cent. Madej, W poszukiwaniu miliardow, p.27

224. Ibid., p.27 and K. Witkowski, op.cit., p.305

225. Zmuda, TL, May 22, 1963

226. ZG, no.12, 1963

227. Wasilewski, TL, May 10, 1963

228. The Parliamentary Commission on the Economic Plan, Budget, and Finance postulated that to counteract waste of materials immediate steps should be taken to build warehouses and stocking facilities. TL, June 4, 1963; cf. Paszynski, Pol., no.37, 1964

229. Madej, W poszukiwaniu miliardow, p.33

230. D. Kac, TL, May 19, 1964

231. Madej, W poszukiwaniu miliardow, p.6. It is
needless to add that considerable shortages of both
wire and cement cause many work stoppages.

232. Wang, GP, no.7, 1961, p.14

233. E. Cieslikowski, ZG, no.20, 1963

234. Madej, W poszukiwaniu miliardow, p.25

235. Wroblewski, Pol., no.13, 1963

236. Madej, W poszukiwaniu miliardow, pp.22-3

237. J. Zelezik, Pol., no.4, 1962

238. Kuzinski, Glowne proporcje..., p.94

239. Zelezik, op.cit.

240. Wroblewski, Pol., no.7, 1962

241. Wang, GP, no.7, 1961, p.10; cf. Matyja, op.
cit., p.6

242. Gora, op.cit., p.57

243. B. Maloleprzy, Pol., no.37, 1962

244. A. Jedrzejczak, Pol., no.24, 1962

245. Szyndler-Glowacki, ZG, no.17, 1964

246. Maloleprzy, op.cit.

247. Jedrzejczak, op.cit., J. Kopinski, GP, no.6,
1959, p.3. A conservative estimate indicates that the
national economy loses approximately 4 to 6 billion zl.
annually or 1 to 2 per cent of national income due to
poor quality of production. Ibid.

248. Maloleprzy, op.cit.

249. Gora, op.cit., p.18

250. Gutowski, Pol., no.17, 1963

251. Kalecki, in Mierniki oceny..., p.230

252. It should be pointed out here that the piece
rate wage system greatly contributes to deterioration
of quality by its one-sided emphasis on the quantity
of output. P. Solski, TL, May 30, 1964

253. Misiak, ZG, no.36, 1963

254. Gutowski, Pol., no.22, 1963. The upkeep of
capital assets is also neglected due to the high cost
of repairs which, because of shortages of spare parts,
involves the production of spare parts by the user.
A director of a metal fabricating enterprise questioned
on the subject of repairs commented that in many cases
only two alternatives are open to him, namely, to over-
pay for the repair of machines or to accept their
idleness. "In many cases" - he said - "I have to
produce on premises the spare parts needed without
having the necessary equipment for such an undertaking. It should not be surprising that they are at
times 15 to 20 times more expensive than in specialized establishments." Lewicki, TL, May 11, 1963

255. C. Kulik, TL, April 15, 1964

256. It was reported that in 1962 over 20 per
cent of the working hours of repairmen were spent
in direct production. Gutowski, Pol., no.22, 1963

257. J. Bolkowski, GP, no.12, 1950, p.687

258. Kuzinski, Glowne proporcje..., p.58

259. For example, in June, 1963, Tonsil fulfilled
its output plan by 72.2 per cent, in September it
fulfilled the plan by 104.9 per cent, in October by
118 per cent, and in November it fulfilled the plan
by 121.4 per cent. H. Weber, ZG, no.10, 1964

260. Pol., no.44, 1962

261. Ibid.

262. Doberski, GP, no.10, 1961, p.25, Struminski, in Mierniki oceny..., p.32, Mierniki oceny..., p.134, and Lesz, in Mierniki oceny..., pp.18-23

263. Struminski, in Mierniki oceny..., pp.35-6; cf. G. Zalski, ZG, no.13, 1963

264. J. Zakrzewski and Z. Zarudzki, ZG, no.1, 1963, Lesz, in Mierniki oceny..., pp.21-3

265. Struminski, in Mierniki oceny..., p.36

266. Lesz, in Mierniki oceny..., p.23

267. Zakrzewski and Zarudzki, op.cit.; cf. ZG, no.50, 1964

268. Jedrychowski, ND, no.4, 1962, p.5

269. See, for example, Gomulka's appeal to metallurgists and miners to overfulfil their production plans. TL, May 12, 1963; cf. Matyja, op.cit., p.1

270. Jedrychowski points out that increase in profit results from two factors: increase in production and cost reduction. The socialist economy is vitally interested in maximization of both, and it would therefore follow that if those two factors are used as performance criteria simultaneously with profit they would not be contradictory. But the variables of paramount importance are the rate of increase of output (value of the marginal product and hence the problem of valuation) equated with the rate of increase of costs. Cost reduction alone is not a sufficient test as costs may even rise but the sacrifice should be compared with the benefits ensuing. Notwithstanding the above, the actual cost reduction index is of dubious validity. As a rule one cannot demand increase of output and simultaneous cost reduction.

271. Pol., no.9, 1963

272.   Jedrychowski, TL, December 12, 1959

273.   The foremost question is which criteria will
the planner use for determining the most desirable
product mix and could the trade centrals' suggestions
be considered good guides?   Even Jedrychowski doubts
this. Mierniki oceny..., p.8

274.   MP, no.4, 1964, item 15

275.   Fick, ZG, no.2, 1965

276.   Ibid.

277.   Gutowski, ZG, no.42, 1964

278.   Bober, ZG, no.20, 1964

279.   Weber, ZG, no.32 and 33, 1964

280.   Fick, ZG, no.2, 1965

281.   These proposals date back to the late 1950's.
Kalecki, ZG, no.29, 1957, B. Minc, Aktualne zagadnienia...,
p.377, and Dudzinski, ZG, no.50, 1959

282.   At the price formation stage high material
costs would favor the size of value added since they
would increase the size of profit.   Therefore, proposals
were advanced to calculate profit merely as a surcharge
on labor. Z. Mawarski, ZG, no.17, 1963. This, of course,
abstracts from capital intensity and may impede technical progress.

283.   Mierniki oceny..., p.138

284.   Ibid., p.139

285.   Madej, Zysk..., p.64

286.   By relating the wage fund to value added a zero
or even negative price is assigned to labor at the planning stage since replacement of 100 zl. of labor for
50 zl. of materials increases value added by 50 zl.
Strict regulation of the wage fund mitigates this

phenomenon. Maximization of personal income in the
form of wages, ceteris paribus, increasing costs and
decreasing profit, conflicts with profit maximization
as a performance criterion.

287. Rog, in Mierniki oceny..., pp.191-2

288. A. Czechowicz, in Mierniki oceny..., p.67
and Iszkowski and Rog, op.cit., p.10. "The real
situation... is the popular estimate of the relative
merits of the economist and engineer. It is probably
no exaggeration to say that to most people the
engineer is the person who actually does things and
the economist the odious individual who sits back
in his armchair and explains why the well-meaning
efforts of the former are frustrated. In a sense
this is true. But the implication that the forces
which the economist studies and the engineer is
likely to disregard are unimportant and ought to be
disregarded is absurd. It needs the special training of the economist to see that the spontaneous
forces which limit the ambitions of the engineer
themselves provide a way of solving a problem which
otherwise would have to be solved deliberately."
Hayek, in Collectivist Economic Planning, p.8

289. The standard processing cost employed in
the clothing industry excludes indirect materials.

290. Mierniki oceny..., p.140 and Iszkowski and
Rog, op.cit., p.10

291. Mierniki oceny..., p.141

292. S. Romanowicz, ZG, no.40, 1964

293. S. Bukowski, ZG, no.26, 1964

294. Jedrychowski in Mierniki oceny..., p.5

295. Hatt, et al., op.cit., pp.130-1

296. Misiak, ZG, no.18, 1964

297. Szyndler-Glowacki, Pol., no.48, 1962

298. Obodowski, ND, no.6, 1964, pp.160 and 163

299. Spotan, GP, no.7, 1964, pp.44-5

300. Fick, ZG, no.19, 1964

301. Fick, ZG, no.31, 1964

302. Dudzinski, ZG, no.6, 1965

303. Madej, Zysk..., pp.65-76 and E. Lipinski,
Ekon., no.3, 1964, pp.506-7. Vide the highly publicized
proposals of Professor E. Liberman to enhance the role
of profit in industrial managment in the U.S.S.R.
E. Liberman, Voprosy Ekonomiki, no.6, 1955 and no.8,
1962, Pravda, September 9, 1962. For analysis of
the Liberman proposals see, inter alia, Nove, Soviet
Survey, April,1963, pp.112-18 and Zauberman, Slavic
Review, December, 1963, pp.733-44

304. "Modern theory no longer undertakes to prove
that perfect competition is an ideal. But it can
show what the effects of given deviations from competition
will be.... Economic theory is slowly developing the
mental instruments that are necessary in order to
'rationalize' planning and to tell planners what they
must do and avoid in order to attain certain given ends...
To say that pure theory is of no interest for practice
is as unreasonable as to say that pure mechanics is
of no interest for building the machines we want. The
ends themselves, that is to say, the kind of society
or culture we want, we must choose ourselves. No
science can do more than indicate the means of attain-
ing whatever it is we want." Schumpeter, History of
Economic Analysis, p.1145; cf. Robbins, An Essay..., p.24

305. E. Preobrazhenski, Novaya ekonomika, (Moscow:
1926), p.11

306. Brus, ZG, no.6, 1964

BIBLIOGRAPHICAL ABBREVIATIONS

AER   American Economic Review

Biuletyn PKPG   Biuletyn Panstwowej Komisji Plan-
                        owania Gospodarczego (Bulletin of
                        the State Commission for Economic
                        Planning)

CJEPS   Canadian Journal of Economics and
                        Political Science

DU   Dziennik Ustaw (Official Legal
                        Gazette)

Econ. of Plan.   Economics of Planning

EiOP   Ekonomika i Organizacja Pracy
                        (Economics and Organization of
                        Work)

Ekon.   Ekonomista (Economist)

Fin.   Finanse (Finance)

GM   Gospodarka Materialowa (Economics
                        of Materials)

GP   Gospodarka Planowa (Economics of
                        Planning)

JPE   Journal of Political Economy

MEE   Mala encyklopedia ekonomiczna
                        (Concise Economics Encyclopedia)

MER   Mala encyklopedia rachunkowosci
                        (Concise Accounting Encyclopedia)

MP	Monitor Polski (Polish Monitor)
MRS	Maly rocznik statystyczny (Concise Statistical Yearbook)
ND	Nowe Drogi (New Ways)
Oxf. Econ. Papers	Oxford Economic Papers
Pol.	Polityka (Politics)
Prob. of Com.	Problems of Communism
QJE	Quarterly Journal of Economics
Rach.	Rachunkowosc (Accounting)
RES	Review of Economic Studies
RESt.	Review of Economic Statistics
RS	Rocznik statystyczny (Statistical Yearbook)
SE	Studia Ekonomiczne (Economic Studies)
Slav. Rev.	Slavic Review
Sov. Stud.	Soviet Studies
TL	Trybuna Ludu (People's Tribune)
WNBP	Wiadomosci Narodowego Banku Polskiego (National Polish Bank News)
ZG	Zycie Gospodarcze (Economic Life)

Note   In all cases diacritical marks have been omitted
from Polish names and words for typographical
reasons

CONCISE BIBLIOGRAPHY

This selected bibliography is confined to chosen
works in book or pamphlet form by Polish and Western
contributors to the subject. Limitation of space does
not permit **going** beyond a scant recognition of Soviet
publications. Many references to articles in period-
icals and newspapers appear in the notes to each
chapter and will not be repeated here.

ALTON, T.P.   Polish Postwar Economy. New York, 1955.

ARAKIAN, A.   Industrial Management in the U.S.S.R.
   Translated by E.L. Raymond. Washington, 1950.

BALASSA, B.   The Hungarian Experience in Economic
   Planning. New Haven, 1959.

BALCEREK, J. and GILEJKO, L.   Problemy samorzadu
   robotniczego (Problems of the Workers' Self-management). Warsaw, 1961.

BARTNICKI, M.   Inwestycje i ich efektywnosc w piecio-
   leciu 1961-65 (Investments and Their Efficiency in
   the 1961-65 Five-Year Plan). Warsaw, 1959.

BERGSON, A.   The Economics of Soviet Planning.
   New Haven, 1964.

BERLINER, J.S.   Factory and Manager in the U.S.S.R.
   Cambridge, Mass., 1957.

_____   Soviet Economic Aid. New York, 1958.

BETTELHEIM, C.   Studies in the Theory of Planning.
   New York, 1959.

BIEN, W.   Ewidencja srodkow trwalych i amortyzacji
   (Recording of Fixed Assets and Depreciation).
   Warsaw, 1962.

BIENSTOCK, G. et al.   Management in Russian Industry
   and Agriculture. New York, 1944.

BISHAEV, M.A. and FEDOROVICH, M.M.   Organizatsiia
   upravleniia promyshlennym proizvodstvom (Organization

of Management of the Industrial Enterprise).
Moscow, 1961.

BLASS, B. Fundusz plac w mechanizmie zaradzania przedsiebiorstwem uspolecznionym (The Wage Fund in the
Management of a Socialized Enterprise). Warsaw, 1965.

_____ Zagadnienia systemu finansowego przedsiebiorstw
przemyslowych w panstwach socjalistycznych (Problems
of the Industrial Enterprises' Financial System in
Socialist States). Warsaw, 1964.

BOLESTA, J. Zasady prawne ustalania cen (The Legal
Principles of Price Setting). 2 vol. Warsaw, 1963.

BORNSTEIN, M. and FUSFELD, D.R. The Soviet Economy.
Homewood, 1962.

BORYSIEWICZ, J. System cen srodkow produkcji w przemysle
na przykladzie hutnictwa (The Price System of
Producer Goods in Industry With Reference to Metallurgy). Warsaw, 1955.

BRUS, W. Ogolne problemy funkcjonowania gospodarki
socjalistycznej (General Problems of the Functioning
of a Socialist Economy). Warsaw, 1961.

_____ Prawo wartosci a problematyka bodzcow ekonomicznych (The Law of Value and the Problem of Economic
Incentives). Warsaw, 1956.

BRZEZINSKI, Z. The Soviet Bloc - Unity and Conflict.
New York, 1961.

CAMPBELL, R.W. Accounting in Soviet Planning and Management. Cambridge, Mass., 1963.

CHLEBOWCZYK, A. et al. Materialy do badania relacji cen
(Data for Analyzing Price Relations). Warsaw, 1958.

CSIKOS-NAGY, B. Polityka cen w gospodarce okresu
przejsciowego (Price Policy in an Economy of a Trans-
itional Period). Translated from Hungarian. Warsaw,
1961.

CZERWINSKA, E. Samodzielnosc finansowa przedsiebiorstwa przemyslowego (Financial Autonomy of an Industrial Enterprise). Poznan, 1963

DOBB, M.H. An Essay on Economic Growth and Planning. London, 1964.

_____ On Economic Theory and Socialism. London, 1955.

_____ Political Economy and Capitalism. London, 1937.

DMITRIEVA, P.I. Rentabel'nost' promyshlennogo predpriiatiia i puti ee povysheniia (The Industrial Enterprise's Profitability and Ways to Enhance it). Moscow, 1960.

DRUSKA, H. (ed.). Fundusz zakladowy, fundusz za osiagniecia ekonomiczne, fundusz premiowy (The Enterprise Fund, the Fund for Economic Achievements, the Premium Fund). Warsaw, 1961.

Dyskusja o polskim modelu gospodarczym (The Discussion on the Polish Economic Model). Collective work. Warsaw, 1957.

Dyskusja o prawie wartosci ciag dalszy (Continuation of the Discussion About the Law of Value). Collective work. Warsaw, 1957.

Dyskusja o prawie wartosci i cenach w ZSRR (Discussion on the Law of Value and Prices in the U.S.S.R.). Collective work. Warsaw, 1958.

ERLICH, A. The Soviet Industrialization Debate 1924-1928. Cambridge, Mass., 1960.

FEDAK, Z. Ewidencja i kalkulacja kosztow w przemysle (The Recording and Calculation of Costs in Industry). Warsaw, 1957.

_____ Rachunek kosztow produkcji przemyslowej (Cost Accounting of Industrial Production). Warsaw, 1962.

FEDOROWICZ, Z. Finanse w gospodarce socjalistycznej (Finance in a Socialist Economy). Warsaw, 1962.

_____ Kierunki przebudowy systemu finansowego przedsiebiorstw przemyslowych (Directions for Reconstruct-
ing the Industrial Enterprises' Financial System).
Warsaw, 1958.

FICK, B. Bodzce zainteresowania materialnego pracownikow przedsiebiorstw i zjednoczen a funkcje ekonomiczne
tych jednostek gospodarczych (Employees' Material
Interest Incentives of Enterprises and Associations
and the Economic Functions of these Economic Units).
Warsaw, 1965.

FIEJKA, Z. Wydajnosc pracy w przemysle polskim (Labor
Productivity in Polish Industry). Warsaw, 1962.

FISZEL, H. Efektywnosc inwestycji i optimum produkcji
w gospodarce socjalistycznej (Investment Efficiency
and Optimum Production in Socialist Economy).
Warsaw, 1960.

_____ Prawo wartosci a problematyka cen w przemysle
socjalistycznym (The Law of Value and the Problem of
Prices in Socialist Industry). Warsaw, 1956.

_____ Zagadnienia cen i rachunku ekonomicznego (The
Problems of Prices and Economic Calculation).
Warsaw, 1958.

GLINSKI, B. Teorie i praktyka zarzadzania przedsiebiorstwami przemyslowymi (Theory and Practice of Management of Industrial Enterprises). Warsaw, 1964.

GOLDMAN, M. Soviet Marketing. New York, 1963.

GORA, S. Bodzce ekonomiczne w gospodarce socjalistycznej
(Economic Incentives in Socialist Economy). Warsaw,
1961.

GORDON, J. (ed.). Ekonomika przedsiebiorstwa przemyslowego (Economics of Industrial Enterprise). Warsaw,
1962.

_____ Ksztaltowanie cen wyrobow przemyslowych (Price
Formation of Producer Goods). Warsaw, 1963.

GRANICK, D. Management of the Industrial Firm in the
    U.S.S.R. New York, 1954.

_____ The Red Executive. Garden City, 1960.

GROSSMAN, G. (ed.). Value and Plan. Berkeley, 1960.

HATT, S. et al. System planowania w Polsce (The Plan-
    ning System in Poland). Warsaw, 1964.

HAYEK, F.A. (ed.). Collectivist Economic Planning.
    London, 1935.

HOLZMAN, F.D. Soviet Taxation. Cambridge, Mass., 1955.

_____ (ed.). Readings on the Soviet Economy. Chicago,
    1962.

JANZA, W. and TYPOLT, J. Zagadnienia ksztaltowania cen
    w nowym systemie zarzadzania przemyslem Czechoslowacji
    (Price Formation Problems in the New Administration
    of Industry in Czechoslovakia). Translated from Czech.
    Warsaw, 1960.

JASNY, N. Soviet Prices of Producers' Goods. Stanford,
    1952.

JEDRYCHOWSKI, S. The Fundamental Principles of Economic
    Policy in Industry. Translated from Polish. Warsaw,
    1957.

KALECKI, M. Szkice ekonomiczne (Essays in Economics).
    Warsaw, 1958.

KANTOROVICH, L.V. Rachunek ekonomiczny optymalnego
    wykorzystania zasobow. Translated from Russian.
    Warsaw, 1961. The Best Use of Economic Resources.
    English translation. Cambridge, Mass., 1965.

KARPINSKI, A. Poland and the World Economy. Translated
    by L. Szwajcer and H. Yaris. Warsaw, 1960.

_____ The Polish Economy 1961-1965. Translated by
    E. Lepa. Warsaw, 1962

KASER, M. Comecon. London, 1965

KIERCZYNSKI, T. Istota akumulacji pienieznej przedsiebiorstw socjalistycznych (The Nature of Monetary
Accumulation of Socialist Enterprises). Warsaw, 1960.

_____ Przedsiebiorstwa deficytowe w gospodarce
socjalistycznej (Deficit Enterprises in Socialist
Economy). Warsaw, 1962

KONDRASHEV, D.D. Tsenoobrazovaniye v promyshlennosti
SSSR (Price Formation in Soviet Industry). Moscow,
1956.

KOOPMANS, T. Uses of Prices. Chicago, 1954

KORNAI, J. Overcentralization in Economic Administration.
Translated by J. Knapp. London, 1959.

KRENCIK, W. Badania polityki zatrudnienia i plac w
gospodarce socjalistycznej (Analyses of Employment
and Wage Policy in Socialist Economy). Warsaw, 1962.

KRISHNAMURTI, B.V. Pricing in Planned Economy.
Bombay, 1949.

KRUSZCZYNSKI, S. Polityka ekonomiczna i planowanie
gospodarki narodowej (Economic Policy and Planning
the National Economy). Poznan, 1964.

KRYGIER, K. and WITKOWSKI, H. Gospodarka materialowa
w przedsiebiorstwie przemyslowym (Administration of
Materials in an Industrial Enterprise). Warsaw, 1962.

KUZINSKI, S. Glowne proporcje rozwoju gospodarczego
Polski Ludowej (Main Proportions of the Economic
Development of People's Poland). Warsaw, 1960.

_____ O czynnikach wzrostu gospodarczego Polski
Ludowej (About the Economic Growth Factors of
People's Poland). Warsaw, 1962

KWEJT, J. Elementy teorii przedsiebiorstwa (The Principles of the Theory of the Enterprise). Warsaw, 1959.

LANGE, O. Economic Development, Planning, and International Cooperation. Cairo, 1961.

_____ Ekonomia polityczna. I. Warsaw, 1963.
Political Economy. Translated by A.H. Walker.
New York, 1963.

_____ Essays on Economic Planning. New York, 1958.

_____ Niektore zagadnienia centralizacji i decentralizacji w zarzadzaniu (Some Problems of Centralization
and Decentralization in Management). Warsaw, 1962.

_____ The Political Economy of Socialism. The Hague,
1958.

_____ Some Problems Relating to the Polish Road to
Socialism. Warsaw, 1957.

_____ Introduction to Econometrics. New York, 1962.

_____ (ed.). Zagadnienia ekonomii politycznej
socjalizmu (Problems of Political Economy of Socialism). Warsaw, 1959.

LERNER, A. The Economics of Control. New York, 1944

LEWIS, W.A. The Principles of Economic Planning.
London, 1952.

LIPINSKI, E. Rewizje (Revisions). Warsaw, 1958.

_____ Teoria ekonomii i aktualne zagadnienia gospodarcze (Economic Theory and Present Economic Problems).
Warsaw, 1961.

LIPPINCOTT, B.E. (ed.). On the Economic Theory of
Socialism. Minneapolis, 1938.

MADEJ, Z. W poszukiwaniu miliardow (In the Search for
Billions). Warsaw, 1962

_____ Zysk w gospodarce socjalistycznej (Profit in
Socialist Economy). Warsaw, 1963.

MAIZENBERG, L. Ksztaltowanie cen w gospodarce narodowej Zwiazku Radzieckiego (Price Formation in the National Economy of the Soviet Union). Translated from Russian. Warsaw, 1955.

MALYSHEV, I.S. Obshchestvennyi uchet truda i tsena pri sotsializme (Social Accounting of Labor and Price Under Socialism). Moscow, 1960.

MARCZEWSKI, J. Planification et croissance economique des democracies populaires. 2 vols. Paris, 1956.

MATUSZEWICZ, J. Rachunek kosztow w przedsiebiorstwach o produkcji jednostkowej i maloseryjnej (Cost Accounting in Enterprises of Non-standardized Production). Warsaw, 1962.

MATYJA, E. Rola cen w mechanizmie funkcjonowania przedsiebiorstw i zjednoczen (The Role of Prices in the Functioning Mechanism of Enterprises and Associations). Warsaw, 1965.

MEADE, J.E. Planning and the Price Mechanism. London, 1953.

MICHALSKI, S. Instrumenty finansowe w mechanizmie funkcjonowania przedsiebiorstw i zjednoczen (Financial Instruments in the Functioning Mechanism of Enterprises and Associations). Warsaw, 1965.

Mierniki oceny dzialalnosci przedsiebiorstwa przemyslowego (Performance Criteria of an Industrial Enterprise's Activity). Collective work. Warsaw, 1964.

MINC, B. Ekonomia polityczna socjalizmu (Political Economy of Socialism). Warsaw, 1961.

_____ Planowanie i polityka gospodarcza (Planning and Economic Policy). Lodz, 1961.

_____ Zarys teorii kosztow produkcji i cen (Outline of the Theory of Production Costs and Prices). Warsaw, 1958.

MISIAK, M. (ed.). Bodzce ekonomiczne w przedsiebiorstwie

przemyslowym (Economic Incentives in the Industrial Enterprise). Warsaw, 1963.

MISZEWSKI, B. Mierniki oceny dzialalnosci przedsie-biorstw przemyslowych (Performance Criteria of Industrial Enterprises' Activity). Warsaw, 1963.

MONTIAS, J.M. Central Planning in Poland. New Haven, 1962.

NEMCHINOV, V.S. (ed.). Primenenie matematiki v ekon-omicheskikh issledovaniakh (Application of Mathematics in Economic Research). Moscow, 1959.

NOVE, A. The Soviet Economy. London, 1961.

_____ and ZAUBERMAN, A. (eds.). Studies on the Theory of Reproduction and Prices. Warsaw, 1964.

PAJESTKA, J. Funkcje ekonomiczne przedsiebiorstw i zjednoczen (Economic Functions of Enterprises and Associations). Warsaw, 1965.

_____ Zatrudnienie i inwestycje a wzrost gospodarczy (Employment Investments and Economic Growth). Warsaw, 1961.

PASIECZNY, L. Kierownik a bodzce materialnego zainter-esowania (The Manager and Material Interest Incentives). Warsaw, 1963.

PIOTROWSKI, W. Ekonomika przemyslu (Economics of Indus-try). Lodz, 1962.

PIROZYNSKI, Z. and WINTER, E. Budzet panstwowy Polski Ludowej (The State Budget of People's Poland). Warsaw, 1961.

PLOCICA, A. Podstawy cen srodkow produkcji (The Bases for Producer Goods' Prices). Warsaw, 1964

Polityka gospodarcza Polski Ludowej (Economic Policy of People's Poland). Collective work. 2 vols. Warsaw, 1962.

PORWIT, K. Zagadnienia rachunku ekonomicznego w planie
    centralnym (Problems of Economic Calculation in the
    Central Plan). Warsaw, 1964

ROBINSON, J. An Essay in Marxian Economics. London, 1942

_____ Collected Economic Papers. II. Oxford, 1960.

RUMYANTSEV, A.F. (ed.). Ekonomika sotsialisticheskikh
    promyshlennykh predpriyatii (Economics of Socialist
    Industrial Enterprises). Moscow, 1959.

SCHUMPETER, J.A. Capitalism, Socialism and Democracy.
    New York, 1950.

SKRZYWAN, S. and FEDAK, Z. Rachunkowsc w przedsie-
    biorstwie przemyslowym (Accounting in the Industrial
    Enterprise). Warsaw, 1960.

Spor o ceny (The Price Controversy). Collective work.
    Warsaw, 1958.

SPRYCHA, Z. Koszty wlasne w nowych zakladach przemysl-
    owych (Production Costs in New Industrial Establish-
    ments). Warsaw, 1961.

SPULBER, N. The Economics of Communist Eastern Europe.
    New York, 1957.

_____ The Soviet Economy, Structure, Principles, and
    Problems. New York, 1962.

STRUMINSKI, J. Polityka cen w Polsce Ludowej (Price
    Policy in People's Poland). Warsaw, 1958.

STRUMILIN, S.G. Problemy sotsializma i kommunizma v SSSR
    (Problems of Socialism and Communism in the U.S.S.R.).
    Moscow, 1961.

SULMICKI, P. Proporcje gospodarcze (Economic Proportions)
    Warsaw, 1962.

SWEEZY, P.M. Socialism. New York, 1949.

TINBERGEN, J. Centralization and Decentralization in

Economic Policy. Amsterdam, 1954.

TURETSKI, S. Zarys planowego ksztaltowania cen w ZSRR
(Outline of Planned Price Formation in the U.S.S.R.).
Translated from Russian. Warsaw, 1962.

WAKAR, A. Morfologia bodzcow ekonomicznych (The
Morphology of Economic Incentives). Warsaw, 1963.

_____ et al. Materialy do studiowania ekonomii
politycznej socjalizmu (Aids for Studying the
Political Economy of Socialism). Warsaw, 1963.

WELLISZ, S. The Economics of the Soviet Bloc.
New York, 1964.

WERALSKI, M. Kierunki reformy polskiego systemu podatkowego (Ways of Reforming the Polish Tax System).
Warsaw, 1960.

_____ Rola budzetu w planowaniu gospodarczym (The
Budget's Role in Economic Planning). Warsaw, 1963.

WILES, P.J.D. The Political Economy of Communism.
Cambridge, Mass., 1962.

WIERZBICKI, J. Zagadnienia akumulacji pienieznej w
gospodarce socjalistycznej (Problems of Monetary
Accumulation in Socialist Economy). Warsaw, 1964.

WOJCIECHOWSKA, U. Problemy tworzenia funduszu zaklad-
owego (Problems of Enterprise Fund Formation).
Warsaw, 1961.

ZABKOWICZ, L. and DOBERSKI, W. Eksperymenty ekonomiczne
ich wyniki i przyszlosc (The Economic Experiments,
Their Results and the Future). Warsaw, 1958.

ZAJDA, J. Zagadnienia przebudowy systemu finansowego
gospodarki narodowej (Problems of Reconstruction of
the National Economy's Financial System). Poznan,
1960.

ZAUBERMAN, A. Industrial Progress in Poland, Czechoslovakia, and East Germany 1937-62. London, 1964.

ZIELINSKI, J.G. Rachunek ekonomiczny w socjalizmie
    (Economic Calculation in Socialism). Warsaw, 1961.

ZVEREV, A.G. Voprosy natsionalnego dokhoda i finansov
    SSSR (Problems of National Income and Finance in the
    U.S.S.R.). Moscow, 1961.

ZWEIG, F. Poland Between Two Wars. London, 1944.

Z zagadnien cen srodkow produkcji (Some Aspects of
    Producer Goods' Prices). Collective work. Warsaw,
    1956.